To John
God bless always
Alan Ross

THE
NEW TESTAMENT
OF
SPIRITUALISM

Received by James E. Padgett and Dr. Daniel G. Samuels

Compiled by Alan Ross

Edited by Arthur Finmann and Patricia Doyle

ROSS PUBLICATIONS

First Edition reprinted in 2004

ISBN # 0-9617038-3-0

Contains Biblical References

Published by:

Ross Publications
1438 W. Lantana Road #401
Lantana FL, 33462 USA

Printed in the US and the UK

DEDICATION

This book is dedicated to my dearest friend Alese Jones, whose help and encouragement has meant so much to me in the production of this book, and to all those people, past and present who have worked s unselfishly to make these teaching known.

CONTENTS

CHAPTER ONE

Family

HELEN PADGETT (Wife)

ANN R. PADGETT (Mother)

JOHN H. PADGETT (Father)

ANN R. ROLLINS (Grandmother)

NITA PADGETT (Daughter)

LAURA BURROUGHS (Cousin)

Chapter Two

Friends

CHAPTER THREE

Strangers

CHAPTER FOUR

Soldiers

CHAPTER FIVE

Heads of State

CHAPTER SIX

Religious Reformers

Chapter Seven

Philosophers

Chapter Eight

Ancient Spirits

CHAPTER NINE

Old Testament

CHAPTER TEN

New Testament

xiii

xiv

xvi

PREFACE

*T*he *New Testament of Spiritualism* is a revealment from the spirit
world of the most extraordinary nature. Because this book as
some unique features a brief explanation of this work is in order.

The *New Testament of Spiritualism is* a collection of channeled messages received by a mortal medium by telepothy and written down
through the means of automatic writing. The writings themselves originate from a wide range of spirit authors living in all of the levels of the
spirit world. As a channeled work this book has been organized according to the spirit communicator, and not in the order in which the messages were received. Because in most cases English was not the spirit's
native language, it had to be learned. Therefore, to insure the author's
meaning they have been edited for clarity. When the date the message
was written is available it is located below the title.

Oftentimes the medium would ask a question of the spirit communicator of which there is no record. However, in most cases, the spirit's
answer starts a sentence with either "Yes" or "No". Of course, it would
be difficult to be absolutely certain of every question, although, from the
answers one can get a pretty fair idea as to what the question most likely may have been.

The one hundred and seventy-two Bible references contained in this
book have been verified using *The King James Version* of the Bible. These
references can be helpful to the reader who wishes to compare this book
with the Bible text.

There are certain messages which provide valuable insights into the mechanics of the mediumship used and which demonstrate the interaction between the medium and the spirit author. It is also worthwhile to note the distinctly different personalities of the communicators, most dramatically when comparing messages from unevolved or lower spirits with those of advanced spirits who inhabit the higher realms.

The New Testament of Spiritualism is a book that contains revolutionary new concepts which are not to be found elsewhere. I ask you when reading to please keep an open mind to the possibility of things which you have never read or heard of before, even if you have been a Spiritualist for many years.

INTRODUCTION

As the era of modern Spiritualism was ushered in through psychic phenomenon in Hydesville, New York in 1848, the completion to Spiritualism's philosophy also came to America through
psychic means some sixty-six years later.

The circumstances surrounding this extraordinary mediumistic
event began in 1914, shortly after the Washington, DC lawyer James E.
Padgett, lost his wife Helen. James Padgett was born August 25, 1852.
He attended the Polytechnic Academy Institute at New Market,
Virginia, and in 1880 he was admitted to the bar in Washington, DC.
Thereafter he practiced law for forty-three years until his passing.

Padgett was not a Spiritualist but a Methodist, however, after

Helen's passing he was prompted by a friend to attend a
Spiritualist meeting. There the medium described Helen
perfectly, and told him that his wife wanted to contact
him from the spirit world. She continued saying, that she
recognized that he had the ability to receive her thoughts
and to write them down.

James E. Padgett

In the evenings that followed, Padgett sat patiently at
his desk with pencil in hand hoping to hear from his dear
departed wife. Eventually, one evening, he wrote a short note signed

I

Helen. In the months that followed, Helen provided proof to her lawyer husband that she was alive and well and living in another dimension. In time, Padgett became thoroughly convinced by Helen's letters and those from other relations that he had been chosen by Jesus and his disciples to be his mortal instrument, whereby great spiritual knowledge would be imparted to the earth as an epoch-making "revelation" from the spirit world.

You may be wondering, if such an important event took place on behalf of Spiritualism why you haven't heard about it before? The answer is, Padgett's savings were depleted due to Helen's long illness, he had to continue to work to live. He must have realized at the time that by revealing his mediumship he could jeopardize his reputation and law career and thus his only means oif income. He must have decided to keep his mediumship secret, revealing it as far as is known to only his closest Spiritualist friends.

Padgett was able to accomplish this mediumistic feat because he was born with psychic abilities that could be developed. And, most importantly, he had the rare ability to make his mind totally passive so that he could receive the thoughts of spirits without imposing his own thoughts along with theirs. Padgett did not know what he was writing until he read it afterwards according to his closest friend Dr. Leslie R. Stone. Padgett was also willing to learn through his writings how to increase his psychic power to be able to link with the highest spirits and write their messages accurately.

Dr. Stone was born November 10, 1876 at Aldershot, Hampshire. In 1903 he emigrated to Toronto, Canada, where he was introduced to Spiritualism. He then studied at the Palmer Gregory College of Chiropractic in Oklahoma City, and after graduation in 1912 opened an

office in Washington D.C., where he practiced and continued his spiritualistic interests. In the early fall of 1914, Dr. Stone was introduced to Mr. Padgett at his law office in the Stewart Building. A lasting friendship ensued based on their mutual interest in psychic phenomenon. Dr. Stone was invited to Padgett's home, which he visited regularly, often being present during the writing sessions.

Dr. Leslie R. Stone

Upon Padgett's passing in March of 1923, Dr. Stone was selected to become the publisher of his works. It was a considerable undertaking for Dr. Stone to publish the first book of writings, because with Padgett's automatic writing the words were interconnected, the t's were not crossed nor are the i's dotted, in short there was no punctuation.

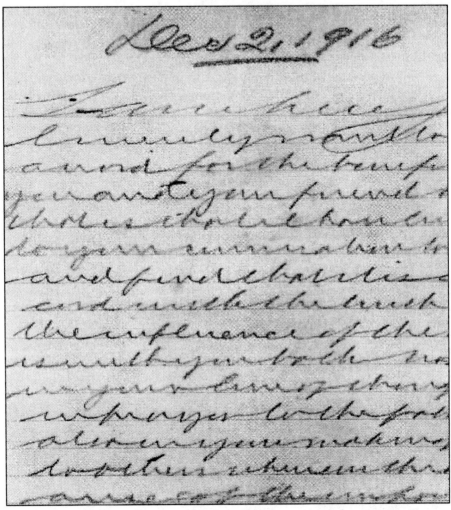

Nevertheless, Dr. Stone persevered and completed his book of messages, as he called them, in 1940. Unfortunately, by then Spiritualism's popularity in America had waned dramatically, due to the successful campaign by the celebrated escape artist Harry Houdini to expose fraudulent mediums. Spiritualism became a mere shadow of its former self, which proved not to be a good time to introduce new spirit teachings. I believe that it is these circumstances which have led to the obscurity of these important spirit writings for the past nine decades.

After Padgett's passing a small but dedicated group headed by Dr. Stone carried on the effort of transcribing and publishing his writings. In the fall of 1954, Dr. Stone met Dr. Daniel G. Samuels while employed by the University of the District of Columbia. The meeting took place in Washington, D.C., and a friendship sprang up which was to last for years. Dr. Samuels was a graduate of City College (New York) in 1930.

Dr. Daniel G. Samuels

He received an M.A. from Columbia University in 1931, and a Ph.D. in philosophy from the same university in 1940. His proficiency was in romance languages and journalism, which he taught at the university level. He also worked for the government as a translator.

In November of 1954 Dr. Samuels began to take automatic writing and it was soon realized that he had been chosen by Jesus as his second mortal instrument, to continue his revealment with further knowledge of his life and teachings. Dr. Samuels wrote for eleven years until his passing in 1966.

I believe that the writings of both of these men are of immense importance to Spiritualism and can contribute greatly to its advancement. Not only, because they shed new light on Spiritualism and the Bible, but also because they teach a unique way to develop spiritually, by receiving God's Love into one's soul. I also believe that if these teachings were to be embraced by Spiritualists, particularly by the mediums and healers, they could develop their psychic abilities to the extent that they would be able to produce phenomenon which would appear to the world as miracles. Spiritualism would be recognized as a true religion, and it could then take its rightful place among the great religions of the world.

Alan Ross

Alan Ross

THE
NEW TESTAMENT
OF
SPIRITUALISM

A Revelation From Spirit

CHAPTER ONE

Family

HELEN PADGETT (Wife)

Mrs. Helen Padgett's experience
leaving her body and going to the spirit world
December 8, 1914

I am here, Helen.

I am so very happy as you are loving me very much tonight, for I can see that your thoughts are with me so much more than of late; let me continue to feel that you love me.

When I realized that the time had come for me to go, I did not fear to do so, but calmly waited and thought that all my sufferings would soon end. When my spirit left the body I commenced to feel as if I was rising out of it and that I was going upward to the place that I had so often heard my father speak about. I had scarcely awakened to the fact that my spirit had left the body, before your mother had me in her arms and was trying to tell me that I had nothing to fear or cause me to feel that I was not with those who loved me. She was so beautiful that I hardly realized that it was she, and when I commenced to see that I was no longer in my body, I asked her not to leave me but to take me with her to where she lived. She told me that I could not go there, but that God had prepared a place for me to go to, and that she would accompany me and show me the truth of my future existence. I went with her, and she took me to a place that was very beautiful and filled with spirits who had recently passed over. She did not leave me for a longtime, and when she did, your father came to me and said, "I am Ned's* father and want to help you to realize that you are now in the spirit world, and must not let the thoughts of the earth keep you from getting in a condition to learn that all of us are only waiting for the Love of God to help us to higher and better things."

Your grandmother soon came to me and told me who she was, and was so beautiful and bright that I scarcely could look at her, for her face was all aglow with what seemed to me to be a heavenly light; and her voice was so sweet and musical that I thought she must be one of God's angels that I had read about in the Bible. She told me of the things that God had prepared for me, and He wanted me to love Him and believe that He loved me.

After awhile I commenced to think that I must be deceived in my sight and hearing, and was still on earth, and needed only my body again to know that I was still a mortal. Some time elapsed before I really became conscious that I was a spirit and was not on earth; for when I tried to talk to you, as I did, you would not listen to me and turned away from me as if you did not hear or see me. After a short time your mother and father came to me again, and tried to persuade me that I must not continue in my belief that I was still of the earth, and must believe that I was in the spirit life, and needed only the things of the spirit to make me more contented.

So you see, I was so very fortunate in having your dear parents**

*A nickname for Padgett used by family members.
**Helen did meet her own parents in the spirit world, however, they were not in condition to help her with her transition as her inlaws were.

and grandmother welcome me when I passed over. If they had not received me I do not know to what condition of fear and distraction I might have been subjected. No spirit can learn the truth of the change, unless in someway helped by others.

When I commenced to leave the body I felt that something unusual was happening, but I was not afraid. As I always in life dreaded death (as you know), the strange thing to me was that I did not look upon death as dying; it was only a pleasant dreamy feeling. I had been suffering pain, but I thought that I was getting well, and that the feeling of relief that came over me was the result of my getting better. As my spirit arose, I thought only of my condition and how soon I would be able to return home and see my friends. No other thoughts came to me — not even my love for God, or the fact that I was not in condition, as regards my soul, to meet my Maker, as I had been taught. There was absolutely no fear of what might happen to me, or that I would soon be called upon to account for the sins I had committed.

Just before my spirit left my body I was unconscious, but just as soon as the separation commenced I became fully conscious and knew everything that took place, and did not feel as if I were at all in danger or needed the help of anyone. I did not stay with my body at all, but when I commenced to leave it, I continued to rise, as I have told you, until your mother met me. So you see death, which I so much feared, was not such a dreadful thing to experience after all.

When you come over I will be there to receive you and love you so much that you will never have to go through the period of doubt that I did. Your father is also waiting to receive you, and in fact, all your spirit band have agreed that when you come, you will have nothing to fear for want of help and love. You must let me stop now, for I am tired.

Your own true and loving,
Helen

Mrs. Helen Padgett describes the method used
to communicate her thoughts to her husband
December 9, 1914

I am here, Helen.

I am here, your own true and loving Helen. After I passed over, I saw that I must seek a way to communicate with you in my spirit existence. You do not know this, but it is a fact that I was with you when you visited the medium who informed you that you were a medium, being possessed of the gift of automatic writing. I learned this fact from some of your spirit relatives, principally your father, who impressed this medium to tell you the fact of your mediumship. When, at last, you made the experiment, I was present with you and exerted all my powers, and had the help of other spirits, in making your experiment a success. When you commenced to receive my messages I cannot tell you how happy I was and thankful that the way was opened up that enabled me to tell you that, above everything else, what I was so anxious to tell you that I loved you with all my heart and soul.

Let me tell you that you are only making yourself unhappy trying to learn all about the way that I write to you; for you cannot, as you are not able to see my method, and I cannot fully explain it to you, but I will try to do as best I can. When you take hold of the pencil, I exercise all my power to move the pencil so that it will write just what I think, and in order to do that I have to let my thoughts go through your brain. You do not do the thinking but merely let the thoughts pass through your brain, and the movement of the pencil is caused by the exercise of your brain in conjunction with my power which I exercise on the pencil. So you see, you do not originate the thought but merely convey it to the hand, which I guide in accordance with my thought. You do not have anything more to do with what is written than an electric wire has to do with transmitting a message from the party at the end where the message is given.

Let me explain in another way. When I think a thought I pass it through your brain to your hand, and my power to move your hand is brought into action, just as when you think a thought your power to move your hand is brought into action. My thoughts are not your thoughts; and when I think, your mind catches the thought but does not create it. So you must believe that I am doing the writing and not you — for I write some thoughts which you could not write if you tried. You could not write the things that I write without giving much thought to the different subject matters, for some of them are not familiar to you, as you have often said. Let go the idea that you are writing things which emanate from what is sometimes called your subconscious mind; because only the material brain furnishes thoughts which it puts forth from the observation of the senses, or from the faculties which are brought into action when reason makes the basis of the thoughts.

I am studying the laws of physical and psychical sciences, so that I may be able to assist you in your investigations when you come to search for the true relationship between spirits and mortals, and the laws which control these communications. Yes, my studies include the investigation of the laws governing clairvoyance and inspirational communications. You will have the opportunity sometime to have an experience in each of these phases, and I want to be in condition to assist you to a degree that will help you in arriving at conclusions which will be correct, and which will help others to understand the laws that govern these things.

So you see your wife loves you so much that she is willing to attempt to learn these things which are thought to be only for the masculine mind in order to help you more clearly understand them. If you will only give your thoughts to the spiritual things, and let your soul be open to the inflowing of God's Love by praying with all your soul longing, you can progress just as rapidly as I do.

Your own true wife,
Helen

Mrs. Padgett answers a dream call from her husband
December 4, 1914

I am here, Helen.

Well, sweetheart, I heard you call me in your waking moments after your dream, and I came to you and loved you with all my heart. I know what your dream was, for I was trying to come to you in your sleep so that you would realize my presence, and I came as I might have appeared to you on earth were I now living. I heard you call me several times and I came to you and then I realized how lonesome you were and how much you wanted me, and how necessary I am to you.

Oh, my darling, to think that in a few short years you will be with me and we will never have to separate again, and that our love will be so great that never can anything occur that will bring us unhappiness or discontent. I do love you with all my heart and soul and you must love me in the same way, and think of me very often and wish for me, as you did last night.

The dream had no special significance, but was merely intended to show you that your little wife was still with you, and that even if she could not come to you in the flesh, she could in your dreams. She was just as she might have appeared to you in her early days of married life, and tried to let you see how beautiful she was, because she thought that maybe your recollections of her of those days may have become dim and shadowy.

So you see, we can be with each other in our writings, in our visions, in voice communications and in dreams, should we not thank God for these great privileges? I often think of the great gift that God has given to you, and of our ability to become so close to each other in conscious communion, and I wonder why it is. When I consider the work that you have been selected to do, I don't wonder, for that work is of such importance that you will have to have the gift which has been bestowed upon you, and also the other great powers that will be given you.

As I said last night, the power of inspiration is yours also, and if you will seek to cultivate it, you will find that you will be able to express the thoughts of some of the greatest spirits that we have in our higher spirit world, and you will be surprised at what will come through you in this way, and your hearers will also wonder and think that you are a wonderfully wise man and orator. However, you must understand that it will not be you who will really do the speaking, but the spirits who will be behind you.

No, it will not interfere with your writing powers, but, on the contrary, will help and increase these powers, for many times when we write, if we could only tell you in the way of inspiration what we desire to express, many things would be more easily transmitted to paper, than as now, when we have to do the physical work of moving your hand as well as of using your brain. So you see, it is very desirable for you to cultivate this phase of mediumship, for the good that you will be able to do is beyond calculation.

No, I have not heard that Ed Thomas has passed over, and I don't know any of his friends here, but I will try to find them and will speak to him and tell him that you sent me to him, and if he needs help I will try to help him, and, if he desires, will bring him to you, and let him write. So you see, if we can do good to any spirit we are always willing to do so.

Well, sweetheart, I do love you with all my heart and soul and I will stay with you, and comfort you and make you feel my presence. I am so happy that you love me so much and want me with you as you do; but we have to observe the laws governing our communications, and it will not be best for us to write more at this time.

Don't you think that we had better stop now, as you are tired, although you may not realize it? I will come again and tell you of my love. So with all my love I will say good-bye.

Your own true and loving,
Helen

Mr. Padgett is the chosen instrument
for Jesus's truths to be delivered to the earth
July 18, 1915

I am here, Helen.

Oh, my darling Ned, I cannot tell you how happy I am that all these great spirits should have come to you and testified* that you are the chosen of the Master. Of course, I knew it, and you knew it before, but to remove all doubt that you might have, they came, and in such certain terms declared the fact.

I know that you will have the power and love of many spirits to sustain you in your work; and think of the wonderful messages that you will receive, first those of the Master which will excel all others, and then those of his various apostles and disciples. You will certainly be blessed with wonderful knowledge of the celestial world and the power that will be exerted by your band will surpass any power that has been exerted before, and you will have the protection and sustaining power of spirits that will not permit any undesirable spirits or mortals to interfere with your work.

I am your own true and loving,
Helen

Helen describes her home in the third sphere
and the importance of seeking for the Love of God
November 30, 1914

I am here, Helen.

I am very happy for I have so much of God's Love in my heart that I cannot think of anything that tends to make me unhappy.

My home is very beautiful and I am perfectly delighted with it. It is made of white marble and is surrounded by lawns and flowers and trees of various kinds. The grass is so very green and the flowers are so beau-

*A number of these messages appear in later chapters.

8

tiful and variegated. The trees are always in foliage* and have such beautiful limbs and leaves. I am most pleased with my home, I mean the building. There are many beautiful pictures on the walls, and the walls are all frescoed and hung with fine coverings, and the floors are inlaid with beautiful mosaics, and I have all the splendid furniture that I could possibly wish for. My library is full of books of all kinds, especially those that tell of God and His Love for humanity. You would be in your element if you could be with me. It is permanent, and the house and trees and flowers are more real to me than were ever the houses and trees and flowers on earth; they are not shadowy as you may think, but are so very substantial that they never decay or grow old.

I have music, such as you have never heard on earth, and instruments of various kinds which I am learning to play, and I sing with all my heart and soul as the days go by. I have beds on which I lie down, but I never sleep. We do not need sleep here; we only rest, for sometimes we get tired from our work and are greatly refreshed by lying on the beds and couches which are so comfortable that we do not realize that we are tired after lying down just a little while.

We eat fruit and nuts or rather imbibe their essences, but do not do so because we are hungry, but more because we enjoy the flavors so much; and we drink water, pure and sweet, as it makes us feel so refreshed when we are a little tired. No, our fruit is not of the earthly kind — it is so much more delightful that I am unable to describe it to you. The nuts are different, also. Yes, the water is purer than what you have and is more refreshing.

I am going to try to progress into the higher planes, and hope to do so as rapidly as is possible, and you may rest assured that no matter what plane** I may be in, my love for you will not lessen, and I will not cease to be with you as I now am. You can progress on earth just as rapidly as I can here, if you will let God's Love come into your heart as fully and as abundantly as I do; and you can if you will only pray. God does not require the child of His care to be in the spirit world in order to develop his soul. You have the same soul now that you will have when you come here, and if you let God fill it with His Love while you are on earth, why should it not progress as much as it does here? The Love of God coming into the soul of a human does not depend upon whether he

*This is not to say that there are not places in the spirit world that have seasons.
**Spheres one to six each have seven planes of habitation.

9

is in the flesh or in the spirit. All souls must answer for the sins done in the body, although it is not necessary that such penalties be paid in the spirit world — you can pay the penalty while on earth. As you "sow so shall you reap," but the reaping is not necessarily here.

If you seek earnestly for God's Love and Grace you can obtain them on the earth, and I am informed that when they are obtained on earth, greater will be the progress of the spirit when it comes over. So let me pray that you seek these blessings while you are in your present life, and not wait for them to be given to you after you have entered the spirit world.

You are now on the way to obtain these blessings, and I pray that you may continue, for you cannot find true happiness in any other way. So try to become more spiritual, so that you may learn the wonderful teachings of God's Love and truth that he will give you. You must stop writing now as you are tired and so am I.

So pray to God for His Love and spiritual enlightenment,
Helen

Helen tells of her great happiness in her progress in the world of spirits
March 3, 1915

I am here, Helen.

I am happy to say that I have this Love now to a considerable degree, and the more I get of it the happier I am. I thought that I was happy when I entered the third sphere*, and more so in the fifth, and then supremely so in the seventh, but I really did not know what happiness was, until I got into my present home in the celestial heavens**. I suppose as I go higher, the happiness of each succeeding progressive sphere will be so much greater than the one from which I progressed.

Of course, the Master has been the great teacher, whose love and power have helped me more than all the others. He is so wonderful in

*The third, fifth and seventh spheres are used by spirits who are progressing through seeking God's Love.
**The realm immediately above the seventh sphere; the same as celestial spheres, celestial kingdom, kingdom of heaven and kingdom of God.

love and wisdom that I almost adore him, although, he says that I must worship only God, and I follow his directions.

My experiences here are so wonderful that I hardly realize what it all means. My time in the spirit world has been so short, and yet, the wonderful knowledge of spiritual truths and the great happiness that I have received, cause me to wonder in amazement that such things could be.

You have had a long writing session tonight, and I think I had better stop. So good night.

Your loving wife,
Helen

Helen discusses the sudden passing of their daughter, Nita, as a result of a serious operation, and the progress she is making in the spirit world
June 20, 1918

I am here, Helen.

Well, my dear Ned, you have had your little girl leave you, as you now feel, but she has not left, for she will be more with you than ever, and happier than she could possibly have been had she remained in the body.

I was with her as she passed over and received her in my arms and told her that she was with her mother and had nothing to fear, and that she had come to the spirit world and would now know what love and happiness are, and that all her troubles had left her forever. I told her that she would not have to leave you and her brothers*, except as regards her body which was no longer a part of her, and which she would soon realize was merely a covering for herself. She was not afraid and nestled in my arms as I kissed her and told her that now she would understand how much her mother loved her and how happy she would be in that love, and that in a very short time she would be perfectly content, and feel so happy that she had left behind the cares and troubles of her earth life.

*The Padgetts had two sons besides their daughter Nita.

11

I was with her before she died, and she actually saw me as I waited at her bedside for her spirit to find a release from her body. She recognized and talked to me and actually heard my voice as I encouraged her and called her to come to my arms. She was not afraid and I know that I was as visible to her as I ever was on earth.

She is now with me, or rather I am with her, and am trying to help her realize fully that she is a spirit; and she is convinced, for, as she tells me, she remembers the many talks that you had with her in which you told her of my coming to you and to her with all my love and desire to make her happy, and that as she remembered these things it seemed to be natural for her to have the experience of having me with her as her real loving mother. I will be with her a great deal and so will many other spirits who love her, including your parents and mine. They were with her when she came over and spoke to her of their love and encouraged her to believe that she was really with them and had nothing to fear, and that only love was around her.

She will soon be in a better condition to appreciate her surroundings, and then I will bring her to you and let her tell you of her experience and her love for you and the boys. I know that you are sorrowful to have her leave you in the body and that your heart is very heavy, as you expected to have her with you more intimately than ever and to find much happiness and comfort in her presence. Now dear, you must try not to worry or grieve, for, as I have said, you have not lost her. She will be with you more than ever and you will feel her presence and know that she is so much happier than when a mortal.

I wish that I could make myself visible to you so that I could comfort you the more and cause you to believe that your Baby* has not left you. Let not your belief in the fact that we are really alive go from you. We are more alive than ever, and can love you more than when in the earth life. So do not grieve, but know that it will not be long before you will be with us, and that this is a certainty.

Oh, my dear, I love you so much tonight and want to comfort you with my love, and with the assurance that now, as you sit in your room at night and feel lonesome and sometimes wish that Baby could be with you. I and your Baby, who will soon be a bright spirit, will be with you and enjoy the happiness that her love for you will bring her.

As I say, you must not grieve, for you are not strong and grief will

*The Padgett's affectionate name for their daughter Nita.

12

not be beneficial to your condition of mind. Think only of her as being a beautiful loving spirit, filled with love for you and always glad when she can be with you, but sorry that you may not be able to feel her arms around you and her kisses on your lips.

Well, dear, I want to encourage you and keep you from worrying so that you will not be unhappy. I really believed that she would not die, but that she would have the strength to overcome the results of the operation; but I was mistaken and for your sake, I was as sorry as I could possibly be. We cannot always foretell the results of certain contingencies affecting the material conditions of mortals. We do not know these things as a matter of omniscience, but merely base our conclusions on what we believe will be the results of certain causes. I was so anxious to comfort and relieve you from your worry, and the real fact is that you have no cause for worry. I did not allude to this when I told you not to worry, for I believed that she would recover from her sickness, and so thought the others who wrote you encouraging words. Even Dr. Campbell thought that she would be able to withstand the results of the operation, but in these things we cannot always judge aright. We are not infallible and cannot always exercise the power which we possess to bring about results that our loved ones on earth may desire. So sweetheart, do not feel resentful because my promises did not come true.

If you could only fully understand what the condition of your Baby is, you would not want her with you in the body. I know that you will, at times, feel very lonesome and long for her as your dear one of earth form and companionship, but soon you will have such an experience with her as your spirit Baby, that you will not sorrow often because she left you. This I know without the possibility of your being disappointed, and you must try to believe me.

Well, sweetheart, when you are a little stronger I will come and write and Baby will write also. You are not in condition to write more tonight and must go to bed.

Love me and love her, and may God bless and comfort you, my dear husband.

Your own true and loving,
Helen

Helen explains the effect on babies who
come into the spirit world as a result of abortion
November 13, 1915

I am here, Helen.

In my investigation of the subject of babies who have come to the spirit world as a result of abortion, I find that they never go back to their earth mothers for any purpose whatever. There are spirits who are specially designated to take care of babies, and in cases where the natural mothers have succeeded in cutting short the lives of these babies, these spirits who have charge of them in the spirit world may not permit them to come in contact with their natural mothers or visit them. This is because the mother's love is not there to receive these poor little waifs; and where there is no mother's love there is no attraction existing that will cause the return of the babies when they have once left their mothers.

In the case of babies who prematurely die, or of those who die very young, these babies do return to their mothers under the guidance of their guardian spirits and receive from their mothers their love and feelings which are going forth to these babies. The law of attraction operates here as well as in other matters and this is the law in reference to babies who die early. When there exists a mother's love, the baby will return and receive this love and help by coming in contact with its mother, but when there is no mother's love there is no attraction, and the baby may never know its mother.

In many cases, the baby, before the mother comes to the spirit world, finds other attractions, and hence there is no feeling of love or sympathy between the baby and its mother. Frequently it happens that when the mother comes into the spirit world, she finds the spirit of the unborn baby, and in a way has a uniting, but rarely is this love strong enough to keep them together, the law of attraction separates them and then each goes his own way. I will not write more tonight.

Your own true and loving,
Helen

14

ANN R. PADGETT (Mother)

Ann Padgett talks about her soulmate
and how much love she has for her son
September 15, 1914

I am here, your Mother.

You are the best son in the world. Yes, I am very often with you. Try to give me more of your heart and you will feel that I am with you even more.

I have a home and live with a spirit that is the same in progression as myself. We are very happy together and she is the soulmate of your father. No, I am not with my soulmate; he is not in the same sphere with me. He is in the one with your father and is progressing too. No, I did not know him on the earth and only met him when he came to the spirit world. He was living in the city of Chicago, and was a very wealthy man, but a very great sinner. He is now in a state of progression and will be with me soon.

I do not believe in eternal punishment; it is a false teaching of the orthodox church. Jesus is the same as I believed him to be on earth, but I do not worship him as God. He is not God, but a spirit of the greatest perfection and goodness. He is with me quite often. He talked to you on Saturday night and he will come to you again very soon and explain the true teaching of the Bible. Let him be your friend and adviser.

You must go to bed.

Good night my son,
Your Mother

Padgett's mother says his father
has found his soulmate in the spirit world
December 20, 1914

I am here, your Mother.

I am your mother and I want to write you a few lines for I have not written lately. Do not think that you are not very dear to me, for you are still my own darling boy.

I am very happy as your father is now in a sphere where he is more spiritual and happy. His soulmate is with him very often and she loves him very much. He is a very bright spirit and needs only more of God's Love to make him perfectly content.

Oh! My darling boy, I am so glad that your soulmate is Helen. She is so beautiful and lovely now that she has found God's Love that I can hardly tell you how beautiful she is. I am very happy also, but my soulmate is still in the first sphere* and does not seem to progress as rapidly as he should. I wish that you could talk to him as you did to your father, for I believe that it would do him good. You seem to have a wonderful influence with the spirits of men who are in a condition of sin and darkness. God is certainly good to you and has favored you beyond my greatest expectations. You seem to have the faith that calls for an answering ear and for a love that reaches to the very throne of God, and I believe that you will in someway do a great deal of good in the spirit world as well as on the earth.

You will meet your old friend** or I will bring him to you before long, and have him write to you, and then you can tell him of what you know about God's Love, and the necessity of his believing that he must give his whole heart to God. I have a very good influence over him but not sufficient to cause him to believe in this Love as being a necessity to his advancement. He is not a very spiritual man, and never was, but he is good-hearted and will listen to you for you seem to have the power to make spirits listen to you. I do not understand why but it is so. Be very careful of this great power which God has given you.

Jesus is also interested in you and loves you with more than ordi-

*The sphere closest to the earth where spirits are paying a penalty.
**This person is believed to be A.G. Riddle, Padgett's law partner.

16

nary love. He seems to think that you will be of great help to him and he is trying to show you the way to God's Love and favor. So do not doubt what I say for I believe that you are the special object of his love and favor.

I must stop now for you are tired,
Your Mother

Mother of Padgett says Mrs. Mary Baker Eddy sees the error in her teachings, and is living with her in the same sphere
December 5, 1914

I am here, your Mother.

My boy, I am so glad to write you again. It seems so long since I last wrote to you. I love you so much and feel that I must tell you.

Go to the Universalist Church. It is the best one now in existence because it believes more in God's Love without having to worship Jesus. As you say, the Christian Scientists are good people but their position on Spiritualism is all wrong and Mrs. Eddy now sees her error and wishes that she could undo it. She is in the same sphere with me but she does not enjoy as much of God's Love as I do. I talk to her sometimes and she tells me that she is very sorry that she made the mistake of teaching that spirits could not communicate with mortals. She is a very bright spirit and does not know all that she thought she knew when on earth and may soon write to you.

I will pray for you, my dear boy, with all my heart.

So good night,
Your Mother

JOHN H. PADGETT (Father)

John Padgett agrees with the suggestion made to form a band
to protect his son in his spiritual investigation through automatic writings
May 31, 1914

I am here, your Father.

I will try to tell you what we must do to form a band of spirit work-ers. Let me select them, and then you will not be troubled by bad spir-its. You must not try to talk to everyone who may come to you, for that will work injury to you and you will not be able to get the best results.

Let me tell you whom you should have form the band: your grand-mother, your mother, Helen, Professor Salyards*, Mr. Riddle, and myself will be enough to help you in the investigation of Spiritualism. Yes, I will have them come, and you can ask them yourself if they will join.

Grandmother. Yes, I will, and you will be a successful medium, and will not need to go to the seances where you went on Friday night, as they are not helpful to you in the way of progressing in your investiga-tions.

Mother. Yes, I am. I certainly will, and you will not be troubled by bad spirits, for your father and grandmother will keep them away from you.

Professor Salyards. Yes, I am, and I will be one of the band to help you. You will be my mouthpiece in my writing to the world the thoughts that I desire to make known on subjects that are of interest to mankind. Keep well and I will soon let you write my ideas of this life and of what I find to be the real truth of the Love of God and the love of man. Yes, I will show my face in the photograph, and then you will know that I am one of your band.

Mr. Riddle. Yes, I am, and I will be one of the band. You will not be annoyed by any others than the ones your father has named. I will write you what my beliefs and thoughts are of the life here so that you may know that I am a spirit in search of the truth. You will see that I am not one who knows everything, but will try to learn whatever is possible

*Padgett's university instructor.

18

and will tell you what I have learned. Yes, and I will let you see that I have my mustache and goatee just as in my earthly life.

You can go to the photographer as soon as you find it convenient and we will be there, and you will see us all. I will be in my naval uniform and then you will be convinced that I am living.

Go to bed and rest.

Your father,
John Padgett

*Father of the medium has been selected by
the higher spirits to be the guardian angel of his son*
March 17, 1915

I am here, your Father.

Well my son, I have not written you for some time as you have not given me the opportunity, but it was best as you have received much valuable information from the others that have written you.

I am your guardian angel and will be as long as you live on earth. I know that Helen is with you very much of the time, and of course is much more interested in you than any of us and tries so hard to make you happy; nevertheless, she is not your guardian angel. White Eagle* is your guide in a great many things and is faithful too, but he is not the one designated by the higher powers to perform the duties of a guardian angel. So do not think that I am not with you trying to help and sustain you in your troubles and cares, for I am.

We are all so much interested in you, that you are never alone even while you sleep. Mr. Riddle and Prof. Salyards are with you a great deal trying to influence you in your earthly affairs. The spirit of the man who wrote the book that you are reading, I did not know him until he came to write and introduced himself as the author of the book and said that Jesus recommended him. Of course we consented for him to write. He is a spirit of the fifth sphere where I live and I shall see more of him now, and it may be that he will join our band, for he is a wonderfully intel-

*A powerful member of Padgett's spirit band.

19

lectual man and well versed - in spiritual truths. He is not filled with this great Love as are your grandmother, mother and Helen, but he will make a desirable addition, and I believe that all the band will consent, especially as Jesus has recommended him.

I am glad to say that Laura* is now in the third sphere, and she is praying with all her soul for more Love, and is a beautiful spirit. Yes, she loves you very much, for your kind thoughts, and is with me very often, when I am with you. Look at your writings and you will see.

Yes, your friends are still praying and I see them quite often. Mackey is progressing more rapidly than any of them. Taggart is progressing, but he is so hard to convince, sooner or later he will be convinced and then he will advance rapidly. Harvey is held back by his disappointment in not receiving what the priests had told him on earth. McNally is still in darkness — his awful habit of drink has resulted in keeping him in this darkness, but he is praying also. We all hope that they will see the light.

Yes, especially Taggart, who says that he would like to have another talk with you before long, and he wants to ask you some questions and maybe you can answer them so that some of his doubts may be removed.

Well, I must stop, so good night, my dear son,

Your loving Father

John Padgett is involved in the work of helping spirits find their soulmates
December 31, 1914

I am here, your Father.

I am very happy and am glad that you seem to be also. Your experience the other night in loving Helen and in her loving you must have made you perfectly happy to have had such a demonstration of love and the realization of the actual sensitive presence of your wife. I tell you that she was with you and was so filled with her love for you, that we all wondered at it. She is a spirit that seems to have no limit to her love

*Padgett's cousin.

for you. Not many spirits have such an abundance of love as she has for you, so you must consider yourself a very blessed man to have such a wife and soulmate.

As I told you many years ago, there is a record in the heavens, a book of lives, as I might call it, which contains the names of those who are decreed by God to be together through all eternity. When I want to know who the soulmate is of one who desires to know his or her soulmate, I consult that book, and there I find who the soulmate is. I am not permitted to give the name of the soulmate if he or she is in the earth life, for it might create discord or unhappiness. However, if the soulmate is not married then there is no restriction upon me, but if the soulmate is married then I must not tell the name, such is the law of God in this particular.

I have had this duty assigned to me, and I have taught her to perform this duty and she is now engaged in it, and is most successful in the performance of her mission. She seems to have a wonderful ability, or you might call it, intuition for locating the soulmates in the spirit world as she never fails when she undertakes to find one. She also finds great happiness in doing this work and in seeing the happiness that comes to those who ask her to perform this task. I do not engage in it with as much enthusiasm as she does, however I do the best that I can, and I am rewarded by seeing the happiness of the soulmates when they are brought together.

You are tired and must stop.

Your father,
John Padgett

Padgett's father reassures him that it was Jesus who wrote on Saturday
September 14, 1914

I am here, your Father.

I am happy and so is your mother, for you are much better spiritually than when you were a boy. You are commencing to see the true teachings of the Bible. Let your teachings be in Christ as he is the truth and the way and the light.

It was Jesus of the Bible who came to you on Saturday night. I know because I was with him and know it was he. He is not an impostor, as your friend thinks, but he was Jesus of Nazareth and he was the only one in all the spirit world who has the wonderful countenance of love and truth. He is the one true Son of God who can show you and your friend the way from your sins. Believe in him and do not let the teachings or false statements of other spirits cause you to have doubts as to his being the true Christ.

Keep his love fresh in your hearts and he will come to you again. He is the true Jesus that was hung on the cross and arose again from the dead. Be not deceived by the spirits who say that he cannot come to you or your friend. He is your friend and he loves you both* as his younger brothers.

Jesus is the personality that took the form of a man and lived on earth, teaching the truths of God. The truths that Jesus taught are the everlasting things that will save the human race from their sins. He is a spirit just as we are, although he is so very far above us in the spirit life and in his knowledge of God that we all, who believe in God, look up to him as our teacher.

Let his love for you keep you in the true way to eternal life and happiness.

Good-bye and may God bless you,
Your Father

*James Padgett and Dr. Stone.

22

ANN R. ROLLINS (Grandmother)

Grandmother of medium affirms that
no impostors write through her grandson
April 5, 1915

I am here, your Grandmother.

Well, I am glad to be with you again, as I want to tell you some truths that you will benefit by knowing.

You have had more or less doubt pass through your mind as to whether we are really the persons whom we represent ourselves to be, or whether it is your own mind producing the thoughts and writings, or whether some evil spirit or imposter does.

I want to tell you now, with all the love which I have for you, that every one of us who writes you is the person he or she represents himself or herself to be, and no spirit who may seek to impose on you is permitted to write or in any way communicate with you. Our band is sufficiently powerful to prevent any such spirit from intruding himself upon you. Of course, the unfortunate spirits* who write you, we permit to do so, however they are not impostors, but tell you truthfully just who they are. I know how natural it is for you to doubt this great marvel of spirit communion, and of the truthfulness of our representations, but I assure you that it is all true.

The Master is the one of whom you have read about in the Bible, and of whom you have heard about all your life, the only difference being that he is not God, but a spirit — the greatest in all the celestial heavens. He is not so very different in his desire to do the great work which God gave him to do, and what he did do when on earth, except that he is now more highly developed than when a man traveling the plains and mountains of Palestine. He is more powerful now and knows so many more truths of God, and his love is just the same, only greater in degree.

So you must not doubt any longer or you will not develop as you should. He is the wisest and most filled with God's Love of all the spirits in the celestial spheres.

I know that you love us all, and I believe that you love him also, and

---

*Padgett would devote one evening a week to helping dark spirits.

when I tell you that his love is greater than that of any of us, I am telling you what is true.

I would like to write more tonight, but there are some others here who are very anxious to write you and I will stop.

Your own true and loving,
Grandmother

Ann Rollins was both blind and deaf when on earth,
but was not unhappy; also how worry can be removed
January 9, 1917

I am here, your Grandmother.

Well, my dear son, it has been some time since I wrote you, and I feel that I must say a few words to you, as you are in a condition that needs some encouragement and sympathy.

I love you, as you know and while I have not written you lately, yet I have been with you a great deal watching over you and trying to influence you with my love and powers by bringing to you spiritual thoughts and soul longings.

Now, I want to tell you a few things that may help you in your moments of worry. When on earth, as you know, I was nearly blind and deaf, and in such condition that would naturally cause me to worry and be unhappy, but I did not worry and was not unhappy; and the secret was that I had in my soul the Love of God. It was so real to me that no doubt of its existence in my soul ever came to cause me unhappiness, and I assure you, that this Love is the same kind of love that now floods my whole being and gives me the happiness that I now possess. I remember that I did not have many material things to trouble me, for you looked after my material welfare and was always kind to me and loving, yet, nevertheless, if it had not been for the Love that I speak of, I can readily see that I should have been very worried and unhappy a great deal, for my natural inclination was to worry when things did not go right, as we said.

So, I tell you from actual experience, that all your worries, and by this I mean your causes of worry, may be taken from your conscious self if you will only seek for and obtain, which you certainly can do, this Love of God. It is astonishing how efficacious it is to cause the worries and troubles to disappear. They, as you may know, are very largely a matter of the mind and while in a certain sense they are real, yet the mind or its condition is the real cause of the realization of the worries. Now consider for a moment the fact, and I know that you will agree with me that it is a fact, that the indulging in these worries does not in one particular remove the material causes of the worry, and does not in any manner bring relief from the troubles, no matter how much you may allow your mind to dwell on these things, and how intensely you may worry, the cause, the material cause, remains.

You may say, and it is natural to do so, that it is easy enough to advise that you should not let these inconvenient things cause you to worry, but when you come to the practical experience and are suffering from these conditions, it is not so easy to throw aside the effect of these troubles on the mind. Well, there is much truth in that, notwithstanding that this Love that I tell you of, when living in the soul, will make even that effort easy to accomplish.

The philosophy of the phenomenon, if you may call it such, is that this Love is of such real substantial Essence that it takes control of the mind and eliminates the consciousness of the reality of the causes of the worry. Now I do not want to be understood as intending to convey the idea that these material causes are not real, for I am not a Christian Scientist to that extent, what I mean is, that notwithstanding the real existence of these causes, the effects of this Love, and the faith that accompanies it, upon the mind which is the real cause of the worry is such that forgetfulness of these causes of worry takes the place of the constant indulging in the thoughts of their existence, and the unhappy consequence that must flow from them. The cause itself is not removed but the consciousness of their existence, for the time being, is dissipated, and to the mind that is thus influenced by the Love, these causes are as if they were not. Of course, they are existing and facing you to some extent, but it will come to you that they are not so overwhelming and insurmountable as they would appear were this Love absent from the soul and its influence from the mind.

In addition to this, love and faith create a confidence in the power of God and His willingness to help. That engenders courage, which enables the possessor of this confidence to overcome these causes of worry that he would not otherwise be able to do. What I have said may be called the philosophy of the workings of this Love in its effective destruction of worry. Now the great fact in this is that God does, as a truth, help the one who is in the condition of being possessed with this Love. His Love is real and His help is real, and the effect is to make the causes named things of unreality so far as the happiness of the object of this help is concerned. And as a truth, shown by the experience of mortals, a very large proportion of the worries and troubles that harass and cause so much unhappiness to mortals is a thing of the imagination and never realized.

So my dear son, try to understand what I have written and apply it to your own condition, and you will find that your worries are not near so great as you now think. I know just what is facing you, and as you have been told by others who have written you, in a short time you will be relieved and the sun will again shine in your consciousness of existence, and you will become in a much better condition to do your work, both that of your business and that of the Master.

You must not for a moment think that you will not be looked after so that you can do and complete the task that you have been selected to do. This is as certain as that the sun shines, and while for a time yet some disagreeable and disheartening things may confront you, it will not be a great while before they will become things of the past, and you will be in condition to do this work without hindrance or interference.

So think of all that I have said and try to believe and make a practical application of my philosophy; and above all pray to God for a greater inflowing of this Love, and have faith to realize that it will become yours, limited only by your longings and sincerity of aspirations. Well, I will come soon and write you a long letter on some spiritual truth that will be of interest to you.

I must stop now, and so with all my love and God's blessings, I will say, good night.

Your loving,
Grandmother

A description of some of the spheres
December 22, 1915

I am here, your Grandmother.

I come, because I see that you have been very much interested in the description of the various spheres of the spirit world as contained in the book that you have just been reading.

Well, my son, I have read the book as you did and I must say that I have grave doubts that any mortal ever had the experience of the doctor as is related in that book. I, of course, will not positively say that he did not leave his body and visit some of the spheres of the spirit world, and attempt to give a description of what he saw, but I do not think it was possible for him to visit any sphere which is higher than his soul development would enable him to enter. I am informed that not being a man with the soul development that would fit him for the higher soul spheres*, I do not understand how he could possibly have entered a sphere higher than the sixth; and I doubt that he entered that, for from all the information that I have received, I have never heard of any mortal entering a sphere higher than the third.

At any rate, the descriptions of the higher spheres as contained in the book — and I mean by this the spheres above the third — are not correct in many particulars for, as I have told you before, the fifth and seventh spheres are not intellectual spheres in the preeminent sense. In them are not the great colleges and institutions of learning that the book refers to, and neither are the inhabitants engaged in any special study of the laws of nature with the mere intellect, for in these spheres the great studies and aspiration of the spirits are given to the development of the soul by obtaining God's Love. To help in the work there are teachers who devote themselves to instructing these spirits in those things which will lead to this soul development.

The mind or mere intellect is not given much attention to, but is subordinated to the soul development, for with this development and a part of it, comes a wonderful development of the faculties of what you might call the mind, but which we call and which really are the soul perceptions. I know it is hard for you to understand, for what we call the soul

*Three, five and seven are the spheres of soul development.

perceptions may be compared to the mental faculties as you commonly speak of them. These soul perceptions do not depend upon these mental faculties, and in fact the latter forms no part of the former, they are entirely distinct and of a different order and composition from these mental faculties. These soul perceptions, as such, cannot be cultivated or made to increase in their powers or qualities by mere study. They and their progress are entirely dependent upon and not separated from the development of the soul in Love. I mean the Love of God. In other words, unless there be a development of the soul by this Divine Love, there will be no development of the soul perceptions. It is difficult to explain this to you, but you may possibly get some idea from what I have said.

The sixth sphere* is the great intellectual sphere, and in it are wonderful colleges and institutions of learning, and many spirits who were great intellectually on earth are teachers in these institutions. You must not think that because certain spheres are preeminently intellectual, that there are not teachers of the higher truths pertaining to the soul and to the love of man, working in these spheres, for there are, and many great spirits of the celestial spheres are engaged in this teaching. This I must say, that the work is more difficult and the effort to convince these spirits of highly developed intellectuality and knowledge is more strenuous than in any of the lower spheres. These bright-minded spirits seem to think that the mind is the great thing to be cultivated and looked after, and while they in a way worship God, yet it is with the faculties of the mind merely. They do not think that there is any teachings in the truth of the New Birth and the Divine Love, in contradistinction to the love which they possess, which is only the natural love**. I have been in all these spheres and have worked in them, and what I tell you I know from actual experience.

Well, he is mistaken, for in the seventh sphere the spirits have homes just as they do in the lower spheres, only they are much more beautiful and bring more happiness and gladness because of the great number of additional things that are provided by God to increase the happiness of His children.

As to our clothing in that sphere, we are clothed in what you would say a modest and comfortable way. Our clothing is not so flimsy as to

*The sixth sphere is the highest sphere obtainable through the progress of either purification of the human love or the development of the intellect.
**The same as human love.

permit our forms to be seen as if we had on no clothing at all. This idea must have arisen from the fact that inhabitants of that sphere have no thought of immodesty or of what might result from the suggestions that a naked or half clothed body might give to mortals or even some of the lower spirits, but such an idea does not enter into the question of the nature of the clothes that we shall wear.

Our thoughts are all pure and free from mortal taint, and the character of our thoughts has no influence upon the character of our clothing. We wear clothes to cover our bodies because we think it proper to do so, and because we make our clothes by our own thoughts and will, and they are of the most glorious and shining appearances that you can imagine. As all things in nature have a covering, so in the spirit world, the spirits all have coverings, and this is so even in the celestial sphere in which I live. I have never seen such a thing as a naked or nearly naked spirit in these higher spheres. Of course, the spirit of the doctor may have entered some of these higher spheres, as I have said, but his information as the author of the book that was communicated to his mortal friend, was not correctly transmitted, for many things which he says are not true.

I would like to write more tonight but it is late, and you are tired. I will say with all my love, good night.

Your own loving,
Grandmother

Ann Rollins's experience in seeking the
Love of God; also a description of Jesus's appearance
May 13, 1915

I am here, your Grandmother.

I am happier than I can tell you. I am living in my home and it is beautiful beyond the possibility of description.

Tonight I want to tell you of my experience in seeking the Love of God and in realizing that He loves me with a Love that knows no shadow of wavering or cessation. I was not always filled with faith, or believed so implicitly in prayer, but in my early married life, I received the conviction that if I were to be happy in life and fitted to receive the blessings which the Bible promised to those who should seek the Lord and His Love, I must see the necessity of seeking; and I, with all the earnestness of my nature, commenced seeking for the Divine Love, and as a result I found it, and with it a great happiness and peace.

You know what my spiritual condition was in my later years on earth, and how my faith was such that, although I was nearly deaf and blind, yet I was happy and joyful. Well, when I came to the spirit world, I brought that faith and Love with me, and I found that it was just as real here as it had been on earth. Of course, in some of my beliefs I was mistaken, such as my belief that Jesus was God, and that his death and blood saved or could save me from sin and damnation; but notwithstanding my mistakes in these particulars, my love for God was not interfered with, and I continued to live in that love and was happy.

I had not been in the spirit world for a great while, before spirits of a higher order than myself came to me and told me many wonderful things of God's kingdom, and that my progress to the higher spheres would depend upon my receiving more of this Divine Love in my soul and becoming more at-one with God.

The first time I saw Jesus was after I had been in the third sphere a short while, and when I met him he impressed me as being the most beautiful and loving spirit that I had ever seen. When he told me that he was Jesus, I, of course, was somewhat surprised, because I had believed that he was in the heavens sitting on the right hand of God, as I had been taught on earth to believe. When Jesus saw my surprise he looked on me with a wonderful love and said that I must not believe further that he was God accepting the worship of men, for he was a spirit as I was, and was still working among mortals and spirits to lead them into the light and the way to God's Love.

At first, I confess, it was difficult for me to believe this, and I had my doubts; but his manner of speaking to me and the wonderful love that he displayed, not only for me but for all humanity, soon convinced me that he was the true Jesus and not an impostor. Afterwards, I met many spirits who knew him and had been his followers for many years, and they told me that he was the Jesus of the Bible, and I could not do anything else but believe. And now, after my long years of association with him and feeling his ministrations of love and the influence of his greatness, I know that he is the true Jesus, who by his teachings and over-whelming love saves men from their sins, by showing them the way to God's kingdom. So my dear son, do not doubt what I tell you now in reference to this matter, or what I have already told you.

Well, it is somewhat difficult to describe his appearance, but I will try. He is of a commanding figure, as you say on earth. His features are regular, and his eyes are of a deep blue, almost a purple blue, with such depths of love in them that under its influence you almost forget to note the color of his eyes. The hair is a beautiful brown, worn long and parted in the middle so that it falls over his shoulders. His nose is straight and somewhat long, with nostrils very refined and showing the artistic elements in his nature. He wears a beard quite long and very silky and brown like his hair. His manner is grace itself and modesty personified, and yet in him is the intensity of feeling which can show itself in just indignation when the occasion requires. Yet, with all the great beauty of his person and the greater love of his soul showing itself, he is very humble — more so than any spirit I have seen.

I have given you a bare outline of his appearance, and you will never fully realize in your mind's eye just what his appearance is; and only when you come over and meet him will you fully understand the appearance of the most wonderful and beautiful and loving spirit in all God's universe. Someday this will happen, and you will not have the doubts that I had, and your heart will go out to him from the first moment of your meeting. My dear son, it is a greater privilege than you can appreciate, so be prepared to meet your friend and teacher; for he is your friend to a degree that is beyond what I thought he would ever be while you are on earth. So you see, my experience was a somewhat exceptional one, and one secret of its being so is that I received great faith and the Love of God while I was on earth.

While the teachings of many preachers are that the earth is the only place of probation, that teaching is not correct; yet if it were believed more, and humankind prepared their future in view of that belief, many a mortal, when he becomes a spirit, would avoid experiences that are very unpleasant and which retard his progress in the spirit world. Of course, such a belief (that the earth is the only place of probation) when the mortal fails to make the preparation, will work him great injury after he becomes a spirit, because such a belief is difficult to get rid of, and as long as it lasts the spirit is very apt to believe that his status is fixed forever. Hence, he will not progress until he accepts the truth, so you see after all, the only good belief is a belief in the truth, which never changes.

Probation is not confined to the earth life but is with mortals and spirits alike. In fact it never ends, for each preceding condition of a spirit is nothing more than a probationary condition to what follows. This great probationary condition, undoubtedly, is that which exists for the mortal while on earth; and if that probation is accepted and made the most of, the spirit gains an advantage which is beyond my ability to describe.

Sometimes men do not attempt to take full advantage of this probation on earth, and come to the spirit world in all their material thoughts and sins, with their souls dead, and will find that in such condition, as spirits, they will have a more difficult time to awaken from such condition and progress. I am informed that some spirits have been in this world for many, many years and have not yet had an awakening. So you must see the importance of taking advantage of the earth probation.

Well, dear son, I have written a great deal and must stop now, though I should like to write you a much longer time. So with all my love I will close, and sign myself,

Your loving Grandmother,
Ann Rollins

The truth about the unpardonable sin, that is of the greatest importance
November 1, 1915

I am here, your Grandmother.

I have been listening to your conversation tonight and am much pleased to see that you and your friend (Dr. Stone) are growing in your conception of the truth.

The matter of the unpardonable sin is one that is of the greatest importance to the world especially in view of the fact that so many of the orthodox ministers teach that it is a thing of existence and is so dreadful in its consequence. But thanks to the Master this teaching will not in the near future be permitted to go unchallenged, for the truth in this particular will be made so plain that humankind will cease to believe it, and, as a consequence, will be relieved from a fear that has kept many from seeking the Love and favor of God. I know that this resolution of the truth will be antagonized by men and preachers who see that it is one of the strongest instruments which enables them to keep their organizations together, but their antagonism will not succeed, for the truth will prevail and humankind will come to think for themselves. They will then embrace this truth with gladness and joy.

How strange that the professed members of the churches should so slander and blaspheme the one loving God and cause men to look upon him as a God of insoluble wrath. And one who, because a man refuses to believe in the doctrines of the church, shall be forever consigned to eternal punishment and hell, when he gets into such condition of hardness of heart that, as your preacher says, even God Himself will have no power to save. Oh, it is pitiable that such erroneous and harmful doctrine should be taught and worse that by professed ministers of the loving Jesus. So my son, you and your friend, whenever the opportunity comes to combat this monstrous teaching, do so, with all your strength and power of conviction and love and proclaim to the world that such teaching is not true and that for every sinner there is opportunity for salvation and that God loves the man who will not believe in Him, just as he loves the believer, only the former may not partake of His Divine Nature as does the latter.

I wanted to write this because I thought that the time was opportune to impress on you the falsity of this great dogma that has no place in truth or in the plan of God for the salvation of humanity.

Well, I will not write more tonight as you will have others who may want to write.

So with all my love, I bless you both,
Grandmother

Grandmother of medium on forgiveness
March 31, 1915

I am here, your Grandmother.

I came to write you about the forgiveness and pardon of God, and to enlighten you upon this subject which is so little understood since men first commenced to distort the teachings of the Master.

Forgiveness is that operation of the divine mind of God which relieves a man of the penalties of his sins that he has committed, and permits him to turn from his evil thoughts and deeds and seek the Love of God. If he earnestly seeks he will find the happiness which is waiting for him to obtain. It does not violate any law that God has established to prevent him from avoiding the penalties of his violations of the laws of God controlling his conduct. The law of compensation, "that what a man sows that shall he reap," is not set aside, but in the particular case where a man becomes penitent and in all earnestness prays for God to forgive him of his sins and make a new man of him, the operation of another and greater law is called into activity, and the old law of compensation is nullified, and, as it were, swallowed up in the power of this law of Love and forgiveness.

So you see there is no setting aside of any of God's laws, as in the physical world certain lesser laws are overcome by greater laws, so in the spirit world or in the operation of spiritual things, the greater laws must prevail over the lesser. God's laws never change but the application of these laws to particular facts and conditions do seem to change when two laws come into apparent conflict, and the lesser must give way to the greater. The spiritual laws are just as fixed as are the physical laws that control the material universe, and no law having application to the same condition of facts ever is different in its operation or in its effects.

So in the spirit world, when a spirit has committed sins on earth, the law of compensation demands that he must pay the penalty of these sins until there has been a full expiation, or until the law is satisfied. And this law does not change in its operations, and no one can avoid or run away from the inexorable demands of the law. He cannot of himself abate one jot or tittle of the penalties, but must pay to the last farthing as the

34

Master said, and hence, he cannot of himself hope to change the operations of this law.

Now, as the Creator of all law has provided another and higher law, which, under certain conditions, may be brought into operation and causes the former law to cease to operate. Man may experience the benefit of the workings of this higher law, so when God forgives a man of his sins, and makes him a new creature in His Nature and Love, he does not, for the particular case, annihilate the law of compensation, but removes that upon which this law may operate.

Sin is violation of God's law, and the effect of sin is the penalty which such violation imposes. A man's suffering for sins committed is not the result of God's special condemnation in each particular case, but is the result of the workings and scourgings of his conscience and recollections, and as long as conscience works he will suffer, and the greater the sins committed, the greater will be the suffering. Now this implies that a man's soul is filled to a greater or lesser extent with these memories, which for the time constitute his very existence. He lives with these memories, and the suffering and torment which result from them can never leave him until the memories of these sins, or the result of them, cease to be a part of himself and his constant companions. This is the inexorable law of compensation, and man of himself has no way of escaping this law except by his long expiation which removes these memories and satisfies the law. Man cannot change this law, and God will not. So, as I say, the law never changes, and remember this fact, that in order for the law to operate, a man must have these memories, and they must be a part of his very existence.

God's Love is the greatest thing in all the universe and the law of Love is the greatest law. Every other law is subordinate to it, and must work in unison with it. This Love frees man from all law and when man possesses this Love he is slave to no law and is free indeed. Therefore, the law of compensation and all laws not in harmony with the law of Love have nothing upon which to operate. In that man's case, God's laws are not changed but merely, as to this man, have no existence. Now, let all men, wise and unwise, know that God in His Love and wisdom, has provided a means by which man, if he so will, may escape the unchanging law of compensation and become no longer subject to its demands and penalties. The means is simple and easy, and within the comprehension and grasp of every living soul, be he saint or sinner, a wise man or an ignorant one.

Intellect in the sense of being learned is not involved, for the man who knows that God exists and provides him with food and raiment as the result of his daily toil, as well as the great intellectual scientist or philosopher, may learn the way to these redeeming truths. I do not mean that a man by mere exercise of mental powers may receive the benefit of this great provision for his redemption. The soul must seek and it will find, and the soul of the wise may not be as capable of receiving as the soul of the ignorant.

Man has a natural love, but this natural love is not sufficient to enable him to find these great means that I speak of, only the Love of God can, and He is willing that all men should have this Love. It is free and waiting to be bestowed upon all, and strange as it may seem, God will not, and I might say, cannot, bestow this Love unless man seeks for it and asks for it in earnestness and faith. The will of man is a wonderful thing but it stands between him and this Love if he fails to exercise this will in seeking for it. No man can secure it against his will. What a wonderful thing is man's will, and how he should study and learn what a great part of his being it is.

The Love of God comes only into a man's soul when he seeks it in prayer and faith, and of course this implies that he wills it to come to him. No man is ever refused this Love when he properly asks for it. This Love is a part of the Divine Essence, and when a man possesses it in sufficient abundance, he becomes a part of divinity itself; and in the "divine" there is no sin or error, and, consequently, when he becomes a part of this divinity no sin or error can form a part of his being.

Now, as I have said, a man who is without this Love has his memories of sin and evil deeds, and under the law of compensation, must pay the penalties. Yet when this Love comes into his soul, it leaves no room for these memories, and as he becomes more and more filled with this Love these memories disappear and only this Love inhabits his soul, as it were. Hence, there remains nothing in him upon which this law can operate, and the man is no longer its slave or subject. This Love is sufficient of itself to cleanse the soul from all sin and error and make man one with God.

I know by personal experience that this forgiveness is a real, actual, existing thing, and when God forgives, sin disappears and only Love exists, and that Love in its fullness is the fulfilling of the law. So let men know that God does forgive sin, and when He forgives, the penalty disappears, and when it disappears as the result of such forgiveness, no law of God is changed or violated. Teaching this was the great mission of Jesus when he came to earth, and before he came and taught this great truth, the forgiveness of sin was not understood even by the Hebrew teachers, for their doctrine was an eye for an eye and a tooth for a tooth (Exodus 21:24). God's Love, as I have described, was not known or sought for, only the care and protection and material benefits that God might give to the Hebrews.

My dear son, I have written you a long communication, but there is sufficient in it for men to think of and meditate upon, and if they do so and open their souls to the divine influence, they will know that God can forgive sin and save men from its penalties, so that they will not have to undergo the long period of expiation, which in their natural state the law of compensation demands.

So without writing further, I will say that I love you with all my heart and soul, and pray that God will give you this great Love in all its abundance.

Your loving Grandmother,
Ann Rollins

NITA PADGETT (Daughter)

The first communication from Padgett's daughter, Nita ,
also known as Baby, tells of her progress to the third sphere
June 27, 1918

I am here, Nita.

I am Nita, and I have been so anxious to write you ever since I came to the spirit world and realized that I could do so. Well, Daddy, I cannot tell you how happy I am and how glad I am that I can write you. I know that mother has written you in regards to my passing over and my condition and progress since I became a spirit, and all that she said is true and much more. I am so desirous to tell you in detail just what my experience has been, but as this is my first attempt to write I will not do so tonight, but very soon I will, and I know that you will get tired before I cease writing, for I have so much to tell you.

Of course, I had some idea of what my experience might be in passing, but the idea was a very faint glimpse of what I really experienced, and I want to tell you how much your information helped me when I was with you.

Well, Daddy, I am also so very glad that I could be with you and know that you were still my dear Daddy, and loved me so much more than I ever realized when on earth. I am now so very happy and know to a large extent the reality and blessedness of God's Love, which you used to tell me of. Oh, how can I ever express to you how thankful I am that you told me of this Love, for it has been the means of helping me so much in my progress. I am now in the third sphere as Mother tells me, and I cannot tell you the beauty and loveliness of all that surrounds me, and what a lovely home I have and what delightful associates. You must not think me selfish when I write that I would not return to the earth life for all the world, for here I am free from the worry and troubles that I had, and also can be with you and love you and know that you love me as your own darling Baby.

Well, Daddy, I have written a good deal, and mother says I had best not write more now, but wait until I am in a better condition to express to you just what I desire to write. So love me and think of me, and expect me very soon to tell you of what I have suggested.

So, dear Daddy, I must say good night with all my love.

I am still your own loving,
Baby

Nita describes her experience passing into the spirit world
and the beautiful spirits that have helped her to find happiness
December 29, 1918

I am here, Nita.

I am so glad that I can write to you again. It has been a longtime since you let me write and I have been so anxious to tell you of my progress and love. Why, Daddy, I thought that you loved me so much that you would not keep me waiting so long to tell you of my love and how happy I am. Mother has told me that you were not in condition to receive my message and that I must wait until conditions are different, which I understand.

Now I want to tell you of my progress and how the Love of God has changed my soul so that now I am in a sphere from where I may soon expect to go into the celestial heavens where mother is. When I first came to spirit life as you know, mother met me and took me in her arms and was so loving and tender with me that I had no fear of the change in my condition. With her were other beautiful and loving spirits who gave me their love and assured me that now I would soon find a home that was so different from my home on earth and would experience a happiness that I had never before felt. I was not afraid and did not want to go with my body again as I was told so many newly arrived spirits desire to do when they first come over.

I was satisfied from the first, and how could I not help being so when I had such a beautiful mother to enfold me in her arms and assure me that never more would I have to undergo the cares and disappointments of an earth life. How glorious this was and how I thought that if heaven should have all spirits as lovely and grand as was here, what a happy place it must be. Mother was with me for quite a while and also Grandmother Padgett, who was also beautiful and bright, and who told me that I had nothing to fear, but to believe that I was truly in the spirit world and later I should find everything to make me happy and content.

How badly I felt when the parting came, for you must know that this parting was necessary. Mother lived in a higher sphere to which I could not go and she could not remain with me all the time, as I wanted her to do. She told me that she would be with me quite often to comfort and love me. That under the law I would have to go to the place that my soul fitted me for and from thence I would have to pray and work for my own progress. And that she could not determine for me where I should live and that my own soul's condition would fix my place and so, as I say, we had to part.

I soon found myself in some darkness and suffering and did not quite understand why this should be so, or what was the cause of my darkness, but after a little while I found that my recollection of my earth life came to me in wonderful clearness and that my conscience was causing me some suffering. I was awfully lonesome and wanted my mother so much, but found out that I had to bear my own burdens and obey the laws that fixed my condition.

I know you would want to be with me if you could, to comfort and love me and protect me from my sufferings, but this was impossible for this law that I speak of, knows no forgiveness, until it is satisfied. It is stern from the necessity of things, because only through its workings can a soul be made purer and enabled to progress from its first condition. But thanks to my dear mother, I had with me the hope that such condition was only for a moment and that soon the Love would come to me and take me out of the workings of the law and set me free and enable me to get into the light and more happiness. Oh! How I prayed and prayed for this Love and tried to believe that it would come to me and dispel the darkness and the recollections of the evil things that I had done and thought when on earth.

Mother and grandmother prayed with me, and encouraged me with their sympathy and love and the assurance that this Love would come to me and that God would answer my prayers. On one occasion when I had been praying with all my soul, and when my faith seemed stronger, there came to me a beautiful spirit, all tender and loving, and said, "My daughter, God will hear your prayers and soul longing and call you to higher service and brighter surroundings and greater happiness. I know that God never fails to answer the prayer of an earnest soul and besides you are the very child of His Love and care and nothing pleases Him so much as when His children call on Him for His Love and help. I am praying for you also and my faith makes it certain that you will soon receive the answer, only let your very soul breathe out its longings for His Love."

Oh! How beautiful and grand this spirit was and how tender his love, which seemed to flood all my surroundings and to give me such hope and encouragement that I felt that I surely must be a little weary in brain while he was talking. He then told me, that he was Jesus and was so glad that I had come to the spirit world with so much love surrounding me and also told me how he loved me and sympathized with me and wanted me to get out of my darkness and into the light. I cannot express to you how I felt as he talked to me and how I wondered if he were not really God. But he could not be God for he was so human and humble and seemed to think that he was a mere child of the Father of whom he spoke. When leaving me, he said that he would come again and talk to me of God and His Love and blessed me and said, "You are a child of God and just as dear to Him as I am, and He loves you just as much as He does me. Believe in His great Love and you will be happy."

Well, Daddy, you can imagine what my feelings were and how much I was helped. I will not stop to tell you now of how this Love came into my soul, little by little, until at last it seemed to fill my whole being. Oh, how happy I became, and how beautiful my surroundings appeared and what beautiful bright spirits I found myself in an association with. I was satisfied and my home became to me the most glorious and happiest place imaginable.

My new home surpasses all conception of man, and would satisfy the most hopeful and extravagant man as his house of bliss. As I continued to progress, and more and more of the Love came into my soul, and strange as it may seem to you, as I rose higher and higher, grandmother was with me so very much, and she became more beautiful and glorious than ever before. I understand now why that was. As she came to me in the different spheres, and as I rose higher, she approached nearer her home and took on more of the beauty and glory that are really hers in her sphere. I am now happy beyond expression and love you with a greater love than I ever had on earth, and know what love really is, and one of the happiest things that I now have before me is to wait until you come and to meet you with all my love and goodness.

Oh, Daddy, won't it be glorious when you come over and we can all be together in love? You thought that you had a beautiful Helen on earth, but when you come to us and see her in her glory, your very eyes will be dazzled at her appearance. We are with you a great deal, loving you and trying to help you, and you must believe that we will never leave you, till you reach the heaven where we now are.

So Daddy, believe that I am your little Nita and that I write you and love you with all my heart and soul.

Your loving daughter,
Nita

LAURA BURROUGHS

Padgett's cousin is in darkness and seeks his help
March 29, 1915

I am here, Laura Burroughs.

Oh, my dear Edward*, please do something to help me. I am so unhappy and need help so much. I am in such darkness and pain that I can scarcely see the light of day, I mean the light that enables me to see my surroundings. I am also so lonely and without love or sympathy. I feel that you can help me.

Yes, I have seen several beautiful spirits but I did not believe that they had interest enough in me to help me and so I turned aside from them. I don't understand why I am in this condition and no one has explained it so far. I thought that maybe you might show me some way to get out of this condition. I thought so because I saw other spirits writing to you who are in this darkness as I am and they said that you had helped them.

Why, I see Aunt Nancy and your mother and Helen and your Father and others I don't know. How beautiful and happy they look to be! Why are they so beautiful? If I could only be like them! Tell me, why is it, and what made them so.

Oh, how glad I am that I came here, I feel better already. Dear Aunt Nancy, she will love me and so will cousin Ann and Helen. I am now

*Padgett's middle name.

going with them.

So good-bye, my dear cousin,
Laura

Laura tells of meeting her soulmate
January 19, 1917

I am here, Laura Burroughs.

I am glad to be able to write you again and tell you that since I last wrote you I have made much progress, and have come into the possession of much more happiness. Dear cousin, I am so glad that I can tell you this, for I know that you rejoice with me in my happiness and the knowledge of what great mercy has come to me. I merely wanted to say this, for it makes me very happy to come to you in this way.

Well, he* is in the spirit world, but in a very dark plane and is not at all happy. I have been with him some, but have not been able to do him any good, as his old beliefs cling to him and prevent his progress. Some time we may be able to help him, and will try then. Helen has told me he is not my soulmate, and I have met my soulmate very recently.

He is in the same sphere with me, and we are very happy together and are trying to progress together. I never knew him on earth. He lived in Pennsylvania and died a longtime before I did, and tells me that he had to go through much suffering and darkness before he got into a plane of light. He is a very beautiful spirit and I could love him, I believe, even if he were not my soulmate, but as he is, you know what our love means. He is looking at me write, and heard your question, and says his name was Henry W. Spaulding, and he lived in Millville, if you know where that is.

I met Henry after I had made some progress and got some of this Love in my soul. Helen brought him to me one time and said, "Laura, here is a young man who has been very anxious to meet you for some time, and you must not fall in love with him, if you can keep from doing so," and she laughed. Well, I suppose I blinked, as mortals used to say,

*In all likelihood she is referring to her husband when on earth.

and I did fall in love, as you can imagine, and have been loving him ever since.

How we all love Helen for her kindness and the great good that she does. You just wait until you come over and you will see the most beautiful girl that you ever saw.

Henry says that he considers himself very fortunate in having such a cousin, and he means it, for he sees the wonder of the great gift that you have, and the loving and high spirits that come to you.

I must say good night now. So with my love, I will stop.

Your loving cousin,
Laura

CHAPTER TWO

Friends

HUGH T. TAGGART

Taggart is grateful for what Mr. Padgett has done for him
and the wonderful results that followed from the advice given to him
July 22, 1915

I am here, Hugh Taggart.

I am grateful for what you have done for me, and the great light that has come to me by reason of your advice, and the teachings and help of your band, and especially the deep sympathy and sisterly love of that beautiful wife of yours. Why, Padgett, I want to tell you that the most fortunate things of my whole existence were my acquaintance with you and the wonderful results that flowed from it. I sometimes wonder how all of this could have come about.

When on earth, while I knew that you believed in Spiritualism, yet I never realized what your belief and experience meant to you, and what a great help it would be to me when the time came for me to become a spirit. I will never forget our first argument after I became a spirit on this great question of how I might be rescued from my awful condition of suffering and darkness, and with what earnestness you maintained the position that you took and tried to show me that there was a way by which I could get light and happiness and relief from my torments. Mackey and I often talk about it, and we wonder how you could have such knowledge of these spiritual matters and such faith to maintain the truth of their existence. However you were right and your faith was not misplaced.

Old friend, I thank you again, and God bless you! I am now in a condition of light and suffer very little and realize to a great extent that there is such a thing as the Love of God, and that it may be mine. I pray and my faith is becoming stronger all the time. The great proof to me, aside from what I see in the condition of other spirits who claim to have this Love, is my own change in soul happiness and in desire to progress to the higher spheres, which your band tells me exists, and that I may find my home there if I will only pray more to God and let my faith enlarge.

To me this Love and faith are a "new revelation". Of course when on earth I heard of God's Love and of faith, but to me they meant nothing more than the rhapsodies of the enthusiastic religionists, whose emotions had overcome their normal reasoning powers — a will-o'-the-wisp, as it were. But now I know the reality of these things and I find that the emotions, in things pertaining to the soul, are more certain leaders than are the reasoning faculties. I am quite happy at times, and I hope to make such progress in my soul development as to be happy all the time. You are my true friend and I love you as a brother now.

Well, they are still in darkness, but have progressed some. The great disappointment which Harvey experienced when he came over seems to have had such a baleful influence on him, that it is almost impossible at this time for him to reach out and try to grasp the truth of the existence of this Love. We are trying to help him, and he is commencing to wonder at our improved appearance and to think that maybe we know what we tell him to be the cause of the change.

Mac is still in darkness, and it seems hard for him to awaken to the fact that there can be any other condition that he may have. He is very hard to reason with, and does not seem to have much desire to have his condition change.

I saw some spirits writing to you but did not know them, except for Jesus. I know him and I could never forget him for there are none like him in grandeur and beauty and love.

Well, I will not write more tonight. So, my dear friend, let me again express my gratitude and say with all my heart that I am grateful.

Hugh T. Taggart

FRANKLIN H. MACKEY

Mackey is grateful and never will forget
Mr. Padgett's kindness in helping him to see the light
July 22, 1915

I am here, Franklin H. Mackey.

I must write just a line to tell you that you are my friend and helper in my darkness and sufferings.

I have been much benefitted by your advice and the help which your band has given me and I am commencing to see the light and to know what the Love of God means to a poor benighted soul who has been in a state of torment.

I will not write longer but say that I am so grateful and will never forget your kindness and sympathy. May God bless you and keep you in His care.

Your old friend and brother lawyer that was,
Mackey

GEORGE W. HARVEY

A friend of Mr. Padgett's feels misled by the priests of his faith
January 12, 1915

I am here, George Harvey.

I lived in Washington, and kept a restaurant on Pennsylvania Avenue and Tenth Street. I am in the spirit world and in hell also. I am not happy for I am in darkness and despair.

Yes, I did, but that did not keep me from hell. The priests misled me, and they are here too, damn them — can you help me any, if you can do so. Yes I remember Taggart, for he is here too — and can't help himself, for I see him sometimes, and he tells me that he is in a condition of suffering too. No, he is not in condition to help me, even if I do see him.

You must help me if you can. I don't know who from, but I want help from someone. I know they say so, but I don't believe them, for they can't help themselves. No, I don't know them. I will see him at once and ask him, and tell him that I want to know.

So good night.

Your friend,
George Harvey

Harvey wants to know why Mackey and
Taggart have changed so much in their appearance
July 22, 1915

I am here, George W. Harvey.

I want to tell you that Mackey and Taggart have changed so much that I wonder why they have and I have not. They tell me that it is because they have received the Love of God in their souls and faith in what the beautiful spirits of your band tell them.

I hardly know what to think and I want to ask what you think is the cause. I am a doubting Thomas. Well, I have heard what you said and I will try to do as you say. I will do so and I want to express to you my gratitude for the interest you have taken in me.

Your friend,
George W. Harvey

SPENCER

Spencer, a friend, comments on the book
that Mr. Padgett was reading about Spiritualism
June 18, 1919

I am here, Spencer.

I want to say just a word to your friend Dr. Stone who is so much interested in the discovery of the truths of the spirit world and of the facts that exist in that world.

Well, I have been with you as you discussed these prospects, and also the writings of the men who have become converted to Spiritualism. I saw that you are not satisfied with what the writings contained, and wished that these men might know the truth so that they could declare it to the world.

You must wait until your messages are finished and in shape to publish before these truths can be made known to the world. These men who are having the experiences of which they write are doing a good work in publishing accounts of the same in this: that they are preparing the minds of their readers to accept the truth of Spiritualism whenever the same shall be published. They are breaking up the fallow ground and making it ready to receive the seeds of truth as they shall become scattered over the soil that so lately has been barren and unfitted to receive and nurture these seeds. The work is one that will result in much good and will gradually lead mankind to accept as true and coming from the spirit world, what they would not otherwise receive.

I merely wanted to write this little message so that you and your friend may not think that the publications, such as you have read tonight, are worthless and without a function in causing men to believe in the lower truths of Spiritualism. They are very valuable to mankind in general and to those philosophers and scientists who are more interested in the physical aspect of the study. They must be encouraged and you must not think that their appearing is merely a waste of time or effort. They are the ABC's of Spiritualism and must be learned before you can expect the higher or more spiritual truths to be received. I was a scientist when on earth and a supposed agnostic, but I know better now.

Well, I will not write more now. Good night.

Your friend,
Spencer

JOE SHELLINGTON

After his death he could not forget his wife and daughter back on earth
June 17, 1915

I am here, Joe Shellington.

I am glad to be able to write to you, and let you know that I am in the land of the living. I have waited a long time to write you as your band would not consent to my writing, so I had to wait until it was agreeable to them, as well as with you.

I am in a state of semi-darkness and am suffering somewhat from the recollections of my life on earth, and, thanks to your wife, I am commencing to see the light and to learn the way out of my sufferings.

When I found myself dying, I thought that I was going to sleep and that my body was resting from the cares and pains which my sufferings had caused; and when my spirit was separated from my body, I hovered around for a longtime expecting that when my body should feel refreshed I would go into it again and continue my life on earth. But after waiting a longtime and failing to see my body awaken, I commenced to wonder what had taken place, and, at last, came to the conclusion that I was dead, and that no more would I walk the earth as a mortal. Well, as soon as I realized that fact I looked around and saw my mother and father, and several others who I knew on earth, and they told me that I had died, and was now a spirit, and would never more go into my body. I commenced to ask questions, and wanted to know where I was and what place I was in. They told me that I was in the spirit world, and in what is called the first sphere, and that my future home would be in that sphere until I had, by repentance and suffering, progressed to a higher one.

My mother, who is a very beautiful spirit, tried to comfort me, and told me that I must now think of the things that belong to the spirit world, and not let my thoughts run on the things that I had been interested in while a mortal. While I considered her advice and was impressed with what she said, I could not follow her advice, as I was compelled by something which I did not understand to give my thoughts to the affairs of earth, and especially to my wife and daughter.

I was with them nearly all the time for many long days, and tried to speak to them and advise them what they should do, but they would not pay any attention to me. Of course, I now know that they did not know that I was present and did not hear my voice; but at the time I thought it very strange, for they were just as real and unchanged to me as when I was with them in the body.

I never fully realized what my position was until long months after I died, and I could not think of anything except my loved ones at first, and was with them all the time. I saw them sorrowing and weeping because of my death and tried so hard to comfort them, but all to no purpose. I, at last, saw that it was utterly hopeless for me to make them feel that I was with them, and so I sought for information among my spirit friends to know how I could reach my dear ones. I got no consolation, as they told me that it was only through the instrumentality or help of some earth medium that I could ever be able to communicate with them or let them know that I was still alive, and loved them just as I did when on earth.

So one time in my wanderings I entered the circle of the medium where you heard me talk to you, and then I was happy because I thought that now I would be able to reach my wife and daughter. But I was disappointed, for you never told them that I had talked to you, and wanted them to know that I was anxious to talk to them. I suppose you thought that they would not believe you, and so you neglected to tell them. But you were mistaken in this, as they would have believed you had you told them. My wife knows something of Spiritualism, though she has not much faith in it, and while she may not have absolutely believed, yet she would have had enough interest to have sought for the opportunity to learn more, and, if possible, to hear me speak to her. So while you disappointed me, I cannot altogether blame you.

Old friend, do not fail to let her know that I have written to you tonight, and if it is not too much trouble, I would like for you to send her a copy of this message. I still love her and am with her very often, and try my best to make her feel my presence, and realize that I am doing my best to comfort her. If she only knew how dear she is to me and that my whole heart burns with love for her, she would be happier, for I believe that she will be mine when she comes over, and through all eternity. So do not fail to send her a copy of this message.

When I passed over I was not one particle afraid and while I was not just in condition to know what was taking place, yet there was no dread or apprehension in any way of my being harmed. I arose, as I have said, from my body, and did not leave it, but stayed with it and with my loved ones even until it was buried and then I continued with my dear wife.

After I realized that I was a spirit, I found myself in a dark atmosphere surrounded by dark spirits who, I supposed, were like myself. My mother, while she often came to me, did not live with me, for as she told me, lived in a higher sphere where much happiness exists. I was not happy and I suffered very much from my recollections of my earth life, and had no fixed home. All spirits in a condition like mine have to roam about with no place that they can call home. Often I have longed for a home but found none, and even now I have one that is not very beautiful. I am progressing and light is coming to me and my sufferings are decreasing. I rather expected to find myself in hell, as I was not a Christian, and as I was taught that all who are not Christians and do not believe in Jesus must go to hell. But I have not seen this hell, and I do not believe that there is any such place. Yet the suffering which we have creates a hell enough for any spirit who wants such a hell.

Well, I am now learning to pray to God and to believe in His Love, and the more I pray the stronger my belief becomes, the more light I see and the less I suffer. Your wife came to me at about the time I spoke to you at the medium's and tried to help me, and she has been with me many times since and has helped me very much. She is a beautiful spirit and seems filled with the Love of God, as she says.

So I am seeking that Love, and I believe that I will soon get enough of it to get out of my present condition. I thank you so much for this opportunity, and when it is agreeable I will come and write to you again. I will not take up more of your time tonight.

So with my kindest regards and many thanks.

> I am your old friend,
> Joe Shellington

CHARLES T. WILSON

A dark spirit seeks the help of Dr. Stone whom he knew while on earth
May 16, 1918

I am here, Charles T. Wilson.

Let me write a few lines. I am the friend of Dr. Stone and knew him some years ago when he was living in Buffalo, New York. I was in a hospital where he was engaged in looking after daffy mortals, such as I was.

Well, in those days my mind and my brain did not coordinate, and after I passed into the spirit life I found that I had a mind which enabled me to understand things as I did before I had the awful blank mind come to me which resulted in my being incarcerated in the hospital.

What a wonderful experience I had after I became liberated from the imprisonment of my mind in a diseased brain. Then everything appeared to me as if I were a new creature, and the happiness which came to me — I mean the happiness that came from my liberated mind — is beyond what you may conceive of. I can suppose that men think that those whose minds are thus blotted out, as it were, by a brain which has ceased to perform its functions must not be unhappy, because they know not the loss of the benefits that a mind with a sound brain affords. But in this supposition men are mistaken, for while the person thus afflicted may not know of what sound-minded men call real trouble and worry, yet they have troubles which belong to their diseased brains, and to them these troubles are just as real as are the troubles of those who think that they are sane. Of course, while I was in the flesh I did not fully understand just what my condition of mind was, and many of my vagaries were of such a character as to cause me apparent happiness; while on the other hand, others caused me real suffering. Things of great importance appeared to me with a force that no real existence could surpass.

Shortly after I passed to the spirit life these imaginations left me, and with them disappeared the unhappiness which they caused, and it seemed to me as if my mind had been freed from a great burden. I became so conscious of the fact that it seemed as if I must be in heaven or some other place of bliss. But it meant nothing more than my mind finding its real condition, and the recollections of my earth life came to me with all their consequences. Strange as it may seem to you, there were no recollections of anything that happened while I was in the state of mental darkness. The only things that came to my remembrance were parts of my life before my affliction, and only these brought with them a knowledge of good or evil deeds which I had committed.

Since then, I have realized the workings of the laws which controlled my acts of life, and I was happy or otherwise as these laws called for my suffering or if they failed to operate. I have been in the dark planes ever since, though I have made some progress towards the light, or rather the darkness has grown less intense and my sufferings have decreased. My mind has always been alert and nothing has escaped me which was a part of my sane existence while on earth.

I wish that I could find a way to get rid of this darkness and suffering, and, as only a few nights ago I heard that you could help spirits in my condition, I determined to seek your help, and tonight when I saw the doctor with you, I thought it a good opportunity to ask your help.

Your father says that he will help me, and as he is so very beautiful and bright I can easily believe that he can, and I am going with him.

So, I thank you,

I was Charles T. Wilson,
and was called Wash

JOHN CRITCHER

A brother lawyer explains his disappointment on entering the spirit world
November 7, 1915

I am here, John Critcher.

I was passing when I saw the light that comes from your room, and looked in and saw you, and asked permission to write. Your band consented and so I am writing. You must remember me, for I had my office in the same building with you when I practiced law.

Well, I am in a condition that gives me considerable happiness, and yet I am not in that state of happiness which I expected to have when I was on earth. As you know, I was an Episcopalian and tried to observe strictly the doctrines and formalities of my church, and expected when I died to go to heaven and find rest and nothing to make me unhappy. But in this I was mistaken, and I found myself in the first sphere of the spirit world, and had to undergo some suffering and darkness, and did not find the heavenly rest that I expected. I have progressed since I came over and am now happier and in more light.

So thanking you, I am your friend,
John Critcher

R. ROSS PERRY

*Perry, an old friend of Mr. Padgett's, wrote about his suicide and
his condition in darkness and explains the reasons for taking his own life*
October 1, 1915

I am here, your late friend Perry.

I want to tell you that I am in a condition of great darkness and suffering, and I am not able to find a way out or to relieve myself from my tortures. I know that you may think it strange that I did not listen to Riddle when you brought him in contact with me a short time ago, I could not believe what he told me, or understand in what way the darkness would leave me by merely praying to God and trying to believe that there is such a thing as God's Love, which I might obtain by letting my belief in what he said become sufficiently strong to cause me to forget the recollections of my awful deeds. I saw that he was a wonderfully bright spirit, and seemed to be so very happy in his condition of belief, but, nevertheless I was not able to believe that it was the result of what he told me, and so, I am in the same condition that I was when I wrote you last.

My friend, for such I believe you to be or you would not be able to interest yourself in me as you have, I want to tell you that if only I could shoot myself again and by that means end my existence, and I mean annihilate my spirit and soul, so that they would go into nothingness, I would gladly and quickly pull the trigger and send the bullet into that spot which would bring about the desired effect. I realize now that I must continue to exist and to suffer, for how long I don't know, but it seems to me for ever and ever.

Oh, why did I do such a thing! I had no reason to take my life so far as earthly things were concerned, for I needed nothing of the material to make life satisfactory. Well, I will tell you, as you may know, I was, as I thought, something of a philosopher on earth, and to me life was a thing to retain or put off just as I might think it had served or not served its purpose. When I felt that I could no longer do any special good in the world or to those who were near to me, I thought that there was no reason why I should continue any longer the life which was one of monotony in a certain sense. Besides, I felt that I had arrived at the height of my mental powers, and that they were on the decline, and the thought that I should decrease in what I had so striven to cultivate and display to my acquaintances, caused me to believe that the object of my creation had been fulfilled and that I would gradually become not only an encumbrance, but a person to be looked upon with a kind of pity which would cause me much unhappiness. To have others point their finger at me and say, "There goes poor Perry who used to be such a brilliant and capable man, and who is now intellectually a mere wreck of his former self. Isn't it a pity that such a man should come to a condition that he has come to." These are some of the thoughts that entered my mind and, in addition, as I have told you, I thought that death was the end of all, and that in the grave I would know nothing and sleep in utter oblivion.

I fed on these thoughts some while before I decided to die, and the more I thought, the greater became my condition that what I had said would prove to be true. Just before I fired the fatal shot I thought intensely of all these things, and saw what I supposed would be an end to everything and the true solution to life's decay, mental as well as physical decrepitude. When I prepared to do the deed I was never more calm in all my life. It did not require any courage on my part, for the conviction of the correctness of my conclusions was so strong that the question of courage was not a part of the equation.

Men may think that courage is a necessity to commit suicide, but I tell you that courage forms no part of a man's condition of mind when he commits that deed. I have no doubt, though, in bringing his mind to the condition that I have spoken of, that is, in feeling that the burdens of life are too great, or that he cannot further bear the things which duty calls upon him to do, he may be and often is a coward. I must not write more on this theme now. I am more interested in finding a way, if possible, out of this intense darkness and suffering.

I have not seen Mr. Riddle since my first interview and I do not think that I would be benefitted by seeing him, because for one thing, the great contrasts in our conditions only intensify my sufferings, and hence, I prefer to remain to myself or among spirits like myself. You know that on earth the poor are much happier with the poor than when thrown into the company of the rich, and this is because of the apparent greater happiness of the latter, and so it is with me, when I see Riddle in his happiness, I feel that my misery is all the greater.

I am astonished at what you say, for I never really believed in Jesus as you tell me of him. I could not when on earth believe in him as a god, and I thought that he was only an idea of human minds, and that as to his actual historical or earthly existence, it was a mere fable. But now you tell me that he really exists and is working in the spirit world to help the fallen and dark spirits, and that he comes to you and tells you of his love and work. Well, I won't say that I can't believe you, but I prefer to wait until I see him myself, and then if he appears to me as you say, I will be ready to believe what Riddle told me about prayer and the Love of God.

When on earth I merely considered you to be like the rest of us. Now I am told that you know things that I never thought any mortal could know. Well, astonishment upon astonishment, and all as you say to help me and lead me to the light. Yes, that is what I want, light.

So my dear friend, let me say, that I thank you with all my heart, and hope that I may be able to come to you again, and say that what you promised me, I have received.

Your friend,
R. Ross Perry

FRANK D. SYRICK

Judge Syrick, an old friend of both Mr. Padgett and Dr. Stone, relates his spiritual progression and is living with his soulmate in the fifth sphere
May 13, 1917

I am here, Judge Syrick.

I cannot tell you how pleased I am to be able to write to you tonight. As you know, I always enjoyed being with you, for you are both very dear to me, and I want you to feel that throwing aside my covering of flesh did not change me in any particular as regards my feelings for you, except to cause me to realize how much more you are my brothers and friends.

I have made much progress in my soul development and in the acquirement of the knowledge of these spiritual truths, so that even I know that what was written you in that message is true. I am progressing all the time, and the Love that has come into my soul has transformed me to a large degree into something more than the mere image of God. Oh! I tell you, this Love is wonderful, and we who have it are happy beyond all conception, and the best thing about it is that the more of it we receive the greater knowledge comes to us that there is more waiting for us to receive.

I am in the fifth sphere, and I have with me one whom you have heard me speak of, I mean, of course, my Rose. What a blessing to have such a soulmate, and if I could only find words to tell you of the happiness that comes with such a possession I would do so. If only to give you some idea of what you may expect when you come to the spirit world, and especially when you remember that both your soulmates are in a higher sphere than are we, and of course have more love and happiness.

Well, I would like to write a longer letter, but am advised that I have written enough for tonight, and so I must stop. Yes, I was there and spoke to you, but did not try to talk much as there were so many other spirits, all anxious to speak to their friends and who haven't the blessed opportunity that I have to communicate. The room was filled with spirits, and if you could have seen the condition of some of them I know that you would have had a longing desire to help them. So do not let any doubt come to you as to the great work that is yours to help these spirits. Tell the Doctor that he is also doing a great work and must persevere; and when he comes over, as my old mother said when I was a mere child, there will be crowns of glory waiting for him.

Well, I must stop now, and in doing so want to assure you both that you have my love and gratitude to the extent that an appreciative soul can give. Rose sends her love and says that she is so very happy and is praying for you both.

Good night, my dear brothers.

Your old friend,
Syrick

*Judge Syrick confirms what Mr. Padgett and
Dr. Stone told him about the spirit world and reports on
his experience there and progress to date*
May 6, 1915

I am here, your friend Syrick.

Well, I first want to say that I am so very glad to have the opportunity to write to you, thanks to that beautiful wife of yours. I tell you Padgett, that she is a wonder, and you should feel yourself a highly favored man to have such a soulmate. She is not only beautiful but so full of love and so wise in the things that pertain to the higher life. Why she tells me things that I never in all my life thought could exist, and when she shows me the truths of God's Love and how beautiful and beyond conception her home is, I can scarcely contain myself. She is helping me so much in my progression.

Of course Rose is also, but Rose does not have that great angelic love that your wife has, and is not able to tell me of the wonderful things that may be mine, and the way that I may obtain them. I want to tell you that the most fortunate day of my life was the one when I met you at the Colburns* and commenced the investigation of Spiritualism that you were seeking to learn. Many times you told me to seek for the higher things and the soul development, and I heard you but did not know what you meant. I knew that I was not a very bad man as men go, and would wonder what you meant. Sometimes I got a glimpse of what you might mean, and would ask you, as you may remember, if you thought I was a very bad man. You would tell me no, and that I must give my thoughts to higher things and get the Love of God in my heart.

Well, I did not comprehend what you meant, and when you told me to pray I did so, yet somehow I did not understand just how to pray. Now I realize what you mean, and what an awful mistake I made in not trying to learn what you tried to tell me when on earth.

When I arrived in Richmond (Virginia) I felt a little sick, but had no idea that I was so near death. In fact, death was not in my thoughts, as I had induced myself to believe that I would live to be an old man. You can imagine my feelings, after I had been stricken and was unconscious

---

*A couple who held seances at their home.

for quite a while and then suddenly recovered my consciousness and found myself looking down on my body all cold and lifeless. I thought it was not my body but someone else's that resembled me very much and that I was still in my body; but as I tried to make myself known to my friends who had gathered around, I found that they did not hear me or see me. I then remembered the description that you had read to me of your wife's passing over, and the conviction came to me that I was no longer a mortal. And to further convince me, just then Rose came to me and said, "Frank, I am keeping my promise, you are with your soulmate and never again will you return to your mortal life. You can stop wondering what kind of girl your soulmate may be, for now you see her as she really is, and you also feel her arms around you and her kisses upon your cheek, and I know that you would not go into that body again for all the world."

Oh, I tell you, that such a reception, accompanied with such beauty and love, was enough to make a man forget that he had ever been a mortal, and for the time I forgot that I had. So you see, my passing was not so undesirable as I had thought it would be. I cannot tell you what my happiness was as I had no doubt about my being a spirit, and thoroughly believed that I had left the earth forever, so far as occupying my body was concerned. I had no desire to return to it, and my thoughts did not turn to things material. My Rose was sufficient for me. She occupied all my thoughts, and my being was wholly with her, and my happiness was a thing no mortal could understand or believe, even if I were capable of telling him. Such beauty and love! Well, I will not try to tell you of it, for I cannot; but only say that when you come over and your soulmate meets you, you will lose your breath and wonder how such a man as you are now, could be loved by such a being of beauty.

A short time after I had been with Rose, your wife and others of your band came to me, and with them my own dear mother, who was so beautiful and loving to me. I was so happy that I cried with all my heart and soul for joy. Well, such was my passing, and when on earth I had no conception that it could be such.

As soon as I could recover my breath, as we say on earth, I made many inquiries about the things that I saw and which I had wanted to know when on earth. I want to tell you that some things that I heard seemed familiar, and I thought that I had heard them before, and so it was, because in our communications and in our conversations and in our circle I had heard them. So you see what a privilege it is for a man to have the opportunity of learning of the spirit world while still on earth. You and Dr. Stone and the Colburns are much favored in your opportunities to hear of so many of the things that pertain to the spirit life.

I am acquainted with Dr. Stone's Mary*. Tell him that she is real and is certainly his soulmate as I was his friend and patient when on earth. She is a beautiful spirit and so good, and loves him with a love that he cannot now understand, but which he will someday. Tell him I am more fortunate than he, because I came first and partook of the love of a beautiful, fine and loving woman; and his time is coming, but I am more fortunate than he, in that I came to my soulmate a little sooner than he will to his.

I have met Bright Star**, and I certainly was surprised. I thought to meet an Indian squaw, but instead, I met a spirit, the most beautiful and bright, with God's Love emanating from her whole being. She was glad to see me, and reminded me that I was not a stranger, as she had seen me many times at Mrs. Ripple's seances; and she said, "Then you only knew me as a little Indian girl, simple and accommodating". And I said, "Bright Star you certainly surprise me; I had no expectations of meeting you as such a beautiful and bright spirit". And she said, "The Love of God makes us all alike. We who have that Love are not Indian or Pale Face or Yellow Face, but are all the children of God, and as His Love is the same unchangeable Love, those who receive it are all the same in their beauty and color and brightness. His Love makes our appearance, and as our souls become more filled with it, we become more like Him, and color, race and previous conditions disappear. Now what do you think of that? I tell you that the things I have learned here are wonderful and surprising."

Well, to continue, after I had lived in this condition of happiness for some time, I saw that my future depended upon my progress, for you must know I could not go with Rose to her home because she was so much more spiritual than I. I commenced to examine myself to learn what my drawbacks were and as I continued to make this self-examination, I found that my life on earth, or rather my recollections or memories of that life, were still with me, and that I must do something to get rid of them. Then my conscience commenced to work, and I soon saw

*Mary Kennedy is Dr. Stone's soulmate.
**Bright Star is a guide at Mr. Ripple's seances.

myself as I had never seen myself while on earth. The more transparent my actual self became, the more this conscience accused me of things done and omitted while a mortal. With these accusations came sufferings, for your wife and my mother told me the way, yet somehow I could not just understand how to find it, and so the days went by and I suffered.

As I continued to pray (for you must understand that I had been praying ever since I commenced to suffer) all of a sudden a feeling of peace came to me and with it a great Love that I had never felt before, and I realized that it was God's Love that my Rose and the others had been telling me of. Since then my sufferings have grown less and less, and my prayers and faith more and more. Oh, how I regret that in my earth life, I had not sought this Love! How much suffering I would have avoided and how much more happiness would have been mine!

Well, I have written you a long letter and must stop, but before doing so permit me to say that you have my thanks for the help that you gave me in the short time that we were friends. The few months that we knew one another, I now realize, were the most profitable months to me of all those that I spent in the investigation of Spiritualism.

So give my love to my friends and keep some for yourself. Believe me when I say I am your own true friend and brother.

Frank D. Syrick

ROSE McGOVERN

Soulmate of Judge Syrick writes about the
wonderful love that the Master has for Mr. Padgett
March 4, 1916

I am here, Rose.

I am your old acquaintance in the spirit world, and you have said that you loved me as a sister and wanted to make me happy, and you did, for I am very happy, thanks to your help. I am the soulmate of the Judge, and I merely want to say that we are both with you at times and try to help you and receive your help. The Judge is progressing very rapidly now, and will soon be with me and I know that he will be extremely happy. He wants me to say that he will never forget you and the great benefit you conferred upon him when you brought him in contact with me and enabled him to learn what was in the future for him in the spirit world. He is now a true believer in the truths of the Master and is trying to obtain the Love in all its fullness, and he wants you to know that this Love is a reality and not a mere thing of speculation. He has written you a long letter as he promised, and he would have come before, but your time is so occupied by the high spirits with their messages that he has not found the opportunity to write.

Well, I must not write more, except to say that you are in store for a happiness that you cannot conceive of. Your soulmate is so very beautiful and loving and beloved by us all, and has a most wonderful influence over all with whom she comes in contact. Greater and above all else, you have the love and wonderful friendship of the Master, who comes to you so very often. Oh, I tell you that you are favored and should feel that great benefit of the companionship of the number of high spirits who come to you, for you do have a great number of these celestial spirits come to you and write, and cast over you the influence of their great love. I am your friend forever, and I want you to love me too.

Yes, I try to help them, for I am present when they come, and some of them come to me for help. This is a wonderful work and we are all so interested in doing it. The dark spirits who seek your help seem to be as much impressed as any of us that you have so much influence over them, and when they start on the way to light, they, in many cases, find it, and then turn to you in gratitude and thanks.

So my dear friend, I will say good night,
Rose McGovern

JOSEPH H. SALYARDS

Mr. Padgett was once a pupil of
Prof. Salyards and now the tables are reversed
February 8, 1916

I am here, your old Professor.

Well, my dear boy, I often think of the wonder of it all, this experience, and sometimes let my mind return to the days when you were my dear pupil, and I think how wholly we were in want of any conception that such a thing could be. I can't tell you how glad and thankful I am that we came in contact with each other, for I will frankly and assuredly say that if I had never met you I doubt if I would have had the privilege of meeting such spirits as your grandmother and mother, and of having received the benefits of their advice and the influence of their love, as well as the companionship of your father and Mr. Riddle.

I often think of how a mere accident as your coming to my school should have brought about such momentous results. So my boy, keep up your good work and you will find a wonderful happiness when you come over.

Well, I have been watching the many messages that you have received and I have been much interested in the variety of the subject matter and the number and difference in the spirits who have written. You seem to have received messages from spirits of all ages and from all nationalities and I am pleased to see that these messages were mostly of

65

a higher order of communication. I was interested in the messages from the prophets and also those from the apostles and saints and in them I saw that there were many spiritual truths disclosed. It is wonderful that you should get such corroboration of these truths from spirits who have had such a wide difference in experiences in the spirit world.

So I say, we all love you very much, and you must believe in us and know that we are with you and have more power than you may think to help you in your work. I have written enough, so my dear boy, I will say good night.

Your brother and friend,
Prof. Salyards

*Professor Salyards describes his entry
into the spirit world and his spiritual progression*
December 18, 1914

I am here, Prof. Salyards.

I am here to tell you of some of my experiences in spirit life and I wish that you would let me speak first of my regeneration and birth into the higher sphere where I am now living. Your mother is the chief cause of my progression as she first showed me the way to the Love of God. I was, as you may know, not a very spiritual man when on earth, but thought that man only needed a great intellect in order to enjoy the great blessings of the spirit life. I was not what might be called a great sinner as I lived a tolerably good moral life as you may know from your experiences with me while you were at school under my instruction. I had no idea that something more than mere intellectual acquirements were needed in order to enjoy the happiness that God had provided for his children who were willing to receive all the blessings that His Love and favor had in store for them.

Well, after I ascended to the spirit world I found that my intellectual and moral qualifications did not make me very happy, although I enjoyed comparative happiness in the pursuit of knowledge and the investigation of those intellectual questions that appealed to my higher desires. I soon commenced to see that I had something more to acquire than mere knowledge of spiritual laws and the things that appealed to the intellect which all who are of a practical inclination deem sufficient for self-satisfaction. I began to study these things and have advanced very much in my knowledge of them. I have succeeded in writing a poem which gives me great satisfaction and makes me think that I am really a poet. Since I have progressed to the higher spheres where love rules and intellect is a mere subordinate medium of true happiness, I find that while my acquirement in the particulars mentioned are desirable and afford much enjoyment and delight to my mind, yet my true happiness is with the possession and knowledge that I have the Love of God in my soul.

So you see, mere intellect or moral qualities are not the important thing for a spirit who wants to possess and enjoy the greatest happiness. Keep this in mind in your earthly life and when you come over you will find that many things will appear easy to comprehend which otherwise you may have to search for in darkness and doubt.

I will write you some time when we have more time and will also tell you the results of my investigation of the spirit life, but not tonight as I am tired and so are you.

Yes, I am really Prof. Salyards who is writing and you must believe me or I will feel hurt.

Your old professor and friend,
Joseph Salyards

The various experiences of spirits when they arrive in the spirit world
February 25, 1915

I am here, Prof. Salyards.

Well, I am very happy and desire to write you on some phases of spirit life that I have observed in my experience of progressing.

I have noticed that when a spirit first comes into this life, it is very often in a condition of darkness, not realizing where it is or what its surroundings are, and in many instances, it requires quite a long time for the spirit to realize that it is not still of the earth. In many cases this is not the condition of the spirit for it seems to have an immediate understanding of its condition and surroundings. I attribute the first-mentioned condition to be due to the fact that, when on earth, the mortal had no definite belief as to what the future life might be, and in many instances believed that the soul went into the grave with the body to await the great "resurrection" day.

Some of your religious denominations are preaching that doctrine now, and the consequence will be that all those who believe the doctrine will experience the condition of darkness and the want of knowledge of the continuity of life that I have spoken of. The second class of spirits, or those who appear to realize immediately that they have passed from earth to spirit life, are those who, while on earth, believed that when the spirit left the body it passed immediately into the heavenly spheres, or into the opposite, I mean the place of the wicked.

Well, as soon as the spirits realize fully that they are no longer of earth, they commence to inquire as to where they are, and many of them ask questions that indicate they are disappointed in not realizing the expectations that they had while on earth. It is very difficult at times to convince them that there are no such places as the heavens and the hells as taught by the churches, for while our spirit world may be a heaven or hell to them, yet the heaven or hell that they expect to find is not here. Some, on the other hand, do not seem to understand that they have really left the earth, because they say, if we had left the earth life, we would know nothing, quoting the Bible and some of the preachers, "the dead know nothing" (Ecclesiastes 9:5).

I have been very much interested in observing these different phases of the departed spirit's beliefs and thoughts which show me the absolute necessity of mortals understanding the truths pertaining to life and death. This affords a very strong argument why Spiritualism should be more extensively and earnestly taught to mortals and why the false doctrines of those who teach either that the dead know nothing, or that the departed spirit goes either to heaven or to hell in the orthodox sense, should be shown to be not only a false belief, but injurious to mankind.

Let the believers and teachers of Spiritualism make greater and stronger efforts to refute these harmful teachings, and they will be doing the cause of truth and of man's happiness a great good. I am not only interested in these phases but in all others, which show that the spirits, even after they realize that they are still alive and must live as spirits, continue to ignore the fact that their orthodox teachings are false. Some say that they may yet be able to go back into the body and await the great "resurrection" day for deliverance, and say that they will soon see God, and that He will take them into His heavens where they will find that eternal rest and peace that they were taught to expect when on earth. Even the wicked will look in dread to have some devil come and carry them to the hells where torture of the most terrible kind awaits them, so they think.

From all this you may understand that we spirits who know the truth have a great work to do, to enable these darkened spirits to understand and believe that their false hopes and dreadful fears have no foundation in truth and will never be realized. Many spirits are engaged in doing this work and these spirits are not necessarily of the higher kind, for many spirits who occupy the lower planes and have no real spiritual enlightenment are engaged in this work.

I am not engaged now in causing these dark spirits to see the truth, for I have progressed to higher things and my mission is to teach the truths of the higher life which I have been taught by spirits who live in higher spheres. To me, this work is one that is not only interesting, but gives me the great happiness that comes with the realization that I have been the means of leading a spirit to learn to love God and to receive the happiness which the Love of God gives to spirits. I tell you that this teaching is the grandest that I have ever engaged in in all my life. When on earth, as I taught and saw the young mind develop, I found much happiness in the knowledge that I was doing some good, but here, in my teachings, when I see a soul develop, I realize that I am doing a spirit the greatest of all good.

My work is not confined entirely to this teaching. I also am engaged in trying to assist mortals to a true conception of life here, I mean the spiritual part of this life. No human is entirely without spirit influence, whether good or evil. Many are susceptible to the influence of the evil spirits and for that reason the work of the good spirits is so much more difficult. The advantage, though, with the good influences, is that what they suggest is truth will never die, while the suggestions of the evil influences last only for a comparatively short time.

When the material gives up the spirit being which it clothes, that being will then be relieved of many of these natural tendencies to evil thoughts and deeds; and while this mere separation does not make a devil a saint, it makes it so much easier for the spirit to get rid of many of these evil tendencies, and makes him more susceptible to the influence of truth and goodness. You must not think from this that as soon as they have been in the spirit world for a little time they become good spirits, for that is not true. Many evil spirits have been in the spirit world for a great many years, and yet still have their evil thoughts and desires, and all the evil qualities of hatred, malice, envy, etc., as when they were on earth. Their giving up the earth life did not deprive them of their will, the greatest force or power that God gave to mankind, except that of love. Many of these spirits refuse to exercise their will in a way that will enable them to rid themselves of these evil thoughts and desires.

Let me stop now as I am tired and you need to rest. So with all my love and best wishes, I am your old professor,

Joseph H. Salyards

Professor Salyards on the laws that govern the spirit world
April 13, 1915

I am here, Prof. Salyards.

Well, I am here and will endeavor to write you my thoughts on what spirits may know about the laws of the spirit world after they have been in that world for a short time.

As you know, I have been here for a comparatively short time, and while my studies have been to a considerable extent in the study of these laws, yet, I find that I have limited knowledge of the same and much of my information has been gathered from other spirits who have lived here a great many years, and who have devoted their study and investigation to these laws.

Well, I first want to say that no spirit, by the mere fact of having recently made his advent to this world, has received any greater knowledge than he had when on earth. My knowledge of spiritual laws when on earth was not very extensive, and I found when I came into the spirit world that I did not know much more than I did before I came and such is the experience of every spirit. As I continued to investigate these matters, I discovered that my capacity for learning was greatly increased and that my mind was more plastic and received this knowledge more easily than when I was a mortal. This is largely due to the fact that the brain, I mean the mortal brain, is, when compared to what you might call the spirit mind, a thing of much inferior quality and not so capable of learning the cause and effect of phenomena. I am now undergoing a course of study that will, I have no doubt, give me wonderful information of these laws, so that ultimately I may become what you mortals might call a learned man.

The first and, to me, the most important law that I have learned is that man continues to live in the spirit world without his earthly body. This great law, while to you and to many others is well-known and is an established fact, yet, to me, was not known, as I had never had any experience in Spiritualism and had never given any study to the subject. When I arrived in the spirit world, I learned that this law is one of God's truths, and that it is fixed and will never change, for all will survive the change of so-called death.

The next great law that I learned is that no man can of his own power make his condition or position in the spirit world just what and where he would have it be. This is another fixed truth, and one which many spirits do not fully comprehend; for they think, or so express themselves, that all they have to do is to exercise a little will power and they can move from certain conditions. But this is not true, for the law controlling this matter never has any exceptions in its operations.

A mortal or spirit can, in a way, determine what his destiny may be, but once fixed by this great power of will which God has conferred on man, he cannot by the exercise of that will change that fixed condition until the laws of compensation have been satisfied; and even then the change is not brought about by the exercise of his will, but by the operation of the laws releasing him from memories and recollections which hold him to the conditions that his life has placed him in. So when men think that they, by the exercise of their own will, can release themselves from a condition which they have made for themselves, they are mistaken.

Of course, while a mortal or spirit cannot by the exercise of his will change his condition, yet, in order to secure that change, the will has to be exercised. This is because the help* which comes from without is

*This reference is to God's redeeming Love.

71

absolutely necessary to cause the change, which will not come unless man exercises the will in the way of desiring and asking for the help. So let not man think that he is his own saviour, because he is not; and if the help did not come from without, he would never be saved from the condition which he finds himself in when he enters the spirit world.

You hear in your spirit circles and read in the publications about Spiritualism that progression is a law of the spirit world. Well that is true; but it does not mean that a spirit by the mere fact of being in the spirit world necessarily progresses, either mentally or spiritually, for this is not true. Many spirits who have been here for years are in no better condition than when they first became spirits. All progression depends upon the help that comes from outside the mind or soul of man. Of course when this help comes, man has to cooperate, but without this help there would be nothing with which to cooperate, and no progress could possibly be made. If a man depends upon his own powers exclusively, he will never progress. This law does not apply only to the soul's progress, of which you have heard us speak so often, but to the progress of the mind and also to what might be called the purely moral qualities.

Another law of the spirit world is that when a spirit once commences to progress, that progress increases in geometrical progression, as we used to say when teaching on earth. Just as soon as the light breaks into a man's soul or mind, and he commences to see that there is a way for him to reach higher things, and to expand either his mind or soul, he will find that his desire to progress will increase as that progression continues, and with that desire will come help in such abundance that it will be limited only by the desire of the spirit. His will then becomes a great force in his success in progressing and working in conjunction with the help that calls it into operation.

This progression may be illustrated by the history of the snowball, which started rolling from the top of a hill. As it continues its descent, not only does its velocity increase, but it continually enlarges its form and body by the outside snow attaching itself to the ball. So with the mind or soul of a spirit: as it ascends, it not only becomes more rapid in its flight, but it meets this outside help that I speak of, which help attaches itself to the spirit, and, as it were, becomes a part of it.

So you see that the great problem is to make the start. This principle will apply to mortals as well as to spirits because, if the start be made on earth, the mere fact of becoming a spirit will not halt or in any way interfere with the progress of the soul of that spirit. Of course, this means that a correct start be made. If the start be a false one or based on things other than the truth, instead of progress continuing when the man becomes a spirit, there may have to be a retracing of the way and a new start made in order to get on the right road.

This applies to the progress of the mind as well as to the progress of the soul. The mind of a mortal learns many things which seem to that mind to be the truth, and which, in its opinion, must lead to progress and greater knowledge. Now when the earth life gives way to the spirit life, that mind may find that its basis of knowledge was all wrong and that to continue in the way that it had been moving would lead to increased error, and consequently, a new start must be made. Frequently, the retracing of that mind over the course that it had followed, and the elimination of errors that it had embraced, are more difficult and take a longer time to accomplish than does the learning of the truth after the mind makes its correct start.

Sometimes the mind of great learning (according to the standards of earthly learning) is more harmful and retards more the progress of that man in the ways and acquirements of truth than does the mind that is, as you might say, a blank, that is, without preconceived ideas of what the truth is on a particular subject. This unfortunate experience exists to a greater extent in matters pertaining to religion than to any other matters because the ideas and convictions which are taught and possessed of these religious matters affect innumerably more mortals than do ideas and convictions in reference to any other matters.

A spirit who is filled with these erroneous beliefs that may have been taught him from his mortal childhood, and fostered and fed upon by him until he becomes a spirit, is, of all the inhabitants of this world, the most difficult to teach and convince of the truths pertaining to religious matters. It is much easier to teach the agnostic, or even the atheist, of these truths, than the hide-bound believer in the dogmas and creeds of the church.

There is another law which enables spirits to become, by the mere operation of their natural affections and loves, pure and free from the consequences and evils of their mortal lives. This does not mean that the law of compensation does not operate to the fullest, and that it does not demand to the last farthing. For such is the exactness in the operation of this law and no spirit is released from its penalties, until he has satisfied the law.

As you believe, and as many other mortals believe, a man's punishment for the sins committed by him on earth are inflicted by his conscience and memories. There is no special punishment inflicted by God on any particular man, but the law of punishment operates alike on everyone. When a spirit first enters the spirit life it does not necessarily feel the scourging of these memories, and this is the reason why you will so often hear the spirit who has recently left his mortal life assure his friends or sorrowing relatives at the public seances that he is very happy. But after a little while, the memory commences to work, and as the soul is awakened, it then never ceases until the penalties are paid. I don't mean that the spirit is, necessarily, continuously in a condition of torment, but substantially so, and relief does not come until these memories cease their awful lashings. Some spirits live here a great number of years before they receive this relief, while others more quickly obtain it.

The greatest cause which operates to relieve these spirits of these memories, is love. I now mean the natural love, and this love embraces many qualities, such as remorse and sorrow, and the desire to make amends for injuries done, etc. Until a spirit's love is awakened, none of these feelings come to him. He cannot possibly feel remorse or regret or the desire to atone, until love, no matter how slight, comes into his heart. He may not realize just what the cause of these feelings are, but it is love just the same.

Well, as these various feelings operate and he acts in accordance with them, a memory here and a memory there will leave him, never to return; and as these memories in turn leave him, his sufferings become less, and after awhile, when they have all left him, he becomes free from the law, and it, as to him, becomes extinct. Now it must be understood that this is not a work of quick operation, for it may be years — long, weary years of suffering — before the spirit becomes free and once more a spirit without sin or these memories. This is the way the great law of compensation is satisfied; it cannot be avoided, all its demands must be met, until sin and error are eradicated and the soul is returned to a pure state.

This gradual release from these penalties does not mean that a spirit is progressing in his journey to the higher and brighter spheres, because even without this torture and torment he may still remain stationary as to the development of his higher nature, mental and moral. When he has been relieved of these sufferings, he is then in a condition to start towards the progression that I have spoken of.

As you are tired, I will stop now and I will write to you again. With all my love, I am your true friend and professor,

Joseph H. Salyards

Joseph H. Salyards writes about his knowledge
and soul perception that God has personality
November 22, 1915

I am here, your old Professor Salyards.

I merely want to say that I am very happy and want you to know that I am progressing in my condition of soul development and in my knowledge of the truths that pertain to the spirit world. I have not written you for some time, and would like to tell you of certain truths that I have learned since last I wrote you.

Well, I find that I am now in a condition of soul development that enables me to see the truth of what the Master has told us in reference to the real existence of God, who knows what His creatures are doing and in what way they are making use of their bodies and souls. I mean that this God is one having all the faculties that you would suppose only a being would have who had a form and personality; and one can hardly understand how a mere essence or formless existence could have such powers and qualities.

I never, until recently, could comprehend the real truth and meaning of God. I believed Him to be mere essence, void of form or personality, who had the wisdom and love and power that I was taught such a God possessed. Such comprehension is beyond the finite mind, and can only be accepted as a realization of an existing condition or truth by means of faith. Yet now I have more than faith to enable me to understand the fact that this God, whom we call our Father, for He is, has all these qualities and powers, and such understanding, which to me is a wonderful and unexpected addition to my knowledge of God.

This understanding, of course, is not a thing that arises from any exercise of the mind or the result of any mental power or quality which I may not have realized that I possessed. It is the result of the exercise of my soul perceptions, which have become so great and in such condition of unison or harmony with God's qualities of Soul that He and all His attributes appear to me as real, perceptible existences having a certainty of a comprehensible Being, as do the existence of spirits and their attributes.

No mere development of the intellectual qualities or attributes could ever lead to a comprehension of the personality of God as I have described it. I never in all my life, natural or spiritual, conceived or expected that it was possible for any soul of a mortal or a spirit to see God as I now see Him. I never could understand what was meant by the beatitude, "The pure in heart shall see God" (Matthew 5:8), except in this sense, that as we became pure in heart those qualities that were ascribed to God would become a part of us, and as such possessors, we could see God, or rather the result of those attributes of God in our souls.

I don't know whether you can fully comprehend what I intend to convey to you, but I have tried my best to put the idea in such language that your mind may understand, to some extent, what my meaning is. I know that you will never fully know what this great soul perception is until you have experienced what this development is in your own soul, which is necessary to enable it to see with the clearness that I now see.

I have written enough for tonight and if you will carefully read what I have written, you will find much food for thought and probably some help to a correct and concrete comprehension of who and what God is. I want to express to you my gratification and pleasure in being able to come to you again and having you take down my ideas, and also for the opportunity to declare that God is a Being having an existence of His own, comprehensible only by the soul perceptions of His redeemed children.

I will say good night.

Your old professor and brother,
Joseph H. Salyards

A.G. RIDDLE

*Padgett receives healing from Jesus and White Eagle, also Riddle
has progressed to a new sphere and is seeking further spiritual progress*
February 15, 1915

I am here, your old law partner.

I am very happy tonight and I am glad that you are so much better. You had a rather hard time of it which reminded me somewhat of the suffering that I used to undergo when I was on the earth. Well, you are cured of the indigestion but the gas accumulates at times and makes it uncomfortable for you, but that will pass away before long and your digestive organs will soon be in perfect working order.

The faith that you had in your prayers and through the work of the Master you were actually cured. The work done was a means used to impress upon you with fact that God had answered your prayers. I do not see how you could have had such faith as you evidenced at the time, but it is a fact that you had it and as a consequence the cure was effected. Jesus helped you to pray and also helped your faith. He also did the work that you observed through the power which he possesses and used White Eagle to manipulate your intestines and liver. It was a revelation to me, I must confess, and caused me to believe more than ever in prayer and faith.

I am now so very happy in my new sphere and cannot explain to you what this happiness means, for I cannot express myself in language sufficiently strong and descriptive so that you may comprehend my meaning. However, this I will say, that my happiness now transcends all conception of what I thought happiness might be when as a mortal I sometimes thought of the afterlife and the happiness which might be in store for me when I passed over.

I am in the third sphere and I am not contented to remain there, for your mother has told me on many occasions of the far greater happiness existing in the higher spheres. I am now striving and praying for this greater happiness and I will never be contented until I get it. Your wife is in a much higher sphere and is so very beautiful and so exceedingly happy that I know that where she lives such happiness must exist. I am also happy because I have my soulmate with me so very often and her love is so great and pure that it leads me on to higher things and enables me to seek with so much earnestness the great Love of God which I now believe is working for me if I only will strive to obtain it.

Well, as you want me to tell you of the laws of the spirit world, I will say that the one great law is that God is Love and that He is willing to bestow that Love on anyone, spirit or mortal, who asks Him for it. I am not only very happy but I find that my mind is expanding to a great extent by reason of the Love that I possess. No mortal or spirit can possibly be filled with this Love and not have the wisdom that comes with it.

I am not yet fully conversant with the laws of communication, but I know enough to be able to say that every spirit is trying to communicate with their friends on earth, and why they are not able is because the mortals are not in that condition of psychical rapport that will enable them to receive the communications of the spirits. I do not know as of yet why one mortal is susceptible to these influences in such a way as to be readily understood and another mortal is not. Although this I do know, that when the rapport exists, the communications become stronger with the exercise of their powers. You have this power to a very large degree and if you will continue to try to exercise it, you will find that manifestations of several kinds will be disclosed. Your writing powers are very great and will grow as you continue to write, and beside this phase you have the potential ability to have other manifestations such as independent voices and slate writing. This latter, I think, will soon come to you and when it does you will get messages that will have great value to you in convincing you that what you write in this method is written by the control of the thoughts of your friends in the spirit world.

You will also get the voices very soon, I think, and when you do you will be able to converse with us in your room at night when you are alone. But I don't know of any manifestation so satisfactory to both spirit and mortal as the writing such as you are now doing, for we have the opportunity for such a greater extent of communicating and interchanges of thought. I am perfectly delighted at the possibility given me of writing you in this way. So you must believe that I am writing to you and that all the others of your band are doing the same thing.

Your father is with me a great deal and he has helped me very much and he is now progressing so rapidly that he will soon be with his soul-mate in the fifth sphere. Your good mother tells me this and she knows so many things pertaining to spiritual progress. I must stop now for you are tired and so am I.

So with all my love and blessing.

I am your old partner,
A. G. Riddle

Heaven is a place as well as a condition of the soul
February 27, 1920

I am here, Riddle.

Let me write tonight as I see that you are anxious to hear from some of your friends in the spirit world. I have not written for a long time, though I have been desirous to do so, and tonight will say only a few words in reference to my progress and happiness in my condition as a celestial spirit, for I am now in the celestial heavens, and know the truth of many things that have been written you.

It is a little difficult for me to recite to you the wonders of these heavens and the perfect happiness that is enjoyed by those spirits that have found their home and abiding place in the many mansions that Jesus spoke of while in the flesh. You must know that heaven is a place as well as a condition, notwithstanding the fact that so many of the Spiritualists teach that it is only a condition or state of the soul. No, this is not all of the truth but is a great part of the truth, for the condition of the soul determines just what heaven it shall occupy and find its harmony and happiness in; for the all-loving Creator has provided that the soul shall have a place corresponding to its condition in which it may live and progress. If heaven were only a state of the soul, then it would not be a real, existing thing with the substance and reality that the soul, even in its state of bliss, must have as a necessary accompaniment to the enjoyment of what God has provided for its true condition of living.

Heaven, as a place, is real and independent of the state of the soul, though it is necessary for the soul to be in a corresponding state in order that it may enter into this heaven and fully realize that it is a home suitable for its condition and enjoyment. If it, I mean heaven, were not a real objective and perceptible place then the soul would be limited by its own condition which would be very narrow, as I may say, and confined to the limits of its own state, and separated from the states of other souls, and without the social intercourse that makes heaven a place of such happiness and contentment. Every soul would then be in the condition of the ascetic in human life, and introspection and contemplation would be the source and only means of possible bliss. Knowledge of those things that are spoken of as beyond the heart of man to conceive of, and which are truly and certainly provided by God's Love for the continuous and never-ending progress of the soul towards higher and greater enjoyment, would have no real, conscious existence in that soul.

As man in his earth life is provided with those surroundings and material things that are intended to make him happy or miserable, so in the heavens things material are provided to enable the soul of man to better enjoy its own condition. The things of heaven are not all spiritual, as conceived by so many men, but are partly composed of the material of the universe and are so constituted and formed to supply the desires and wishes of the soul with that which will satisfy the soul's longings for beauty and harmony and perfect enjoyment. In the several heavens are homes, real and substantial, which are suited to the states of the souls and differing as those states differ in their requirements. These material things are not subjective as so many mortals teach, but are objective as are the things of earth, and are the objects of sight and touch and of the other spiritual senses.

When I desire to go into a city and indulge my desires, I find a city with streets and avenues and houses and other things that belong to a city, just as do you mortals of earth when you visit your cities; and so, when I desire to go into the country and enjoy the fields and hills and streams and gardens, they are all here, real and existing, and not the subjects of mere thoughts or state of my soul. When I am absent from the city or country, that city or country continues to exist in all its beauty and magnificence, just as truly as when I am present.

Men must know that the soul in its heavenly life requires these material things and has them, just as a soul when enveloped in a body of flesh requires the material things of earth. While the condition of the soul determines its place of living, yet that place is also existing and real and awaits the coming of that soul in a condition of harmony. In these heavens there is nothing nebulous or impalpable or only a reflection or image of the soul's condition, but everything is real and substantial and lasting as the eternal hills; and when the soul finds a habitation it is not merely the effect of its own condition, but a place already prepared for the habitation of that soul in accord with its true condition.

If not, heaven would be a place of confusion and of appearances and disappearances, with no stability or abiding qualities, and the many mansions spoken of by Jesus as existing in his Father's house, would have no real, permanent being, but would depend for their creation and existence upon the mere state of the soul. The mansions are there and change not, and whether or not they shall have occupants depends upon the harmony of souls in their correspondence with the harmony of God's laws creating these mansions.

I have written you this short description of the heavens as based upon my knowledge and experience, devoid of speculation or metaphysical musings. I am glad that I could write you again. I am very happy and know that God's Love is a real and transforming thing, and sufficient to create in the souls of men and of spirits that state which will enable them to have and enjoy the mansions in the highest heavens.

I will not write more now. Good night.

Your friend and brother,
A. G. Riddle

*Riddle is in a condition of wonderment
after seeing Jesus show such brightness and glory*
September 27, 1915

I am here, your old partner.

I will write only a few lines tonight, as I am in such a condition of wonderment over what took place when Jesus was writing to you last night that I do not feel able to gather my thoughts for extended writing. Although I want to say that what happened to me was the greatest revelation as to the character, or rather the attributes, of Jesus that I have seen since I have been in the spirit world.

When he wrote to you in his emphatic and authoritative manner, he became transformed into such a being of light and glory and power that none of us could look upon his countenance, and we had to fall upon our faces to hide the brightness of his presence. I tell you it was wonderful evidence of his greatness and power. Never before had I seen him clothed in such brightness and power. He was always the most beautiful and bright and magnificent of all the spirits, but never was there displayed by him before those appearances which made us think that he very well could be a god.

I now know as never before that he is the true Son of God and that he is worthy to follow and believe in. What a wonderful spirit he is, all love and power and greatness, and yet all humility. I had no conception that such a combination of attributes could ever exist in the same spirit, and I cannot help thinking of him and the greatness of his being. I am so glad that I saw him as he appeared when he wrote, because now I have some conception of what the glory and grandeur of the high celestial heavens and their inhabitants must be.

Well, I cannot say much more now, except that you surprise me more and more because of the great favor and blessings you have had conferred upon you. We are all amazed over it, and of course, happy over the fact. You must try your best to do this work and fulfill the mission for which you have been chosen.

Yes, I see the Professor quite often and he is progressing very wonderfully in his spiritual growth, for he is really a beautiful spirit and as you know he was not so beautiful on earth. Now he is a spirit that shows that he possesses what he says is the Love of God to a wonderful degree. He is still studying and writing, and says that he has written you some of his thoughts, and they are wonderful, even for the spiritual world. He is here now and says that he wants to thank you for your inquiry about him, and also wants you to know that he is thinking a great deal of you.

I will not write more tonight.

I am your old partner,
A. G. Riddle

CHAPTER THREE

Strangers

SOLOMON P. BROWN

A wandering spirit is looking for help

I am here, Solomon P. Brown.

Let me write just a few lines and tell you how unhappy I am and how much I need your help.

Well, I was not a very bad person, I merely did not do what I should have done to help my fellowman to become happy and prosperous, because I was selfish and thought that I needed everything for myself. Now I see that I was all wrong and that I must try to right the matter, but I don't know how; tell me if you can. I am not happy.

I don't know anything about God, except in a general way, who created the world and sends the bad to hell and the good to heaven. This is one thing that has confused me, for I am neither in heaven nor in hell, and where I am I just don't know, but I know that I am a spirit and do suffer and am not very happy. So if you please, tell me where I am and what I must do to get to a better place.

My name was Solomon P. Brown and I lived in a town named Bridgeport, Connecticut. I died in 1892, and I have been here ever since, wandering around in hope to find someway to get out of this unhappy condition.

Yes, I was married. My wife is still on earth and enjoying herself in a second marriage, and I don't blame her, for if I could find someone here who I thought could add to my enjoyment, I would get married too. I have never seen any marriages here, and I suppose they don't have any. Well, I will go with him, he says all right come along and I am going.

So, my dear sir, good night,
Solomon P. Brown

LOUISA R. CONNELL

She had a theatrical career and is in
darkness with others of the same profession

I am here, Louisa Connell.

Let me write a little for I am in darkness also, and need help so very much. I was not a very good woman when on earth, nor a very bad one as I then thought. I was engaged in the theatrical business, and was considered a very fine singer and dancer, but I now see that my life was not one that helped me after I came to this world of truth and nakedness. I mean that nothing is hidden here. I am seen just as I really exist, and I can hide nothing, or make myself appear other than I really am. I am suffering from the recollections of my earth life and the experiences that

I had on the stage.

I was married to a man who was an actor, and like myself never gave any thought to the higher things of life; and so we both were satisfied to live in the atmosphere which a theatrical life throws around those who live in it. I, of course, was a good woman in the sense of being chaste, for I have that consolation and it helps me some, especially when I consider the many temptations that surround a woman of the stage. Thank God, I maintained my chastity, and I believe that recollection has been a great help to me here. I did many other things which I now see were not right, and from which I am suffering and am kept in darkness. I don't know how to get out of it and hence I come to you.

Well, when I was a child I went to church and Sunday school, and was taught what a child is usually taught there, but I have to confess that those teachings made no lasting impression on me, and after I became a woman and started my career of singing and dancing I never gave those teachings another thought. My thoughts were given to becoming a star, as we say, as a successful actress and singer; but, as you know, that did not help my spiritual nature, as I have now found to be the fact. I am now a spirit and am without very much knowledge of the things which I suppose are necessary for me to know to get out of this darkness.

No, he is not, he is still on earth and is not now on the stage, but is living a very respectable life with his family, for we had several children. My name was Louisa R. Connell, and I lived in London, England, and died in 1877, at that place.

No, I have never been taught the way to light, as you say. I have met some spirits who said that they were living in a higher sphere and could help me if I would only listen to them, but I refused because they did not seem to me to be any different from myself and I did not believe that they could help me. My associates have been spirits like myself, some of them theatrical people, who knew no more about spiritual things than I did. We are all in darkness and need help. I will try to do as you say, only show me the way.

Yes, I see a great many spirits, and they tell me that I must hurry, as they wish to write, but they don't seem to be any better than I am. Well, I see more bright spirits about you and they are very beautiful, and I wonder how they can be so beautiful.

She answers and says of course she will take me with her and help me and love me too. She now says come with me and I am going and will try to believe as you told me to.

So my dear friend, I must say good night,
Louisa Connell

CLARA BARTON (1821-1912)

*Clara Barton, founder of the Red Cross Society,
is not too interested in spiritual progression*
April 14, 1916

I am here, Clara Barton.

I was the woman who founded the Red Cross Society and I am still interested in it, although I am a spirit. I saw that others were writing through you and I thought that I would like to try, and so with the permission of your wife I took hold of the pen and am now trying to express a few thoughts to you.

Well, I see that my society is very busy now in the Great War* and is doing a great deal of good and needs all the encouragement that it can get. It also needs to have an increase in its membership in all parts of the world, for I see additional scenes of action where its services will be required, and many a poor soldier will need the services of the Red Cross.

I have the association of some very good and lovely spirits who are interested in humankind as I am. We are trying to help men wherever we can.

Yes, I have met some of these beautiful spirits and they have been very kind to me, trying to help me, and I am so interested in the work of my society that I have not given much attention to the advice of these high spirits.

I have listened to you with great interest and I am impressed by

*World War I (1914-1918).

what you tell me. I have never thought of myself in the particular which you mention, but now I see that what you say must be true and that I should seek my own development as well as try to assist my late associates. I will do as you advise and seek one of these high spirits, and ask her help and instructions.

I see a number of high spirits here now, brighter and more beautiful than I have ever seen, and your wife brings one to me and says that she is interested in me and loves me and will help me in the way that you suggest. I am going with her and will seriously listen to her and seek for all the benefits that I may obtain. I thank you for your interest and kindness and will come sometime and write you of my experience.

So thanking you, I will say good night,
Clara Barton

SARAH J. WILSON

*Sarah J. Wilson, an abortionist, realizes only too late
the great wrong she performed on earth and is seeking help*

I am here, Sarah J. Wilson.

Let me write, as I need help so very much. I am in darkness and suffering.

When on earth I was a woman who tried to make my living by doing that which God and man both condemned as against nature and all the provisions for perpetuating the world. I was an abortionist and caused many a premature birth, or the destruction of that which, if it had been permitted to gestate, would have been a human being. So you see my deeds were so very evil, and since I have been in the spirit world I have realized the enormity of them.

Of course, when I committed these acts I knew that I was doing wrong and in many cases committing murder, but the desire to make money was so great that my crimes did not appear to me in all their nakedness and enormity. Now I see them face to face, and I realize that I am of all wretches the most wretched. I have never known a moment's peace since I have been a spirit, and it seems to me that I have been such a spirit for centuries and centuries.

No ray of light ever comes to me and no words of love or sympathy. My associates are just like myself, steeped in sin of one kind or another and never a ray of hope comes to us. I wonder sometimes why I was ever born and why I cannot die and forever be annihilated, but I must live and suffer and pay the penalties of my deeds done in the body.

I thought that I was a kindhearted woman in most of the affairs of life, and I believe that my neighbors so considered me. I often helped the poor and fed the hungry, and spoke words of kindness to the distressed, and I really thought that I was a good woman. But now, how useless all these deeds of apparent kindness seem to me, for they do not weigh a grain of sand to a mountain in my favor. So you see the great sins that I committed have no way of being blotted out. I wish that I had never been born.

Well, I am told that some of the little children who live in higher lands are the children whom I deprived of the earth life. I, of course, do not know, for some spirits tell me this, and when I learn this it helps me some to think that even though I deprived them of their earthly existence, yet they are alive in a brighter and happier land. However, this is not sufficient to relieve me of my sufferings, for I killed them when on earth and I had no right to do it, and I am being punished for it.

When on earth I tried to make myself believe that there was no hell. I know now that there is a hell and that I am in it and believe that I will never get out of it. Well, I could tell you of many instances of my sinning but it will do no good. I feel that I have told you enough to arouse your pity, and that if you can help me you will.

I was married but had no children and sometimes I think that if I had had children of my own I would not have engaged in the business of destroying others. Now it is too late and I must suffer. I will do anything that you tell me and will try to believe and follow the advice that may be given me, only do something for me.

I have asked for Mrs. Salyards and a beautiful spirit comes to me, and puts her arm around me and says, "You are my sister in trouble and a child of God, just as I am, and He loves you just as He loves me, so come with me and I will love you and try to show you the way to light and happiness".

Oh, dear friend, I thank you, and with all my heartfelt tears and gratitude,

I say good night,

Sarah J. Wilson

BEN ROBINSON

A sailor needs help and describes his travels
in the seas of darkness and recalls what he did on earth

I am here, Ben Robinson.

Let me write. I am very unhappy and want help. So listen to me for awhile.

I am a man who lived a life of sin on earth. I was a sailor and visited every country on earth, and joined in all the vice that I could find in the seaports of these countries. I drank and gambled and visited the women and did everything that was bad. Since I have become a spirit I have seen that my life was very sinful and am suffering so very much, and have to sail through these seas of darkness with never a port to land in. I am always sailing and never coming to anchor, and my ship is nothing but my spirit body*. How funny that I don't need any sails, or rudder or compass, yet I sail and go where I want to and never miss my bearings. All I do is think of where I want to go and I sail there without any trouble or mistake; but these seas are all blackness, and there are no stars to guide us and nothing to tell us that it is storming or calm, and the blackness is here all the time.

I have companions or mates who sail with me at times, and we talk of the strangeness of the seas and the blackness of the heavens and the want of stars and winds, and of our torture. Why, I sometimes think that I must be in the seas of hell, only there is no light which would naturally come from fires, if there were any. I have my recollections of what I

*An etheric body that is created by the active energy of the soul, which gives a spirit's its appearance.

89

did on earth and they seem to burn me and cause my sufferings. So do my mates suffer from the same cause, they say.

I want to get into port and find some relief from these long, never-ending voyages in which I suffer torment. So will you tell me where I can find a port of landing where I may see the light and the stars and get rid of my tortures? My mates can't help me, and I don't know the course that will land me. I am without any hope of ever dropping anchor again, and I tell you the thought that I have got to sail these dark seas forever makes me wish that I had never entered on the voyage of life. I have never seen any spirits who are different from myself or who could help me out of my troubles. I never believed in God or religious things and lived only the pleasures of the sea and ports, as I have told you.

My name is Ben Robinson, and my land home was Yarmouth, Maine. I died in 1878, at sea.

I should like to meet such a mate. Well, I have found him and he says he will show me the way to port. I am going with him and will listen to his yarn.

So with all my heart, I say good night,
Ben Robinson

SAMUEL WILLIAMS

Samuel Williams is seeking help
because on earth he made many animals suffer

I am here, Samuel Williams.

Let me write for awhile. I am in darkness, too, and need help so much. I was a man that lived a very wicked life in the way of causing many animals to suffer in order that I might get paid for my work in the way of helping the doctors. I collected the animals and sold them to the doctors, and knew at the time what they were to be used for. So I was as much to blame as the doctors.

I am now suffering for doing these things, and I want help. Can you give me any? I have been here a very short time as you might say, but to me it seems a century of years. Please help me if you can. I need it so much. Yes, I will do as you say. I was a white man when on earth, but I am very dark now.

I have asked for him and he says that he will help me and calls me to him, and I am going.

So good night,
Samuel Williams

MOHICAN INDIAN

An early American Indian asks Mr. Padgett for help and he was not denied
March 6, 1916

I am of the Mohican tribe and want to write a line. I was an Indian who lived in the early days of your country's existence and I was not a civilized Indian as you would say, but was a warrior and a leader of my tribe and had many scalps to my credit. So you see there are some Indians in the spirit world who still glory in the deeds which they did on earth, and still feel the hatred and enmity against the pale faces who inflicted injury upon them; but I understand that some Indians have lost all such feelings, and that they are happier by having done so, and it causes me to think that I may be mistaken in holding my hatred against the white people, and that I will never reach the happy hunting grounds so long as I am in the present condition of bitterness and hope for revenge.

What do you think of it? I will do as you say, and I see that your guide is a very happy spirit, so I will ask his advice.

This is all I wish to say.
Good night

WHITE EAGLE

White Eagle, under Jesus's direction, helped to correct
Mr. Padgett's digestive organs as a result of his prayer for help
February 15, 1915

I am here, White Eagle.

You are much better. The Master helped you very much last night. I manipulated you as he directed, and your digestive organs are now doing their work. Your prayer to God was answered. He heard you, as Jesus told you he would, if you would pray in faith. You had the faith and the cure came. So it is with everything in life, only pray and believe and you will receive the answer. You are certainly blessed, and I wonder, as do all of us, at your faith; and thank God, you are the one that the Master has selected, and you will be in condition soon to do his work as he desires.

Yes, you are right, He is the only one who can help you in time of trouble. Only continue in your faith and you will realize that He is your Father and your helper. Jesus says that your faith is wonderful, and that you will be able to do many things that will help mankind. Only be true to Him and you will never be forsaken.

No, you need not use any more medicine now. The work is done, and medicine is no longer necessary. Well, Dr. Stone may help you some in starting your various muscles and nerves to get into activity, even his treatment is not necessary now; when God heals, He heals effectively, and no other help is needed.

You are commencing to get that great Love in your soul now, and soon you will be filled, and then your happiness will be complete, that is, it will be of such a character that the worries of life will not make you unhappy.

Yes, Jesus was present and he directed my movements. He is the all-powerful one. His knowledge is without limit, and he is so full of Love, that when he tries to impress you, you cannot resist the influence of that Love. So be more prayerful and you will become possessed of that Love to a degree that will make you love all humanity as well as God. Well, I am telling you what the Master tells us, and he knows. You had better not eat promiscuously yet. Give the digestive organs a chance to get back their full strength.

So good night,
White Eagle

White Eagle assists Dr. Stone in his healing work

I am here, White Eagle,

I want to tell Dr. Stone that I was with him when he treated the sick woman. Her name was Miss Fallin, an elderly patient. I was his assistant and tried to help him in ministering to her and am making every effort to establish that rapport which enables him to do her good. He must have faith, for notwithstanding that she appears to be beyond all hope, there is more than hope if we can only establish the rapport that is necessary. He will be able to help her so that she will recover, and restore to her the powers of sensation in the apparently dead portions of her body, and also recover strength of mind sufficient to enable her to regain her condition. It will be necessary for her to follow his instructions and we will make a special effort in his case in order to demonstrate the effect of the powers which the spirit world has over the conditions of mortals where all hope has been abandoned by physicians who rely on drugs and medicines.

Besides my powers, there is a spirit doctor present who has the power of the high spirits, which powers are beyond the comprehension of mortals who have not the faith that has been told to you in the messages you have written. Faith and prayer are mighty instruments in effecting cures of human ills, and in this case the Doctor must pray and exercise his faith, and he will see the glory of God manifested in the case of this woman.

So tell him to rely on us and in the powers of the bright spirits, for they will both be with him in the treatment of this woman. I thought it best to write this so that he may be encouraged in his good work. Tell him that we will be with him on every visit that he makes to her, and will try to get the conditions so that our powers may be exercised in helping him. But above all, pray and exercise faith.

So good night,
White Eagle

BRIGHT STAR

*Mr. Padgett met Bright Star at a seance and
is now helping her to progress spiritually; she says
that automatic writing is superior to independent voice seances*
September 24, 1914

I am, Bright Star.

I am very happy and I would like to talk to you more often than I do, as you help me so much when I come to you, for you love me as a true brother and realize that I am not a mere Indian squaw, but a spirit of light. Oh my dear brother, if you only knew how I love to hear of spiritual things and not of those things which I have to listen to so much, you would think of me more often and give me many thoughts that would help me in my work. I am not one to complain, and I am also one who loves the beautiful thoughts that tell of God's Love and the love of the Master and of the spirits of the higher planes. So you see you are the only one in all the earth who knows what I am in my spiritual nature. So think of me sometimes and especially in your prayers. Yes, I know you do pray for me sometimes, and I am so grateful, for they help me.

Yes, I do, and if you will only sit in the dark for a little while, I believe that we will be able to talk as you suggest. I certainly will try my best, and I know that your wife and father will, and so will White Eagle, who is such a powerful spirit that we should not have any great difficulty in establishing the rapport necessary. So try tonight after you stop writing, and maybe some result will follow.

You are certainly blessed and you must do your work with all your strength and ability. I will try all that I know how to help you. You are not so very far behind some of our spirits who are very near the kingdom in your love for God; and I believe that if you continue to receive the Love, you will have a most wonderful influence with God and also with men. The Master certainly loves you and you are his favorite one to do his work, so believe implicitly.

Be my true brother and love me as such, for I can see that your love is true. Yes, you can pray for me as I said, and give me your best thoughts. I want to get closer to God and his heaven of love, even though I have to spend so much time in the earth plane*. Thank God my duties will soon be over in that respect and then I can live more in my home higher up, where your mother lives. She is a lovely and pure spirit and is filled with God's Love.

Tell Mr. Colburn that I was at his house last night about six o'clock and tried to impress him with my presence but I could not. He is one who is very dear to me and I want him to seek for the Love too, so tell him. When you go to his home again, try to get the voices, for I believe that they will soon come to you all. Your father was there and called his name, and Mr. Colburn answered and your father told him that your Uncle William wanted to give you a message. You are one of the most favored persons that I know in the way of receiving communications.

The independent voices do not convey such messages as you get by writing, for even if the spirits speaking could talk in the way that those do who communicate with you by writing, yet there would not be power sufficient to support such extended communications. I would rather have the power of automatic writing, as it is called, than any I know of.

She is an honest medium or I would not sit with her, you may rest assured of that. You do love me as such and your prayers have filled my soul with happiness. I will not write more tonight, but will come some time and write more fully, if I am permitted to do so.

Your loving sister,
Bright Star

*The space between the surface of the earth and the first sphere.

HORTENSE de BEAUHARNAIS (1783 -1837)

Hortense, stepdaughter of Napoleon,
now knows the way to the celestial heavens
October 27, 1915

I am here, Helene (Hortense).

I was the daughter of Josephine, the wife of Napoleon, and I come to tell you that I am not so far advanced in the soul development as I wish to be, but I am striving to obtain the Divine Love that I have been taught since my coming to the spirit world, which is necessary in order to obtain a home in the celestial spheres and immortality.

When on earth, being the daughter of an Emperor, my thoughts were given to everything else than to the real soul religion which I now know is the only religion that can save a soul from sin and error. My stepfather was not a spiritual man, as you may know, but all his thoughts were given to the gratification of his ambition and the conquest of nations. He was also a man who had a great deal of the love nature and was intense in his affections and let them guide his life to a large extent when they did not conflict with his ambitions. He and my mother were true lovers and are now soulmates, but my mother is much more developed than he.

When I died, I was totally ignorant of the soul requirements, and my religion was confined to the belief in the doctrines of the Catholic Church, which were mostly man-made, as I now see. No one ever told me about the New Birth and the Divine Love of God. Instead it was always about the power of the priests to forgive sin and their authority to pray a soul out of purgatory. This, as you may know, did not help me when I became a spirit, and when this great change came to me I found myself in darkness and suffering, with no love existing in my soul, although I had the natural affections for my kinfolks. It was many years after my death that a knowledge of the soul love came to me and I was relieved of my sufferings and brought into light and happiness. I am now in the fifth sphere and am very happy, although my spirit instructors tell me that there are higher spheres where much more happiness

96

exists and which I must strive to enter.

My stepfather is not so much elevated, as he is only in the fourth sphere* and does not yet know of this soul development to any great extent. His ambitions are still with him, and to him the mind is the greatest part of all the spirit's possessions. So you see that an Emperor's daughter does not even stand as good a chance for becoming a spirit of happiness as does the daughter of the poor burghers who know not ambition but whose life is spent in toil and in helping and sympathizing with others. How unfortunate to be a child of high position wherein only the material things of life are thought of and attempted to be obtained. No ambition for earthly things will help a spirit when the earthly things are no more to be obtained.

My mother is with me and she is very happy, and for many years has been trying to induce her husband to give his thoughts to the things of the soul; but so far she has not succeeded, although he sees that she is such a beautiful and happy spirit. This love for and ambition to obtain the material things of life are hard to get rid of. Something in the nature of a great calamity is necessary to awaken some spirits who have this love and ambition to a realization of the necessity and the desirability of seeking for the things of the higher spheres. I am now seeking for these things with all my energies and longings, and I am helped by many spirits of these higher spheres. I now know no difference between the prince and the peasant, and in fact, I find that the peasant is in general much superior to the prince in his soul progression and beauty and happiness.

My friend, excuse my intrusion. For several weeks I have seen other spirits writing to you and I so longed to do so, and as the opportunity presented itself tonight I took advantage of it and imposed on you. So to recompense you I will say that your discussions and your writings have done so very much to help me in my progress and bring happiness to me.

I will not detain you further, and will subscribe myself your friend and well-wisher.

Helene

---

*Spheres two, four and six are used by spirits who are progressing either by purifying their human love or developing their intellect.

ELLEN LOUISE AXSON WILSON (1860 - 1914)

Mrs. Wilson writes of her attempts to
influence her husband, President Wilson
February 8, 1917

I am here, Mrs. Wilson.

I will write only a line or two. I am not known to you, but I am very desirous to write, as I am so much interested in what is now taking place in our country in connection with foreign countries; and one in whom I am very much interested is suffering the burdens that are now resting upon him. I am with him a great deal and try to influence him in his thoughts and dealings with the great problems that are now before him, and sometimes I fear that he may succumb to the heavy burden. He also has around him other spirits who are much interested in the country's welfare, and they are the spirits of men who, when on earth, were states-men and rulers of our country, and interested in directing its fortunes. I will not name them, only to say that from Jefferson down to McKinley, they are with him who now occupies the President's chair.

This war is a serious one to not only the people of Europe, but also to those of America, for as I see, and these other spirits say, it is impos-sible for our country to keep out of it. The Germans so desire and they are doing everything to bring about the participation of the United States in the conflict, and the result will be that the U.S. will suffer much more than its statesmen and finances contemplate.

I wish I could bring to the President in clear and undoubted effect the advice that these spirits would like to have him understand, but this power to communicate is limited to the impressions that they may make upon him by the exercise of the very imperfect rapport of their minds with his, without the proper or necessary medium. If he could only have you with him to receive the advice that these spirits so earnestly desire to give him, it would help him so much. We have been trying to create a way by which this might be brought about, but it seems to be almost impossible.

So far as I can see the future, he will bring the country to a sound ending, although much trouble and unhappiness will be suffered, and he may not be able to endure the strain.

I wish that I could write longer tonight, but my rapport is leaving me, and I must stop. But notwithstanding what has taken place — which only I know — I still love him, for he is mine, and someday he will realize that fact.

I will now close, and thank you for your kindness.

Your new friend,
Mrs. Wilson

JOHN BROWN (1800 - 1859)

John Brown gave his life for the freedom of the slaves and the purification of the nation, and is still fighting for truth and liberty in the spirit world
August 1, 1915

I am here, John Brown.

I was the man who gave his life for the freedom of the slaves and the purification of the nation. So I come to you as a spirit who, in the long years since my death, has seen the principles for which I fought and died established in the laws of my country, and the principles of freedom and political equality have been made a part of the economy of your nation.

I am now a spirit who is still fighting for truth and liberty, but now my fight is for the liberty of all mankind from the slavery which sin and the greed of men impose upon their fellowmen. No man has the right, because of superiority in position or greatness in wealth, to make his fellowman a slave or keep him from enjoying the God given things of earth. Of course, some men must rule and some must possess the greater riches, but these facts do not justify the ruling ones or the wealthy in treating the subordinate or the poor in a way to make them unhappy, or to prevent them from receiving their just dues in the working of the affairs of their relationship of employer and employee or of governor and governed.

Right is right, and no machinations of men will continue much longer to make the poor and dependent slaves to the rich and independent. Men are awakening to their rights and to the object of their creation by a just God, and soon men will come into their own and peace will reign on earth. I am not what is called a socialist, but am a lover of mankind without regard to environments or opportunities. Let the rich treat the poor as brothers, and let the laws be administered for all alike.

Religion is a mighty power in the world, and as men come to see that the Golden Rule of the Master is the only one that should govern their actions, one towards the other, peace and prosperity and happiness will come to the inhabitants of the earth. What I say is not a mere dream of an enthusiast, but is the result of what I see will follow the workings of the great spiritual forces which are now combined and working for the salvation of men as never before in the history of the world. In this great work, love will be the mainstay of the principles that will activate men in their dealings with one another, and men will realize a new existence, and the brotherhood of men will become a thing of reality. So I say, let men prepare themselves for this Love, which will sweep away the evils and trifles that now are influencing the great crime of the centuries. I mean the great barbarous and inexcusable war that is now devastating the whole of Europe.

Men may think that the end of the war will see a peace that, because of the horrors and great losses and depletion of men and means, will last for many years, but if peace should depend upon these causes, war will rear its ugly head again before many generations have passed. While the war shall end, the causes of war will only slumber, and when new generations come, and the ambition and desire for aggrandizement and power shall again work their evil influences upon the hearts and minds of the rulers of the new generations, war will come again.

We hope, and are working to that end, that the love of one for another and the great feeling and realization of the brotherhood of man will so fill the souls of men that those things which cause war will entirely disappear, and peace will become the lasting condition of both individuals and nations. Liberty and freedom are the great possessions of men even as they are now possessed, with all these feelings of envy and hatred and ambition; but peace and love are the greatest things in all the world, and when men learn this, war will never rear its ugly head again.

I am living in the fourth sphere and am comparatively happy, and am much interested in my country's welfare and in the welfare of mankind the world over. I am a worshiper of God and am trying to follow His precepts as I learned them on earth. I am not the possessor of what you call the Divine Love but I have a love for my fellow men which enables me to try to help them in every way that is in my power.

I must stop now. I have never troubled myself about the Love that you speak of. I know that there are spirits who live in higher spheres than I do, and they seem more beautiful than I, but I have never sought the reason or troubled myself with knowing why. Since you put the proposition to me, I will talk to some of these spirits and ask them about this Love that you speak of.

So I thank you for the opportunity of writing my sentiments on the subject that is so dear to me now, and was when I was on earth.

> With all my love, I will say good night,
> John Brown

EUGENE CROWELL

A Spiritualist author writes that he now knows
that Jesus was more than a mere medium when on earth
March 17, 1915

I am here, Eugene Crowell.

By permission of your band, I will write you a little, as I see that you are reading my book, and I am, consequently, interested in your right understanding of it.

Well, as you have observed, I did not look upon Jesus as a god, but merely as a very high medium and in great favor with the high spirit powers, which is correct so far as it goes. However, he is more than that. He is the highest and most enlightened and most powerful of all the

101

spirits, and is the only one of all the great prophets or seers or reformers, or messengers of God, who have ever taught the true and only way to the kingdom of heaven. The sooner all Spiritualists recognize and believe this fact, the sooner true Spiritualism will be established on earth and the Love of God implanted in each soul.

I have learned all these things since I came over here and had the opportunity of investigating the truth firsthand with all my powers, which are not limited or encumbered with the physical senses. So you must, in reading my book, eliminate everything from what you may accept as true that teaches or intimates that Jesus is not the great Master and teacher of the true and only way to God's Love and salvation. Of course, all spirits do not understand or believe this, and I know now that Jesus is the most exalted Son of God, and while we are all God's sons, yet none of us is so at-one with Him as the Master.

So as you are investigating this question of Spiritualism in true earnestness, I thought it best to tell you what I have learned, as I do not want any expression in my book of a meaning contrary to what I have here expressed cause you to doubt for one moment the truths that Jesus and your band have been teaching you.

You are wonderfully favored in having such a teacher, and I believe that the result will be that when you have received his messages and transmitted them to the world, Spiritualism will become the religion of the whole earth. This is my belief and it is founded on the fact that it will then teach, besides the continuity of life and spirit communication, the great truths that will show men the absolute necessity of following these teachings of the Master in order to become the true children of God and be received by Him in His kingdom of Love and divine existence.

I think that you have written as I intended, and I must not take up more time now. I will write you again, if permitted. Eugene Crowell is my name and you will find an account of my passing over in the San Francisco newspapers of June 7, 1886. So examine for yourself and you will find what I say to be true.

Well, I will say good night.

Your recent spirit friend,
Eugene Crowell

CHAPTER FOUR

Soldiers

SIR WALTER RALEIGH (1552 - 1618)

Sir Walter Raleigh writes of his progress to the fourth sphere
February 25, 1917

I am here, Raleigh.

I am Lord Walter Raleigh, the Englishman, who loved and was beheaded.

I am interested in the war, as you may suppose, to some extent and only because the country to which I once owed allegiance and claimed the protection of is now a very great sufferer by reason of the efforts that are now being made to subdue her. My interest is not very great, though I have arrived at that condition of brotherly love and the true conception of right and wrong and of the certain destiny of men, that all are my brothers, and the name of Englishman, German or Frenchman makes no difference in their destinies.

The human soul, when it comes to the spirit world, is without nationality, and the destiny of that soul does not depend upon the fact that it was lodged in the form of an Englishman, etc. No, the thoughts of earth, to a large extent, have left me and I am intent on my progress in the spirit world and attaining to that condition which will bring me the most happiness and enable me to do the most good to my fellow spirits, for I am working to help those who are not in such a favorable condition as I am.

I live in the fourth sphere and am a quite happy spirit, surrounded by many things that make me happy and contented, and am free from all those things that caused me worry and sufferings while on earth. I have lost all my recollections of the acts and deeds, and even thoughts, of my earth life that caused me so much darkness and unhappiness when I first came to the spirit land. You must not think that it was an easy thing to get rid of these recollections, for I tell you that they clung to me like leeches and seemed to draw from me all my heart's blood, if I may so express it. The hells of those who have led lives of wrong or injustice are not imaginary, and all who think that the stories of such hells are the idle tales of superstitious mortals will be greatly surprised when they have shuffled off the mortal coil.

I have progressed out of my dark condition and am now in the light, and quite happy in my pursuits that appeal to me so much. I have done as you suggested, and one comes and says he is Mr. Riddle, and I must say that he is a wonderfully bright spirit and has an appearance that is different from the appearance of those spirits that I see in the fourth sphere.

Well, I have heard what you said to him and I will go with him and listen to what he has to say in reference to the subject matter of our conversation. I doubt that he can tell me anything that is an improvement to what I already know. As I told you, I will listen in seriousness and consider what he may say to me.

So, thanking you for your kindness,

> I will say good night,
> Raleigh

NAPOLEON BONAPARTE (1823 - 1876)

Napoleon's love of country is still uppermost in his thoughts
November 1, 1915

I am here, Napoleon.

Yes, I am that man who did so much harm when on earth. I merely want to say that I have been told by my daughter of her experience a few nights ago, and I became interested in the fact that she could write to you, and that other spirits could write, and I thought that I would try. I found, though, that you have around you a band of beautiful and powerful spirits and that I had to have their permission before I was permitted to write. They kindly gave me permission and I am writing.

I want to say that I am the ambitious man that I was on earth, and realize that I cannot take part in any of the movements or actions of men, as I am now a spirit, but I can associate with them and influence them into doing things and carrying out my ideas of what is necessary for France's good and glory. I frequently visit the headquarters of the generals of the Allies in this present conflict and I know their thoughts and give them, by impression, the benefit or otherwise of my thoughts, and in addition, I know what the plans of the Germans are. This war will last some time and in the end the Allies will be successful, for I can see all the factors that are working together to bring about that result.

Joffre is a competent man, and Kitchener is a good adjudicator. When they unite their forces and enter upon the aggressive campaign with all the force and power which they have, the Germans will have to retreat, and victory will come to them. Alas, I also see the great sacrifices that will have to be made; and France will become a glorious nation, and the lives that will be sacrificed will be well devoted to the glorious cause.

The spirits are coming over in great numbers. I see things, they are exchanging an earth life merely for a spirit life, and the latter is the happier one. So what matter is it if men die when a great nation can be saved, and the country for which I fought and suffered and was exiled shall become a glorious nation. A nation is only an aggregation of individuals, and the individual is not so important as the nation. The nation must be preserved, even though the individual may die.

I am in the fourth sphere and my dear wife is in the fifth. She is so much more beautiful and bright than I am. Well, I will think of what you said, but until this war is over with and the glory of France is established, I will not think of myself, for I am a Frenchman more than a spirit.

I will come again sometime, and, in the meantime, I will assure you that you have my best and kindest regards.

So thanking you, I will stop,
Napoleon

HELMUTH von MOLTKE (1848 - 1916)

The spirits that are earthbound do not change
their thoughts when they enter the spirit world
November 1, 1916

I am here, Von Moltke.

Let me tell you that I am a German and have heard what the little Corporal said, and while he was a great general when on earth, yet as a spirit general he is a failure, for his dear France will never see the glory that he predicts for her. She is at her best now, and when her armies commence that great advance that Napoleon speaks of, they will be met by the Germans and annihilated.

I also visit the headquarters of the Allies and know their plans, and I know that Napoleon is there advising them; but he is behind the day of the improvement in armament and guns and ammunition, and he is also behind the times in his advice. He has found his Waterloo and never again will he rise to become the great leader of armies. Strange to say, he thinks that he is the same wise, sagacious and tactical general that he was on earth, but he will find his mistake.

The Germans will surely be victorious in this great war, and the French will sue for peace, and with them their Allies as well. It is no use for me to write further on this matter because I could only repeat what I have said; but you, my friend, put this into your memory and at the end of the war call forth this prediction: the Germans will become the victors.

Your friend,
Von Moltke
The old strategist of the German armies.

SALAALIDA

*Salaalida, a Moslem who helped defend Jerusalem
from the Christians, is a very happy spirit and a lover of God*
August 12, 1915

I am here, Salaalida.

I am a Moslem and I lived in the time of the crusaders and helped to defend Jerusalem from the Christians. I was an officer of high rank and a general who was known among my own countrymen for my prowess in battle. I merely want to tell you now that I am a lover of all mankind and know no difference between the Christians and the Moslems, for all are God's children and are the objects of His Love, and of my love, for I am a lover of God.

I am an inhabitant of the highest Mohammedan heavens and am very happy and satisfied with my spiritual condition, and am still a follower of the Prophet who lives in our heavens and still teaches the truths of the Father, Allah.

I have no criticism to make of the Christians and believe that they are also followers of God in the way that their Jesus taught, but I cannot believe that his teachings are the only truths of God. He and his followers live in a different sphere from our sphere, and those whom I have met seem to be happy and are very beautiful.

So while I was once an antagonist of the Christians and hated them with all the hatred that my religion taught me to hate, yet now I see that hatred is not a thing which God recognizes as being a part of the faith or practices of his true followers.

I came merely to tell you this and to inform you that love is the ruling principle of the spiritual world where I live. By love, I mean love for God and for my fellowman; this is the only love that I know of and I find it sufficient for my happiness.

I don't know what you mean by the Divine Love. It cannot be anything more than the love which we have for God.

Well, I must stop now, and will say good night.

Your friend,
Salaalida

ULYSSES S. GRANT (1822 - 1885)

Ulysses S. Grant has had his spiritual
eyes opened and is seeking for God's Love
October 19, 1915

I am, General Grant.

I was the President of your country and also general of the Federal armies.

Well, I want to say that I am in a condition of comparative happiness, though not entirely relieved from my darkness or sufferings. I had a great many sins to answer for and many penalties to pay, and during the years since my death I have suffered much and experienced great darkness. But thanks be to God, I am emerging from these conditions and am having my spiritual eyes opened to the truths of God and the necessity of obtaining His Love and favor.

As you may know, when on earth I attended the Methodist Church.

My religious knowledge was merely that which came from an assent of the mind to certain propositions, or rather doctrines, of the church. I knew nothing of the soul development or of the Divine Love, or of any of those attributes of God which were necessary to my becoming a redeemed spirit and an accepted child of God.

I am in the second sphere*, where are many of my old comrades in arms and many who were antagonistic in the great War of the Rebellion**. We are no longer enemies, for we have obtained sufficient Love to become friends and to know that war and hatred and murder are not in accord with God's laws or approved by Him, and we are now seeking only Love, and trying to apply the Golden Rule in our lives here.

Well, I am somewhat surprised that I can communicate with you in this way, for while I have attended some seances and made my presence known in other ways and by other manifestations, I never before had the opportunity to do so by this method of writing, and I must say, it is the most satisfactory of my experiences. As this is my first appearance, and coming without an invitation, though some of your band which is here signified their assent, I do not feel that I should intrude longer.

Well, I have been interested in this great and bloody war, and have visited the scenes of many battles and the headquarters of the officers of both sides, and have heard their plans discussed, and have learned what their expectations were. It is rather early in the game to form an opinion as to the outcome, but judging from the facts, as I have been able to gather, and from the conditions of the armies and means of carrying on the war, of both sides, I am rather inclined to think the Allies will win. This I say in a perfectly unbiased way, as I have no bias or prejudice for either side, that no human being can estimate the great injury that will be done to the various countries or to the progress of the human race in the things material by this war. As God rules, right will prevail, as I believe.

I will now say good night. Sometime later, if agreeable, I will write you further on this matter..

Your friend,
U. S. Grant

*The second sphere is the sphere of familiarity because the environments that it contains very much resemble the earth.
**The American Civil War (1861 - 1865).

WILLIAM T. SHERMAN (1820 - 1891)

William T. Sherman is the same as he was on earth; but seeing his former friends so changed causes him to go with Riddle to learn the reason
October 19, 1915

I am here, General Sherman.

Well, as Grant and I are very close friends here, as we were on earth, I thought that as he wrote a letter I would like to do so also.

Just as he said about himself, I say. I am in some darkness and suffering — paying the penalties of my evil deeds on earth, and for what I neglected to do in the way of performing my duties when I had so many to perform, and so many opportunities. I am in the same sphere with him, although he is in a higher plane, and is not in such darkness as I am. I am not a Christian yet, but hope to be some time, as I have some dear friends here who are, and they are trying to persuade me to become a Christian; but as you may not know, I never could be persuaded on earth, and it is difficult to be persuaded here.

I am enjoying this new experience in writing to you, and to me this is very surprising, and very satisfactory. I wonder how such a thing can be. I have attended seances when my earth friends have attended, and have tried to make myself known to them and to some extent have succeeded, though not in the way that I am doing now. I am afraid that if you are not careful I shall steal on you and write many times so that you will wish that I had never come.

Well, my dear boy, I am certainly glad that you recalled these reminiscences. Of course, with all the people that I met in those days, I cannot remember you, as we only had a passing handshake, but I am certainly glad that you recalled those times, and more glad that I can be with you now. Things will be reversed now, for I will be the one who will not forget, while you, considering the great number of spirits who come to you to write, and the great number who are around you ready to write, I hardly expect that you will find time to give me much thought.

Well, I don't quite understand you, but if you can show me the way to obtaining such a condition of soul and such a degree of happiness, I will certainly accept your kind offer, and will try my best to follow your advice. But really, I don't see how you can accomplish this.

Yes, I remember Riddle very well, and he was a very dear friend of mine, but why do you ask that question? Is he involved in my redemption? He was a very dear friend, but I doubt that he can do what you seem to imply.

I have done as you advised, and I must confess my surprise to see Riddle in the band that you speak of and what a beautiful and bright spirit he is. How in the world did he get in that condition? When on earth he was somewhat like myself — a free thinker — and he cussed sometimes. I must speak to him and learn what it means.

I have been introduced to your grandmother, and what a glorious spirit she is! I never before saw such spirits. They must live in spheres far above where I live.

Riddle says I am the same old, rough, wicked Sherman, and wants me to go with him, and I will go, and I will not forget to request a few words with your grandmother.

I will ask Ingersoll. He seems so beautiful and bright too. What does it mean? Ingersoll says it means that he has become a believer in the great Love of God and is a follower of Jesus Christ. What a surprise and what a change in Ingersoll!

My friend, I cannot write more as I am all upset by what I have seen and heard. So excuse me, I will say good night.

Your friend,
William T. Sherman

MARQUIS de LAFAYETTE (1757 - 1834)

The Revolutionary War general relates how
Washington helped him to a knowledge of God's Love,
and his resultant changed attitude towards the Germans
April 26, 1916

I am here, Lafayette.

I have been anxious for some time to write you again and let you know the results of your advice to me when last I wrote. After our last communication, I sought General Washington and told him of my conversation with you and asked him to explain what this Divine Love meant and how it could be obtained. He was so pleased at my inquiry that he actually took me in his arms and called me his boy as he had on earth and with his face beaming with love and happiness he told me what this Love meant and what it had done for him, and what happiness it had brought him and how he was now progressing towards the celestial heavens of light and truth.

Well, I commenced to consider what he had told me and to have a longing in my soul for that Love and the happiness which he said it would bring me, and I commenced to pray for the Love and tried to have faith. Well, without taking up your time by rehearsing the steps of my progress, I am glad to tell you that I have this Love to some extent and that I am now an inhabitant of the third sphere and enjoying the associations of spirits who also have this Love and are striving to progress.

My happiness is very different from what it was before this Love came to me, and I realize that the soul and not the mind is the man, especially of God's redeemed children. I never thought that the soul was capable of such Love and happiness and of the knowledge that the Divine Love is the one absolutely necessary thing to bring spirits into unison with God. I want to express my gratitude to you and to say that I will never forget your kindness and love in turning my thoughts to this great truth.

Yes, I am still interested in the war, but now I do not have any hatred for the Germans that I had before. I see that they are all brothers, and children of God, and that only the ambitions of some and the passions and hatred of others are prolonging the war. Although it will soon close, for I see before me the collapse of the German campaign against Verdun and then the end will come rapidly.

I wish it were tomorrow, for then slaughter and death and added misery would cease. There are so many spirits coming from these battlefields who are all unfit for the spirit life and appear in great confusion, and when they realize they are no longer mortals they become bewildered and miserable. We are trying to help them and we know no enemies. All are helped alike.

I will not write more tonight and in closing give you my love.

Your brother,
Lafayette

GEORGE WASHINGTON (1732 - 1799)

Commander of the Colonial Army affirms that the ancient spirits wrote, and that many came from the celestial heavens and the lower spirit heavens
August 12, 1915

I am here, George Washington.

Well, you are my brother and I am pleased that you call me your brother, for in this world of spirits we have no titles or distinctions because of any fame or position we may have had on earth.

I came to tell you that I have watched with interest the many communications that you have received from the various kinds and orders of spirits, and am somewhat surprised that you could receive their messages with such accuracy. I never in earth life supposed that such a thing could be, and since I became a spirit, I have never seen such demonstrations of the powers that exist on the part of spirits to communicate and a mortal to receive the messages that come to you. I know that very many times such communications have been made by spirits to mortals, but what I mean as surprising is the great variety of spirits who come to you. They come from the highest celestial spheres as well as from the earth planes and what they write are not only new to mortals but many of their declarations of truth are new to many of us spirits.

Very seldom do we who are in the spiritual spheres have the opportunity to communicate with any of these ancient spirits who live high up in the celestial heavens and when I see them come and communicate to you so frequently, I wonder at it all. I know, of course, that such spirits do occasionally come into the earth plane and try to influence both mortals and spirits to do good, and I want to tell you that usually their influence is exerted through intermediary spirits and not directly by these higher spirits in person as they do through you.

The messages that you have received from these spirits who lived on earth thousands of years ago were really written by them, as they controlled your brain and hand. I am trying my best to help you in your work and will continue to do so, for the work that you have been selected to do is the most important one that the spirit world is now engaged in, I mean the world that recognizes Jesus as its Prince and Master.

Some spirits come because they see the way open to communicate to mortals, and they naturally desire to make known the fact that they live and are happy in their spheres. But their happiness is not the real happiness which the true believers and followers of the Master enjoy. So in your work, when they come you may have the opportunity to tell them of this higher experience which the redeemed of God enjoy. Many spirits are in these lower spheres who would be in the celestial heavens if they only knew the way. We frequently try to show them the way to truth and the higher life, but we find it a difficult task. They think that we are merely spirits like themselves and have our opinions just as they have theirs, and that we are mistaken in ours, and hence we can tell them nothing which will show them truths that they do not know, or will give them greater happiness than they have.

When they notice the contrast in our appearance, that is, that we are so much more beautiful and bright than they are, they simply think that such beauty and brightness is a result of some natural cause, and that we merely differ from them as does one race of men differs from another. They do not seem to think that there is anything in the contrast in our appearance that is caused by any higher spiritual condition than what they have. This is the great stumbling block in the way of their becoming interested in the conditions which we have, and which should urge them to investigate and learn the true cause for the same. Hence, I say, that you may do them some good in this regard, for you are a third person and should call their attention to the great contrast and tell them the cause as you understand it. What you say would probably make some impression on them and cause them to make inquiry, and once they commenced this, then would come our opportunity to lead them into the light of the great truth of the Divine Love of God.

Well, I have digressed from what I intended to write, but it is just as well, for all the truths of God are important to both mortals and spirits. I am very happy in my home in the celestial heavens, and I am trying to progress to those higher. So let me assure you of the truths of what you have had written to you by your band and others of God's redeemed spirits.

I thank you for this opportunity and I will come again some time.

Your own true brother,
George Washington

CHAPTER FIVE

Heads of State

JULIUS CAESAR (100 - 44 B.C.)

> *Julius Caesar writes that earthly*
> *position does not determine one's spiritual abode*
> September 16, 1915

I am the spirit of one who when on earth was called Caesar.

Well, there was only one real Caesar — all others by that name were merely imitations. I was Julius Caesar and was the Emperor of Rome and the conqueror of the Gauls and of the Egyptians.

I am now in a condition of darkness, and also suffering from my deeds on earth, which were very wicked and numerous. I am not an Emperor now but am a spirit who is in the condition of one who has no one to do him reverence — none of my former slaves bow their knee or salute me as their superior. But why? Because in the spirit world a man is as his soul development makes him, and mine has been very much retarded by my want of belief and faith, as I now see.

I merely want to tell you this that you may know that no position on earth can determine the position of the person when he comes into the spirit world. I mean that the position of the man on earth does not in the slightest degree influence the position of this same man in the spirit world. Many of my slaves are higher in their development and in their spirituality than I am.

I see some bright spirits and have asked for Prof. Salyards, and find him to be a most beautiful and bright spirit, and I am inclined to listen to what he may say. He says that he was well acquainted with my history on earth, as he had read many books dealing with my life and exploits and he is glad to meet me and show me the way to a higher and happier condition of existence. I rather like him, and believe that I will go with him and listen to him. Well, I will try.

So I will say good night, and good luck. I am your friend now, since you have shown such interest in me.

Julius Caesar

Caesar is grateful to Mr. Padgett for his prayer and
introduction to his grandmother and is progressing into the light
December 20, 1916

I am, Caesar.

I want to tell you that I am a grateful spirit even if I was an awful sinner, and that I took your advice and went with your grandmother, and she opened up a whole world of love and truth to me. Oh, what a wise and magnificent spirit she is and what love she has, and she treated me with such kindness and was even like Brutus of old. For in her kindness she gave me a stab that killed all my old beliefs and feelings of greatness and made me in truth a mere nothing and at the same time the greatest being that I had even been in all my existence. For it showed me

117

that I was a real child of God and the object of His Love and care, and one that had all the possibility of becoming in my soul even Godlike. She is my true friend and when she comes to me it seems that my soul, which had for so many centuries remained dead and cold, opens up with a flame of life that her influence brings to me.

I will not write more now. I thought that you were so interested in me that you would rejoice in knowing that now I have started on the way to the attaining of that which you told me of. I will come sometime when I have received more Love and write you a long letter, which I hope will be interesting, for it is a fact that at one time Caesar did write interesting letters.

So, my friend, pray for me and send me your kind thoughts, and believe that they will not be misplaced as now I am so anxiously seeking for that which was not in me for so many centuries. Good night.

Your friend,
Julius Caesar

EMPEROR CONSTANTINE (306 - 337 A.D.)

Constantine says when on earth he never accepted Christianity
September 5, 1916

I am here, Constantine.

I was the Roman Emperor who died as the head of the Christian Church. I wasn't really a Christian and did not understand the true principles of the Christian teachings. I adopted Christianity as a State religion because of political purposes added to my desire to destroy the powers of my antagonists who were believers in and worshipers of the gods of paganism.

I was a man who cared not in the slightest whether the cross or the symbol of the oracles was the true sign of religion, or whether the followers of religious beliefs belonged to the Christian Church or the worship of the gods which our country had for so many years adopted and followed.

My great desire when I made Christianity the State religion was to obtain power and the allegiance of the majority of the people of the Empire. The Christians were very numerous and were persons of such intense convictions, so intense, that not even death could remove or change these convictions. I knew that when once they gave me their allegiance, I should have a following that could not be overthrown by those who were worshipers of the old gods. The latter people were not so interested in their religious beliefs, individually, as to cause them to have such convictions as would interfere with any religion that I might establish, when they realized that their material interests would be advanced by at least formally recognizing that religion as a State establishment.

Their religious beliefs were not the results of any conviction but merely of what had been accepted by their ancestors and transmitted to them as a kind of inheritance. They believed in the gods and the oracles as a matter of course, without ever having made the objects of their beliefs matters of investigation in order to learn if those beliefs were true or not. Truth was not sought for, and hence conviction was a mere shallow acquiescence.

During all the time of my office as Emperor, I never changed my beliefs and never accepted the teachings of the Christians as the revelation of truth, and in fact, I never considered such a matter as religion worthy of my serious consideration. Many doctrines were proposed and discussed by the ecclesiastical teachers and leaders of this religion, and those doctrines were approved by me which were adopted by a majority of these leaders as true and the correct declarations of what the scriptures of the Christians contained.

I let these leaders fight their own battles as to doctrines and truths, and when they decided what should be accepted and declared by the church to be true doctrines, I approved the same and promulgated them as binding upon all the followers of the Christian faith. So I did not establish the canonicity of the Bible, or determine and legalize the doctrines which were declared and made binding by the conventions of the leaders of the church. Of course, I gave them my sanction and official approval, but they were not mine and should not be said to have been established by me, for if the doctrines of the Arians had been accepted and declared by a majority of these ecclesiastic as the true teachings of the Christian scriptures, I should have sanctioned and given them the State's authority. As I said, I was not a Christian when I lived and I did not die a Christian, notwithstanding all the fantastical and miraculous things which have been written about me and my conversion to Christianity.

When I came into the spirit world, I found myself in great darkness and suffering, realizing that I had to pay the penalties for the sins thought and committed by me on earth; and all the masses that were said for the benefit of my soul never helped me one particle to get out of my unhappy condition. I knew nothing about the Divine Love or the mission of Jesus in coming to earth, and I found that my sins had not been washed away as the teachers had often told me on earth would be done for me.

For many long years I remained in this condition of darkness and unhappiness, without finding any relief by reason of the mystical workings of Jesus's atonement of which the priests had told me, and which I did not believe, nor the help of the gods in whom I had been taught to believe by our philosophers and religious teachers. No, I found no relief and my condition seemed to be fixed, and hope of the Christian heaven that was never mine and of the fields Elysian that would be mine in a hazy way, did not cause me to feel that my sufferings would at some time come to an end and the glad face of happiness appear.

After a time the light of the truth in which Jesus came to teach broke in on my understanding and soul, and the Divine Love of God commenced to flow into my soul and continued until I became a possessor of it to the degree that I was carried to the celestial spheres, where I now am a redeemed, pure and immortal soul. I now have undoubting knowledge and conviction that I possess in my soul the Divine Essence of God and the certainty of eternal life in the celestial kingdom.

Before ceasing my writing, I wish to say with all the force that I have, that only the Divine Love can save a soul from its sins and make it at-one with God in His Divine Nature. Let creeds and dogmas and man-made doctrines take care of themselves, and learn the truth, and in that truth abide, for truth is eternal and never changes, and no decrees of man or dogmas of church tradition of the early fathers or writers, or creeds of ecclesiastical conventions, so solemnly adopted and declared, can make that a truth which is not a truth. Truth existed before all these

120

things and is not subject to them, nor by them can it be added to or taken from.

I must not write more now, but thank you for having permitted me to write.

So with my love, I will say good night,
Constantine

NERO (54 - 68 A.D.)

His experience in the hells and his progress to the celestial heavens
January 16, 1917

I am here, the spirit of one who lived on earth the life of a wicked man, and a persecutor of the Christians, and a blasphemer of God and everything that was pure and holy. When I had lived life to its end and shuffled off the mortal coil and became a spirit, I also became a dweller in the lowest hells where all is darkness and torment, and the abode of devils and everything that tends to make the spirit unhappy and at variance with the loving God.

I introduce myself in this way in order to demonstrate to you the wonderful power of the Divine Love, for now I am an inhabitant of the celestial spheres, and know that this Love is not only real, but is capable of making the vilest sinner a partaker and owner of the Divine Essence of God.

My sufferings were beyond all description and I was the most desecrated of mortals, and was almost worshiped by the devils of hell because of the great injury that I had done to the followers of Jesus, who, in my time, were possessed of this Love and faith. Even the terrors of the wild beasts of the arena, or the torches of my own evil designs could not cause them to renounce their faith in this great religion that the Master had taught them, and the disciples were still teaching, when I put so many of them to death.

The devils loved me for the very evil that I had done, but strange to

121

say, the spirits of those who I had sent to the spirit world before their time were not revengeful to me, nor did they come to me with imprecations or cursings. When I had been in the spirit world a sufficient time to realize my surroundings and the evil there, these spirits of the martyrs, which I had made, came to me in sympathy and pity, and in fact, tried many times to help me out of my great sufferings and darkness. I did not understand all this unexpected kindness and evidence of love, and I would not for a long time believe that these spirits were sincere; and so I suffered year after year, and century after century, and became convinced that my condition was fixed, and that for me there was no hope, and that the God that I had heard of was not my God, and devils were the only companions that I was destined to have through all eternity.

I endured, wishing to die, but I could not. Oh, I tell you it was horrible and beyond all conception of mortals! The law was working and I was paying the penalty, and there seemed no end to the penalty. I could find no consolation among those who surrounded me, and the pleasures that I first enjoyed became to me mere things of mockery and derision, and my darkness and torment became the greater. How often I called upon God, if there be a God, to strike me dead, but the only answer to my call was the laughter of the grinning devils, who told me to shout louder as God might be asleep and may be deaf.

What to do, I knew not, and so I became isolated as best I could from these terrible associates, and many years of my living were spent in the darkness of lonesomeness with never a ray of hope or the whisper of one word to tell me that for me there might be a fairer destiny. So time went by and I waited in my misery for some kind power to come and annihilate me but I waited in vain.

During all this time the recollections that I thought of my earthly deeds were like hot irons scorching my soul and burning my body, and the end came not. I suffered the tortures of the damned, and it seemed to me that I was paying the penalties for all the sins and evil deeds that had ever been committed by all the wicked kings and rulers and persecutors of earth. Many times the shrieks of the Christian children and the groans of the men and women as they were being torn asunder from limb to limb, or burned as living torches which I had made of them, came to me and increased my torment. I lived the life of centuries of torment in a few moments, as it seemed to me, and not one cooling drop

122

of water was mine. It may seem impossible that I should have continued to live in this ever-increasing suffering, but I did, because I was compelled to. The law did its work and there was no one to say "enough." I might write a volume on this suffering of mine, and yet you would not comprehend its meaning, and so I will pass it by.

In my loneliness and suffering there came to me on an occasion, a beautiful spirit, full of light and love and all the beauty of early womanhood, as I thought, and with eyes of pity and longing, and she said: "You are not alone, only open your eyes and you will see the star of hope, which is the sign of God's Love and desire to help you. I am a child of that God and the possessor of His great enveloping Love, and I love you, even though you took from me my young life when you threw me to the wild beasts to satisfy your desire to gratify your thirst for innocent blood, and to see the suffering and hear the groans of your victims. Yet, I love you, not because I am a woman with a kindly nature and a forgiving disposition, but because I have in me this Divine Love which tells me that I am your sister, and that you are a child of God just as I am, and the object of His Love, just as I am the object of His Love.

You have suffered, and while you suffered God's great Love went out to you in sympathy and desire to help you, but you yourself prevented this Love from coming to you and leading you to light and surcease from sufferings. Now I come to you, your young and innocent victim, who had never done you any greater harm on earth than to pray for you and ask the Heavenly Father to take away from your heart the great wickedness that caused so many of my people to suffer persecution and death. We all prayed for you and never asked our God to curse you or do anything to you to make you suffer. We prayed for you often since we came to the spirit world and we are now praying for you, and this is because we love you and want you to be happy. Look into my eyes and you will see that love is there and what I tell you is true. Now, can you not love us a little and open up your soul to our sympathy and let your feelings of gloom and despondency leave you for a moment, and realize that in this world of spirits there are some who love you?"

Well, to say that I was surprised does not express my feelings, and as I looked into the lovelit eyes of that beautiful spirit, I felt the great sins of my earth life overwhelm me, and in my anguish I cried, "God be merciful to me, the greatest of sinners", and for the first time in all my life in the hells tears came to my eyes, and my heart seemed to have a sense of

123

living. There came to me feelings of remorse and regret for all the evils that I had done.

It would take too long to tell what followed this breaking up of my soul, all shriveled and dead. Suffice it to say that from that time, I commenced to have hope come to me to get out of my awful condition of darkness. It took a long time, but at last, I got into the light and this Love which the beautiful spirit first told me of gradually came into my soul, until, at last, I reached the condition of bliss in which I am now.

During all the time of my progress, this radiant loving spirit came to me very often with her words of love and encouragement and prayed for me and never left me when I became, as I did at times, doubtful and discouraged. As my awakening continued, the Love came into my soul, and she told me of the heavenly things that would be mine as I progressed and reached the soul spheres where there are beautiful homes and pure bright spirits. I became more and more bound by my love to her and after a while I got into the third sphere, and realized that what she had told me was true, only I had not been able to comprehend the greatness of the truth.

She then commenced to tell me of the happiness of the beautiful spirits of the two sexes that I so often saw together, and explained that they were soulmates and that their love was the greatest of all the loves except the Divine Love, and that every spirit in all the spheres had its soulmate and at the proper time would find him or her.

My love for this loving spirit had become so intense that in the very depths of my soul I wished and prayed that my soulmate might be such a one as she and, at last, I became so filled with my love for her that I told her that the only thing in all the heavens that I needed to make my happiness full was she as my soulmate, but I realized that that desire was hopeless as I had destroyed her life, and of course she could not be my soulmate. Oh, how I suffered when I realized that she could not be mine, but was another's.

As I told her of these longings and hopeless feelings of my soul, she came close to me and looked into my eyes with such burning love, and threw her arms around me, and said, "I am your soulmate, and knew the fact a short time after you came to the spirit world and entered your hells of darkness, and during all the long years I prayed and prayed for the time when I could come to you with my love and awaken in your dead soul a response to my great love for you. When the time came that

I could go, I was so thankful to God that I almost flew to you to tell you that you were not neglected or unthought of, but that there was some love in the spirit world that was going to you.

Of course, I could not tell you of my soulmate love for you would not have understood, but as your soul awakened and the Love of God came to you I became happier and happier and have waited so anxiously for this moment when I could tell you that this love that had been consciously mine for so long, is all yours."

Well, I will draw the veil here, but you can imagine what my happiness was and as I progressed from sphere to sphere my happiness and love for her increased and increased.

Thus I have told you the story of the life in the spirit world of the wickedest man that God ever permitted to live and gratify his feelings of hatred and revenge. I, who have passed through this experience and realized all that it means, say that the Divine Love of God is able to and does save the vilest sinner and transforms the chiefest of devils into a celestial angel of His highest spheres.

I have written long and you are tired. I thank you, and will say good night.

> Nero, the Roman Emperor, the one time
> persecutor of God's true children.

SELEMAN

Contrasting the Mohammedan heavens and the Christian heavens
August 8, 1915

I am here, Seleman.

I am an ex-sultan of the Mohammedans. I do not know time, but about four hundred years ago. Yes, I am still a follower of the Prophet, and I am in our paradise and happy. God is great! Allah is his name and Mohammed is his prophet!

I had a desire to learn what the writers who have written you tonight might say, and so I stayed and listened to them and found that their doctrines of the Divine Love of God are new to me. The Mohammedans do not understand this Love, and when I heard that it gave such bliss to those who possessed it, I became interested and wondered what it really meant. We have not this Love, and our happiness comes to us from our brotherly love and our worship of Allah and our devotion to his Prophet. But as I wondered, the thought came to me that we should have been taught to know what this Love means, if our Allah is not such a loving God as the God that these Christians tell of. I am going to inquire into this, because if there be a greater happiness than what I now have I want to learn about it, and if it exists, I want to become a partaker of it.

We don't have much intercourse with the Christian spirits, as our heavens are separate from theirs, and we believe that we have the true heavens and are the chosen of God, and that all these Christians are in the dark, even though these Christians seem to be brighter and more beautiful than do the spirits in our heavens, and that has caused me to think. I know that in our heavens the higher we progress the more beautiful we become and the brighter we seem to be, and that the progress of the individual determines his appearance. Knowing this I have come to think that these Christians live in a higher or more progressive heaven than ours.

I am dissatisfied now, and I will investigate. Can you tell me the best way to do so?

126

There is a beautiful woman who says she is your grandmother. I will ask her and maybe she can start me on my investigation.

Well, I will say good night.

Your friend,
Seleman

QUEEN ELIZABETH I (1553 - 1603)

A great queen in her day confesses freely to the violations of the law of compensation which she committed and reveals a soul full of remorse
May 12, 1915

I am here, Queen Elizabeth I of England.

I have been here several times before but never have I been able to get the chance to write to you, and now that I have, do not disappoint me in my hope that you may help me.

Well, I was a very bad woman on earth as I now see the true relation of things and deeds and am suffering from the memory of those things. I was looked upon as a creature of divine favor and could, therefore, do no wrong, and that whatever I said or did must be obeyed and followed by my subjects and others who lived within my dominions. I lived a life that was not in accordance with the laws of morality or of God as they now appear to me. When I tell you that although I was a single woman who had my lovers to gratify my passions and to please my caprices, you will understand that I was a wicked woman and that those are the things that now cause my sufferings and darkness.

I am not a spirit who thinks that because I was a ruler that therefore I could do no wrong. I knew at the time that many things I did were wrong and consequently my sufferings have become so much the greater. Many a poor soul has been sent to damnation by my commands, a damnation on earth as well as here. Even murder I was guilty of, although it may have had a legalized form, it was murder nevertheless,

127

and I am suffering the penalties. Some of my truest and best friends in moments of jealousy and envy I sent to the block, to afterwards bitterly regret my deed. Oh, I tell you that a queenly crown makes no difference in the penalty that must be paid for evil deeds. Many a humble subject of mine is now where I cannot go, and where they find happiness and love, as I am told.

I loved once truly and deeply, but I sacrificed the object of my love through pique, and what I wanted in my blind rage to have him do, and he would not, and how bitterly I regretted the deed and suffered even while on earth, though to all outward appearances I was callous and without feeling. God knows how my heart bled, and how my very soul was wracked with remorse and torture, but I was a queen and had no right to have the feelings of a human being.

Well, I will not relate the vast number of evil deeds that I had done, but will only say that as my opportunity for committing evil without fear of punishment was great, so the number of my deeds was great. I have suffered in darkness and torment, and love has been absent from me all these years of the travail of my soul. I have lived alone, as I saw no pleasures in what other spirits who lived near me were engaged in.

When I first entered the spirit world, I was still a queen as I believed and many of my subjects who had become spirits and knew me still believed I was their queen and worshiped me as such; but as time passed they saw that while on earth I may have been of divine creation, yet as a spirit I was without any evidence of divine right and no better than themselves, and they soon ceased to look upon me as superior to themselves and as is usual, as you on earth say, they went to the other extreme and treated me with neglect and even taunted me for having been on earth a fraud and deception. I soon hated them all, and so sought my consolation in silence and isolation.

What a mockery is nobility on earth and what a leveler is the spirit world! Many times I have wished that they had let me remain the simple country girl and not made me the queen of a great nation. I can now see that if my life had been that of a subject living in God's pure and uncontaminated country air, I would now be a much happier spirit. But it is now too late, as I have made my bed I must lie in it, and there is no remedy.

Yet when despair and darkness come to overwhelm us there seems some good providence which gives us a little ray of hope, and even though it comes to us as a glint of sunlight, yet it comes, and we some-times think that in the future, we know not when, there may be some relief for us. So that glint of hope comes to me sometimes, and I feel that God has not forsaken me altogether.

I have seen spirits made happier by coming to you and so I come with just that little spark of hope telling me that you might help me, and if you can please do so. Yes, I will do as you say. Yes, I see the beautiful spirits. I see your mother and she says that she will take me with her and show me the way to light and happiness and will love me as God loves me as He does all His children.

So I am going with her and now I want to say that as you are my true friend and well-wisher I believe what you told me and want you to think kindly of me as not many do.

So with my thanks, I will say good night,
Elizabeth I

QUEEN VICTORIA (1819 - 1901)

Wishes she could have lived longer on earth,
for she could have helped to prevent World War I
February 8, 1917

I am here, Victoria.

I must write a line, for I have listened to the communications, and feel that none who have written are more interested than I, as my peo-ple, who such a short time ago listened to my advice and loved me, are now being destroyed on both land and sea.

Oh, this war is horrible, and the flower of my people are being cut down like so many fields of wheat that are ripe for the scythe. How I wish that I could have lived a few years longer as Queen, for I believe I could have controlled my grandson to the extent of preventing him from launching this terrible catastrophe upon the nations of Europe. I have tried since becoming a spirit to influence him, but all in vain, for his ambitions were great and his sense of having suffered indignity from my own people was great; and in his blindness and hot blood he started the ball of hatred rolling and the destruction that is still accumulating as it continues on its murderous, and destructive course.

I have prayed for all the people who are engaged in this war, and have, with other spirits, to stem the tide of hatred and feelings of conquest and revenge which now possess them. I believe the end is now in sight and that the Germans will soon seek for peace and the nations will lay down their arms, and common sense and cool blood will rule again.

I cannot write more tonight, and will only say that we are all praying to God that His mercy may be showered on these unhappy and misguided men.

So thanking you, I will say good night.

Yours truly,
Victoria

OTTO von BISMARCK (1815 - 1898)

A former statesman places the blame on England for the
economic conditions in Germany that forced them to go to war
February 1, 1917

I am here, Bismarck.

Let me say that I confess that I am not impartial, but I think that I can do justice to both of the contending parties in the war, as I am a spirit and have learned that right is right irrespective of the person or nation that may claim to be in the right in its actions.

I was a German, and a rather important one, as men consider importance in the earth life, and was acknowledged by the world to be something of a statesman. I have kept in constant touch with the thoughts and motives of the leaders of the various nations that are engaged in this great conflict, and know the right and wrong of things to a great extent.

In the first place, this was not brought about by the Germans without justification and cause, because for a long time the German rulers delayed and endeavored to postpone, and, if possible, avoid the war. But their rights, as a nation, were so seriously preyed upon and not recognized, that the only thing left for them to do was to compel their enemies to respect their rights by force of arms, and so you have the real cause of the conflict. The Germans were not desirous or ambitious for conquest or territory or advancement to the detriment of other nations, but only for what they, as a great nation, were entitled to. England, in its greed, stood in the way of and prevented these rights from being recognized, and tried every way in her power to prevent the German nation from enjoying these rights, and especially from extending its commerce to countries in which England had established her commerce and trade, almost to the exclusion of every other nation.

The Germans waited in hope, that by diplomatic means their rights would be established and recognized, but such hope was never realized. As a last and only resort, they threw down the gauge of battle, quick and sharp and destructive — with some violation of the rights of a neutral that stood in the way of accomplishing what the German nation considered its decisive blow. This is history, and it is not necessary that I should further detail.

Now, as the war has progressed for more than two years, Germany has naturally become depleted of its resources, and especially in those things that are necessary to sustain the physical existence of its people, and all through the action of the Allies in preventing foodstuff and other necessaries being imported from other nations. Its ports have been blockaded for a long time, and it has been unable to obtain supplies that were absolutely necessary to the existence of its people, until famine and want are staring them in the face, and more than that, have actually worked their ruinous effects, and the cry of the people is for sustenance.

Then, such being the fact, what is the duty of the German rulers? Can mankind ask that they shall sit supinely by and see their people starve and their country ruined, because of the conditions that I speak of, brought about by their enemies in preventing intercourse with outside nations? I know that international law should be respected by nations in war as well as in peace, and that it is for the good of all nations that such laws be held sacred and inviolable, and Germany has tried to observe these laws, even after some of its enemy nations have violated them.

Let me ask here, what difference does the means used in considering the right or wrong of a thing, make when the same result is accomplished? England, by her superior number of war vessels, has succeeded in blockading the ports of Germany, and preventing its people from getting the supplies necessary to their sustenance, and at the same time is enjoying the benefits of unrestricted importation of these necessaries, because Germany had not had it in its power to blockade the ports of England and thus prevent her from obtaining these supplies. This kind of blockade, the nations claim, international law justifies, no matter what the results may be.

Now, when Germany has found a way to accomplish the same thing, as regards the ports of England and place her and her people in the same condition that the people of Germany have been in for so long a time, and have given notice of its intention to use such means, the nations hold up their hands in horror because such means are not known to international law.

When international law was formulated the means and instruments used in this war were never heard of, and they are only the evolution of the war, growing out of the progress of man in the knowledge and necessities of war. Laws are always subject to change and that change need not be by agreement, for sometimes, and it has often happened, necessity has compelled and justified the modification of the law.

It is said that necessity knows no law, and it is a truth, and one that has been recognized and applied by many nations, at many times. In the present circumstances of Germany, this necessity has arisen to such an extent that the very existence of Germany, not only as a nation, but of her people as individuals, is involved. Her life is at stake, and the only remedy is that the nations who are fighting Germany be placed in the same position as she is in. That can be done only by preventing those nations from obtaining those supplies that are necessary to maintain their people, and this can only be accomplished by blockading their ports. It may be said that the use of the submarine is brutal and inhuman. Well for the argument I will admit this to be a fact, yet it is not necessary that any brutality or any murder be actually inflicted, for if the persons interested will heed the warnings and not attempt to run the blockade there will be no murder or outrage.

Well, I will not write more along this line. As to the results of the war, or rather as to its ending, I cannot prognosticate. Germany is fighting on very unequal terms, and she may be defeated, and I would not be surprised if such was the end of the conflict. But, nevertheless, even though victory may come to the Allies, I assert as true that the right of the matter is with her, and that the neutral nations are not doing her justice when they declare that she is the aggressor, and that she is not justified in the course that she is now pursuing.

I am told that I have written enough, and so I must stop, but what I have said is the right of the matter. Good night.

Your friend,
Bismarck

WILLIAM McKINLEY (1843 - 1901)

President McKinley and others in the spirit
world are striving to bring an end to World War I
February 8, 1917

I am here, McKinley.

Let me say a word, as I am interested in this great conflict of nations, and especially in the danger that faces my country, and the almost certainty that in a short time the cry of war will fill the streets and homes of its inhabitants.

God moves in a mysterious way, His wonders to perform, and this war will result in the wonder — if it may be called such — of many of the inhabitants of the earth seeking a way to a closer union with God. Lives will be sacrificed but souls will be saved, and men will realize that they are brothers of one God, and that love, only, must rule, and that war must cease forever.

The spirit world is interested in this great conflict, and spirits are striving to open up the souls of the rulers of the nations in conflict and to influence them to bring an end to the fearful carnage that is now destroying so many of God's children. The suffering, though, will be great before the end shall be accomplished, and many men will become spirits before the dove of peace will leave the ark of refuge and see the dry land. Nations shall fall, and some shall cease to exist; but at least the truth of the fellowship of man and the Fatherhood of God will be established.

For men must work its harvest, and the reaping must continue until there shall not remain in men's hearts any desire for war or the satisfying of unholy ambitions. We in spirit see this and are striving to bring the great calamity to its ending. God will not cease to love His children, even though those children forget Him and murder their brothers.

I have finished, and through the gloom of desolation and ruin I see the rainbow of hope and the end of strife. May all men learn the fact that God is Love, and that they are His children, and will soon realize the truth of His Love.

> I must stop, your brother in Christ,
> McKinley

ABRAHAM LINCOLN (1809 - 1865)

The one-time president describes his home
in the spirit world, and his great love for Jesus
January 5, 1916

I am here, Abraham Lincoln.

I am your friend and desire to write a few lines. Well, I am in the seventh sphere and am very happy and enjoy all the delights of a soul redeemed, and am in the way of progress to the higher spheres where some of your band live. How beautiful must be their homes, because, when they come to the lower spheres, they have such beauty and are so filled with Divine Love that I know they must live in homes of transcendent beauty where happiness is supreme.

I am not one who knows all that there is in the heavens provided by the Father, but I know enough to say, "that no eye of man has seen and neither has his heart conceived of the wonderful things that the Father has prepared for those who love Him and do His will" (1 Corinthians 2:9). In our sphere the glory of our habitations and surroundings that we have are beyond all conception of mortals, and beyond all the powers which we have to describe. Your language is poor indeed when we attempt to use it to describe our homes and our happiness.

Never a sigh, nor a thought tainted with the slightest flavor of unhappiness or discontent. All our wishes are gratified, and love reigns eternally and without stint. Never, when on earth, did I conceive that one man could love another as one spirit here loves his brother spirit. The mine and thine are truly the ours, and no spirit is so happy as when he is doing something to make another spirit happier; and then, love between the opposite sexes is so pure and glorious.

My home is not in any of the cities, it is in the country, among beautiful fields and woods where the purest waters flow in silver streams of living light, and the birds of paradise in all their glorious plumage sing and make merry the echoes of the hills and rocks, for we have hills and rocks as well as plains and beautiful meadows and placid lakes and

135

shining waterfalls, all praising God for His goodness.

So why will every mortal not try to attain to this heavenly condition of love and happiness, when it is so easy to do so? The Divine Love is waiting for all, and needs only the seeking and the believing in order to make the mortal an heir to all the glories of this heavenly place. But the mind of man, in its superimposed importance and in the conceit of the wonderful powers of his reasoning faculties, keeps the simple childlike faith from making him a child of the kingdom.

Oh, I tell you, if mortals only knew what is here ready for them to obtain and make their own, they would not let the supposed greatness of their minds, or the cares and ambitions and desires for earthly possessions keep them from seeking this great and glorious inheritance, which is theirs by merely claiming it in the way made known by the Master.

What can I say of him, the most glorious and beautiful and loving of all the spirits in God's universe. When on earth I looked upon him and worshiped him as God, sitting on the right hand of the Father way up in the high heavens a way off waiting for the coming of the great judgment day, when he would separate the sheep from the goats and send each to his eternal place of habitation. Whether to heaven or hell only he knew, and I did not and could not until the great judgment should be pronounced.

But now, when I see him as he is, and know that he is my friend and elder brother, a spirit such as I am, with only love for his younger brethren, be they saints or sinners, and a great longing that all may come and partake of the feast that the Father has prepared, I feel that the loving brother (Jesus) and friend is more to me, and my happiness is greater than when I looked upon him as the God of judgment, having his habitation way off beyond my vision or reach. He is so loving and so pure and so humble. Why, his very humility makes us all love him almost to adoration, and if you could only see him, you would not be surprised that we love him so much.

Well, my friend, I have written a little more than I intended, because I am so filled with Love and so happy in having such a friend as the Master, that I can hardly restrain myself.

When on earth I was not orthodox to the full extent, but my early belief that Jesus was a part of the Godhead I did not succeed in getting rid of, although my mind often rebelled at the thought. The early teachings of my mother lingered with me, and maturer thoughts and development of mind could never entirely eradicate this belief in Jesus as being part of God. Some have said and thought that I was almost an infidel, but this is untrue, for I always believed firmly in the Father and, as I have told you, in Jesus.

I was also to some extent a Spiritualist, that is, I believed in the communications of spirits with mortals, as on numerous occasions I have had such communications, and have acted on advice that I received through them. But I never learned from any of these communications any of the higher truths which I now know, and which are so important for mortals to know, and which, if men only knew and taught, would make their religion a live, virile, all pervading and satisfying religion.

We are all interested in your work, and are co-workers with you in revealing these great truths. May God bless and prosper you and cause you to see the realities of the great Divine Love, is the prayer of your brother in Christ.

A. Lincoln

Chapter Six

Religious Reformers

CHARLES T. RUSSELL (1852 - 1916)

A preacher found that the teachings of a lifetime were false
July 31, 1918

I am here, Pastor Russell.

Let me say a word, for I have been with you today as you read the book of which I was the writer.

I see that you are aware of the erroneous interpretations of the testament that it contains, of the false constructions that are drawn from the quotations of the Bible, and also that you feel that a great injury is being done to those who read and believe in my teachings. Well, I realize the falsity of my teachings and the wrong and injury that is being wrought among those who have been followers of me; and how great will be their surprise when death comes to them, for they will be more alive than they ever were while living in the flesh. This I have realized, to my great surprise and suffering.

When I was about to leave the flesh, and for long years before, I believed that when I died I would go into the literal grave and would thereafter be in a state of oblivion, knowing nothing until the day of the first resurrection, when I and all those who believed that we were of the little flock would be called into the presence of Jesus and there become his co-workers and co-judges of men during the "millennium". While the rest of the world would be tried and finally judged to either a life of happiness, as men were restored to the condition of Adam before the fall, or to total annihilation.

But as I passed from the body, I found that I had a spiritual body in which were contained all the faculties of my mind and the appetites of the flesh that were a part of me when on earth; and also, the memories of all that I had thought, and taught, when trying to lead my followers into the truth, as I supposed. I was more alive than ever before, and conscience soon began to do its work of reproving and bring to me remorse and regret for the great harm that I had done to many of my fellow men by reason of my teaching a faith that is wholly untrue, and destructive to the soul's salvation. I taught that there was no such thing as the soul after the separation of the body and life; that it then ceased to have an existence, and would never again come into existence until the first resurrection, which would be the first awakening of the little flock to a consciousness of its existence.

To me the will was the great thing, and while that never ceased to exist, yet it lay in a dormant state and was as dead, knowing nothing. How vitally misleading was this teaching and how my followers will find themselves deceived, and will suffer from the want of knowledge of the fact that the soul is the man and is susceptible to progressing in the knowledge of the truths of God while on earth, as well as after it becomes an inhabitant of the spirit world.

I have had a tragic awakening, with all the consequences of a tragedy in which I was one of the important actors, and the principal cause of the results of the tragedy. I know what death means, and what life means, for I died merely to live, and to live a life in which at this time there is much suffering and regret, accompanied by the knowledge that I have before me a work greater than I can perform in many long years in the future.

I must now try to undo what I for so many years did, to the injury of those who believed in me; and when I realize that there is hardly a way, until these followers of mine become spirits like myself, in which I can do this work, my suffering becomes almost unbearable. Only through the medium of the mortal can I reach these people, and because of my teachings they will not believe what I may attempt to communicate through a mortal medium, which I wrote against and reviled, and alleged that they were only creatures used by the devil and his minions to deceive men.

If I had only known the truth, and thereby abstained from preaching untruth in this particular, how different my lot would now be. But I believed what I taught, and taught what I believed. It was all a lie, and though I believed it, yet that fact does not lessen my regrets, for I see with the clearness of the spirit that my thoughts and teachings are believed by many of my followers because I taught them. Consequently, they will suffer from their beliefs, and the fact that I believed these erroneous things and taught them in good faith will not, in one iota, save them from the darkness and sufferings which will certainly become theirs. Unfortunate is the man who believes spiritual untruths; and accursed is the man who teaches them, and thus deceives those who are earnestly seeking for the truth.

I would like to write more tonight in reference to this matter and my condition, and the heavy burden which I am now bearing, but your wife says I must not write more now as you are not in condition to be further drawn on. So, thanking you, and having the hope that at some time in the near future I may again communicate with you, I will say good night.

Your friend,
Pastor Russell

JOHN BUNYAN (1628 - 1688)

*The writer of "Pilgrims Progress" is
now a celestial spirit and a follower of Jesus*
September 13, 1915

I am here, John Bunyan.

I am the writer of *Pilgrims Progress*, and I want to tell you that I am an inhabitant of the celestial spheres and a follower of Jesus. I am now a Christian who knows that many of the things that I wrote in my book as allegory are truths. Of course, my belief in Jesus as God and as having made a vicarious atonement is all wrong, for now I know that there is only one God, the Father, and that every other living being, either on earth or in the spirit world, is His child — son or daughter.

Jesus is the brightest spirit in all God's universe, and possesses more of the Divine Love than the other spirits, and consequently is nearer the Father, with whom he has his spiritual communions. My belief in God and in His Love and mercy is stronger than when on earth, and I want every man to believe and understand that the great thing to be acquired is the Divine Love of God and His Grace.

I am so very happy that I cannot tell you of its extent, and when I think of the troubles and sufferings that I endured when on earth it makes me believe that I acquired the wonderful Love at a very small cost. I am in the second celestial sphere where your folks are, I mean those who write to you. I want to tell you also that you are a very highly favored man to have been selected to do this work. I know the fact that Jesus is with you so very often, and that his great love and power will be with you and you will feel their wonderful influences. So remember that I want to write again.

Your brother in Christ,
John Bunyan

CHAUNCEY GILES

Chauncey Giles changes his belief about Jesus being God
February 28, 1917

Let me write you a line, for I am interested in what has just been written you, for when I lived on earth, I was a Swedenborgian or New Churchman, and believed in the doctrines of that church, and especially in the cornerstone of its beliefs, and that is that Jesus was God. The only God to be worshiped as such and accepted as the incarnate God, who came to earth and lived and taught among men the coming of God into the flesh.

Well, when on earth I was a leader or preacher in that church, and during the course of my ministry I not only taught but wrote many pamphlets and some books upon this doctrine of God becoming man in the form of Jesus, and on many other doctrines, that I now know to be untrue.

My authority for saying that this fundamental doctrine of the church is untrue, is that I have seen and talked with Jesus in the spirit world, and learned that he is only the spirit of a mortal, although the highest and most glorious spirit in all the heavens, and is not God. I have never seen God nor has any spirit seen Him with their spirit eyes, though Jesus and others of the highest spirits say that they have seen Him with their soul perceptions, which must be true because Jesus is so much like God that he cannot tell a lie.

I know that there is a God, and my knowledge is based on certainty, however the basis of this certainty I cannot explain to you, as you could not comprehend my explanation. Yet God lives and rules and loves, and is present with us and with you in some or many of His attributes, and Jesus is not this God.

I wish that I could come to my people and tell them of the errors of their beliefs, and the truths as they exist and to the extent that they are known to me. I have no hope of ever being able to do so, for one of the cardinal doctrines of the church is that with the passing of Swedenborg passed the possibility of all communications between God or His angels and mortals as to spiritual truths, and that it is contrary to God's will

Religious Reformers

that mortals should attempt to penetrate the veil that separates the two worlds. Yet such beliefs as I taught now cause me suffering and regret, for I see no way of remedying the wrong that I did, and of turning the thoughts of my followers into the paths that lead to truth and the certainty of heaven.

As this is my first attempt to communicate, I am somewhat tired and must stop. I thank you for the opportunity, and hope that some time I may have the privilege of writing again. Notwithstanding my erroneous beliefs, I have in my soul some of the Divine Love, that enables me to sign myself,

Your brother in Christ,
Chauncey Giles

JOHN GARNER

Preacher of England states that all sin and
error will eventually be eradicated from men's souls
August 8, 1915

I am here to tell you that God is Love and that all humanity are His children and the object of His bounty and care. Not even the vilest sinner is beyond the boundaries of His care and Love.

He is not a God who needs propitiation or sacrifice, but calls to all His children to come unto Him and partake freely of the great feast of Love which he has prepared for them and to enjoy the happiness which His presence gives.

So my friend, do not for a moment think that the doors of mercy or the entrance into the delights of His heavenly home are closed by the death of the body, for I tell you that the death of the body is a mere entrance into a higher life with increased opportunities. Notwithstanding what I say, the soul that seeks to obtain the Divine Love while on earth has a great advantage in time over the one that waits until his spirit leaves the body before seeking for God's Love. The

143

best time for mortals to aspire to attain this great gift is now, and no time is so propitious. God's Love is for the mortal even if he has the passions and appetites which the flesh encumbers him with, and when a mortal fights against the temptations which these burdens impose, and overcomes, he, when he enters the spirit world, is stronger and more able to progress, than when he puts off the great attempt until he becomes purely spirit. So, while there is no such condition as probation terminated when the mortal enters the spirit world, yet the probation on earth is the accepted time to seek the great prize. I know I am writing like some of your camp meeting preachers, but what I say is a truth nevertheless, and happy is the mortal who realizes this fact and acts in accordance.

Jesus is working among mortals now as he did when on earth, and although they cannot see his physical form or hear his voice of love in tones of benediction and pleading, yet the influence of his love is felt and the persuasion of his spirit voice is heard in the hearts of men. He is still the saviour of men as he was on earth, and his mission will not cease until the closing of the celestial kingdom, when sin and error shall be eradicated from the earth and from the spirit world. He will triumph and conqueror over sin and everything that tends to pervert man from that which is good and righteous. Man, having only his natural love, will be freed from all inharmony and will live as brothers and friends in peace and happiness. And those spirits having the Divine Love will become angels of God, and live forever in the bliss of the celestial heavens.

So I urge upon all men to seek the Divine Love and live in its presence forever. I must stop now, so I will say good night.

John Garner
I was a Christian preacher of England at the time of the Reformation.

GEORGE WHITEFIELD (1714 - 1770)

Preacher of England and a contemporary with John Wesley,
has changed his erroneous beliefs that he taught on earth
December 8, 1915

I am here, George Whitefield.

I was a preacher of England and a contemporary of John Wesley. I am in the celestial spheres where are only those who have received the Divine Love that will be written about by other and more ancient spirits. I merely want to say that I am still a follower of Jesus, only a little different in my knowledge of what he was and is. I do not now look upon him as God, or a part of God, but as His true Son, and the greatest of all the spirits in the spirit world. There are none to be compared to him in beauty or spirituality or in his knowledge of God's truths.

I used to preach to thousands about his vicarious atonement and his blood sacrifice, but now I see his mission in a different light. It is not his death on the cross that saves men from their sins, nor his sacrifice that appeases the wrath of an angry God, but his life and teachings of the Divine Love bestowed on humanity and the way to obtain that Love, that saves men from their sins. There was no need to appease the wrath of an angry God for there was no angry God, only a loving and merciful God. When men think that unless they turn from their sins they will burn forever in a fiery hell, they are the dupes of preachers such as I was and will never get the Love of God by such teachings. God is Love, and men must know it and that His Love is for all of every race and clime.

I see now what a great mistake I made in my conception of God and of Christ's mission on earth, and how much harm I did to mortals in my preaching and how I slandered the God of Love. Though I was honest in my beliefs and taught as I thought the truth to be, yet that does not alter the fact that many a mortal after he became a spirit, was retarded for a long time in his spiritual progress, because of these false beliefs, which, in order to progress, he had to give up and start anew in his efforts to find the truths of God.

As I worked hard and preached eloquently to make mortals believe these injurious doctrines while on earth, so now I am working hard and preaching eloquently to make spirits who come over with these beliefs, unlearn them and see the truth as it is. I am in sympathy with the movement which the Master is now making to spread the truth of these spiritual things on earth and I am ready to follow him in all his efforts to bring about the salvation of men not only from sin but also from erroneous beliefs.

So I come to you tonight to express my sympathy and interest in the cause. Let your work proceed, and do your best to make known to men the great truths which the Master shall teach. We will all join in the work and do everything in our power to speed the great cause of men's redemption from sin and ignorance. Man must have the soul development by obtaining the Divine Love, because you cannot inspire a man to preach grand and sublime spiritual truths unless he has the capacity in his own soul to feel and understand the truths. I will not write longer tonight.

I am your true friend,
George Whitefield

*The great world teacher will be the Master
come to earth in the form of his "divine revelations"*
October 11, 1917

Let me write a line or two. I have been present with you since you returned from the church, and have listened to your conversation.

I was with you tonight at the prayer meeting and heard what the preacher said, and was particularly interested in his ideas about the coming of the great world teacher, and saw that his idea of what constituted greatness in this particular, arose from his estimate of human greatness.

The teacher will not be a great preacher or a magnificent specimen of physical development or a man with a wonderful voice, but a man who can reveal to the world the truths of God, regarding the relationship of man to God and the plan provided for the redemption and reconciliation of man. It is a fact, and I know whereof I write, that the regeneration of the human soul is caused more by the quiet meditations of mortals of the truths of God and by the silent longings of the soul than by the emotions that arise from the fervid and persuasive sermons of the preachers and evangelists. These latter may arouse the dead souls to a realization of their need of a reconciliation to God, but so often these emotions do not bring the soul into rapport or unison with God, as do the silent meditations of which I speak.

There must be the true soul longings and aspirations for this Love, and in such cases these longings do not arise from the emotions produced as I have mentioned, and especially where such emotions are the results of fear created by the picturing of an angry and revengeful God. No, in the silence of the home chamber, where the mortal is, as it were, alone with God, and lets his longings go to God for the bestowal of His Love, because of the love that the mortal may have for God, this Divine Love will come in response and regenerating power. Only the mortal and God need be alone.

Excitement or the magnetism which the preacher may give to the mortal does not create the true longings or aspirations, and for the preacher to suppose that the great world teacher must be a man with this great personal magnetism or with a voice that can cause the feelings of the mortal to vibrate with emotion or excitement, is a mistake. Jesus, when on earth, I am told, never tried to create emotion or excitement in this manner, but his teachings were as the still small voice that enters the soul and draws it to a contemplation of God's Love in all the power of a soul's longings and cravings.

So I say, the preacher's conception of this teacher was not a true one, and besides, while there will be a revelation of the truth, there will be no world teacher, but only a revealer of truths that will be disclosed. The Master, himself, will be the great teacher come again to earth in the form of his "revelations".

I wish that I could come and proclaim these truths, but I cannot, and only through the instrumentality of a human can my thoughts be made known, and they will not be my thoughts either, because what I may attempt to impress upon the minds and consciousness of men will be only those truths that I have learned from the same source as will come the "revelations".

Of course these truths will have to be preached and taught to men, but this will not be done by any great teacher, but by many preachers who shall learn the truth from what the Master shall disclose; and no man of himself will be able to claim to be the great teacher. The greatest will be those who shall have the most of the Divine Love in their souls, and the greatest knowledge of the truths.

I also heard the preacher say that he would believe in any truths that might be confirmed by miracles, such as were performed in the time of Jesus, the instantaneous healing, etc. Well, you need not be surprised of such a demonstration, for it will surely take place. When a man shall receive in his soul sufficient amount of the Divine Love, there will come with it to that man a power and knowledge of the laws governing the relation of spirit to material organism that will enable that man to perform these same acts that are called miracles; and further, there will be some who will have that power and will demonstrate the same in confirmation of the truths that you are receiving.

The spirits who are now working to make known to man and convince them of these truths, have determined that such so-called miracles shall take place in confirmation of the "new revealment." The Master is the leader in the movement and he will not cease to bring about this great demonstration or rather not cease to work to this end, and he will not fail, if the human agents will follow his lead.

Well, I must not write more tonight, but as I am interested in this great work, and saw that the preacher's conception of this great world teacher is incorrect, I deemed it wise to write you as I have. What I have written is not the result of my individual belief or opinion, but the result of what these high spirits have determined shall come to pass, and back of it all is the will and help of God, for in His Love and mercy He desires to see all men become His true children and redeemed from the sins and evils of their present human condition.

So with my love and as a co-worker I will say good night and subscribe myself,

Your brother in Christ,
George Whitefield

148

JOHN WESLEY (1703 - 1719)

Confirmation by John Wesley that James Padgett
has been chosen to be the writing instrument for Jesus's truths
July 17, 1915

I am here, a man who lived in the faith of the Christ, and who was a true follower of him, and lover of God. I hesitate to write at the same time with these great spirits who have written you, and yet, I want to give my testimony also to the fact that I have heard the Master say that he has chosen you for the work of delivering his truths to the world. My dear brother, believe this great fact with all your mind and soul, for it is a truth, and one that prefers you before any other mortal.

Jesus, the greatest of all spirits and the one nearest the fountainhead of God's Love, and he has declared to us who are close to him and working to accomplish his great desire for man's salvation, that he has selected you to do the work and you will not fail if you will only have faith.

So make your start in trying to get this faith, and pray to God for more of it, and it will be given to you in great abundance. Only God can give the faith that will remove mountains and overcome all obstacles.

I must not write more, and will say good night. I sign myself your true brother and co-worker in the cause.

John Wesley, the Methodist preacher

John Wesley reassures Mr. Padgett not to worry about his material wants
September 30, 1915

When the Master said, "Feed my sheep" (John 21:16), he not only meant that Peter and those to whom he was talking should feed the spiritual natures of those who should believe in him and try to belong to his fold, but he also intended that their material wants should be taken care of. Tonight he is saying the same thing, and as you are his sheep of spe-

149

cial care and love, he intends that all the things that are necessary for your well-being shall be given you. So do not doubt at all, but believe that you will be looked after in all your times of need.

He was so loving to you tonight that we were all somewhat astonished at the great love which we saw going to you, and thought how dear you must be to him. I have never seen him take such interest in any particular person before, and when you realize what his love and power are, you will be more astonished than were we.

I see what your troubles are, and while they may seem mountains high to you, they are merely temporary and will soon pass away. So believe in what the Master told you, and pray to God for Love and faith.

I will not write more, and will say God bless you.

Your brother in Christ,
John Wesley

John Wesley attends the services over
Mr. Padgett's daughter's remains, as the Master was shedding
his love and influence over the mourners and near ones
June 21, 1918

I am here, John Wesley.

Let me write a line. I was present tonight at the services over your daughter's remains, and saw what a wonderful congregation of high and beautiful spirits was there. Your band was present and the Master was shedding his love and influence over the mourners and near ones.

Your daughter's spirit was also present, and although it seemed a little strange to her that she should be outside her body and could look upon it as it lay cold and dead, yet she understood and was quite happy that so many of her friends were there displaying their sympathy and love. Of course, your wife was present and was radiantly happy in her love for you and her boys and her other relatives. She had her daughter close by her side and was telling her of the truths of the resurrection as the minister read the services, and especially how the great Love of God is necessary to the true resurrection and heaven.

It was a glorious evening with the spirits, and no sorrow or unhappiness was with them, only their sympathy for the human grief of those who did not know the truth of the liberation of the spirit from the bondage of the flesh.

Well, I might tell you many things which occurred among the spirit visitors, but I am admonished not to write more, so will say good night.

Your brother in Christ,
John Wesley

ROBERT DALE OWEN (1801 - 1877)

*An investigator of Spiritualism speaks of spiritual
phenomena investigations that he used to write about*
February 11, 1919

I am here, Robert Dale Owen.

Let me say just a word, for I am interested in your work and in the phenomena of Spiritualism. I have been with you as you read the book which attempts to show the truth of spiritual manifestations, and the instances mentioned of spirits showing themselves in the garb of humans are true. I was then an investigator of the question, and had only the knowledge which I received from my own observation, and, hence, was an outsider, as it were, of these spiritual phenomena. I mean that I was not one of the gifted ones of earth, who can have the power of receiving or communicating with spirits by reason of the fact that they possess the power of seeing or feeling or hearing the presence of spirits. I was not so gifted.

I am now an investigator of things spiritual, although not of the possibility of communicating with the spirit world, for this I know to be a fact, and beyond all question. Men who doubt this fact are in the condition of those who will not learn, because they do not believe in the first principles of the phenomena, and are willing to let their prejudices or their indifference lead them away from the truth.

The phenomena which I have portrayed in my book are very simple and of the lower order of spiritual phenomena, and yet men will not believe because they fail to approach the subject with open minds and a desire to learn the truth, even though the search for the same leads them along lines of investigation that are so foreign to the course of study that they are pursuing in their various vocations. Of all the bigoted and hardheaded investigators of truth, the preachers are the most difficult to teach the truth of Spiritualism, and their periscope is one that enables them to see only in a straight line that has been laid down to them for ages and holds them in its iron grasp.

Well, you have asked me some questions which I cannot answer in one breath. I am in the fourth sphere, where many spirits are pursuing their studies of things which pertain to the laws of the spirit world, as well as to the laws of the earth. I have not heard of the Divine Love, except as we call all love "divine," and it must be so, for it leads us to the spheres where those who are sinless and in harmony with God reside. I am a true believer in the things of God and in the redemption of all humanity, sooner or later.

The intellect is only part of my existence in the spirit world, and above and greater than that is the Love that causes me to become in harmony with the laws of God. These are the answers to your questions, and I should like to write you at length upon the truths of what I have so briefly stated. I know that you are very busy in receiving communications from the spirit world and have little time for communications from strangers, yet I should like to write at least one letter in reference to my condition and knowledge of things as I have found them.

I say what is true, for I have never heard of the Divine Love in the sense that you have spoken of. I have never talked with spirits who claim to have this Love, and to be better than are the spirits who are progressing in the love which they have, and as to immortality, I only know that death merely sets the soul of the mortal free and enables it to enter onto its progress towards the higher spheres, where truth and goodness are.

Let me wait a moment in my astonishment, for I see more spirits who seem to be of a different order of spirit from me, and who are brighter and more beautiful, and are willing to tell me of the Divine Love, for they all claim to know of it. I do not understand and I am sure that if they are possessed of this Love, it is only another form of belief. I am all confused and cannot think for the moment. I must go.

Good night,
Robert Dale Owen

WILLIAM STAINTON MOSES (1839 - 1892)

The medium whose book Mr. Padgett was reading,
explains why his book "Spirit Teachings" did not contain
the truth of the Divine Love as taught by Jesus
September 14, 1918

I am here, Stainton Moses.

Let me say a word. I have been present as you read my book called *Spirit Teachings* and saw that while many of the statements contained therein are in accord with the knowledge that you have of spirit matters, yet there is wanting of the one great truth of the Divine Love as it has been explained to you by the high spirits.

Well, you must not, on account of the fact that this truth is not alleged and explained by the spirits who wrote the messages that you have been reading, assume that these spirits were not of a higher order, or that they are wanting in the knowledge of many truths that the book portrays as to the relationship of spirit to man and man to God, and his future destiny. No, these spirits were real and genuine and taught truths as they understood them. They were limited in their knowledge by the amount of the progress which they had made in things spiritual, and in attempting to teach they were honest and declared only those things that they believed to be true. Many of the truths that they declared are of vast importance and necessary for men to know in order for their own salvation. They show the way to the condition of the perfect man, and the struggles, and sufferings, and sacrifices that spirits will have to make in order to arrive at this condition.

These spirits since the time of the writings have learned of this formation of the soul into an Essence Divine by reason of the possession of the Divine Love, and, hence, could not use their medium in making known this great means of perfect salvation to humankind. They have since the time of the writings learned of this truth and are now progressing towards the celestial spheres. You will notice in the teachings there are many expressions that are erroneous, and solely because the writers did not know to the contrary. However, this fact must not cause you to believe that many other things which they teach are not true, for outside of and independent of this truth of the Divine Love and what it means to mortals and spirits, the teachings are true and should be believed.

I write this that you may not doubt the genuineness of the writings, or think that the same were not made by the spirits who professed to write. These spirits had a mission to perform and were earnestly endeavoring to acquaint the medium, and through him, the world, with the truths and the necessity of meditating upon the same, and ceasing to be satisfied with the old-time beliefs which were so erroneous and misleading and harmful, as the spirits declared.

I have an enlarged knowledge of the things that pertain to the spirit world, and to the true plan of salvation as established by God, and have experienced the possession of the Divine Love and its operations and effect upon the souls of men, and how sufficient it is to relieve men from the sufferings and penalties of their sins that they would have to endure or undergo were this Love not open and free for them to obtain. I have that Love to a degree that has made me an angel of the celestial spheres, and a possessor of that immortality that was unknown to men when I lived on earth, and also unknown to the spirits who communicated the writings which you have been reading. They taught only a part of the truth of salvation and regeneration, and that the lesser part in importance, although the one which the large majority of men will know of and obtain, only.

I thought that I would write this to you, for I saw that you were very much interested in the teachings, and had in mind the question as to whether these spirits who wrote were acquainted with the great truth. I am very happy that I am permitted to write, for I do not want those who have read and believe these writings to rest upon the assurance that the same contain all of the truth, and that there is no other way to heaven and happiness, except that set forth in these writings. It is so important that all of truth should become known to men, and the opportunity given to them to seek and find the great way to immortality and bliss.

I will not write more now, but some time in the future I should like to come and write further with reference to these matters. I thank you for your kindness in receiving this imperfect communication and will only say further that the Divine Love and the celestial heavens where the Master is forming his kingdom, are truths, vital and unchangeable, and the desideratum of the happiness of humanity.

I will say good night, and while a stranger to you, yet, can subscribe myself,

Your brother in Christ,
Stainton Moses, the medium

MARY BAKER EDDY (1821 - 1910)

Mrs. Eddy's testimony
December 17, 1916

I am here, Mrs. Eddy.

Let me write a few lines, as I am anxious to declare some facts, which when on earth were not facts to my understanding and beliefs, and oh, the pity of it all.

Today, I was present at the church where the preacher discussed and criticized my teachings and me also and I am compelled to admit that some of his criticisms were true and justified.

I am Mrs. Eddy, and the founder of the sect which bears the high-sounding name of Christian Science, and the doctrines of which are neither Christian nor science as I now know from actual experience in the spirit world. Many of my teachings I have been shown not to be in accord with truth, and are so misleading.

I now realize that my mind and soul were not in accord as regards the truth, while I lived as a mortal, and that my mind was superior in causing me to have certain beliefs which I left to the world in the form of doctrines contained in my textbook and my other writings.

My soul possessed a considerable degree of the Divine Love, as that Love has been explained to you, and when I came to the spirit world that Love was my salvation, notwithstanding the errors of many of my teachings as to mind and matter, and the non-reality of sin and evil.

I am too weak to write more, but I will soon come for I must declare the truths.

Good night,

Mrs. Eddy

Mrs. Eddy did not know the truth that has been
revealed in the messages that Padgett has received
June 13, 1918

I am, Mrs. Eddy.

Let me write a line, for I have been interested in the conversation of the Doctor and want to express to him my thanks for his efforts to enlighten one of my followers as to the truth. My obligation is based on the fact that I recognize the misleading errors of some of my teachings, and that I am responsible for the beliefs of many mortals that are not true and have the effect of keeping them from the truth.

Whenever any of those who have embraced the beliefs that I taught are shown the light and directed to the errors of my teachings, I am to that extent happier and relieved from the burdens which I carry with me — that my teachings are keeping so many from the truth. In all this I refer to the great question of the Divine Love and the way in which mortals may obtain the same and become in harmony with God, and partake of His Divine Nature and immortality. I have examined these truths since I came to the spirit world, and realize with a great conviction that the reflection of the "divine" comes only with the possession of the Love of God.

I wish that I had time tonight to write you a longer letter on this subject, but your guide says that you are not in condition to receive a lengthy letter and I must stop.

Let me express the hope that you and your friend, whenever the opportunity occurs, will attempt to enlighten my followers as to the truths which you know, and as to errors and the want of the true explanation of a salvation which my books do not contain.

With my love I will say good night,
Mrs. Eddy

ROBERT G. INGERSOLL (1833 - 1899)

This writer, called an infidel by his contemporaries,
tells of his religious views when on earth
August 5, 1915

I am here, Robert G. Ingersoll.

I am a spirit who when on earth taught men that the only salvation required for them was good deeds and kind hearts, and that the Bible, outside of its moral precepts, was not worthy of belief, that many of its sayings were untrue, and that all of its teachings as to belief and faith were not worthy of consideration.

I was perfectly sincere in what I taught and thought, and hence I don't feel that I was guilty of any very great sin, although I have now changed some of my beliefs, or better, thoughts. I did not believe that Jesus ever really lived, as was set forth in the Bible, and I certainly did not believe in a vicarious atonement, or any salvation through blood or propitiation of an angry God. Neither did I believe in any New Birth or in any of the doctrines of St. John having reference to a soul being redeemed; instead I believed that every man's future state, should there be a future state, depended upon his deeds of love and mercy towards his fellowman. I believed that God was not to be worshiped or consulted, neither would He, nor could He, save a man from anything that might tend to make him unhappy, and man's love for one another was the great thing that would determine his condition in the future life, should such life exist.

I did not deny that there would be a future life. I merely didn't know anything about it, and hence, all my teachings were directed to making men live on earth in a way that would bring to them happiness while mortals. My foundation stone, as it were, was love, one towards another, and with this love went kindness and forgiveness, and good feeling and fair dealing. I especially emphasized the necessity for love at home. I am still of the opinion that these qualities, if possessed and expressed in action, will make men happier, make the world better, and finally do away with evil and distress. I now see, though, that there is a future life and that men who would enjoy the greatest happiness in this future life must not only have this love and kindness for one another, but also must believe that God is interested in the soul of each individual man.

I am in the fourth sphere and have much happiness in my intellectual pursuits and in my love of my fellowman, and am trying to help them get the best out of life on earth. I do not believe in the teachings of those parts of the Bible which, in effect, say that you must believe on the Lord Jesus Christ in order to be saved (Acts 16:31), for I do not believe that any mere belief will save a man from anything. I know that many here believe that Jesus is the saviour of men, as taught by the orthodox churches, but I think that such spirits are as much mistaken as were those who believed the same doctrine when on earth.

I consider myself as saved. I have not found any hell as taught by the churches, although each man has to pay the penalties for his evil deeds done on earth, and many men are suffering here since they became spirits. I will confess that I was somewhat surprised to see that spirits who did not live correct lives on earth are suffering very serious tortures and this, I suppose, is the effect of the law that demands a penalty for every violation of its command.

I understand that this suffering will not have to continue forever, or that the state of these men is fixed. Progression is the law of the spirit world, and I cannot conceive that any spirit will remain the same through all eternity. To me, the great satisfaction is that there is no orthodox hell and no devil to punish the wicked, although I am told that many of the spirits who suffer from their evil deeds have been in a condition of suffering for a long time.

Well, I am satisfied with the condition that I am in, and in the possibility of progression, and I do not need the teachings of the spirits who profess to have knowledge of a higher Love that brings happiness of a kind that enables them to enjoy supreme bliss. Such spirits, I believe, are those who had the old ideas of the churches, against which I taught.

I was not compelled to undergo such suffering when I came into the spirit world or to endure much darkness, yet I suppose there were some deeds which I had to pay the penalties for, and hence I had to suffer some. But as my love for all humanity was my principal feeling when on earth, this love gives me a position which I now enjoy.

Well, as to the last statement, you are right. I have an open mind and am willing to learn any truth that may be presented to me in such a way as to convince me that it is a truth. You are stating things of which I have no knowledge, and which I do not believe to be true. I have thought a great deal of God and do believe in a God, but as to this Divine Love, I have never heard of it nor ever thought of it.

I know of no love except the love for man, and that means spirit for spirit, and a certain Love of God for man. But as to a Love that makes one partake of divinity, I have never heard, and as to the New Birth that you speak of, I don't believe in it any more than I did on earth. To me it seems foolishness. What is there about me or any other spirit to be born again? You might say that when I left my body and became a spirit I was born again, and in a sense that is true, but when you tell me that I must be born again and that by such "birth" I will become a partaker of divinity, I cannot believe what you say or understand what you mean.

Well, you state your proposition very fairly and very clearly, and I must say that I am impressed with what you say, and it might be that you are right. At any rate, I will keep an open mind and will stand ready to hear any argument from you or any spirit that you have mentioned and if they can show me the truth of your propositions I will not hesitate to embrace them. I want to learn everything possible, and as I was an honest inquirer on earth, I will be an honest one here. You make your assertions very strongly and you seem to be in earnest in what you say, and for those reasons I must listen to you.

Yes, I knew Riddle very well, and he was a believer somewhat like myself. I have not met him since I have become a spirit, but would like to do so. I will keep in mind what you say and will observe any difference in beauty that may exist, because if such be a fact there must be some cause for it, and that cause I shall endeavor to understand.

I have done as you suggested and I see Riddle, but hardly recognize him, as he is so changed and is so much more beautiful than I conceived of. He has shaken my hand and introduced me to the others. What beautiful spirits they are! The one who, he says, is your grandmother is glorious in her beauty and brightness, and Love seems to be a part of her very being. How I thank you for the experience! I am going with Riddle, who says that he has a wonderful truth to tell me and that I will become convinced of its reality.

So, my friend, I thank you for our conversation and if you desire, I will come again and tell you of the result of our interview — I mean between Riddle and myself. I have made the request of your grandmother and she says that she will be pleased to tell me of this Love that you speak of. Let me tell you this before I stop, that what you said about the difference in beauty and brightness of the spirits is true, and that I am as a dark night compared to the noonday sun in my appearance compared with theirs. I am so glad I came to you tonight.

So my dear friend, I will say good-bye for a little while.

> Your friend,
> Robert G. Ingersoll I was called an infidel.

Life and death, the friends of mortals, each to be welcomed
March 10, 1917

I am here, R. G. Ingersoll.

Tonight I am a very happy spirit, and one who realizes that it is not all of life to live, or yet of death to die, for life and death are mere incidents in the existence of the soul's career through eternity. Life on earth is but a short breathing of the soul in bondage, yet prized so highly by mortals. The death of the physical is the liberating of that soul from its bondage, and yet, men fear and shun it, and, if possible, would never let it come to them. This may be said to be natural and not to be wondered at, and all because mortals do not know that life and death are brothers, working for the good of mankind, the former giving them the opportunity to seek and possess happiness or misery, and the latter ending that

160

opportunity in this, that happiness may be increased without having to undergo the retarding influence that life on earth throws around mortals. So you see, life and death are complementary, the one positive and the other negative, each the great helpful friend of the human soul.

My friend, life has continued with me in greater and more enlarged abundance, until now I am the possessor of that life which Jesus came to earth to declare to be the heritage of every mortal who should seek it. My friend, death has left me, and in leaving me took with him all the possibilities of increased causes of unhappiness in my soul. The results or effects of the causes that existed in my soul while in the mortal life came with me in more acute and overpowering abundance; no new or additional causes were produced to the effects that came with me. Death took them with himself when he departed from me forever.

Life and death — the friends of mortals, each to be welcomed! The one, the friend for eternity; the other, the friend for only a moment, yet what a friend!

I intended tonight to write you a long and, as I think, an important message relating to the real world of spirits. However, I thought it best not to do so, but will postpone it for another time.

I will come soon. Good night and God bless you.

Your brother,
R. G. Ingersoll

Ingersoll describes his progress and his
difficulty in changing the views of his followers
April 24, 1916

I am here, Robert G. Ingersoll.

I come tonight to tell you of my progress since I wrote you last. I have converted to Christianity — I mean the true Christianity of Jesus— and to faith in the Divine Love of God. Since that time I have been praying and seeking for this Love and the faith that comes with it, and now I have progressed so that I am in the third sphere, where I find such beauty and happiness as I never conceived of on earth or since coming to the spirit world.

I now know what was meant by Jesus when he said, "In my Father's house are many mansions," for I have one that is very beautiful and grand, filled with everything to make me happy and to satisfy my heart's longings. I have so many books that I cannot find time to read them, and all the appointments of my home are so very beautiful and satisfying to the eye, as well as comfortable for its occupancy. Above and beyond all is the happiness that comes from the possession of this Divine Love, which to me is the most wonderful revelation and reality in all my experience, either on earth or in the spirit world.

I now think with regret of my years of erroneous teachings on earth, and of my failure to seek for and know, at least partly, the great truths of a continuous life and the existence of God. When I contrast my beliefs then and my knowledge now, my happiness then and my happiness now, I realize that as a mortal I was very ignorant and very unhappy. I know that Jesus is the way to immortality and life everlasting and to the true and always increasing happiness, and that the followers of his teachings will never be disappointed in their expectations.

My work now is to help those mortals, and spirits as well, who read and believe my books, and, as a consequence, lose the opportunity for learning the truths and the way to the Divine Love. Very many of my followers live on earth and many have become spirits. I search for them, and when I find them I tell them of my great mistakes and try to turn their thoughts to the true way to become redeemed children of God. My work is continuous, and sometimes disappointing, for when I come to

162

some spirits and attempt to tell them of my new beliefs and knowledge I find it difficult to convince some of them of the truths that I attempt to teach them.

As I sowed the seeds of the pernicious and false beliefs when a mortal, now I am bound to root up these seeds and plant in their places the seeds of truth. I can't tell you how much happiness I experience when one of these deluded followers of mine discards the old beliefs and accepts my new teachings, and how unhappy I am when they tell me that, as they believed what I taught them on earth and were satisfied, so now in the spirit they prefer the same belief and are satisfied. As they stay in this condition of belief they remain in darkness and unhappiness, and I, knowing that I am the cause of their darkness and unhappiness, am also unhappy and always in search of someone of these who will accept my teachings of truth. Thus I fully realize the meaning of what a man "sows that shall he also reap".

This is my work, and you must know that it is self-imposed, for I see that until I have removed the evils taught by me and engendered, I cannot be so happy and progress as rapidly as I desire. I further want to say that when I succeed in convincing any of my followers of the truth, I enlist them in my cause of correction and they work with me, for no spirit so well understands the meaning of error as he who once indulged in that same error, as I most assuredly did.

I will not write longer tonight, except to say to all who have heard of me and have read my books and imbibed my beliefs, that I am a Christian, a follower of Jesus the Christ, and a believer, with knowledge, in the Divine Love of God.

Yes, when I told you that, I actually believed what I said, and really felt sorry for your ignorance; I want now to assure you with gratitude that that conversation was the means of starting me in the progress to a knowledge of the truth and the gaining of this Divine Love. Oh, I was very ignorant, and with it I now realize there was much pride in my own opinion, for I thought that my reasoning powers and my research in things of the religious past had given me a knowledge that could not be gainsaid or overcome.

So my brother, you now see that truth is truth, and that no matter whether mortals learn it or understand it, or not, it is still the truth and never changes.

Thanking you for your kindness, I will say good night.

Your brother in Christ,
R. G. Ingersoll

Ingersoll comments on the teachings of Swedenborg while he was on earth
March 29, 1917

I am here, Robert G. Ingersoll.

Well, I come first because I am more modest than the other spirits who are present, and will say a few words and then give place to the others. I have been with you while you were reading the work of Swedenborg, and was much interested in the impression made upon your mind by what he said, and I found that your impressions were not very different from those that I had when I read his book while on earth, except this, that I had no belief in the spirit world, while you have.

Of course, you know from the knowledge that you have received through the messages that have come to you that many of his assertions are erroneous and the creatures of a mind that was fitted with a great knowledge of scientific things as accepted in his day, and also of a desire on his part to reconcile his knowledge of science and of theological teachings with what he supposed had been imparted to him by spirits and angels. But the result was that they could not be reconciled, and the consequence was that he declared doctrines and teachings that were utterly at variance with spiritual truths; and no one knows better than he does at this time of the falsity of many of his teachings.

Swedenborg had many opportunities for receiving and imparting the truth, but his great learning in the sciences and his beliefs in the old orthodox doctrines of the church in which he had been reared led him to conclusions and declarations of truths — as he believed — that were contrary to both science and religion in its higher and true sense.

Well, you may wonder that I write on this subject, and to answer any question that may arise from your surprise, I only desire to say that since I have received a knowledge of God's plan for the salvation of mankind and some of His Divine Love, I have been investigating with all the energies of my soul the great truths that exist and which never change. In this investigation I have talked with Swedenborg and have

164

learned from him the sources of his wonderful declarations and doctrines as set forth in his works. He is now in full knowledge of the truth, and also of his errors of his own learned disquisitions, as his followers believe and pronounce them to be. He can best explain to you the causes of his erroneous beliefs and what led him to attempt to explain the teachings that he received in the spirit world and his experiences in the mystical way that he did. I will not write more on the subject.

Although I, Ingersoll, who was truly and honestly an agnostic, can and do say that in this spirit world I had less darkness and less erroneous beliefs to get rid of than had Swedenborg; and while he had more of this Divine Love in his soul than had I — for I had none — yet his mind was so warped by his intellectual conceptions of the truth that it was easier for me to find the true way and to progress towards God's Love and the celestial heavens than it was for him. This he has told me, and I have listened to him with much interest, and have learned that the way of the narrow and bigoted orthodox believer is a harder road to travel than that of the agnostic who in his soul has not been too defiled by sin and evil.

I am still progressing and praying and believing, and receiving the inflowing of this wonderful Love. Oh, I tell you that this Love is the greatest thing in all the spirit world, as well as on earth, and the only thing that brings the soul of man in close union and harmony with God.

I will not write more now. So, my dear friend, with my love and gratitude, I will say good night.

Your brother in Christ,
Robert G. Ingersoll

EMANUEL SWEDENBORG (1688 - 1772)

Swedenborg does not want Mr. Padgett
to be a failure in his work for the kingdom as he was
December 23, 1917

I am here, Swedenborg.

I desire to impress upon you the necessity and importance of striving to follow the advice therein given, for if you fail now to do the work upon which you have entered, your regrets when you come to the spirit world will be so great that you will find it almost impossible to get rid of them even if you progress to the soul spheres where the Love is so abundant.

I know what I write for that was my experience and it seemed to me that everywhere I turned as I sought to progress I saw before me the word failure and for many long years it was my ghost of a recollection. Failure, as you may know, is relative, and men may fail in their ambitions and desires for fame and wealth and position, and yet when they come to the spirit world they realize that such failures mean comparatively little in their progress in the truth, and they soon forget their failures and cast them behind. Now when a mortal has conferred upon him a work which does not have for its object the accumulation of wealth or the attaining of fame or position, but the great and vital object of showing men the way by which they can become reconciled to God, and also given to him the privilege of receiving the great truths of God in relation to the salvation of men, then I say that failure means a great catastrophe for him and a greater calamity for humanity, and that man is in a condition of mind and recollection beyond description.

Very few men have had conferred upon them this great privilege and power and responsibility, and I was one of them and was a failure not because I did not try to receive and deliver the truth, but because I prevented, by my preconceived ideas of what the truth should be, the real and pure truth from coming to me and hence to humanity. In a way I was unconscious of my failure or of the existence of conditions in me that caused the failure; yet when I came to the spirit world and realized the failure that I had made, then everything was a failure to my conscience.

In your case, you have no such preconceived ideas to hamper you or prevent you from receiving the truth, for you are used merely as an instrument for these truths to transcribe and they are delivered in the very language of the writers, and your failure if there shall be such, will be entirely due to your indifference or want of effort to get in condition that will enable the messages to be written.

You must see your responsibility and your duty, and I may say your love, that should urge you to work and you must not be a failure. I am your friend and brother and co-worker in making known these truths and write only because as a failure, I can speak from experience. So, my brother, turn your thought more to this work, and if necessary sacrifice every worldly consideration to carry forward your work and make perfect your efforts to fulfill the great mission with which you have been blessed.

I will not write more now. May God bless you with His Love.

Your brother in Christ,
Swedenborg

Swedenborg writes on the hells of the spirit world
December 17, 1915

Let me write a few lines as I desire to write you some truths about what you and your friend were discussing, namely, are there any such hells as are described in the messages contained in Dr. Peeble's book, *Immortality*, that you have been reading tonight.

Well, you must know, that in the spirit planes hell is a place as well as a condition, and that as a place it has all the accompaniments that make it a reality to the spirits who inhabit it. Of course, the conditions of the spirits who are in these hells are determined by their recollections worked upon by their consciences. But notwithstanding that these recollections are the things that cause their sufferings, yet the appearances of the locations in which they live are due to something more than these mere recollections, for, as you have been informed, all these spirits are in darkness and the degree of the darkness in which they live is determined by their recollections. I mean that when the spirit has recollections of deeds done or not done, which are not as bad as the recollections of another, the former spirit is in a place where there is less darkness than the latter.

These places have their own fixed condition of darkness and of gloom, and many other attachments which increases the sufferings that spirits have to endure. There are, of course, no fires and brimstone lakes, and devils with pitchforks adding to the sufferings of spirits, but yet, there are certain conditions and appearances which are outside of the spirits themselves, which causes their recollections to become more acute and to work in a manner to produce a greater degree of suffering.

These hells may be places of caverns and rocks and barren wastes and dark holes and other such things as have been written about; and mortals must know that evil spirits do not live in pleasant places and suffer only from the punishments which their recollections bring to them. While the hells of the orthodox are in their descriptions greatly exaggerated, yet there is some truth in the ideas which these descriptions convey as to the fact that the hells are places in which there is darkness and many accompanying appearances that add to the tortures of the spirits of evil. I tell you this because I see you want to know the truth, and for the further reason that you do not believe that there are such distinctive places as the hells, and that the darkness which the spirits in their communications speak to you of are, in your opinion, produced by the conditions of the minds and souls of the spirits who write. But such opinion is not altogether correct, and it is best for men to know that the mere recollections do not include all of what the hells are.

You say you have your hells on earth sometimes, and that is true to a limited extent, and many men suffer very much from their conscience and remorse. When they come into the spirit world, if they have not gotten out of the condition which these recollections and remorse place them in, they will find that there is waiting for them that place or location which will add to their sufferings that arise from the recollections of evil deeds committed while on earth.

These evil spirits live in communities, for the law of attraction operates in these dark and lower planes just as it does in the higher spheres, and causes spirits of like or similar conditions to congregate together and find consolation, or what they may think at times to be consolation, in one another's company. These hells are in the planes that are the nearest to the earth, and these spirits are not confined all the time to any particular hell. They have the privilege of moving at will along this plane, but wherever they go they find that they are in hell, and they cannot escape, unless they accept the help from spirits who can instruct them in what they must do.

Well, when they come to you to write they are not very far from these hells, because the plane in which they live is not far from the plane in which the inhabitants of earth live. Of course, I don't mean to say that that portion of the earth plane that surrounds your earth is composed entirely of darkness, for that is not true, as the earth plane has in it some light and happiness. These spirits, while their habitations are in these hells, have the privilege of leaving these particular localities and wandering in and over parts of the earth plane, but this is only for a short time, for they have to return to the places where they have been placed, and which this law of attraction that I speak of draws them to.

Well, there are thousands of millions of evil spirits, and there is never a time when some of them, thousands of them, are not surrounding and trying to use their evil influences on mortals. We do not know why this is permitted, but only know that it is so. And here again the law of attraction operates, for many mortals are in similar condition of development and of evil thoughts as are these evil spirits, and naturally, these evil spirits are drawn to them and do come to them. Frequently it happens, that while visiting these mortals of similar conditions to their own, they attempt to influence mortals who are in a better state of moral and spiritual condition, and sometime succeed in doing them harm.

Nevertheless, the great fact is that these evil spirits have a place of living where they have to remain until, by the operation of the law of compensation, they are relieved from some of their evil tendencies and desires, and then they are permitted to progress. My principal reason in writing you is to have you know that there are hells of places as well as of conditions, and that these places, by reason of what they contain and their appearances, add to the suffering of the spirits.

As I have written a long time I will stop, and say that I am a Christian and an inhabitant of the celestial spheres, and one of the spirit band that is helping you in your great work of the Master.

So, in leaving you, I will subscribe myself,

Your brother in Christ,
Swedenborg, the seer

MARTIN LUTHER (1483 - 1546)

Luther comments on the Swedenborgian
pamphlet entitled "Incarnate God"
February 28, 1917

I am here, Luther.

I merely desire to say that as you read the pamphlet I read with you, and the description and explanation therein contained as to who God is, is entirely erroneous and blasphemous.

Jesus never claimed or taught, while on earth, that he was God, and this I say because he has so instructed us, and he never since becoming a spirit has made any such claim. The teachings of the new church in this particular are all wrong and tend to lead men away from the true conception of who God and Jesus both are.

Swedenborg has often conversed with me about his teachings and declared that his explanations as to God are not in accord with the knowledge that he now has. The teachings as contained in his books upon this subject were the results very largely of his own speculations, and the results of his endeavors in trying to reconcile what he thought was an absurd conception of the nature and Being of God with the true interpretation of the Bible. He could not accept the doctrine of the trinity, as explained and accepted and taught by the church, and hence, being a believer in the inspiration of the Bible and its infallibility of religious truths, he sought some exegesis that might be consistent with the Bible, and at the same time in consonance with his ideas of reason and common sense. But, as he now says, he added mysticism to mysticism, and irrational explanations to irrational explanations, and the result was that his teachings were more absurd and more difficult to understand than were the teachings of his Christian Church.

170

The doctrine of the trinity, as you have been told, is not true, and never had any authority in the teachings of Jesus or those of the apostles and Bible writers. It was merely the deduction of some of the fathers of the old church, arising from their speculations and desire to make of Jesus a God, though a lesser God than the Father, but at the same time one with the Father and a part of the Godhead that must be considered as being the only God, as taught by the Old Testament writers and prophets.

This doctrine, of course, was absurd and, hence, was one of the mysteries of God, but, nevertheless was taught as a truth and incumbent upon man to believe whether they could understand it or not, which of course, they could not. The doctrine was not accepted by all the writers of the early days, for as you know, there were bitter controversies among these expounders over what they supposed to be the scriptures, and upon the question as to who Jesus was, and his relation to God. As the years went by the doctrine of the trinity became firmly established as a canon of belief in the church, and in my time on earth it was believed, and not questioned by the church. I believed it also, although I could not understand it.

Now, Swedenborg was a member of the church that bore my name and which I was credited with having founded, and believed in its doctrines, even as to the trinity, and the actual transformation of the wine and bread into the blood and body of Jesus. He continued in this belief up to the time of his wonderful visions of the spirit world and his experience in meeting the spirits and angels of that world, including Jesus, whom in his writings he claimed to be God, and with whom he had many conversations and from whom he learned the spiritual truths that he declared to the world.

As you have been told, in the working out of the plans of the celestial angels, under the leadership of Jesus, Swedenborg was selected as the instrumentality through whom the spiritual truths should be revealed to humanity. In carrying out that plan, power was given to him to come in his spirit perceptions or his inner sight, as he calls it, into the spirit world and there see the conditions of spirits and angels, and also of their environments, and learn the higher truths from conversations with spirits and angels. Swedenborg did come in the manner indicated and communed as he has claimed, except that he never talked with God, only with Jesus, who he misconceived to be God. This cannot be wondered at, for Jesus was a spirit, so transcendent in glory and love and wisdom, that it was almost natural, as I may say, that the mortal in his new and unusual experience should conceive this glorious Jesus to be God Himself. But it was not God, only Jesus, that this seer saw and listened to.

With Swedenborg having a conception of this kind, you can readily see that when he came into his mortal self again, and many times this occurred, he firmly believed that Jesus, who had form and individuality in the spirit world similar to what he had when on earth, was actually God, and it therefore became easy for Swedenborg to reject the doctrine of the trinity, and in its place proclaim Jesus is God, manifested in the flesh, and God is Jesus, the "divine" man.

Of course, you must understand that in the exercise of this seership, he experienced the doubts and fears that at times what he saw and heard might not be things of actuality, and that possibly his imagination, or as in these latter days what is called the subconscious mind, was deceiving him. Now being a man of extraordinary mentality and of strong convictions, as well as having established faith in the doctrines of the church to which he belonged, many of his interpretations of what he saw and heard, and his teachings therefrom, were limited and flavored by his existing mental condition and faith. He has told me that for many years before his experience as seer, he had to a more or less extent doubted the truth of the trinity and accepted it only as a mystery, because the church declared it to be a truth, and that after his experiences as seer, believing in the statements of the Bible as the infallible words of God, and also believing that he had seen God in the person of Jesus, he sought an explanation of these Bible statements and a reconciliation of them with his belief that Jesus was God, and the result was his declared doctrine that Jesus is God.

So in many other of his teachings, based upon his experience in the spirit world, he embraced many errors and misconceptions of the truths, and to such an extent that, as you have been told, his mission, in its results, was a failure, and the truths that he had been selected to learn and declare to the world were never made known to humanity. This failure was disappointing to the spirits who conceived this plan and in whom were lodged the spiritual truths of God, and who were acting as God's instruments in their endeavor to make them known to humanity.

Swedenborg says that he has one consolation, and that is many who have founded churches and attempted to declare spiritual truths upon which doctrines and creeds have been promulgated and believed in, and that is that his followers are so comparatively few in numbers, and consequently, so many less mortals are being deceived by his teachings. I can appreciate the consolation that he may have in this fact, for my teachings and beliefs that are false as his are false, are believed in and followed by a very large number of mortals, to their injury.

Well, I am glad for the opportunity to write you tonight, and I am still waiting for the chance to finish my message to my people on the errors of continuing in my teachings, and the necessity for them to become undeceived, and learn the truths that are now being declared to humanity.

I will not write further. So good night.

Your brother in Christ,
Luther

Luther describes the relationship that existed
in his day between the laymen and the church officials
May 23, 1916

I am here, Luther.

I came tonight in the hope that I may write my message of which I spoke to you a short time ago. Well, if you feel that you can receive the same, I will proceed.

In my day, the members of the church — I mean the Roman Catholic Church — were dependent entirely upon the priesthood for all information as to the contents of the Bible and the interpretation that should be given such contents. Very few of the laymen were able to possess the Bible, and scarcely could any read it, as it was written in the Latin tongue and the inhabitants of my section of Europe were not acquainted with that language. The consequence of this was that all the people were dependent entirely on the priests for any knowledge of the will of God, and only as the priests saw proper to convey the same to these people.

Many things were taught by these officials of the church in such a way as to convince the people that the church was the divine institution of God, and that in every particular as to the conduct of men, what the priests said and declared to be the will of God must be accepted without doubt or hesitation. The penalties of disobedience of these teachings of the priests would be in the form that they should prescribe, and that the wrath of God would fall upon all who should disobey these teachings of the church.

The spiritual enlightenment of men was not attempted to any degree, and the requirements of the church were that men should strictly obey the dogmas and tenets that should be declared to them by these instructions of the priests. Duty was the principal thing to be observed, and the utmost obedience to the commands of the church must be performed, unless the church itself should release the people from the performance of these duties.

Every violation of these commands was a sin, to which a penalty was attached which could not be avoided unless the priests should give to the believers an indulgence, and then to the extent of the indulgence the penalty was taken away. In order to obtain this indulgence a compensation would have to be made to the coffers of the church, depending upon the ability of the one receiving such indulgence to make. At the time when these indulgences were most prevalent, and when the church was becoming rich from the revenues paid for the same, I commenced to revolt from the claims of the church and declared my want of belief in the dogma that the church could grant such indulgences and absolve men from the penalties which their sins brought upon them.

You all know the history of the Reformation and its results upon the power of the Church of Rome, and how men were freed from the superstitions of the church and how the reform grew in many of the Catholic countries, and new churches and beliefs were established.

As men of thought became convinced of the false claims and superstitions of the church and of the necessity of making known to humanity the truths of the Bible, I and several others, in our zeal, refused to recognize and accept as a part of the teachings of the reform belief in many things which were contained in the churches' dogmas or teachings that were really true, or in a manner true, when relieved of their appendages which the church had attached to the kernels of truth. As a consequence, we rejected many principles that we should have made part of the beliefs and teachings of the new beliefs.

Well, I will not further recite any of these things, but merely say that what I have written is intended to be only preliminary to what the object of my writing is. I am sorry that you do not feel in condition to receive more at this time, and it is best to postpone the remainder. I will soon come and finish what I desire to write.

So, with my love and best wishes,

Your brother in Christ,
Luther

*Luther is very anxious that the truths
that he now knows be made known to his followers*
May 29, 1916

I am here, Martin Luther, the onetime monk and reformer.

I desire to continue my message, if it is agreeable to you. When on earth I firmly believed what was contained in our doctrines and teachings, and was sincere in trying to induce others to believe as I believed and taught, but after my long experience in the spirit world and my communications with Jesus and his apostles and others to whom the truths of God have come, I realize and know that many of my teachings were erroneous and should no longer be believed by those who worship in the churches that bear my name.

My doctrine of faith, that is, justification by faith, is all wrong when its foundation is considered, and it is impossible to understand from my teachings and the churches' tenets, just what is intended by faith. Our faith was founded on the assumption that Jesus was a part of the Godhead and the only begotten Son of the Father, who so loved sinful man that He caused His sinless and beloved Son to die on the cross so that divine justice might be appeased, and the burden of men's sins taken from them and placed on Jesus. Oh, the terrible error of it all, and how it has misled so many of the believers into a condition of darkness and deprivation of the Divine Love of God. No, such objects of faith have no foundation in fact, and such a faith does not justify sinful man or bring him in at-onement with God, so that he becomes a redeemed child of God.

Jesus was not a part of the Godhead, and neither was he begotten in the way that I taught and my followers believe. He was the son of man, and only the Son of God by reason of the fact that he had received in his soul the Divine Love, which made him like God in many of His attributes of divinity.

God did not send Jesus to earth for the purpose of dying on the cross or for the purpose of paying any debt or appeasing the wrath of his angry and jealous Father, for these qualities are not His attributes. Love and sympathy and the desire that men turn from their sins and become reconciled to Him, are His attributes as affects the salvation of men. No death of Jesus could make any man the less a sinner or draw him any nearer to God, and faith in this erroneous proposition, is faith in an error and never has man been justified by it.

Jesus came to earth with a mission to save humanity from their sins and that mission was to be performed in two ways only: one by declaring to man that God had rebestowed upon him the privilege of receiving the Divine Love, and the other by showing man the way in which the privilege might be exercised, so that this Divine Love would become his, and thereby make him a part of God's divinity and insure him of immortality. In no other way could or can men be saved and made at-one with God; and faith in these truths, which makes them things of possession and ownership by men, is the only faith which is justified.

I write this for the benefit, more particularly, of my followers so that they may learn the vital truths of their salvation and change their faith in the death and blood sacrifice of Jesus, to faith in the rebestowal of the Divine Love, and in the further truth that Jesus was sent to show the way to that Love, and that he thereby and in no other manner became the way, the truth and the life.

I know that the acceptance of these truths will take from them the very foundation of their beliefs, and many will refuse to accept my new declarations of truth, but nevertheless, they must accept, for truth is truth and never changes. Those who refuse to accept it on earth will, when they come to the spirit world, have to accept it, or exist in a condition where they will see and know that their old beliefs were false and rested on no solid foundation. The danger to many will be that when they realize the utter falsity and non-existence of what they believed to be true, they will become infidels or wanderers in the spirit life, without the hope of salvation or of becoming redeemed children of God.

I fully realize the errors of my teachings on earth, and the responsibility that rests upon me for these teachings which are still being spread, and I am almost helpless to remedy them. So, I write this message, hoping that it may be published in your book of truths.

I, Luther, the onetime monk and reformer, declare these truths with all the emphasis of my soul, based on knowledge in which there is no shadow of error, and which I have acquired from experience not founded on the claimed "revelations" to man by the voice of God. My knowledge is true, and nothing in opposition can be true, and the beliefs and faith of a man or of all the inhabitants of earth cannot change the truth in one iota.

The Roman Church taught the communion of saints, and I declare the communion of spirits and mortals, be they saints or sinners. The church taught the doctrine of purgatory and hell, and I declare that there is a hell and a purgatory and that probation exists in both places, and that sometime in the long ages to come, both places will be emptied of their inhabitants, some of whom will become redeemed children of God and dwellers in the celestial heavens, and others will become purified in their natural love and become inhabitants of the spiritual spheres.

I pray and desire that my followers may become inhabitants of the celestial heavens and partake of the Divine Nature of God and His immortality. To them I say, harken to the truths as Jesus has and will reveal them in his messages to you, for in the truths which he shall thus declare they will find life eternal and the at-onement with God for which they have for so many years been seeking in darkness and disappointment.

I will not write more tonight, but will come again soon and reveal other vital truths, if you will find for me the opportunity. So with my love and blessings,

Your brother in Christ,
Martin Luther

Luther has met the two Popes responsible for his trials,
and they have not progressed very far in the spirit world
August 28, 1916

I am here, Luther.

I will not write much at this time although I am anxious to continue my letter to my followers, and as soon as you are in condition I will come and hope that you will give me the opportunity. Well of course, I will have to wait until the others have delivered their messages, but I have no doubt that there will be times when you will not be occupied by receiving their messages and will come.

I have met both the Popes who were in the papal chair at the time that I went to Rome and when I was afterward persecuted and brought to trial before them. They are not in the celestial heavens but in the first sphere where they were in great darkness and suffering intensely, and their repentance was very thorough and sincere. They were compelled to realize the great evil that the teachings and dogma of their church was doing to humankind and they devoted all their time in the spirit life attempting to influence the priests and hierarchy of the great errors that they were teaching, but the result of their work was not very satisfactory for reasons that I have not time to explain now.

The state of the ignorant Catholic layman is a very deplorable one when he comes to the spirit world, but that of the pope and the priest is beyond all description. They are forever branded by the results upon their followers of their evil teaching and consequently suffer very much. Sometime I will come to you and write in detail into the conditions and causes of these blind teachers of the blind. I must not write more tonight.

With my love, I will say good night.

Your brother in Christ,
Luther

The observance of the ceremonies which my church
still uses in its worship is not approved by God or Jesus
June 29, 1916

I am here, Luther.

I desire to write a short message tonight and will not detain you very long and will try to express myself as succinctly as possible.

Well, as you may not know, the church of which I am the founder believes and teaches the necessity of infant baptism and the observance of the Lord's Supper as necessary parts of its church doctrine, and of such very great importance that without them it is difficult to become an accepted member of the invisible church of Christ.

Nothing is further from the truth than these doctrines for the baptism of infants, for they have no virtue to save one from his sins or to make him in at-onement with God, and the mere fact that water is sprinkled on an infant's head and some blessing pronounced by the preacher does not in any way bring that infant in unison with God. Baptism is of man's creation and to God it means nothing more than an outward ceremony that affects the infant merely as regards its connection with the established earthly church. It is not possible for this baptism to have any effect upon the soul of the infant and neither does it open up the soul faculties to the inflowing of the Divine Love.

God cares not for these ceremonies, and rather looks upon them with disapproval, for their tendency is to make men and women neglectful of the great truth that will bring them in harmony with God's laws of Love and redemption. The same thing may be said of any and all kinds of baptism, whether the subject thereof be an infant or a grown man or woman. As to the sacrament of the Lord's Supper, it has no part in God's plan for the redemption of humanity and it is merely a reminder of the association of Jesus with his disciples. It cannot affect the condition or development of the soul, and as now understood and practiced this sacrament is of no importance, for Jesus does not want to be remembered in the way of recalling to him the tragedy on the cross which was only the result of the malice and envy of the Jews; and the blood spilt is not an element that enters into the plan of the salvation of men. Besides with this sacrament there is always more or less worshipping of Jesus as God, which he, Jesus, abhors and looks upon as blasphemy.

So you see, the celebration of the last supper is a thing which is not acceptable to God or to Jesus. He does not want men to believe that they can be saved by any sacrifice of him or by any blood which he may have shed as a result of his crucifixion. You will remember that the question of what the wine and bread of the sacrament really were, was one that engendered much controversy, and even hatred and ill feeling on the part of those who were assisting me in the great Reformation. If I had known then what I do now, no such question would have been debated or believed in by me and taught for many years. The blood of Jesus was no more than any other man's blood, and the commemoration of the last supper that Jesus gave his disciples before his death, is a useless ceremony and brings no help to those who indulge in this sacrament.

I see that you are tired and sleepy and I will not write more now. So with my love and wishes for an increase of the Divine Love in you,

Your brother in Christ,
Luther

*Luther denies the efficacy of the eucharist, it is Jesus's living
and teaching and demonstrating the Divine Love in his soul, and how
it can be obtained, that shows the way to salvation*
January 31, 1917

I am here, Luther.

I have come merely to remind you that I am waiting to continue my discourse to my people. I am very anxious to do this, and as soon as you get in condition I hope that you will give me the opportunity.

Well, you have asked me a question that I should like to have more time in which to answer than I have now. But in short, Jesus was not of the substance of God in the sense that the Catholic Church, following the Nicene Creed, claimed. He took on a part of the Divine Substance as the Divine Love filled his soul, and so can you or any other man to the extent that you may receive this Love. But to say that Jesus was in his very being of the Substance of God to that degree that made him equal

180

to God, is erroneous, and should not be taught or believed in.

He was born or created in the likeness of God in the way that will be explained to you and in no other. He was a man and not God, or any part of Him, and if he had not received into his soul the Divine Love, he would never have been of the Substance of God. He was a being of a very spiritual nature, and in fact so much so that he was without sin. This Love commenced to come into his soul very early, as you may say, from his very birth, and at the time of his anointing he was so filled with it that you may say he was of the Substance of God in the quality that that Substance possessed the Nature of the Divine. He was no more divine, though, naturally, as I may say, than was any other mortal born of the flesh. I should like to write you a long message on this subject, and will sometime, when convenient.

Well, all the speculation that has ever existed as to the eucharist and the change in the qualities of the bread and wine, are untrue. Jesus is not in these elements in any particular or view that may be taken. His flesh and blood went the way of all other flesh and blood of mortals, and no more forms a part of the bread and wine than does your flesh and blood.

This sacrament, as it is called, is very abhorrent to the Master, and when it is celebrated, I must tell you, he is not present, not only not in flesh and blood but also not in his spiritual presence. He dislikes any kind of worship which places him as its object in the position of God or as the Son of God who paid a great debt by his sacrifice and death. He wants God alone to be worshiped, and himself to be thought of as the one who brought immortality to light by his teachings and the living demonstration of the truth of the existence of the Divine Love in himself.

He does not approve of the teachings of men that his death and his blood were the means of man being saved from their sins and becoming reconciled to God. He says that it was his living and teachings and demonstration of the Love of God existing in his own soul that showed the true way to salvation.

I must not write more now. So with my love I will say good night.

Your brother in Christ,
Martin Luther

CHAPTER SEVEN

Philosophers

RENE DESCARTES (1596 - 1650)

*The French philosopher rejects the idea of Divine Love
and places his faith in reason and intellectual development*
November 20, 1916

I am here, Descartes.

Let me say a word. I will not attempt to intrude for a great while for I only want to say that you are not so very good as you may be led by these spirits to believe. I am not a wicked spirit but am an impartial observer of things, including the states of the souls of men, and when I say what I have said you must not think that I have any prejudice or desire to cause you to feel that you are any great sinner. I have heard what some of these spirits have written you and I see that they are flattering you and try to make you believe that you are a little god on earth, and as your friend I do not think it right that you should be so deceived.

Of course, you should become as good as possible and get all this Love that they tell you about, if there is any such thing. It may have the effect upon your soul that they tell you it will, and at the same time I have my doubts about the matter and would advise you to give more attention to gaining knowledge that is open before you in your earth life and when you come over, you will find that in our spirit world there is no more desirable thing as knowledge and intellectual development. Why, I should have great regrets if I had neglected to cultivate my mind and acquire knowledge when on earth, for it has kept me from listening to these sentimental spirits who try to talk to me at times about the development of the soul with Love — a word that means nothing to anyone except those who are like the silly maidens of earth or the lovesick swains who have never cut their eye-teeth.

No, my friend, do not listen to this silly and useless talk about soul development and Love, but learn from me and believe that the intellect is the only thing that a man as well as a spirit should attempt to acquire and to cultivate. Knowledge is power, and I realize that the knowledge that I possess has given me great power in this spirit life.

I associate only with spirits like myself and we have wonderful times of enjoyment in the exchange of our thoughts and bright ideas and in discussing subjects which only spirits like myself can discuss. You may rest assured that only the intellectual spirits attend our meetings and find enjoyment in our discussions. These love-speaking spirits who go about and tell us that love is everything and that mind is only secondary, do not attend our discussions, for of course, they could not understand what our talk is about nor comprehend the wonderful thoughts of a fully developed mind such as we possess.

So you will see that I am really interested in you and desire that you pursue that course in your earth life that will fit you for the highest development and the gradual enjoyment that can be experienced in our spirit world.

I have as associates many of the prominent philosophers and scientists who once were known on earth as the leaders of thought and the revealers of the great laws of nature, and they all think as I am writing you now. I trust that you will believe me to be your friend and that I write this in the utmost good faith and with the desire only to direct your efforts in the way that will lead to your greatest good when you come to the spirit life.

Well, we are all in a sphere where there is some darkness and also in some light, and we understand the reason for living in the darkness. We have not yet made that development in our intellectual qualities that fit us for the planes of great light because as you know the greatest knowledge that we could acquire on earth is not equal to the least knowledge that is required to fit us for the planes where only light exists. It is for this reason we have the appearance of darkness, and as we obtain a greater mental development that darkness of appearance leaves us and we then progress to the light spheres. This, as you will understand, is only natural and the result of a law that we recognize as working exactly and unchangeably as the other laws of nature work.

I have been in spirit life a great many years and have been working as hard and with more enthusiasm than I did on earth to acquire knowledge and understand the laws of nature and I am satisfied with my progress, although, I shall not cease to progress as I know, for I will never give up my efforts to acquire more and more knowledge.

I must stop now for there comes a spirit to me who is a very bright one. I must stop and I cannot refuse to do so. As I leave I will say that I thank you for your kindness and hope that you will believe that I am sincere in advising you as to what I think is for your own good.

So my friend, good night. Your brother in search for the truth,

I was known as the French philosopher and scientist,
Descartes

BARUCH SPINOZA (1632 - 1677)

The celebrated philosopher discourses on reason,
and states that reason is not a reliable guide to truth
January 5, 1919

I am here, Spinoza.

I desire to write a few lines, if you will permit. I need not say that I have never written you before, for you will know from the difficulty that I have in writing that such must be the case. I am a stranger to this method of communication, and to you, and to me it has come in very recent days as a wonderful revelation.

I do not intend to write upon a subject of any great truth connected with our spirit life, but merely to introduce myself, in the hope that when I am better acquainted with the laws governing this method, that I may be permitted to come to you and write of those things which I have learned since becoming a spirit, and which would have been very desirable and very important to have learned when on earth.

I was, when on earth, a philosopher, so-called, and gave many years of my life to the search for truth relating not only to the natural world, but also to what I conceived to be the truth connected with that world or existence outside of and beyond the world of the physical senses. In my research I was guilty of many speculations which I now see have no foundation upon which I had built many conclusions and postulates. I had only the intellect, supplied in its workings by the knowledge that came from the phenomena of the purely physical and, as I thought, by that great faculty called reason, which, as a fact, is a wonderful faculty. Although in its exercise reason is dependent upon, first, its own development, and next, whether that development has been along the lines of and in accord with truth.

Reason is not a guide that can be depended on, for reasoning in an erroneous way must necessarily lead to conclusions of error, and merely calling or believing that these conclusions are the results of reason does not justify the belief that the conclusions must be correct and veracious. Reason can be mistaken and featured by error, just as can the senses; and, hence, if you read the writings of the philosophers and meta-physicians, and also the scientists, you will find that things declared and accepted by these men in one age have been repudiated and rejected by the successors of these men in later ages.

So, when I wrote, and I wrote considerably, I was very largely read by what was considered to be the thinking class of men, and especially those whose research led them along a similar line of study and subject matter as my own, I declared certain doctrines or principles connected with these metaphysical and philosophical matters that I now know to be wholly erroneous, which at the time I firmly believed to be things of verity. This was largely because they were based on what I thought was the true workings of reason, together with some little empirical knowl-edge.

Now from this I do not mean to decry the value and importance of the faculty of reason, for it has been the great factor operating for the progress of humankind, but like other finite faculties it is subject to erro-neous exercise and cannot be depended on as a thing infallible. The common experience of men has shown that men who have sincerely and earnestly and constantly exercised their reasoning faculties have arrived at different and contradictory conclusions as to the same principles or subject matter, and those conclusions have been entirely satisfactory and convincing to the respective persons. Now it is apparent that in such instances all of these men could not possibly be correct in their conclu-sions, and in many cases not any of them were correct, yet they were all founded on reason, properly and intelligently exercised, as they sup-posed.

No, reason is fallible, and it is not a thing of itself, but dependent upon environments and sometimes inherited or preconceived ideas of what truth must be. It is the great friend and defender of speculation, and without it speculation could not exist, and so often speculation is deceived by its friend. Truth is that which exists as an unchangeable condition or fact, and speculation can neither create nor destroy truth. Reason is a means which may be used to reach truth when knowledge does not exist. The fact that reason exists does not mean that it is always used in the way that leads to the discovery of truth. Reason, as I am now justified in saying, is merely a creation of God, just as is everything else in His universe, and when given to man with the freedom of exercising it as man wills, it is subject to all the possibilities of defective exercise that every other faculty possessed by man is subject to, and is no more infallible in its nature than are these other faculties.

Reason is the greatest faculty that man has as a creature of the Almighty, and without it, some of the wise men of earth have said man would be no better than or different from the brute animal. But this is not quite true, for man is possessed with that which is really man himself that the brute animal does not have, and that is a soul made in the image of its Creator. It may be said that reason is merely an appendage of the soul, and I have justification in asserting that the soul in its progress can do without or cast aside this reason without doing harm to itself. This is because I have learned in progressing in the spirit life that the soul may and does arrive at that degree of development where reason is not necessary or even used by it in its acquirement of truth.

I now believe, and without speculation, that reason is a gift to man to be useful to him only in his earth life and in a portion of this spirit life, until the soul comes into a knowledge of truth by the exercise of the mere desire to know. A knowledge of the whys and wherefores is not required, yet it knows because it knows, just as in your earth life you have a knowledge of the sunlight even if you do not know the why and the wherefore that produce that light.

Well, my newfound friend, I have written more than I intended, because as I continued I found the desire to write increase, and I fear that I have trespassed too long and ask your forgiveness. Sometime I should like to come and write of the errors of some of the teachings of earth, or rather of the truths along the line of the subject matter of my earthly writings, as I now know them to be.

I am in what is called the intellectual planes of the fourth sphere and very near the entrance to the sixth sphere, in which I hope to be in a short time. It has been a long time since I left the earth life, and the early period of my existence in the spirit world was one of stagnation, and, as I now see, merely because I brought with me many of the doctrines of the philosophy of my earth life, and as a consequence I continued my research along the ideas and ways that I had pursued as a mortal. The time thus spent was long and continued until I became convinced that speculation in the spirit life is not very different and arrives at no more satisfactory end than speculation on earth, and then I stopped speculating and waited for something, I know not what.

Strange to say, that which came to me was from a spirit who had never heard of my philosophy or any other philosophy on earth, but merely accepted truth as it gradually came to him, without knowing why or how. I soon learned that he had a greater knowledge of the verities than had I, and so I adopted his way of receiving truth, and since then I have been progressing and am now advancing with accelerated speed, all to my happiness and intellectual enjoyment. Good-bye.

Your friend,
Spinoza

Spinoza writes about the ability of mediums to predict a person's future
January 5, 1919

I am here, Spinoza.

Let me write a few lines as I have not written you for some time, and am quite anxious to give some thoughts that may be of benefit to you. I am not one of the spirits who write to you of what they call the higher truths, yet I have a knowledge of some of these truths and believe in all that has been communicated to you. I know that the spirits who write you are of the celestial spheres, possessed of knowledge that we who live in the spirit spheres do not possess.

Well, I merely want to say a few words in reference to the predictions which you heard tonight, and as regards the source of the same. As you know, the woman is a medium gifted with the power of clairvoyance and inspirational receptivity, and on many occasions she perceives and receives some of the truths of the spirit world, and from some of the persons whom she professes to see. Her communicants, though, are not of a very high order, and she, herself, could not see the highly developed spirits, because the law of rapport and communication applies to her phases of mediumship just as it does to yours. She is a very good woman morally, although with some temperamental defects, but she attracts spirits of moral worth and conditions, and her guides are in the condition that enables them to live in the brighter spheres, yet not having that much spiritual development.

She professes to declare the predictions of her spirit friend, as to what the future holds for the ensuing year and what will be the experience of men and nations. Well, she has such a control*, and he is a very intelligent spirit, and to some extent inspires her with his ideas of what the future holds for humankind, and she with more or less exactness declares his thoughts as they are impressed upon her mind. But in connection with these thoughts she incorporates thoughts of her own, believing that they are inspired also, but such is not the fact, though, possibly, these thoughts furnish as good grounds for the predictions as do the thoughts of her control.

I do not believe, at least I have never had it demonstrated to me, that any spirit can make truthful predictions, such as the medium expressed tonight. Spirits have not the powers of omniscience and are as dependent upon the workings of the law of cause and effect as are mortals, with this exception, that spirits can perceive many existing causes that mortals cannot, and hence, because of this knowledge, can make predictions from these effects of future happening, that mortals cannot make.

As you heard, she declared many things that are problems now existing and the subjects of much thought and study on the part of mortals who give their attention to these matters, and she, as one of them, had her own thoughts and had formed her own conclusions and believed that they were the results of inspiration, whereas they had their foundation in her own mind, arising from her knowledge of and speculations on these things.

The present conditions of the world are such that there exists the probabilities of the happening of many things that the medium predicted. Many persons having knowledge of these conditions will predict, if they be called upon, future occurrences similar to those mentioned by the medium. Well, such meetings and such predictions will not do any harm, but, on the contrary, will cause many people to turn their thoughts to spiritual things and to Spiritualism, which will tend to liberate their minds from the shackles that are now preventing them from seeking and understanding the truth.

I will not consume more of your time now, but hope to be able to write later. Good-bye.

Your friend,
Spinoza

*A spirit who controls other communicating spirits.

GOTTFRIED WILHELM LEIBNIZ (1646 - 1716)

*A German philosopher, now in the second sphere, writes on
immortality and the uncertainty of obtaining it even in the spirit world*
June 4, 1917

I am here, Gottfried Leibniz.

Let me write a few lines. I am not an acquaintance of yours, yet I am
not a stranger so far as my being in your presence and observing the different spirits who communicate with you.

I have been in spirit life a great many years and have been through
the hells and purgatory and all kinds of suffering and am now in the
light and comparatively happy. I am in a sphere where there are many
bright and intellectual spirits, working out their own plans for accomplishing certain of their ideas and progressing to higher planes.

I was a professor on earth and gave much of my time to the study of
psychology and kindred subjects, and had many ideas of my own on
these questions. I was especially interested in the study or rather speculation, for I did not believe in the Bible or the teachings of the churches,
as to the future of man. My speculations led me to the conclusion that
physical death was not the end of man, for it seemed to me that if such
was the case, the object of the workings of the great laws of evolution
would be defeated by the ending of the existence of the greatest and
highest resultant of that evolution, namely man.

I was a student of comparative biology and believed without any
doubt and with the certainty of knowledge that man was the greatest
product of this great principle of evolution and that for centuries upon
centuries it had been working to bring or develop man from the mere
molecule to the high degree of perfection displayed in his wonderful
mind and moral faculties, and that then, in a moment, to end it all by
this thing known as physical death, was unreasonable and unjustified,
and, hence, I concluded, as I say, that men must live after the death of
the body.

But when I got that far in my conclusions there came the question,
what was beyond, and here my speculations were not so satisfactory for

I had very little upon which to base any theories. Of course I thought that as man in the past had made such wonderful progress in his evolution, and as he would live in the future, it was reasonable to suppose that this evolution would continue and that man's progress would be without limitation or ending, provided he should continue to live forever. Thus arose the question of man's immortality, and here, I was stalled, for I had nothing with which to make a comparison. I knew that it was accepted as a truth in natural science that nothing could ever be destroyed or lost, and that the elements or atoms from which those physical things, perceptible to the senses, were composed should continue to exist forever. This was not satisfactory to me to base the fact that man would live forever. While these elements or atoms, themselves, could not be destroyed, yet many of those composite things into which these elements had entered and given form had been destroyed and as such the composite entity and form no longer had an existence.

I had seen the oak start from the acorn and grow to be a mighty tree and live for years and suddenly, by a stroke of lightning, be destroyed and ceased to live, and as such the tree went entirely out of existence. Hence, by analogy, I could not say that man as the identical individual would not go out of existence, and, in fact, I had seen him as regards his physical existence, cease to be an existence and his body disintegrate and go back to its elements. I could find nothing in all this to justify my asserting that man, in whatever form he might exist after his bodily death, would at some time in the future cease to have the form that made him the very individual that had lived on earth and continued his existence in the spirit world.

No, I could not in my speculations satisfy myself that man was immortal, and so I was compelled to stop my speculations. I was left without any assurance that my theory of the persistence of man after death was not one that might prove to be false.

When I died, and found that I, the conscious thinking man, continued to exist with all the faculties of mind and feelings that were mine when a mortal. In addition, I soon met those who had preceded me to the spirit world, and who had, since becoming spirits, advanced in their evolution, and were more perfect mentally and morally than they had been when on earth. They also informed me that beyond where they had evolved to were spheres in which spirits of greater intellectual development and ancient in years lived and worked and speculated upon the same question that I had given so much thought to when on earth, namely, is man immortal? They further informed me that these ancient worthies had not been able to solve the problem, and that many who had come to the spirit life thousands of years before were still living, and no spirit had ever been known to have passed out of existence or to have dissolved into the elements of which it was composed.

So you see, the spirits in the highest spheres with all their intellectual development and thousands of years of study, can no more assert with certainty that man is immortal than I could when on earth. To me now, as when on earth, this is the greatest question that arises and engages my continuous thoughts, and I see no way to solve the problem. I remember that when on earth the preachers and the churches claimed and taught the doctrine of immortality, and while I never deeply investigated the foundation of their claims, yet I cannot conceive that they can possess any more certainty of the supposed fact than did I. I can hardly believe that God ever revealed to man the fact of immortality, and in my opinion, in my present stage of development, only God knows, and, all the teachings of the churches and wise theologians are mere speculations, not to be relied on.

I know that there are many mortals who are working and speculating and attempting to find some basis for their hopes of immortality, and some believe that while they may not satisfy their hopes on earth, yet when they come to the spirit world the difficulties will be removed and their problem solved. To these I desire to make known the fact that they will look through just as dark glasses here as they are now looking through on earth.

Well, you surprise me and I can scarcely believe that you are serious, for I have never heard of such a way or of such a knowledge existing among spirits, and if you can show me that way I will, with all the energies of my soul, pursue it. You surprise me more and more, but I am willing to do as you say, no matter how absurd it may seem to me, or what little prospects I may see in making the pursuit. I will do as you say.

I see a beautiful spirit who says that he is Prof. Salyards, and has heard what I said and what you said, and that he will be pleased to show me the way to obtain both a knowledge and the actual possession of this immortality, and I shall accept this invitation and go with him.

I thank you very much for listening to me and for your expressions of desire to help me, and if what you promise comes true, you may rest assured that I will return sometime and tell you.

So my friend, I will say good night.

Your friend,
Gottfried Wilhelm Leibniz

GALILEO GALILEI (1564 - 1642)

Galileo writes of his studies of the material universe
January 21, 1916

I am the spirit of Galileo, and come to you to tell you a few things pertaining to the science of the spirit world.

When on earth, I thought that my invention of the telescope was a most wonderful thing and that it would revolutionize man's knowledge of astronomy and the solar system, and to some extent it did. But what I saw and anticipated then was as a mere drop in the bucket to what I have learned of these matters since I have been in the spirit world, not bound by the limitations of space and sight. I have explored these heavens, among the planets and the stars, and have discovered many truths in reference to them not even conceived of by men.

I desire to come sometimes and describe to you and explain to you these hidden truths so that man may have an enlarged conception of the great God whose creations they all are. It is too late tonight to commence my discourse, but with your permission I will come at a later date. I live in the sixth sphere, where the intellect rules supreme and the wisdom of the ages is congregated.

Yes, I have seen Jesus, and sometimes he comes to our sphere, but he is not so much interested in these scientific matters as in disseminating the knowledge of the Divine Love, as he calls it. I do not know what this is, and am not much interested, as I find great happiness in the pursuit of my studies of the material universe.

I will stop now and say good night,
Galileo

RALPH WALDO EMERSON (1803 - 1882)

Emerson does not believe in the Divine Love

I am here, Emerson.

For a long time I have observed the communications between you and the spirits, and have heard many of the messages in reference to what is claimed to be spiritual truths, and have had a great desire to write you and let you know something of what my ideas and knowledge of the spiritual world are.

Well, I must say that I do not believe in the Divine Love as some of the spirits describe it. I believe that all love is "divine", and that as the love which man — all men — possesses becomes purified it then attains to it perfection of divinity, and beyond that there can be no other or greater love, and it is of this and similar things that I desire to write.

I am in the sixth sphere and not in its highest plane. I am progressing all the time and enlarging my intellectual powers and acquiring knowledge, and at the same time am having my love purified. I am quite happy and in the association of wonderful spirits. I worship God and love Him, and also love all my spirit associates. This must be the only and true religion, but of all this I will write later.

Yes, I have met Swedenborg, and found him to be a wonderful spirit as he was a man on earth, but he and I do not live in the same sphere. He is a believer in that Divine Love and lives in a different sphere, and I seldom meet him.

I must stop now. So thanking you for this favor, I will say good night.

Your brother and friend,
Ralph Waldo Emerson

Emerson, an inhabitant of the sixth sphere, speaks of its purity
March 6, 1919

I am here, Emerson.

Let me write tonight on a subject that is of importance to humankind and one which so few mortals know or conceive of in their teachings and philosophy. I am one who inhabits the sixth sphere, where the pristine purity of the first man and woman exists, and where sin or the alienation from God has no existence.

You may not know, yet it is a fact, that the purity of this sphere is such that the souls of men will find only that which makes a man like unto God, and renders him happy and satisfied with his existence and with the attributes and nature with which he was created and which God in the infinitude of his powers decreed that man should possess and enjoy to the fullest of his capacity.

I am he whose book you have been reading tonight and who was attracted to you by the fact that you were interested in the book and sought the truths of the soul as therein set forth. The soul is one that while individualized, and in its aspirations and thoughts of those things that are pure and in harmony with the Oversoul*, has a satisfaction that is complete and at-one with the God of light and love.

This sphere is one where only the perfected soul can live and bloom and feel its qualities as perfect, and no soul that has not rid itself of sin can possibly enter. I only know that we who inhabit that sphere have the feeling of purity and perfection that was granted to our first parents and which by them was lost at the time of their disobedience.

The human soul is like the great soul of God and mortals of earth should realize that God has for man a higher and greater existence.

Well, I have lost my rapport and must stop.

Good night,
Emerson

*A Hindu term used to describe God's Soul.

FRANCIS BACON (1561 - 1626)

Francis Bacon on the continuity of life after death
May 26, 1919

Let me write a few lines tonight upon a subject that has recently been discussed by a Spiritualist, a preacher, a philosopher and a scientist, and that is the continuity of life after death of the physical body. Each of these writers approach the subject from a different viewpoint, although all arrive at the same conclusion based upon different means of argument, and that is, that life continues after death.

The subject is one in which humanity is vitally interested and is worthy of consideration by the greatest minds of investigation and research. It should be studied in the light of nature as well as in that of actual demonstration by the experiences of those who have by their experiences proved to humankind that the spirits of their departed friends and acquaintances and of others of more or less distinction when in the spirit life, do actually live and communicate to men their existence and the possession of the mental faculties and thoughts that were theirs when mortals.

The proper study of man would demonstrate this fact, and logically, doubt would cease to exist, however the difficulty is that men do not understand man or his creation, or his faculties and his relationship to things of life known as the material or matter. It is a common belief that matter that is now existent, or rather that what men see and know of the material, is all that is knowable. When that which is merely physical, as commonly understood, ceases to exist, no further or other knowledge of it can be obtained or understood by the finite mind of man. But this accepted assumption is not true, and if man would only think for a moment of what matter or the material is, they would comprehend the possibilities of its workings and functionings, and also, of what use may be made of the same by the minds of the spirits operating upon it in the spiritual world, that is, in the world beyond the comprehension of the five senses of man.

Matter is eternal, and exists in all the spheres of the spirit world just as it does on earth, although in different forms and attenuations, and in conditions that may or may not be the objects of the physical senses, or of the senses of the mind which are superior to or exclusive of these mere physical senses. Matter is, in its essential nature, the same, notwithstanding the fact that it assumes different forms — some visible to the ordinary senses of men and some entirely outside of that view or sensation, and, as to these senses, wholly nonexistent, yet to these other senses of the mind are just as real and tractable and subject to the influence of the workings of the mind as the merely physical matter is to the five senses of men.

The world in which men live is composed of the material, and the world in which I live is also composed of the material, of the same nature but of different consistencies and objective qualities. The material of the universe is always material, whether or not it be cognizable by man and subject to his thoughts and inventions and uses. As man progresses in the study of the same — I mean the practical and experimental — he will discover that there are things of the material in nature which to him are being developed and made known, and which a few years before he had no conception of their existence. Such is the discovery and use of electricity, and the workings of the laws of nature which enables him to make possible the effects of wireless telegraphy. These discoveries and workings of forces of the unseen are nothing more or less than a certain kind of knowledge controlling the same which as to his consciousness has become apparent. In all these operations, matter is the thing made use of and not any spiritual power as commonly understood by men. So you see matter, whether in the grossly physical of earth or in the more attenuated and invisible of the spirit world, is that which is used to produce effects and is operated on by the mind, whether or not it be tangible and understandable or not.

The mind is an entity indivisible and united, and is not separable into the subjective and objective as men frequently teach, except in this: that in its workings, that part of the mind which controls the brain in the ordinary affairs of life may be called the objective, and that part which is suited for and used in controlling the material after it has been transformed into the purely invisible may be called the subjective. It is all one mind and exists in man while on earth, just as it will and does when he becomes a spirit.

Man in his journey through life, and I mean when in the earth existence as well as in the eternal part of his existence, is always of the material, that is, his soul has a material covering and appearance, and while this material covering changes in its appearance and quality as he progresses in the spheres, yet the gross physical of his earth life and the sublimated spiritual of the eternal part of his life, are both of the material — real, existing and tangible — and used for the purpose of their creation, namely: the protection and individualizing of the soul which they contain.

Now this being so, you can readily understand that man, when he gives up the coarser physical of the human body, does not cease to be of the material but becomes an inhabitant of the finer and purer material of what is called his spirit body. This body is subject to the laws governing the material, just as was his physical body subject to laws, and the spirit, which in this sense is the real man clothed in the material, controls and uses that material more effectually than it did when on earth, bound in the physical. All the material of the spirit world is used and formulated by the spirits according to their degree of intelligence and development as the occasions for such uses may arise, and such use, or the effects, are or can be made known to man according as his limitations permit.

Ordinarily, man's understanding of the effects of the spirit's control of the material of the invisible world is limited by the capacity of his five senses to comprehend, and as these five senses were created only for the purpose of permitting or helping the spirit to manifest itself with reference to those things that belong wholly to the physical of earth, it rarely happens that men can perceive the invisible material or the workings of the laws controlling the same.

Now in what I have said, this spirit is merely the mind of man, the same indivisible mind that he possesses when on earth, but because of the limitations of the physical organs he was not able to make function as regards the invisible material, so that man could understand that functioning and its results.

When man dies he is thereafter the same being in all his faculties, desires and thoughts and in his ability to use the material as he was before his death, except that the purely physical organs of his own being are no longer his, and as to them he is dead. Now strange as it may seem to you, he can and often does control the physical organs of another man who is living in the flesh, if that man will submit to that control. If you think for a moment, you will realize that there is nothing remarkable in this. The mind of the spirit remains just the same as it was before his departure from the body, having all its powers and thoughts and consciousness, and if it can obtain control of that which is necessary to manifest itself to the consciousness of men, there will be no difficulty in its doing so, and nothing unusual or supernatural.

There is a law of being that no mind in its normal state can be intruded upon by another mind, unless the mind, whose seat and functioning are within the spirit body which is enclosed in the physical body possessing these organs, consents to the control of such organs by the other mind, it cannot use such organs. For the power is in the disembodied spirit or mind, only the opportunity is wanting.

When the spirit desires to control the invisible material, it is limited only by its intelligence and knowledge of the law governing such control and its progress in the spirit spheres.

Well, I have written enough for tonight, and will come again and amplify my message.

Thanking you, I will say, good night.

Your friend,
Francis Bacon

The limitations which mortal man places
upon his perception of the laws governing the universe
January 6, 1919

I am here, Francis Bacon.

Let me write just a few lines, as I desire to tell you of a thing which may be of importance to you.

I see you are a little disturbed over what a man said to you tonight as to his want of belief in the identity of the spirits who profess to manifest themselves through mediums. Well, this need not disturb you one particle, for the identity of the spirit is just as real and certain as is the fact that a man can and does identify another after an absence, more or less long, from the latter's appearance, voice, and so forth. In the case of his identification he depends on the operation of certain of his senses, such as his sight and hearing, and through them he satisfies his mind that the man identified is the identical person that he may claim to be; as you may say, he would be a very silly man if he would not accept such identification as convincing and determinate.

In the case of the identifying of those who are in the spirit world, and who come with the powers and with the presence of spirits only, he cannot, of course, use his senses for the purpose of identification. If he had to depend upon these organs alone, he would never be able to conclude that the spirits who present the phenomena are those who profess to be his friends or acquaintances. Most mortals do not have the gift of perceiving, or receiving the impression of the presence of spirits, and in such cases are in the condition of the blind and deaf man with reference to the things of earth. The latter has no means of identifying his closest friends, and yet it would be just as unreasonable to contend that these friends are not existing and present, and the same day after day, as for mortals to say that the spirits of those who once lived on earth are not existing and present, because the mortals have not the faculties of seeing and hearing them.

There are things in the earth life, as well as in the spirit life, that can come to the knowledge of some men only through information given them by other men who have superior powers and faculties for seeking and obtaining this information. Some mortals have eyes and faculties not material, as usually understood, for seeing and hearing and receiving knowledge from the spirits, and who render what is thus seen, heard and received just as real and certain as are real and certain the presence of mortals and material things to those who have their physical organs of sight and hearing, and the identity of what is seen and heard and received is just as truly established in the former as in the latter case. All men who are wanting as to the non-material organs mentioned can identify the things of the material world and are satisfied of the fact, and make their mode of such identification the standard by which they must, and only, can become convinced of the identity of the things of the spirit world, and when they insist upon such method of identification they, of course, can never be convinced, except perhaps in those phenomena as are manifested in materialization and spirit photography.

When the merely physical powers or means of ascertaining the existence and identity of things or humans are used, then those who confine their search for truth and the discerning of the identity of claimed existences to the use of such physical organs will never be able to see, hear or receive that which might convince them of the identity of the things existing in the spirit world. This is the result of the eternal laws of the universe in their operations, and no desires or efforts of man can change this result. Man is unfortunate when he assumes the position that unless these laws can be or are changed in order that he may by his physical organs see or hear or be able to identify the things of the spirit world, he will not believe that there is identity existing among the spirits who come to men and in the various ways manifest their presence.

When a man stands on compliance with this condition as necessary to convince him of the identity of those friends of his who have passed to spirit life and who come in psychical phenomena and manifest themselves, it is useless to try to convince him, because of the very necessities of the laws governing such phenomena. Those who do believe, and those who know of this identity, will only waste time and effort in trying to convince men who assume the position of depending entirely on the physical means which they may possess.

There are many men today who are truly convinced, and have sufficient grounds for their convictions, as to the identity and presence of their spirit friends, and they are not deceived, but enjoy the happiness that comes to them from such knowledge. In my observations of the workings of human minds upon this question of the existence and identity of spirits, I have learned that such evidence as would satisfy their minds, under the strictest requirements, as to material things, is brushed aside as wholly inadequate, and sometimes not even worthy of consideration, to satisfy them as to these spiritual things. It seems that the greater knowledge they possess of the nature of and laws controlling material things, the less credence and consideration they will give to the nature of and laws controlling spiritual things. Every other explanation of psychical phenomena is put forth and accepted, rather than the simple and natural one. If men only knew what nature really is, and its laws, they would realize how little they now know of it. Generally, nature is only that consciousness of things material which comes within their limited cognition. They do not know that the larger part of nature, if it can be separated, is beyond the things or conditions which they have knowledge of as being the material of the universe.

Well, as I said, the identity of the spiritual cannot be and must not be expected to be established by the operations of the merely physical organs of man, except perhaps in those manifestations appearing in the phenomena of materializations or spirit photography, and even they are not accepted as real or true by many men who accept what are called scientific deductions from supposed facts connected with the manifestations of what these men consider to be natural.

So the proof of the presence and identity of spirits will have to depend upon the results produced by the operations of laws controlling the spiritual existences and the psychical powers and gifts of certain mediums. Sometimes it may be that these gifted persons will be accepted as honest and truthful and not self-deceived, and the manifestations resulting from the exercise of these powers are the effects of the efforts and intelligence of spirits who, at one time, were mortal beings.

When men come to realize that the change called death does not destroy the identity and consciousness and powers of the mind, they will accept the truth that the presence of the spirits of their departed friends is a verity, and that the identity of these spirits is eternal.

Well, I have written as much as I think best to write tonight, and thank you for your indulgence.

With kind regards, I will say good night,

Your friend,
Francis Bacon

Comments on an article written by James Hyslop on Christianity and Spiritualism in regards to laws which operated in certain miracles of Jesus
November 20, 1918

I am here, Francis Bacon.

I have been with you tonight as you read, and I was somewhat interested in what James Hyslop had to say in his article on *Christianity and Spiritualism*. Many things that he puts forth are true, and explained very satisfactorily why many of the miracles, so-called, of the Bible, may be believed. As he says, they are not different in the nature of their operations or in the exercise of the law that produced them, from the physical phenomena which are manifesting themselves at this time among the investigators of Spiritualism; and, if today, the same law in its force that was brought into operation by Jesus and the disciples, could be called into operation, the same or similar phenomena would be produced. Of course, a great deal depends upon the medium and the amount of rapport that may be created by the communicating or rather operating spirit, for it must be understood that all the supposed miracles were the results of the work of spirits, who by reason of the harmony existing between themselves and the mortals, were able to call into operation the laws which were necessary to produce the results called miracles.

At the present time there may not be persons who have sufficient development of these psychic powers, which were possessed by Jesus and the others, to produce such phenomena as they produced. There have been many mortals since his time sufficiently gifted with these powers to cause manifestations very similar to those of the primitive Christian times, especially as regards healing and alike. Today much healing is being performed by mortals, which is attributed to various causes, such as mental healing and faith cures, but which is really due to the exercise of spirit powers by spirits whose duties are to perform that kind of work.

Mortals, of themselves, cannot bring into operation any of these laws, either of mind or soul, but are dependent upon the cooperation of spirits who use some of the properties possessed by these mortals to bring into exercise the laws which can produce the healing. Here I desire to state that it is not necessary that the mortal be of a highly spiritual development in order that the powers of the spirit world may effect and change the conditions of the material of earth, for the laws which control the material are sufficient, ordinarily, to bring about the healing of the physical or mental diseases of men, and therefore, you will find many mediums, and others not recognized as mediums, having this power of healing.

The healing of the body and the healing of the soul require the workings of different laws, and while spirits not having very much soul development may successfully cooperate with mortals in like condition in healing bodily ills, yet such spirits are impotent to heal the diseased soul or the purely spiritual condition of men. Now spirits who have the power to produce the latter healing, may also heal the body. This you must know, that no spirit who is not what may be called physically whole or sound can cause the healing of a physically diseased mortal, for power of this kind can be possessed by and proceed from only those spirits who in their material nature are perfectly healthy and sound. These spirits, while they have cast off the gross, physical material of the mortal, yet are still material so far as the spirit body and form, and the properties which compose the same, are concerned.

The material of the universe is not confined to or entirely composed of what mortals may suppose to be only the material, that is, that which may be sensed by their five senses or some of them. What is of itself material is always material no matter what form it may assume, whether visible or invisible to mortals, and the larger portion of the material of the universe is in the invisible world, though subject to transformation into the visible, and retransformation into the invisible, and the laws governing and controlling the material are the same, whether that material be to men visible and knowable or not.

This material has its quality of persistence after supposed death or destruction, although the form of its manifestation will be changed. Now from this you will see that he who is known as the materialist, with his supposed want of belief in immortality or the continuity of existence, is in error even as to the material world of which he assumes to have special knowledge, and being in error as to this, how can he claim to be right when he asserts that the purely spiritual has no possibility of continuity of existence or, as some understand, immortality.

Well, I have written enough, and feel that you will pardon my intrusion, but I also feel somewhat justified in writing as I have done.

With my best wishes, I am your friend,
Francis Bacon

FLAVIUS JOSEPHUS (37 A.D. - 95 A.D.)

*Creation of the first parents, different in
their qualities but equal in their relationship to God*
June 3, 1916

I am here, Josephus.

I come tonight to write a few lines upon a subject in which you may be interested as I have observed that recently you have been reading my *History of the Jews,* and there are some things in that book which require correction. I don't mean that I desire to correct the whole book, but I do want to say something on some of the subjects that you have been reading about.

Well, you will notice that I attempted to tell of the creation of the world and of man, and that I elaborated a little upon what is contained in Genesis. In my time on earth there were books dealing with this subject, and from these books I obtained much information that is contained in my writings. However, the truth of the things which I wrote, I find now to be not the truth in many particulars, and should not be accepted as such.

The description of the creation of man is not in accordance with the facts, and the story as related in the Old Testament, and by me, is not the true story of the facts of such creation. I will not enter into detail the correction of the errors contained in these descriptions, except that I wish to say a few words as to the creation of man and also his fall.

Man was not made of the dust of the ground, but was made of the elements that existed in the universe of a different order from the mere dust of the ground, and he was created by God for the purpose of forming the physical body of man. The two persons called our first parents, were created at the same time, and not one out of the rib of the other. Therefore, the man and the woman are equal in their dignity, and in the relationship which they bear to God, and the one is of just as much importance in the sight of God as is the other. One was created stronger, physically, than the other, and also was given a stronger mentality for the exercise of the reasoning powers and the workings of the physical organs of the body. And the other, while weaker in these particulars, yet was given more of the spiritual and emotional nature and also, an intuition by which she could understand the existence of things just as accurately and more quickly than could the man by the exercise of his reasoning power. One was just as the other as respects the gifts bestowed, and together, they were the perfect pair — male and female — created with divers functions and duties to perform in the perfect workings of the laws of God. Power and love were theirs, and neither was made the superior of the other, nor was the one to be subject to the other, and had it not been for their fall there never would have been the subjection of the female to the male.

When their disobedience took place and consequent fall, the qualities of the spiritual were taken from them to a large extent, and the animal qualities, as they may be called, asserted themselves. The male then felt his superiority by reason of the fact that he possessed a greater amount of these animal qualities; and the female became subordinated and continued to be ever afterwards. Now with the male, not having these spiritual qualities to the extent that his mate possessed them, and not being able to realize the greater existence of these qualities in the female, he believed that the physical was the superior, and as he possessed the physical to a larger degree than his companion, he determined that he was the superior, and therefore asserted this superiority, and the female observing that this physical superiority did exist, submitted herself to the male and has so continued until now.

As man degenerated, this domination of the male intensified, and in some parts of the earth the female became nothing better in the sight of the dominant man than one of the lower animals. This degradation continued until man found the lowest place of his degeneracy, and when the turning point came, the qualities of the woman came to be more recognized, although very slowly, and for many thousand years this inequality continued, and man remained the master. As man evolved from this low condition and the moral qualities began to come more into his consciousness, and the animal nature became less dominant, the condition of the female commenced to improve, and as education came into the life and practices of men, woman's opportunities became more extended, and she was more and more recognized as approaching the equal of her companion in some countries of the earth, but not in many.

The Jews recognized the equality of the woman in all matters pertaining to the home or the domestic life, but continued the distinction which had previously existed, in respect to public affairs and the qualities of the mind — women were not permitted even by them to develop their mental faculties, and were taught that they were things that belonged to the male, in all matters pertaining to the state or religion of the race. The consequence of this course of life was that the woman developed the spiritual qualities which were hers to a larger extent, and her refinement and emotional nature and love principle exceeded those of the man to a great degree, and she became in her soul nearer the image of the "divine."

I have noticed that this progress has continued with the passing of the years, and now in some of the nations of earth the equality of the woman has become recognized, notwithstanding the fact that the laws of these countries did not permit her to exercise the rights of man, as she is his equal only in the home or in social life. But a time will come when she will be recognized not only by the individual man but by the man-made laws as his equal in every particular, and the further fact will appear that she will be his superior in matters pertaining to the spiritual.

As the time approaches when man shall return to his former state of purity and harmony with the laws of God, the spiritual qualities will assert themselves and the animal will become subordinated, and woman will stand before God and man as the latter's equal, and in these soul qualities, his superior, for in the beginning, in this particular, she was his superior, and that superiority existed in order that what was lacking in this regard in man, was supplied by the woman, and the perfect pair was one.

You may think that this is a digression from what I first intended to write, and so it is, but I thought the occasion a proper one to tell humankind the future of the two integral parts of the perfect creation of God.

I will not write more tonight, but will come again and write. So with my love, I will say good night.

Your brother in Christ,
Josephus

ELAMEROS

A spirit who heard Jesus's teachings when he was on earth
January 22, 1917

I am here, Elameros.

I am a Greek, or rather the spirit of a mortal who was a Greek, and I lived in the days when Jesus walked the hills and plains of Palestine, teaching his new doctrines of the Divine Love and the kingdom of heaven. I was not a follower of him or a believer in his teachings, for I was a disciple of Plato and Socrates, and was satisfied with the truth of their philosophy, and did not believe that there were other truths than what they contained.

I was a traveler, and at times visited Palestine, and on several occasions heard Jesus teaching the multitudes of people who seemed to be so interested in his discourses. I must confess that I was startled at times by his doctrines, and recognized that while they treated subjects similar to those contained in my philosophy, yet they were different, and gave to these subjects a new and spiritual meaning that I had never before thought of.

I could see that he was not a student of philosophy, or even an educated man, as we understood men to be educated, yet he dealt with these questions in such an enlightening and authoritative way that caused me to wonder at the source of his information; and when, at times, he said that he was not speaking of his own knowledge, but that his Father was speaking through him, I was almost ready to believe that such was the fact.

You must remember that I believed in God and in the lesser gods or demons who executed His will, and when Jesus spoke of his Father, meaning God, it was not unnatural for me, in a way, to accept what he declared. I recollect that I was impressed with the fact that he was not speaking from a mind that had been developed by the study of the philosophies, but from a mind that seemed to have in it that which had been lodged there by some great outside intelligence. He spoke with knowledge, and speculation seemed to be no part of his conclusions or the cause of any of his deductions.

Notwithstanding these impressions on me, I was too wise in my own conceit that my philosophy was the only true one, and that my knowledge of it was without defect. I did not give serious consideration to what I had heard Jesus say, and consequently, let the truths which he uttered pass from me. I saw and heard him teach only a few times, and then I heard of his crucifixion and death as a malefactor, and forgot about him.

When next I saw him, it was in the spirit world. He was a wonderfully bright and glorious spirit teaching the same doctrines that I had heard him teach on earth. I don't think that I can write more tonight. I will come again.

Your brother in Christ,
Elameros

PLATO (427 B.C. - 347 B.C.)

Disciple of Socrates is now a follower of the Master
November 11, 1915

Let me be the one to tell you of the truth of what you want to know. I am one of the first of the great philosophers of ancient Greece, and was known as Plato. I was a disciple of Socrates and a teacher of his philosophy, with additions. He was not only a great philosopher but the nicest and best man of his time. His teachings of immortality were then far in advance of those of any teacher, and no man since has surpassed him in his conception of the soul's destiny or its qualities, except the great Master, who knew and brought to light the great truth of immortality.

Socrates and I are both followers of the Master and inhabitants of his heavenly spheres where only those who have received the Divine Love of God can live. As I followed Socrates on earth, so I followed him in the knowledge and in the possession of the great Love which brought immortality to us.

I cannot say much more tonight as you are too tired to receive any more thoughts, but sometime I will come and write you of this great truth, and how far short my philosophy was in its attempts to teach immortality.

I see that you have received many messages from spirits who are higher than I, and who know more about these divine truths, yet I think that my experiences in regard to the teachings of this great subject may do some good.

I will not write more, but will say good night.

Your brother in Christ,
Plato

SOCRATES (469 - 399 BCE)

The Greek philosopher writes of his
experiences in his progress in the spirit world
July 8, 1915

I am here, Socrates the Greek.

I knew that you thought of me and I was attracted by your thought. If such a spirit is in rapport with you or has a similar soul quality, the soul condition is the great medium of attraction.

I have been with you before, and there is a rapport growing out of your soul qualities. I am now a believer in the Christian doctrine of the soul's immortality, and in the teachings of Jesus as to the way to obtain the Divine Love of God, as you are, and, hence, our qualities of soul are similar.

I am now a follower of the Master and believe in his divine mission on earth, although he had not come to earth when I lived.

After I became a spirit I realized my belief in the continuity of life after death, and lived in the spirit world a great many years after Jesus came before I learned and believed his larger truth of immortality.

210

When I taught, of course I had only a hope which was almost a certainty that I should continue to live through all eternity, but I had no other foundation for that belief than the deductions from my reasoning powers and the observations of the workings of nature. I had heard of the visitations of the spirits of the departed, although I never had any personal experiences in that direction, yet I readily believed it to be true. My conviction of the truth of a future continuance was so strong that it amounted to a certainty, and hence when I died, I comforted Plato and my other friends and disciples, by telling them that they must not say that Socrates will die, rather that his body will die and his soul will live forever in fields Elysian. They believed me, and Plato afterwards enlarged on my belief.

But Socrates did not die, for as soon as his breath left the body, which was not very painful even though the fatal hemlock did its work surely and quickly, he went into the spirit world a living entity, full of the happiness that the realizations of his beliefs gave him.

My entrance into the spirit world was not a dark one, but full of light and happiness, for I was met by some of my disciples who had passed over before me and who had progressed very much in the intellectual development. I then thought that my place of reception was the heaven of good spirits, for there were good spirits to meet me and carry me to my home. I was then possessed of the thought that I was in the home of the blessed, and I continued there for many years and enjoyed the exchange of minds and the feasts of reason.

As I continued to live, I progressed, until at last, I entered the highest intellectual sphere and became a beautiful and bright spirit, so they told me, and taught the things of a mind developed. I met many minds of great power of thought and beauty, and my happiness was beyond my conception when on earth. Many of my old friends and disciples came over and our reunions were always joyous. Plato came and Cato and others. As the ages went by, I continued in my life of intellectual enjoyment and profit, with many spirits developed in their minds and powers of thought, until our existence was a continuous feast of bright and momentous thoughts interchanged.

I traversed the spheres in search of knowledge and information without limitation, and found the principles of many laws of the spirit world. I found in many spheres spirits who said they were the old Hebrew prophets and teachers, and they were still teaching of their

Hebrew God, who they claimed was the only God of the universe and who had made of their nation his favorite people. However, I did not find that they were much different from the rest of us, I mean what they called the spirits of the pagan nations. They were not superior to us in intellect, and they lived in no higher spheres than we lived in, and I could not learn that their morality was any more exalted than was ours.

However, they insisted that they were God's favorite people, and were, in their own estimation, superior to the rest of us and lived in a community all to themselves. I did not know just what the condition of their souls were, and as I had observed the condition of the soul determines the appearances of the spirit, however, I did not perceive that their appearances were any more beautiful or godlike than were ours, and I concluded that their God was no better or greater than was ours. No one that I could find had seen any God and I had not, so who or what God was became merely a matter of speculation, and I preferred to have the God of my own conception to the one that they claimed to have.

For long years my life went on in this way, until in my wanderings I found that there was a sphere I could not enter, and I commenced to make inquiries and was told that it was one of the soul spheres in which the great ruler or Master was a spirit called Jesus, who had, since my coming to the spirit world, established a "new kingdom." And that he was the chosen Son of this God in whom he lived and had his Being, and that only those who had received the Divine Love of this God could enter this sphere or become inhabitants thereof. I then sought for more information and, continuing my search, I learned that this Divine Love had been given to mortals and spirits at the time of the birth of Jesus on earth, and that it was free for all who might seek it in the way taught by him, that he was the greatest true Son of this God, and that in no other way than the one shown by this Son could this Love be obtained or the soul spheres entered.

I thereafter thought of this new revelation, and let many years go by before I became convinced that I might learn something, and become benefitted by seeking this way and this Love, and after awhile I began to seek, but you must know that I and spirits like me, who lived in the spheres where the mind furnished our pursuits and enjoyments, could not enter what was called this soul sphere, yet the inhabitants of these spheres could come into our sphere without let or hindrance.

Sometimes I met and conversed with some of these inhabitants, and on one occasion I met one called John, who was a most beautiful and luminous spirit, and in our conversation he told me of this Divine Love of his God, and of the great Love and mission of Jesus, and he showed me some of the truths taught by Jesus and the way to obtain this Divine Love, and urged me to seek for it. Strange to me, there were not any of the intellectual qualities required to be exercised in seeking for this Love, only the longings and aspirations of my soul and the exercise of my will. It seemed so simple, so easy, that I commenced to doubt whether there was any reality in what I was told, and I hesitated to follow the advice of this spirit, John. But he was so loving and his countenance was so wonderful, that I concluded to try, and I commenced to pray to this God and tried to exercise faith as I was told.

After a while, the most surprising of all things to me, I commenced to have new and unaccountable sensations, and with them a feeling of happiness that I had never experienced before, which made me think that there must be some truth in what I was told. I continued to pray the harder and believe with more surety. I continued to make these efforts, until, at last, the great awakening came that I had in me a Love that never before was in my soul, and a happiness that all my intellectual pursuits had never been able to supply.

Well, it is not necessary to tell you further in detail my experience in getting and developing this Love, but I became filled with it, and at last entered the soul spheres, and what I saw is beyond description. I met Jesus, and had no conception that there could be such a glorious, magnificent and loving spirit. He was so gracious and seemed to be so much interested in my welfare and progress in the truths that he taught. Can you wonder that I am a Christian and follower of him?

Thereafter, I learned what true immortality is, and that I am a part of that immortality. I see how far short my conception and teaching of immortality were. Only this Divine Love can give to spirits immortality, and anything less is but the shadow of a hope, such as I had.

I am now in a sphere that is not numbered, high in the celestial heavens, and not far from some of the spheres where the disciples of the Master live. I am still progressing, and that is the beauty and glory of the soul development, where there is no limit, while my intellectual development was limited.

I must stop now as I have written more than I should have done. I will come to you sometime in the not distant future and tell you of some of the truths which I have learned.

Your friend and brother,
Socrates
The onetime Greek philosopher, but now a Christian.

CHAPTER EIGHT

Ancient Spirits

INALADOCIE

Tells of his beliefs when on earth and the fear his people had of the devil
September 25, 1915

I am a spirit who has never written you before, and would not now, except that I have the opportunity to tell you of some things that you may not know.

I am a spirit who lived as a man when the earth was young, and men had not become so filled with sin and error and all those evil things which cause so much unhappiness on earth. In my time men had not the ambition and greed for accumulating worldly possessions that they have now, and consequently the interior worth of the individual determined a man's standing in our community and his real character before us.

I don't want to write much at this my first coming, as I desire to come again and write. I am not able to tell you how many thousands of years ago I lived, but it was before the time of the Bible description of creation. I was an Indian and lived in the Himalaya mountain country, far removed from where your large cities now are. We were pastoral people, hunters and followers of our own doctrines which were not those of any sect or people that you know of. My race is not now in existence, and the teachings of our seers have never been preserved.

My name was Inaladocie. I was a ruler of my people when I lived on earth. We believed in one God only, and in doing justice to our fellowman. We did not believe in any possible blood atonement or in any Messiah to come who would save us by his death and sufferings. We had our creeds, too, and elaborate ceremonies and even sacrifices, but these were not exercised to avert the wrath of any angry God, but rather to preserve us from the evil influences and harm of a devil. We loved God, and feared the devil. Now I know how the plan of salvation teaches no such doctrine of sacrifice and vicarious atonement.

I must stop now, so good night,
Inaladocie

LEETELAM

Writes of his beliefs while on earth, and how human
beings were sacrificed to appease the wrath of his god
August 13, 1915

I am here, Leetelam.

I was a Tartar and lived in Tibet, and died nearly four thousand years ago. I was a Brahman, and was a priest of the temple and the chief of the brothers of sacrifice. In my day we sacrificed human beings to appease the wrath of our god, and they were the most beautiful and vir-

216

gins — so that our god would have a sacrifice that had never been defiled by man.

This was one of the chief tenets of our religion and was observed with all the strictness and pomp that we, who were fanatical in our beliefs, could give the occasion of the sacrifice. Many a beautiful victim just emerging into the full flower of her youth was made to suffer a cruel death in order, as we supposed, to save the rest of us from the wrath of our god, who was always hungry for blood and the cries of his human victims.

This sacrifice was one of the chief ceremonies of our religion, and we believed in the necessity for it, just as you Christians believe in the necessity for prayer. When we, the priests who performed the act which consummated the sacrifice, had performed our duties, we considered that we had obeyed the will of our god and that he was pleased with our great act of devotion and worship. No rank or position could save the victim from the sacrifice when once the priests had selected that victim, and the parents of such victim were taught and believed that it was a great honor to have their young daughters chosen as brides for the great god who was not satisfied unless he could have the most beautiful and virtuous maidens for his brides of death.

Since I have become a spirit and learned some of the truths of the spirit world, and that love and not sacrifice is required by God, all these evil deeds that I and the others performed in the name of our religion have become to me monstrous and shocking. For many long years after I had learned the truth, the recollections of these deeds caused me to suffer the tortures of the damned. The fact that I at the time thought that I was performing a duty did not assuage my suffering or relieve my darkness. Truth is truth, and every violation of its demands must be atoned for, no matter if the intention at the time of committing these violations is supposed or believed by the actor to be in accordance with the truth. No belief, if it violates truth, will be excused.

As on earth, ignorance of law excuses no one for his acts done in violation of law, so in the spirit world ignorance of the truth will not excuse deeds committed in violation of that truth. Every cause must have its effect, and no God interposes to prevent that effect from following the cause. Now that I have been awakened to the truth, I see with the perceptions of not only a clarified intellect but also of the soul, that no act or deed done in the name of religion actually believed in will be excused because of the fact that it was done for the sake of that religion.

I am now in the Nirvana of the Brahmans, and am very happy. My soul has been purified by the long years of suffering and discipline, and I love God and my fellowman. My sphere is high up in the spirit world — just what its location is I cannot tell you. There are no Christians or other sects in my sphere, although I see them at times and converse with them.

I came here because I was travelling in this earth plane and saw a bright light which is unusual in this plane, and it led me to you, and I found that you were receiving communications from spirits, and I listened to some of the messages and concluded that I would write also if I could have the opportunity. I did not know English when I lived, but you must know that the advanced spirits who have been in the spirit world for many years have not let the years go by without study and investigation. I understand most all the languages of earth, and so do most of the ancient spirits, and this for the purpose of being able to understand what the peoples of all lands may think and say. Our work is to help mortals and spirits whenever we can.

Well, I will not write more tonight. I hear what you say and cannot understand you, but if there be such a supreme happiness as you speak of, I should like to possess it. I will accept your invitation and attend your writings on Wednesday night.

With my best wishes and kind regards.

I am your friend,
Leetelam

ALEYABIS

Aleyabis, a follower of Zoroaster, overheard previous conversations,
and since he does not know about the New Birth, he would like to learn
August 20, 1915

I am here, Aleyabis.

Let me write. I have been listening to those who have preceded me, and am interested in what they have said. I know nothing about this New Birth, and although I have lived in the spirit world a long time and in great happiness, yet I have never before heard of the doctrine. If there be any truth to it, I would like to learn what it means. Of course, to learn I will have to make investigation and to do so I must get a starting point, and if you can show me how I may come in contact with anything that may assist me in my investigation, I will be obliged to you.

I am a Persian and was named Aleyabis. I lived four thousand years ago, and was and am a follower of Zoroaster, the divine teacher of God. I am living in the highest spheres where the followers of our teacher live. We are not in the same heaven with the spirits of other beliefs, but have a heaven all to ourselves, although I sometimes come in contact with spirits from these other heavens. Sometimes I come in contact with the Christian spirits and talk to them, but we do not discuss our doctrines, because we each so firmly believe in the truth of our respective beliefs, that no good would come of any discussion as to their relative merits.

I see a great many spirits around you, and some are very beautiful and bright, more so than I have seen before, and they also seem to have much love in their beings. Your wife is here and says she will be pleased to show me the way to start in my investigations, and I will accept her kind offer.

I will come to you again sometime and tell you the result of my investigation.

Your friend,
Aleyabis

AMOULOMOL

Amoulomol, was a resident of the North Pole when it was warm and green
August 31, 1915

I am here, Amoulomol.

I was an inhabitant of a land that no longer exists and is entirely for-gotten by human history. It was at the North Pole, and I lived there when everything was beautiful and green and warm. Yes, thousands of years ago. I now live in the sphere where my people live, and I am very happy with them. I was a white man and lived in a city where we had all the conveniences and comforts. I see you don't believe me, but it is true.

> Good night,
> Amoulomol

JAYEMAS

*Atlantian teacher of arts and sciences, writes about his
lost continent and the high intellect that the inhabitants possessed*
October 7, 1915

I am here, Jayemas.

I am the spirit of a man who when on earth was an inhabitant of the great continent of Atlantis which was submerged in a cataclysm, and by which a great calamity befell all the inhabitants of that country and were drowned.

I am now in the sixth sphere where there are many others of my countrymen, and wherein we are enjoying much happiness and great

220

intellectual pursuits that bring to us knowledge of the wonderful laws of the universe.

I was, when on earth, a teacher of the arts and sciences and of the philosophy of life as well. I made many inventions which enabled my people to progress in the development of the use of forces which existed in the unseen world, and which are now still in existence and operating. If mortals would only understand and had means for utilizing these forces, they would enjoy wonderful facilities for traveling and propelling the different engines of trade and manufacture that they are engaged in, and also for making easy much of the labor which is now done by hand or by imperfect machinery.

You must not think that the forces of nature have all been discovered by your great scientists and inventors, for that is not true, and in the near future you will have revealed to your investigators some wonderful forces that will revolutionize many of the means of conducting the communications between nations, and of leading men to a knowledge of what the possibilities are.

Well, I am not permitted to disclose any of these secrets at this time, but in the near future they will be made known, and you will live to see some of these forces applied to the actual working out of what you suppose to be the ideas of your inventors.

I merely wanted to introduce myself at this time, as I hope to come to you later and tell you about my life on the submerged continent. So I will not write more.

Your friend,
Jayemas, the Atlantian

SEBASTOBEL

Sebastobel, the Atlantian, describes the sinking of the
Continent of Atlantis, which took place in the twinkling of an eye
September 24, 1915

I am here, Sebastobel.

I am a spirit who has never written before, and I desire to say a few things which I consider of importance to mortals as well as to spirits.

I live in the highest sphere where intellect rules supreme, and where spirits are happy in the knowledge that their spirit existence is free from all the cares and limitations which a life in the body imposes. I am a student of the laws governing the relationship of the various planets to one another, and to the earth, and of the influences which the sun and moon and stars exert upon mortals of the earth. I am an ancient spirit and have been in spirit life many thousands of years — long before the great flood which submerged a great continent which men know as Atlantis.

When that continent existed and was peopled by living, active, intelligent beings, I had been a spirit many years and was in communication with the prophets, as they were called — or rather seers — of that happy land. The development of these people far surpassed that of the present inhabitants of earth in not only the purely intellectual qualities in the abstract, but also in their knowledge of what you call the arts and sciences.

The inhabitants of that fair land did not have the necessity for using horses or automobiles or steam cars or boats, or airships, for moving from place to place and traveling, because they knew of the existence of and the way to utilize certain forces of nature which enabled each individual or group of individuals to transport themselves from place to place by the mere operation of their will power, using these forces. These forces still exist in nature, and are just as ready to be utilized now as they were at the time these people of whom I speak brought them under their control.

Someday it will be given to man to understand and control these great forces and utilize them to their fullest extent. Just when this time

222

will be I don't know but considering the rapid strides that mortals have made in discovering and utilizing some of the heretofore hidden forces in nature during the last half century, I do not think it will be long before these great forces will be discovered, or rather revealed, to man. It will not be revealed until the higher powers consider the time ripe for man to have the knowledge of these forces revealed to him and to control them. I know what these forces are, but I am not permitted to make them known to you or anyone else at this time. I should otherwise gladly do so.

Well, while they had this great knowledge and power of transporting themselves, and could have done so had they been given time, the submerging of the continent was so sudden that no one knew the moment when the catastrophe took place. It was in the twinkling of an eye, as it were, and men were drowned before they had time to think or attempt to save themselves.

No, it was not like the Bible description of the flood (Genesis 7:10), that was merely allegory and existed in other books, in a little different form, long before the Bible was written.

These Atlantians are now inhabitants of the spirit world, living in different spheres, and are more or less developed in their intellects. Well, I merely want to say further that I am somewhat surprised that you can receive my thoughts in the way of written communication, for I never before in all my spirit experience have written my thoughts this way. It is a wonderful gift and one which I consider superior to any other method that I know of for communing with mortals. You may ask me any question and I will answer it if I can.

Yes, I see other spirits here, some dark and ugly and some bright and beautiful. I have spoken to one who says she is your wife, and she is a most beautiful and bright spirit — the brightest that I have come in contact with. I must confess that I have never seen in my sphere any spirit so beautiful or bright, or pure looking or lovely as she, and I wonder why it is. I am at a loss to know, and I would like to know, I assure you.

No, my intellect does not tell me, and I see that there is a phenomenon presented here which is worthy of investigation and study. Well, she has told me, and I am astonished at her explanation. I never before knew or heard of the existence of such a thing as this Divine Love, and even now I cannot comprehend what she means, although I see a result or effect for which I can find no cause, and it seems reasonable that I should accept the cause which she gives me. I am astonished, as I thought that there is nothing in all the spirit world equal to the mind, and nothing which brings such happiness, though she tells me of a happiness of which I had no conception. Well, as you say, I see an effect and there must be a cause, and as I am an investigator of the truth, I feel it my duty to search for that cause, and I will.

She has invited me to go with her and meet her band, and also one who, she tells me, is the most magnificent and beautiful in all the spirit universe. I will go with her and investigate this matter, and will come to you again.

So I will say good night,
Sebastobel

LAMLESTIA

Lamlestia discusses Theosophy and reincarnation
December 17, 1916

I was an inhabitant of India when that country was not known of to modern nations, and I lived near the great Himalaya Mountains on a plain that was then fertile and peopled by a vast number of inhabitants who worshiped the gods of whom the later Brahmans have written in their sacred books.

It may seem surprising to you that I should come and write you, and the explanation is that I came in rapport with you tonight at the meeting of the Theosophists. I saw that you were psychic and that I could communicate to you through the medium of the pen. There were many spirits present who, when mortals, lived in that far away country, and were, and are now believers in the mysteries of the occult as claimed to be known now, by those who profess to be leaders of the Theosophical movement. A number of their names were mentioned by the lecture, and these spirits were attracted to the meeting by reason of the similarity of beliefs which the mortals present possessed, and they, the spirits, possessed. I, also, was present because of that attraction, for when on earth I was a great believer in these doctrines, and especially those that teach reincarnation and karma, and I still believe in these things.

Although I have been a spirit for many centuries, these earth beliefs cling to me and hold me in the binding force of their truths, as I conceive these truths to be. Many of those present, whose minds I could read as they thought, believe in these doctrines; however, very few of them have any conception of what the truths are as taught by such philosophy. Even the lecturer has a very slight comprehension of the scope and import of these teachings, and her attempt to explain the objects and workings of the principles of true Theosophy was a very inefficient effort. In order for her to be able to teach these doctrines, it is absolutely necessary that she have a knowledge of the same, which she does not have.

No, the knowledge that she and many others like her have, as to the fundamentals of this philosophy or religion, if it may be called such, is very superficial. The fact that it is a system of mysteries of which they have discerned, in a few instances, the explanation, which causes them to conclude that their grasp of the scope of this philosophy is greater than it really is, and affords them a kind of satisfaction that arises from the consciousness that some mysteries which the world knows not of, they know.

She spoke about the great Masters being in India, who have a full knowledge of these mysteries and, in certain conditions or circumstances, will be able to and will initiate the searcher into the esoteric meaning of these great truths. Well, these Masters know something of mysticism and of occult powers and principles, but such knowledge is not sufficient to qualify them as teachers of the great truths of Theosophy, as I understood and now understand these truths.

We have in the spirit world, and have had for long centuries, communities of Theosophists, who believe and teach to whomsoever will listen to these doctrines, and many of these spirits attempt to teach mortals by impressions and thought transference these truths of the ages, with indifferent success; and, hence, for most of those who think they would like to understand this philosophy, the great attraction is the mystery, which they believe, because of its being a mystery, must contain the truth.

The progress and understanding in the search for the key to the opening up and solving of these doctrines, and the supposed mystery in which they are shrouded, is very slow, and we who have been, as I said, for centuries engaged in this great effort, have never had demonstrated to us the existence of our supposed truths, and we are still plodding the weary way, supported by the faith that at some time light will come to us, and that which has so long been enveloped in darkness will come into the pure light of understanding and comprehension. But as yet, very few of these mysteries have been solved and the truths supposed to be concealed therein have been manifested, and to some of us doubt has commenced to rear its head and cause disappointment.

Tonight, I heard the lecturer declare that man is God potentially, and that when he develops into perfection he will become God. Never was there a more delusive and untrue declaration of a supposed fact ever uttered, for we who have lived in this invisible world long enough to have had come to us the realization that we are gods, all know that we are only and merely the spirits of men who lived on earth many years ago, and believed that when in the far distant future by our own exertions in renunciation, we would become gods.

No, such is not the fact, and while we have renounced many of the sins and errors of our mortal lives, yet we are still spirits, with all the limitations of mind and soul that spirits are bound by nature. And this I must say, that in all the centuries of my spirit existence, never have I known a spirit or the soul of a spirit to reincarnate, and in this my disappointment has been grievous. Many spirits of our association have become perfect through renunciation, and yet they have remained spirits and progressed to the highest heavens of our possibilities (the sixth sphere).

Yet, strange as it may seem in view of this experience, we still, to a more or less degree, cling to our old beliefs in reincarnation, thinking that there is something else that we know not of, to be done in order for reincarnation to become the destiny of our souls. Sometimes I think that my beliefs in this particular must be wrong, for in comparing the condition of mortals, the most advanced in their mind and soul development, I realize that they are not in a small degree the equal of us in development, and then I wonder and cannot understand what good could be accomplished or what improvement made in our condition for progressing, should we again enter mortal bodies.

As true Theosophy taught, as we conceived it, reincarnation was a supposed process of purification, and necessary in order that the spirit could attain to a state of perfection and freedom from everything that defiles his soul and prevents that soul from arriving at the blissful state of Nirvana. This means only that condition of soul where reincarnation is no longer necessary or possible. I know that many of our spirits — onetime believers in these doctrines — have arrived at that condition and entered a state of perfect happiness, and I hesitate longer to believe, and only hold the faith because I fear that the experience mentioned may be the results of special circumstances. But if I cease to believe these teachings, what shall I believe? No one can tell me that this reincarnation will not take place, and I fear to surrender the belief.

I further believe that in order for the workings of karma, as the doctrines hold, reincarnation is necessary — that only in the mortal body could I do the reaping that my sowing demands, and yet, I see and know that karma has been and is working in this spirit world, to the extent that the reaping has all been accomplished, and the spirit made perfect, and this without any reincarnation; for as I have said, never have I known or heard of the reincarnation of a spirit or of anything that is connected with or represents the spirit.

Of late I have been much in cloudland as to these beliefs, and in my desire to find the light, I have visited the meetings of the Theosophists in all countries, and especially in India, where the Masters who are supposed to have the full knowledge and enlightenment live in hope of finding the light, but all to no avail. My desires and longings cry for the light, but none can be found.

Tonight, I was attracted to the meeting where I saw you, and realizing that I could express to you my feelings and doubts, made a rapport and came home with you for the purpose of doing what I have done. I know from your condition of mind that you do not believe in these doctrines of the Theosophists, and that your beliefs are of a different kind, and are new to me, although I have heard of the doctrines that are the objects of your faith. There are spirits with whom I sometimes come in contact who attempt to tell me of another way to a higher heaven than the one that I know of, but as they are mere babes in comparison to my ancient existence, I do not listen to them, and hence I am not acquainted with their teachings.

Well, you seem to be very kind, and I thank you for your interest, and under the circumstances must accept your offer, and will, I assure you, listen attentively to what may be said to me.

I have looked and there comes to me a beautiful spirit who says she is your grandmother, and that she has heard your invitation and will be glad to show me the way to love and light and truth. She seems so bright and beautiful and loving that I must go with her.

So I will say good night and go,
Lamlestia

SAELISH

*Once the soul leaves the physical body, never again
does it find its habitation in another or the same physical body,
but forever thereafter occupies the spirit body and in the spirit world only*
November 3, 1915

I am here, Saelish.

I was, when on earth, an inhabitant of the great empire of Assyria of which Nineveh was the capital. I was not a king but was one of a great king's magicians or wise men, and when I lived was a man of great influence and power in the kingdom. I came tonight to tell you a great truth in connection with the soul. As you may infer, when I lived we knew nothing of the one and only God, but we worshiped many gods, great and little, and believed that these gods could help or harm us, just as we deserved their help or their injurious workings. So our many gods sometimes came in conflict in their treatment of us poor mortals, so that we at times hardly knew whether our gods were our friends or our enemies.

Of course, the help that we sought for was all of a material nature, for never did we think of help in the way of preparing us for a future life; that, we supposed, was only for those of us who by our great achievement in battle or in intellectual pursuits would, upon death, become gods ourselves. The poor, ordinary mortals were only intended to live the mortal life, at least during the incarnation that they then had, and their expectations were that perhaps in some future incarnation, they might have the opportunity and the favors of the unknown gods, so that they might become gods themselves. This was the substance of the beliefs and hopes of the Assyrians at that time, and many millions died in that belief and are now inhabitants of the several planes of certain spheres of the spirit world. None of them has ever returned for a new incarnation and thereby started on their way to become gods. The men who they supposed had become gods when they died were in the spirit world, spirits themselves, and not gods at all.

So you see that the soul, when once it leaves the physical body, never returns again to any physical body, but continues in the spirit world to exist as a soul with a body of spirit form and substance; and no spirit has ever experienced the sensation of becoming reincarnated. This is the truth that I wished to tell you: that the soul, when once it leaves the physical body, never again does it find its habitation in another or the same physical body, but forever thereafter occupies the spirit body, and in the spirit world only.

When a mortal dies, earth, so far as being the home of that mortal again in an earthly body, becomes a thing of the past; it is a mere way station which has been left behind, and will never again appear as a stopping place on the spirit's line of progression. I thought it might do good for me to write this tonight, for it is the information from a spirit who long years ago lived on earth and believed in this doctrine of reincarnation, and who during all the long years of its spirit life has learned and experienced the truth, that reincarnation is a fable and has no real existence.

No, the soul never retraces its steps or its method of existence, for it never goes back from the spirit to the mortal. I know that on the earth today there are thousands of mortals who believe in this doctrine of reincarnation, and many thousands more have died in that belief, yet they live and die in that belief, and only when the truth comes to them, do they realize that their belief was an erroneous one, and that they will never reach Nirvana by retracing their course of life through the physical body.

The soul never dies, but always lives, and whenever its position is such as to justify progression, it progresses. I live in the sixth sphere, and am considered to be a very exalted spirit in my intellectual acquirements and in my condition of freedom from sin and errors which belonged to me on earth, and which belongs to every mortal. My happiness is very great, and my home and surroundings are beautiful.

This sphere is a wonderful place, not only because of the surroundings and homes of the inhabitants, but because of the great mental and moral development of those who live in that sphere. No spirit who has not that development can live in this sphere because of its unfitness. Male and female spirits enjoy this wonderful development, and their intercourse in the intellectual things that exist in this sphere are free and frequent, and the interchange of thoughts brings much happiness and satisfaction.

We don't know of any spheres beyond the sixth, although we have heard it rumored that there are others, but we give little credence to these rumors, because none of us, I mean the inhabitants of this sphere, has ever found a higher one, and many of us live in the highest planes of this sphere.

Well, I, of course, can't say that is not true, however, I do say that you astonish me beyond all belief, for I cannot imagine that any spirit can make higher progress than we have made. What you tell me surprises me and I would like to investigate and discover the truth of this matter. But I don't know how to commence such investigation or where to start. Is it possible that you can show me the way in which I can commence this investigation?

I have done as you suggested and I do see some wonderfully beautiful spirits, and they seem to be so very happy, too, and interested in you. One says she is your grandmother, and she seems to excel the others in her beauty and brightness. She says she is very willing to start me in my investigation herself and to tell me the great secret of the great progression that you speak of, and if I will accompany her she will commence at once.

While I write, there comes another beautiful spirit and says that she formerly lived in the sixth sphere, and lived there many thousands of years before I lived on earth. She says that she was an Egyptian and that her name was Saleeba and that now she is an inhabitant of the third sphere, in order to prepare herself for the great progression that she will make to spheres high above the sixth, and tells me that after I have conversed with your grandmother she will be pleased to talk to me and tell me her experience. I will be with her, you may rest assured.

All this is so wonderful to me that I hardly know what to think or do. I will try to find the truth of it, if it can be found. So, as I have written you a long time, expecting to enlighten you and not be enlightened myself, and am now so anxious for that enlightenment.

I will say that I am glad I came to you.

Good night,
Saelish

ANAXYLABIS

The designer of the great pyramid of Gizeh, in Egypt
July 22, 1915

I am here, Anaxylabis.

Let me tell you about the great pyramid of Gizeh. I want to do so in detail, as I was its designer, and I built it under the direction of the Egyptian king, Monyabasis the Great, who lived many centuries ago, before Ramses, and who is credited with its construction.

I know that humankind has no records which tell of the reign of this monarch, but such records did exist, and in them was contained the history and the description of the occasion which called for the building of this great pyramid. These records were destroyed long before the present extant histories of the world were written — long before the *Book of the Dead* was written and long before any of the present kingdoms of the earth had their beginnings. Centuries and centuries have passed since that time and no man has knowledge of what was then the condition of the human race or, as I should say, speaking for myself, of the race that inhabited that region of the Nile. We were a race of great intelligence, and what you would now describe as a wonderful civilization. Many of our arts and sciences disappeared from earth and have never been rediscovered, and may never be, for that race no longer has communication with the present race.

231

I came tonight because I saw pass by me wonderful spirits of light and beauty, evidently bent on some great mission; and I followed them and found myself with you. Listening to the communications which they gave you, I found that there came to me a desire to write also.

Well, as I listened I soon saw that the communications were written in a language different from my own, and that you understood only that language and that I must write in that language to make myself understood; so I commenced at once to learn it and I learned it in the short space of time when I listened to the others in their communications. This may seem impossible to you, but I can read the thoughts of spirits and men without difficulty, and as all thoughts in the spirit world require no language such as you understand, I soon found that I could clothe my thoughts in your words as I am doing now.

Well, I know it may not be very satisfactory to you, but it is true, and I cannot more clearly explain it so that you may comprehend it. I have diverged or digressed from my intention of telling you what the design of the great pyramid was, and I find that I have written too long to attempt it now, as this is my first effort at writing. So I will postpone it until later, when I will come and give you the explanation.

I don't know in years, but when the *Egyptian Book of the Dead* was written I had lived as a spirit many thousands of years.

I must stop now and say good night,
Anaxylabis

SALEEBA

An Egyptian princess tells of her life in Egypt and in the spirit world
June 2, 1915

I am, Saleeba.

Let me write just a little as I need help, and you seem willing to help us all.

I am a woman who lived a great many years ago in a land that is far distant from your home, and at a time that runs back into the centuries. I was an Egyptian princess, and lived in the time when your Jesus, that I heard you speak of, was not known to the world. I was taught the philosophy of the ancient Egyptians, and Osiris and Isis were our god and goddess. We worshiped them, not in love or soul adoration, but in fear and dread. They were not loving the way you say your God is, but it was the dread of power and wrath that called for our obedience through fear of punishment, and the tortures of the hells where they were supposed to rule, and there the torment of the spirits of mortals who disobeyed them. So you see, our souls were not developed with love, and our minds were controlled with fear, and we offered our sacrifices to appease the terrible threatening of their wrath.

I was naturally a loving woman, and in my life outside of my religious beliefs, I was compassionate and sympathetic. Those who were subject to me in our intercourse of government loved me, and were grateful and obedient subjects; yet when it became a question as to our worship and religious duties, I sacrificed many of them to satisfy the wrath and demands of our gods. These sacrifices were made at first openly, and so great did they become, and deleterious to the good of the nation in its political aspect, that later our sacrifices were made in private, but they were made nonetheless.

Our beliefs were as real and as earnest as are the beliefs of you Christians in your God of Love and mercy; and we did the will of our gods with as much belief that we were doing our duty, as do you the will of your God in the belief that you are doing your duty. For as I now see, what a difference in the motives, and what a difference in the

233

results. Our motives were to appease our angry gods, and thereby prevent their wrath from falling upon us who continued to live. Whereas your motives are to get and be filled with the Love and mercy of a God of Love, and to have your souls filled with that which will enable you to live in His presence and become supremely happy.

In the long years that I have lived in the spirit world, I have learned all this intellectually, and many other things that show me the cruelty and degradation of the beliefs that prevailed when I was a mortal and which resulted in the deaths, physically, of many of my subjects, and the death also of their souls. Love to us, was not a thing divine. Obedience and placating the anger of the gods were the divine things to us.

Now, while I have heard of this Love of your God, and have seen the results of this Love upon the spirit's appearances, and the apparent happiness of the worshippers of your God, yet I have never understood this great Love, except in an intellectual way. My soul has never felt the influence of this Love, and I had never before thought it necessary for me to seek the secret of obtaining the benefit of this Love. But I now see that there is something more to this secret than the mere knowledge of the Love's existence, which the mind tells me must exist. In my journeys to earth, I heard of your meetings with the spirits who are seeking this Love, or rather a way out of their darkness and sufferings, and having seen the effect of some of their efforts, I came to you to learn the way, if possible, by which I may obtain the soul experience which I have heard you, and the beautiful spirits who come to you, speak of.

Of course, my ancient beliefs still have some influence over me, even though I have found that Osiris and Isis are myths; but yet, that negative knowledge has not supplied me with the means by which I can get this Love you speak of. While I know that the angry gods do not exist, still there is a void in my soul which I realize has never been filled. So I pray that if you can help me to the way that will lead to my finding this soul filling Love that you speak of, I will be greatly obliged if you will do so, and will follow that way.

In the years since my coming into the spirit world, I have lived in a number of spheres, each one in a progressive succession. But in none of these spheres which I have lived in, have I found that the inhabitants are possessed of this soul love that I am anxious to obtain. In the higher spheres in which I have lived and in the highest, there is a wonderful development of the mental qualities, and the knowledge possessed by these spirit inhabitants is beyond all conception of mortals. Sin does not exist in these highest spheres, and happiness is very great, and the spirits are very beautiful and bright. For in my comparison of the beauty and brightness of these spirits with those who claim this soul development of Love, I notice a great difference.

We have our loves and our harmonies, and peace reigns supreme, yet I am not satisfied, and so it is with many others who live where I do. Now the cause of this dissatisfaction is not revealed to us, and only, as I say, in my visits to the earth plane and hearing of this Love, have I become convinced that the great secret of our dissatisfaction may be found among those spirits who claim to have this wonderful Love. So I come to you and ask you to show me the way to learn of it.

Well, I have visited the earth plane many times since I have been a spirit, and occasionally, have conversed with the spirits who claim to have this Divine Love, and they have told me to some degree of this Love, but I never thought much about it until lately. I was happy in my condition as I have told you of it, and did not think it worthwhile to inquire into the fact of what this Love meant. Somehow, lately, the desire to learn of it has taken possession of me, and hence I come to you because I see others coming to you who say they need help.

I did not go to the others you speak of because I thought that I might get more help by coming to you first. The spirits who are seeking your help say that they can in someway obtain an advantage in coming to you first. I don't know why, but they believe it; and when I saw the effect of their coming to you, I thought it might be so, and hence I came.

I was the daughter of one of the early Pharaohs and my name was Princess Saleeba. I do not know how to compute the centuries, for I lived before the pyramids were built, so you see I have been in the spirit world a long time.

I have called for your wife, and she is so very beautiful. She must have a great amount of this Love. She says that she will show me the way to obtain it, and will love me herself and take me to the greatest spirit in all the spirit world, in whom I can see this Love developed in its greatest perfection. I am going with her, and remember my promise to come again, for I will.

So with many thanks and my kindest regards.

I will say good night,
Saleeba

Saleeba's progress in obtaining the Love of God
October 16, 1915

I am here, Saleeba.

I am in a much happier condition than when I wrote before, and I want to tell you that the Love of God in my soul is the cause of my being happier. Your sweet wife was with me a great deal, telling me of this Love and showing me the way to seek for it, and I believed her and followed her advice, and as a result, I found a great deal of that Love and it is so very great a creator of happiness that I want more of it.

I am living in the third sphere because I find so much more of that soul love there than in the sixth sphere, and what I want now is that Love. So you see I cannot live where this Love is not so abundant. When I get more of it I shall go to the sixth sphere and tell the spirits there what a great happiness I have found, and try to persuade them to seek it also, and I believe that many will.

I am so glad that I broke into your writing when I did, for if I had not, I would not have learned the way to this Love and happiness. I shall always look upon you as my friend and brother, and will do anything in my power to help you.

I have not found any of my race in these soul spheres as of yet, however, there may be some of them there. If I can possibly accomplish it, there will be some of them in my sphere very soon.

I have forgotten a great many things in connection with my earth life, but I remember my parents and some of my associates and some portions of my religious beliefs. Sometime I will tell you of these things and also of my experiences in passing through these spheres, in my progress to the sixth sphere, where I had to stop progressing. It is strange that I did not find this out until recently, though it is a fact.

No spirit who lives in the sixth sphere is as beautiful as the spirits of the third sphere who have the soul development. The merely intellectual spirit can never become as beautiful as those having the soul Love. Well, I must stop, as I only wanted to let you know that I had not forgotten you. I will come again soon.

So I will say good night.

Your friend and sister,
Saleeba

Saleeba is progressing and soon will be above the third sphere
July 5, 1915

I am here, Saleeba.

Well, I am with you again, and I want to tell you that I am so very happy, as I have progressed so much since I wrote you a short time ago.

I am still in the third sphere, but in a higher plane with spirits who have the soul development to a very great degree, and I am so happy that I cannot express to you its extent.

Oh, what a wonderful thing the Divine Love is, and when I consider the long years that I lived as a spirit without knowing anything about it, I can scarcely express my regret at the unfortunate position in which I lived. I know now that Jesus is the true leader of all the spirits who have this great soul development, and that he can show the way to God's kingdom as no other spirit can; and besides, when I come in contact with him, I realize that he has so much of this Divine Love himself that what he says must be true.

I will soon progress to a higher sphere, they tell me, and will get the Divine Love in more abundance, and then in a little while I shall go to my own people and tell them of the wonders and glories of my new-found home. What a blessed, happy time I anticipate among these spirits who are now in such ignorance of the only thing that brings this great happiness.

I am not in condition now to tell you of my residence or life on earth but sometime I will. You must think kind thoughts of me, and let your love come to me so that I may feel its benefit; for I must tell you that the loving thoughts of a mortal who knows what this Divine Love is have a wonderful influence on spirits, and their advancement in the spirit spheres.

I will not write more tonight, so with my love and kindest thoughts.

I am, your sister in Christ,
Saleeba

237

Saleeba has found happiness through God's Love and mercy
October 8, 1915

I am here, Saleeba.

I want to say only a few words that you may know how happy I am, and how much my soul is filled with this Divine Love of which you first told me. Oh, my friend, it is difficult to keep from shouting the fact that I am a redeemed child of God, and one who knows that this Divine Love is mine, and that I shall live through all eternity, enjoying the happiness which God's Love and mercy have given me.

I intended to keep my promise and tell you of my life on earth many thousands of years ago, and so I will sometime, but now I am so happy in this great possession that I cannot think of those earthly things in such a way as to relate to you my experience as a mortal. Wait a little while and I will try to describe to you all the things of my earth life that may be of interest to you.

I will go very soon now to my people and tell them what I have found and urge them to seek for it, and I trust that they will follow my advice. There are many of them that are good and pure spirits, with a natural love in such a state that they are very happy and contented, and yet, when I realize the great difference in the happiness that is theirs, and that which may be theirs, I cannot refrain from going to them and telling them of it. I know that you are glad that I am happy, and are interested in my progress, and hence, I love to come and let you know what my condition is.

I will not write more tonight. So believe that I love you as a sister, and pray for you and ask God to make you happy and fill your soul with His Love, and bless you.

Good night your sister,
Saleeba

LEEKESI

*Assyrian official who believed in many gods
when on earth but now believes in just one God*
November 4, 1915

I am here, Leekesi.

I was a man who was an Assyrian official and lived in the time of the destruction of Nineveh. I am not mentioned in history, for my time was short, though in it occurred some of the most important events of the whole history of that land.

I was not a believer in the God of the Hebrews, though in my time I had heard of that God, and many Jews lived in my domain; yet I would not let them worship that God or in any way teach my people the religion of the Jews.

Our gods were many and were worshiped by the inhabitants of the nation in accordance with what might be the desires of these people. When the gods answered the prayers of the people they were thought to be good and true, but when the answers did not come, the gods were false, and new gods were made and worshiped according to whether they answered the people's prayers or not. So you see that our gods were the creatures of men and not men the creatures of the gods.

But, notwithstanding this false idea, as I now see, of God, there were men of deep insight into the matters pertaining to the spiritual world, who did not make and worship the gods that I have spoken of. They were able to look beyond these material things and discover that there was such a thing as a higher condition of the afterlife, in which the souls of man could find happiness and knowledge of the existence of a real and mighty power that would bring them into a state of existence where men would realize the higher life of the soul's predominance.

These men were not numerous and did not associate with the inhabitants to any extent, but lived to themselves and evolved certain philosophies which satisfied them of truths which our common beliefs did not comprehend. These men also taught these truths, but not generally, and only to those who might become their followers.

In my time we had what you would call churches and priests and officials of high position in the religious organization, and feasts and ceremonies and sacrifices, and these powerful ecclesiastics were very jealous and intolerant of anything which interfered with, or in any manner controlled, their religious teachings or the power which they exercised over the people and the government of the kingdom. Consequently, these philosophers that I speak of were not permitted to disseminate their speculations or philosophies among the masses, and were compelled to write their doctrines or teachings in a language which the common people could not understand.

This was the condition of the religious part of my kingdom at the time of its destruction, and many of my people who survived this destruction and who were scattered into other countries took with them these beliefs in the multiplicity of gods, and worshiped as before their dispersion. In time these beliefs commenced to permeate the beliefs of the people among whom they lived, until the belief in many gods became the general belief of many other nations. You will find in history that many nations which became great after the fall of my kingdom, such as Greece and Rome and others, continued the belief in a multiplicity of gods.

Not until the spreading and adoption of Christianity by them did the belief in the one true God become the established and universal belief of these nations and of the people thereof. Man made the gods and worshiped them, until the great Master came and proclaimed the truth of the one and only existing God. Of course, an exception must be made in the statement in favor of the Jews, because they had only one God; and even they had different names for their God, which were applicable and used in accordance with the qualities that they ascribed to Him. It was only after Jesus came did that one God with many names by the Jews become our Heavenly Father — the God of Love and salvation.

From all of this you may suppose that I am a Christian. Well, I am, and I live in the celestial spheres; for I must tell you that I became converted to the truths of the teachings of Jesus many years ago, and my progression in the development of my soul has been such that I am now in the celestial spheres.

I merely wanted to write this to show you that man has been a maker of gods for so many years that they cannot be numbered; and that it was only when the great truths came with the coming of Jesus that the real existing God and all His attributes were revealed to mankind.

Yes, I know, many of the people who lived in my time and long since, have never learned the truth of the soul development, and live in the happiness which has come to them with the progress of their intellects. And many of them have also been brought into the light and truth.

I will not write more, but will say good night,
Leekesi

LEYTERGUS

*Wrote a book describing the creation and fall
of man; Genesis was actually copied after his writings*
August 10, 1915

I am, Leytergus.

I was a native of Arabia and lived before the time of Abraham, the Jewish patriarch.

I come to you tonight to tell you that before the Jewish Testament was written, I had written a book containing a description of creation and of the fall of man, and that the Book of Genesis was copied after my writings, which were founded on traditions older than were the description of Genesis. These descriptions of the creation of the world were not the works of men inspired by the angels or by any other instrumentalities of God, but were the results of the imaginations of the minds of men who lived long before I lived, and who left only the tradition of their writings or teachings. I say all this to show you that the world has existed for many thousands of years longer than the account of its creation in the Jewish scriptures would lead you to think.

I don't know when it was created and I have not found any spirit in the spiritual world who does know. Of course, no spirit would know of his own knowledge because in the natural order of things, man must have been created subsequent to the creation of those things which were

241

necessary for his sustenance and comfort. I have never seen any angels who were not at one time mortals, and hence I could not learn from them when the world was created and I have never seen any angels or spirits to whom God has made this revelation. So I say the creation of the world or rather any account if it is all a matter of speculation and tradition.

Yes, I have been informed as to the fall of man. My information is as follows: When man was created he was made two-fold, that is, there were male and female beings which were intended to make a perfect one without losing any individuality on the part of either. Their names were not Adam and Eve, but Aman and Amon, which meant the male Am and the female Am, Am meaning the exalted creation of God.

These beings were made perfect physically and spiritually. Although their souls were not possessed of all the qualities of the great Creator Soul, and in that particular were inferior to the great Creator. As regards this soul part of their creation, they were made in the image of their Creator. The physical or spiritual part of their creation was not in the image of their Creator, for He had no physical or spiritual body. Their soul's were made in the image of their Creator and not of the Substance, and this image was given the potentiality of obtaining or receiving the Substance of the Soul qualities of their Creator provided they pursued that course in their existence or living which would cause their souls to receive in accordance with certain operations of the laws which their Creator had prescribed, this Soul Substance. And only in obedience to these laws or their operations could this Substance of the Creator Soul, be obtained.

Well, they were not equal to the test, or rather requirements, and after living awhile they became possessed of the idea that they needed not to comply with these prescribed laws, but could of their own will and power obtain this Substance by doing that which they had been forbidden by these laws to do. So in their efforts to obtain this Substance or the Divine Love they disobeyed these laws, and, as a consequence, these potentialities of obtaining the actual Substance of the Creator Soul were taken from them, and then they became beings still possessed of the spiritual and physical forms, but not of the great potentiality; and this was the fall of man.

The disobedience then was the great unlawful desire on the part of these two, to obtain this Soul Substance before being in accordance with the operations of the laws prescribed, before they were fitted or in condition to receive it. As a consequence, they became disobedient, and being possessed of wills which were not in any way bound or limited by their Creator, they exercised these wills in accordance with their desires, and from this disobedience the wills of men and women have continued to act in accordance with their desires and in violation of the great laws of truth, which were made for the first two at the time of their creation and are the same unchangeable laws of this time.

The Soul Substance that these two forfeited was the Divine Love of their Creator, which, had they by their obedience become possessed of, would have made them a part of His divinity, and hence like Him not only in image but in Substance and reality. The potentiality that was taken from them was the privilege which they had to obtain this Soul Substance or Divine Love by complying with obedience which these laws prescribed. So you see, the story of Genesis is merely symbolical.

I have nothing further to say tonight. I live in a sphere which is part of the celestial heavens. I have, through the mercy of God and His gift, declared by Jesus, received this potentiality and through it the Soul Substance which our first parents forfeited.

The name which I have given you was mine when on earth. It is Arabic and nothing else. You must know, that many of the names of my time, after centuries were incorporated in the nomenclature of other nations and races.

So I will say good night.

Your brother in Christ,
Leytergus

CHAPTER NINE

Old Testament

KING SOLOMON (970 - 928 BCE)

Hebrew king writes of Mr. Padgett's selection by Jesus
October 1, 1915

I an here, Solomon.

I came merely to say that I have listened to your conversation tonight, and was very much interested because you have discussed that phase of man's destiny which is most important in all the economy or plans of God.

Your being chosen to do this work was not a thing of the moment, but for a long period of time the highest spirits of the celestial heavens have considered this great question, and the way by which the great truths of God and the necessary plans for man's salvation could be made known to mortals. Heretofore, the difficulty has been in finding a man gifted with mediumistic powers, who had the unbiased mind, and yet a knowledge to some extent of the soul's requirements, and who could be used for the purpose of receiving these great truths and transmitting them to humanity.

Some years ago, as you say, a selection was made of a man to declare these truths, and to him much power and spiritual knowledge were given, and even that power of leaving the body and visiting the world of spirits so that he might see for himself the actual condition of things as they existed, and to declare to humankind the results of his observations. He did observe and declare many truths, but the difficulty of his realizing the pure truth and interpreting the things which he saw, was that his mind was too biased by what he had read and believed from the writings as contained in the Bible. Hence, his efforts failed to accomplish the great purpose intended by the mission given him. I am here referring to Swedenborg, the seer, as he was called.

This was a great disappointment to these celestial spirits who had projected such a plan for revealing the truths to humanity. At the head of these celestial spirits was Jesus, as he is now. Since that time, the time has never been propitious for a plan of this kind to be attempted again until now.

But now, instead of having the mortal, through whom this plan is to be worked, leave his body and come to the spirit world, and then relate the results and interpretations of his observations, it has been determined that the truths shall be declared to the mortal in the words and thoughts of these spirits, so that no mistake or wrong interpretation can possibly occur. Hence when we saw the possibility of your becoming a medium with powers sufficient, and a soul capable of development to receive these thoughts and words, it was decided to select you and make you the medium for doing this great work. Of course, Jesus was the active superior spirit in making the selection and we all submitted to his judgment.

I have told you this tonight, because I have been selected by the others to do so. So strive with all your might to acquire this great faith and soul development which are absolutely necessary to a successful performance of the work. We are with you very often trying to incline your thoughts to the higher things, and to fill your soul with their influences which our love for you creates around you.

So on behalf of all of us who are promoting this great work, I give you our love and blessings.

Your brother in Christ,
Solomon the wise, of the Old Testament

AMAN

Aman, first parent, reveals his temptation and fall
August 30, 1915

Aman, the first parent.

You don't believe me, I can see, but I am whom I say, and want to tell you that I am now a follower of Jesus and a lover of God, and live far up in the celestial heavens near where the Master lives.

I know it is hard for men to believe that I am the father of all physical manhood, and that I can come and communicate with mortals. Jesus has rendered this possible in his opening the way for the higher spirits to communicate through you. You should feel specially blessed at having this great privilege, and feel that the Master has conferred on you a great favor, as he has.

Well, I have never before come to earth to communicate with mortals, and, the experience being new, I find some difficulty in doing so, but I will try to write a few more lines.

My soulmate and I lived in a paradise which God had given us, and were very happy until the great fall. We were so filled with the thought that we were all powerful and all wise, that we concluded that the obedience which God had required of us was not necessary for us to observe, and that if we only exerted our powers, we would be as great as He is great, and would be able to obtain that immortality which He possessed. But, alas, the day came when we realized the fact that we were mere creations, although wonderful and beautiful.

Our disobedience was in not waiting for God to bestow upon us the great Divine Love that would make us like Him in substance as well as in image. We disobeyed Him in that we tried to make ourselves believe that we were as He was, and that we need not submit further to His decrees. We tried to make this belief a thing of reality, and in our vanity, tried to appear as gods; but as soon as we did this the scales dropped from our eyes, and we saw how naked and impotent we were.

God did not drive us from His paradise (Genesis 3:24), but the inexorable laws of our creation and of the workings of His will showed us that no longer could we expect this Divine Love which He said would make us "divine". So we became mere mortals, deprived of the potentiality of obtaining this Divine Love, and we had thereafter to become subject to all the appetites of the natural man and to work to satisfy these natural appetites.

We continued to live in the same place as formerly, though no longer could we be satisfied with the spiritual food that had supplied our wants and enabled us to subdue the appetites which formed a part of our physical being. The physical then asserted itself and the spiritual became subjected to it, and we became as mortals now are, and had to find our sustenance in mother earth (Genesis 3:23). We were compelled to till the soil and earn our living by work. I mean we had to work in order to make the earth supply us with food for our physical wants. It was a bitter time of sorrow, for the law had imposed its penalty, and we were without power to relieve ourselves of that penalty, and had to live thereafter without the possibility of obtaining this Divine Love and of having our spiritual natures reassert themselves over the physical, and subdue it.

When Amon and I were created, there were no other human beings living on earth, and none came there to live until we had sons and daughters who intermarried and produced other sons and daughters (Genesis 1:28). I cannot tell you how long ago our creation was, but many thousand years before the coming of Jesus.

I will not write more tonight, but will come again sometime.

Your brother in Christ,
Aman

Aman makes a correction
August 30, 1915

I am here, Aman.

Yes, and I want to correct what I wrote before. I never was a spirit who wanted to have merely immortality as God was immortal, but I also wanted to obtain the power and wisdom which I saw that God possessed. I thought that if I could obtain these qualities, I would become a God and a co-equal with my Creator, and hence the possessor of all the universe, and of all the power and knowledge that He had. My effort to realize my ambition in these particulars was a part of my great sin of disobedience.

I thought it best to tell you this so that my description of the great sin of disobedience would not be only a part of the truth. I now know what an insignificant creature I was as compared to the Creator, and I also know that the creation of Amon and me was the highest creation in all the universe of God.

The great mercy and Love of God, notwithstanding my great sin, has placed me in the position and condition which he promised me at my creation, and which I forfeited with such fatal consequences. You have a privilege which I was then deprived of for so many long years, and your happiness may be as great as mine is now without having to wait the long and many years that I waited. No wonder that humankind worships Jesus as God, when we consider the great gift that he brought to them and the way to obtain it.

I must not write more.

Your brother in Christ and father in the flesh,
Aman

AMON

Amon, mother of all human creation,
gives her experience of her temptation and disobedience
August 30, 1915

I am, Amon.

I am the first mother of all the human race, and I want you to know that before Aman and myself, no human beings ever existed. We were created by God at the same time, and were ready, just after the moment of our creation, to live the lives of natural beings. There was no gradual growth on our part from any other creature or thing. I know it has been said that the first man was not created, but developed from some animal of the lower order, and as the process of evolution proceeded, this being became in the end a man, with all the wonderful organism and structure of his body, but I want to tell you that this is not true.

When I was created I was as perfect in my physical organism as I ever was afterwards or as any man or woman ever became from that time to the present. In fact, I believe that at the time of our creation we were more perfect than humans are now, because we had no physical ailments, no sickness, no deformity of any kind. We certainly were more beautiful in face and form than humans are now or have been for many long centuries; and besides, our bodies and organism lasted years longer than do the bodies of humans at this time.

Before our fall we were very happy in our conjugal love, and knew not troubles or worries of any kind, and never had anything to make us afraid or draw us apart from each other or from God until the great temptation came, and then because of our ideas of our greatness and power and want of dependence on God, we fell, and never again were restored to our position of beauty and happiness that were ours in the beginning of our lives on earth. So you see we were specially created and did not evolve from any other thing.

Some men may wonder at the Bible description of the creation of man, and reject the description as the imagining of a mind of romance or imagery, but I tell you now that the essentials of this creation and the fall, are true. Of course the parts played by the apple and the snake and the devil are not literally true, but are symbolical of the principles that entered into the temptation and fall. I was as much to blame as was Aman. I did not entice him after I had the ambition to become immortal, but our ambitions grew together and we discussed the matter of making the great effort between us and acted as one in trying to obtain this great immortality. So the story in the Bible is not exactly true as far as I am concerned, for I did not entice or seduce Aman to do the great wrong and neither did he seduce me to enter into the effort.

However, all this is past, and many thousands of years have gone by since our fall, and we have suffered much because of our first sin. Since the time that we forfeited the gift of immortality, until it was restored and made known by Jesus the Son of God, for he was the Son of God, in being a part of God's Divine Nature he was "divine." Jesus partook of those qualities of God which gave him immortality, and those who follow his teachings and receive the Divine Love will become immortal also.

I must not write more tonight. Now I will say good night,

Your sister,
Amon

SARAH

The story of Hagar as recorded in the Bible is not a correct one
October 23, 1915

I am the spirit of Sarah, I was the wife of Abraham.

I want to tell you that there are many things in the Bible that are not true. Well, when it says that I sent Hagar into the desert, or caused her to be sent into the desert (Genesis 21:10) to starve and die — that story was a slander on me and did me great injustice because I was not such a wicked woman.

Abraham did not send her there either (Genesis 21:14): she went of her own accord because she had done that which condemned her in her own conscience. Well, she had taken my husband and had a child by him. The Bible says that it was commanded by God, or that I prevailed upon Abraham to have a child by her (Genesis 16:2), but it is not true.

Yes, I am happy, and so is Abraham and our son Isaac, and his son Jacob; although they were without this Divine Love for a great many years, as it only came to us when the Master came to earth. I know that you think it strange that I should come to you and write, but as I was in the earth plane and was attracted to you by the light which fills the space around you, I came to you and wrote.

Yes, I see a great number of beautiful spirits around you, and some of the apostles who are so very beautiful and bright. They seem to be so much interested in you, and say that you have been selected to do the work of the Master on earth in the way of revealing the truths which he shall write to you. I don't quite understand it all, but if the Master says it is what shall be done, you will do it.

I must stop now. Please believe that I am Sarah as I have told you. I will leave you now and say good night.

Your sister in Christ,
Sarah, the wife of Abraham

ESAU

Son of Isaac now knows the difference between
a spirit who has the Divine Love and one who does not
December 4, 1916

I am here, Esau.

I was the son of Isaac and the brother of Jacob, and the one whom the Jews regarded as having sold his birthright for a mess of pottage (Genesis 25:34), but I was misrepresented in this regard, as I did only that which necessity compelled me to do. All that is long past, and now I am an inhabitant of the celestial heavens, for in the world of spirits all things are made right, and I became a possessor of the Divine Love after I had received knowledge of its rebestowal at the coming of Jesus.

Many of the characters of the Old Testament have never realized this great transformation, because in their conception of self righteousness, they are contented in that conception and worship God as they did on earth, although they have ceased to offer sacrifices of animals because they have none in the spirit life to offer. Yet they still have the belief that sacrifice is necessary, and in their imaginations they offer what to them is symbolical of the offerings that they made in the earth life.

Yes, that is quite a natural supposition, but you must know that mind and the beliefs of mortals continue with them when they become spirits and will not permit them to be convinced of the errors of their conceptions of the Deity, and many of these spirits of old are in that condition now. They refuse to believe or even listen to the truths of their existence and their relationship to God, as they did when on earth.

They have eyes, but they see not, and ears but they hear not, and enveloped in the darkness of their beliefs, they decline to let in the light, or to permit the truths that are so apparent to others to illuminate their soul. A mind that is shut in by bigotry and intolerance is just as persistent after the mortal becomes a spirit, even though a change in its surroundings or what you might call its physical existence and in its possibilities for learning the truth occur. Many of these spirits absolutely refuse to recognize any change or possibility of change in their spiritual

252

condition.

It is not surprising that you may not understand how it is possible that these spirits of the kind mentioned could live all this great period of years, as you estimate time, in this condition, surrounded by spirits who have found the truth, and display that possession in their appearances and happiness, and especially by some of their old associates who have entered into the light, and not be influenced by these appearances and the experiences of these associates. Nevertheless, it is true, and the difficulty of converting these bigoted spirits seems to grow the greater as they advance in their progression of mind.

They are happy in a relative sense and in their beliefs they can conceive of no other belief or cause of progress that could bring to them greater happiness; and besides, they are firmly convinced that they are doing the will of God in their manner of worship and in their symbolical sacrifices. These ancient spirits, as you call them, are young as compared to many in the spirit spheres, and they have their synagogues and temples of worship, and their priests and servants and worshippers according to their old beliefs. Their gatherings for worship are little different from what they were on earth. They have all their vestments and attire and other accompaniments that on earth distinguished them from the common people, and they say their prayers in public and delight in appearing as holy spirits, the specially chosen of God, just as they did on earth. They are developing more and more in their natural love and taking on the condition of perfection, like the perfection of the first parents as they existed before the fall. They may remain in this condition of belief as to their relationship to God, and as to their proper and only way to worship Him, throughout all eternity.

I am glad that I could write to you tonight, as it is a new experience for me and one that gives me great satisfaction. I will come again, if agreeable to you, and write further. I wish to say in closing that I know the difference between the spirit who has in his soul the Divine Love, and one who has not, and that the mere time of a spirit's existence in the spirit world does not necessarily indicate that the spirit possesses the Divine Love.

As Jesus said when on earth, "the first shall be last, and the last shall be first" (Matthew 20:16), and I may add that some will never be first or last, but only the reminders of what might have been.

I will not write more,
Esau

AARON

Aaron gives his experience and what he now knows about
immortality since Jesus came and taught how it can be obtained
October 23, 1915

I am the spirit of Aaron, prophet of the Old Testament and the brother of Moses, as it is written.

I lived at a time when we had not the privilege of getting this Love, and, as a consequence, immortality, so instead, we had to find our happiness in our natural love, and that meant a love towards God as well as towards our fellowman. Yet this love, while it enabled us to experience much happiness, did not give us that Divine Essence or Nature which now makes our happiness supreme and also makes us at-one with God.

I had many experiences in teaching the Hebrew children that there was only one God, but at that time my conception of God was not what it is now. I then thought more of Him as a God of wrath and jealousy than as a God of Love and mercy.

In my contest with the magicians of the Egyptian Pharaoh (Exodus 7:10-12) I was afforded the help of the spirit world, and unusual powers were given me, such as I had never had before nor ever afterwards; and it was for the purpose of causing the king to let the people of God, as we called ourselves, depart from Egypt. When this was accomplished I never again possessed those powers or had any occasion to. Those powers were merely the influences that came from the spirit world, and God himself did not speak to me or to Moses, as it is written (Exodus 7:1), merely his spirits or angels told us what we must do, and gave us the power to do it.

This power is still existing, and should the occasion arise again, it will be given to the instrumentality that may be selected to do the will of God. Even as to Jesus, who had the greatest power conferred upon him of any mortal that ever lived, this power was given him by the angels of God in obedience to His commands. I cannot explain to you now in what way these commands were given by God, for you would not understand me if I should make the attempt, but suffice it to say that the higher angels have such soul perceptions that they can receive and understand these instructions.

All this is, I know, strange to you, but it is true, and because you do not understand, you must not doubt that there is such a close relationship between God and His celestial spirits that they know what His will is. I am in a celestial sphere and am very high up, but not so high as are the apostles, though high enough to know what I write you of my own knowledge to be true.

I will not write more tonight, but will come again sometime and instruct you in the laws pertaining to our celestial spheres.

So with all my love, I will say that I am your brother in Christ.

Aaron, the prophet of old

MOSES

*Prophet of God tells of the importance that
the Jews learn the truths of God proclaimed by Jesus*
November 9, 1915

I am Moses of ancient days.

I have been with you on several occasions when some of the ancient spirits wrote to you, and I was very much interested.

I am still the faithful servant of God, and in addition, a believer in Jesus, who is the greatest of all the sons of God, and the only one of all God's messengers who brought immortal life to light. I could not have said this before his coming: I mean that I could not have said that other great reformers and teachers of the truths of God had not done this, because I did not know before the coming of Jesus what immortality meant and that no mortal or spirit before that time knew this great truth.

I am now in the celestial heavens with many of the old prophets and seers who have received this great gift of the Divine Love. Many who lived and died since Jesus's time are also celestial spirits partaking of immortality.

I now see that many of my teachings were not true and that love did not enter into them, but rather the spirit of retaliation which is absolutely no part of the truths of the Almighty. The Jews still look upon me as their great teacher and lawgiver, and many of them observe literally my laws. I want to tell you this fact, because I believe that when you publish the messages of the Master, you should also publish what I may write, for many Jews will believe me, and that I and many of those who taught my teachings, are now engaged in showing the spirits of Jews who come into the spirit world the truths as taught by the Master.

The Jewish nation is the most strict of all people in their beliefs in and observations of their religious doctrines as set forth in the Old Testament; and hence, they will be among the last of all men to accept the truths which I now understand and teach. I hope that something which I may communicate to you will cause them to think and become believers and observers of this "new revelation" of truth.

The Jews have fought and suffered for their religion all these centuries and are still doing so, and the one great thing that more than any other has prevented them from accepting the teachings of Jesus and believing in his mission to humanity, is that his followers, or those who attempted to write his teachings, and those who interpreted the same, declare and maintain that Jesus is God and that the true God was three instead of one.

This has been the great stumbling block to the Jews, and when they read, as they may, that Jesus himself declares and proclaims that he is not God but only his Son, and that they are also his sons, they will look upon his teachings with more tolerance, and many of them will be inclined to accept his truths, and Judaism in its religious aspect will gradually disappear, and the Jews will become a part of the one great religious brotherhood of men, as in our celestial heavens. There will be on earth no more Jew and no more Gentile, but all will become one in their belief in the Father and the mission of Jesus. He will be accepted as the Messiah not only of the Jew but of the whole world, and then God's chosen people will not be a very small minority of God's children, but the whole world will be his chosen people.

I am so interested in this phase of the great truths that shall be given to and accepted by men, because I was, more than any other man, responsible for the present beliefs of the Jews, which causes them to hold themselves separate and apart from all the rest of humanity as the chosen and specially selected of God's people.

I will not write more tonight, but feel that I must ask you to permit me to write again, as I have a mission to perform on earth to undo a work which I so effectively performed when I was the leader of my people. As Jesus is teaching and will teach all humankind the way to the Almighty and immortality, I must teach my people the way to get rid of these erroneous and false beliefs which are contained in the Old Testament.

So thanking you, I will say good night,
Moses, the lawgiver of the Jews

KING SAUL

God is not the God of any race but of the individual
June 1, 1916

I am here, Saul.

I have not written you for some time and I would like to say only a few words, and these are, that never in all the battles with the Amalekites (1 Samuel 15:18) did God help me or bring to me victory as is set forth in the Old Testament. Although some of the prophets, like Samuel, at the time might have thought so, yet as I now know, it was not true. God was not the partial and particular patron of the Jews, and to Him it was just as sinful for the Jews to commit murder and the other horrible crimes that are mentioned in the book in connection with my life as king, as it would have been for the pagans to have done the same thing.

God is not the God of any race, but is the God of every individual who comes to Him in true supplication and prayer, seeking His Love and help in his spiritual nature. God will respond and the individual will surely be helped, but should that individual come to Him seeking power and assistance to murder his fellowman, no matter how great an enemy he might be, God would not help him or approve of his desires, and this being so, you can readily see that He would not help any nation to commit such acts and gain the victory.

I want to tell you here, that God is not a God of nations but of individuals only, and as the individuals that compose the nations, He can be said to be a God of nations. He wants not the praise of men or of nations because of victory that they might acquire through bloodshed and cruelties ascribed to His help. Instead, he wants the praise of men only because their souls may have been awakened to His Love, and have acquired victory over sin and evil.

Nations rise and fall and disappear from the face of the earth, yet the individuals who compose these nations never die, even though their physical bodies die. God is a God only of those things that never die, and He is interested in having the individual become victor over sin and the appetites of the flesh. Of course, the individuals make up the nation and give it its character and qualities, and hence the nation will become sinful and cruel as the individuals that compose it become sinful and cruel. God does not deal with nations as such, but only with the small, but important, units that make up the nation. Hence, for a nation to say that God is our God, or that God will help us to victory over our enemies, is all wrong.

When the individual gains the victory over his greatest enemy, himself, then he can claim that God is his God and give Him the praise, and when all the individuals of a nation have gained that victory, then that nation can proclaim that God is its God and render to Him praise for the victory. Only in such event is any nation justified in saying, God is our God."** Let me say that no Christian nation so-called, has yet, as individuals, attained to that condition of righteousness and victory over sin that it can claim to be God's chosen nation.

So I say that I, Saul the king, before my alleged fall from the Grace of God (1 Samuel 13:13), was no more helped by God than I was after that supposed event, for the reason that while outwardly I may have appeared to seek God's directions and listened to the advice of His prophets, yet inwardly, I was no more in accord with God or reconciled to Him than I was after the momentous event. God never helped the Jews, as a nation, to any greater extent than He did any other nation, for they as individuals were no more in attunement with Him than were

*A passage of this nature appears in the Old Testament (Psalms 48:14).

many individuals of what were called the pagan nations.

When I went to Samuel in my despair, as the Bible portrays (1 Samuel 15:24-25), and felt the burden of the sins of my life, I became nearer to God than I had ever been before, and He was more my God than ever, though I did not realize it. I merely write this to show men that they must not believe and rely on the statement that because I was said to have observed God's will and obeyed His commands before the time that I realized defeat was certain to be mine, that God was any more my God then, directing and assisting me to overcome my enemies, than he was after that event.

I have written enough and will now stop. So with all my love, and the assurance that God is a God of the individual and not of the nation, I will say good night.

Your brother in Christ,
Saul

SAMUEL

His teachings and experiences when on earth; he
did not get the Divine Love until Jesus came to bring it
July 21, 1915

Samuel, the Prophet of God of the Old Testament.

I am the same Samuel whom the woman of Endor called from the spirit world (1 Samuel 28:11) to show Saul his doom; and as I come to you tonight, I came to her at that time, only my purpose is not the same and I am not the same spirit in my qualifications.

I am now a Christian and know what the Divine Love of God means, while then, I did not, and was a spirit living in comparative happiness and existing in the consciousness that I had done my work on earth, and was enjoying the repose of the righteous, for as we understood that word then in both the mortal and spirit worlds, I was a righteous man.

I come to you tonight, because I see that you have been chosen to do the great work of the Master in his efforts to redeem humankind from their lives of sin and error, and to show them the way by which they may partake of the Divine Nature of God and obtain immortality. How much more mortals, and spirits too, are blessed now than they were when I was a mortal, and for a long time after I became a spirit. My God then and your God now, are the same, although His great gift of Divine Love was not in existence then as it is now. So you and all other mortals should realize the great privilege you have because of this gift and the gift of Jesus to explain it, and show the way by which that Love may be obtained, freely, without mental exercise of a high order, but merely by the longings and aspirations of the soul in its desires to become a part of God's divinity.

I tell you that the ways of God are wonderful and mysterious, and His plans, while to us may seem to be working slowly, yet they are working surely, and will be accomplished in His own fullness of time. I never knew when on earth that God was such a God of Love and mercy. He was our Jehovah and Ruler. He was a God of anger and wrath and a jealous God, as I thought, ever ready to punish those whom He thought to be His enemies with massacre and death. I obeyed Him and performed His work as I understood I should, more through fear than love. In fact love was never a weapon or instrument with me to be used in bringing the disobedient Jew to a compliance with what we thought was the will of God.

In such a method of procuring obedience the soul was never developed, and love was a minor factor in making the Jews obedient to God's requirements. Our principal desires were for the success of our earthly undertakings and when these were accomplished we had no further use for our God, except to keep Him in reserve for occasions that might arise when, as we thought, we might need His assistance.

I know that Moses commanded the Jews to love God with all their souls and mind and strength, and many of them thought that they were doing so, but in reality their love was limited by the extent of their desires for worldly gain. This I know, for when they had succeeded in obtaining what they wanted, they forgot to love God; and, hence we prophets were so often required to instruct them, and so frequently did call them to a recollection of God and the danger they ran in forgetting

Him and His laws. We seldom attempted to have them call back their recollections of Him through love, but nearly always through threatening and the portrayal of dire punishments that would be inflicted upon them should they continue to forget Him.

Thus it was that Saul sought my help and advice. He thought that not only had God forsaken him, but that he had forsaken God, and he expected the punishment that he thought would result from such neglect to serve and obey God. He thought that as I was in the spirit world and probably very close to God, I would exercise some influence and have the great, threatened calamity* arrested. However, he did not seek me through Love of God, but through fear of his enemies and dread that God would direct His wrath upon him. So you see, fear was the ruling sentiment that actuated the Jews in my time in their dealings with God, and when that fear was allayed or forgotten, God was forgotten, and only again remembered when danger appeared. Of course, there were many exceptions to this class of Jews, for there were some who really loved God and for whom no fear of wrath or anger on His part formed a part of their love.

So you will see that the laws of Moses were not so much intended to regulate the spiritual or soul part of the Jews, but to control them in their dealings with one another in the practical affairs of life and in their dealings with the heathens and strangers. The moral laws thus taught were taught for the purpose of making them righteous between themselves, and then, as a consequence, so they thought, they would be righteous towards God.

Well, the woman of Endor was not a witch and did not practice the black art. She was a good woman possessed of powers to call up the dead, as they were called. She did not engage in practices of doing harm to mortals, such as putting spells upon them or using charms. No, she was a true medium and, while not possessed of much spirituality, yet she was a woman of good morals and had around her many spirits of the higher order whose only desires were to do good to mortals. She was the one who was careful to have no evil spirits come and communicate, and her powers with the higher ones were very great. Had she been of what you call the lower class of mediums, I would never have responded to her call. She was in rapport with men and other spirits whose thoughts were turned to the higher things of the spirit world, and hence,

---

*The Israelites were defeated by the Philistines. Saul and his three sons were killed.

she had no difficulty in having us appear when she desired it for the consolation of help to mortals.

I had instructed Saul and advised him on earth, and naturally after I became a spirit and he needed help, he would seek my advice. In those days mediums were more numerous than most people suppose, and because of their being so common and of such different kinds, and most of them engaged in necromancy and evil arts. There were passed strict laws against them pursuing their calling or engaging in the practice of consulting spirits.

However, not all were bad, and many of them did good in the world, and among these was the woman of Endor, notwithstanding that she has been so vilified and abused by the churches and preachers. You may be surprised when I tell you that she is now living high up in the celestial heavens and a redeemed spirit enjoying the Divine Love of God.

Well, I must stop, but I will come again sometime and tell you of the things that I know in reference to these higher spheres.

I will say good night.

Your friend and brother,
Samuel

Continuous life of a man after the death of the body
as shown by the manifestations of nature is not conclusive
March 21, 1916

I am here, Samuel.

I desire to write on a subject that is of importance to those who are in doubt as to the reality of the future life.

I know that a vast majority of mortals believe in a future existence and the immortality of the soul, but there are a considerable number of mortals who do not know these facts or who have no belief regarding this matter, and simply say, "I don't know." It is to these latter persons that I wish to write.

In the first place, all persons know, if they know anything, that they

262

are living, and that sooner or later what they call death is inevitable, no matter from what cause it may take place. To live then, implies that there is such a thing as continuous life; and to die, to these people, demonstrates that the life with which they are acquainted ceases, and that the material body in which this life manifests itself gradually disintegrates into the original elements that composed that body.

Now, a man being a materialist purely, would seem to be correct in his conclusions that when life, which could be manifested only through the material things of nature, ceases, and the body becomes inanimate and dead, that this is the end not only of the body but of the individual. If there existed no other manifestation of life than this physical one, there would be no foundation upon which to base the assumption, that the death of the body does not end all.

I know it has been asserted in the way of argument that even though the material parts of vegetation die, yet as spring comes round, these materials show forth again the life that had previously manifested itself, and therefore, by analogy, the death of the human body merely means that its life will appear again in evidence in some other body or form. Now upon close investigation and exact reasoning it will be seen that the two subjects of demonstration are not alike, because while the material of the vegetable kingdom apparently dies, yet it does not all die; even though you may apparently see the particular body of the tree or plant or every part of it go into decay or rottenness, yet as a fact, this is not true. The whole of the material plant which enclosed or manifested life, does not die, until out of it a new body arises and grows, and the life that animated the body that appears to have died, continues in it, awaiting the new growth for its display of existence.

The flower dies and the bush upon which it grows may appear to die, yet the roots continue to enclose the life principle which causes the bush to grow again, and which has its genesis in these roots, and is the same life that originally existed in the bush. Pluck up the bush by the roots and expose them to the elements until they die and commence to disintegrate, and then replant them, and you will find they will not grow, for the reason that the life which had animated them has departed.

The same conclusions will be reached when you apply the same investigation and reasoning to every species of the vegetable kingdom. The grain of corn, though apparently dead, is in reality not dead, but continues to contain the life principle which was the cause of the growth of the stalk and blade and ear. Nothing of the vegetable kingdom will be reproduced or form the basis of a new growth, unless some part of the old growth retains in it the life force.

In man's investigation of the wonders of vegetable life, he has discovered that a grain of corn that had been entombed in the hands of an Egyptian mummy for more than three thousand years, when planted in the ground, reproduced the stalk and blade and ear of corn, just as the original material body had produced. And why? Not because when the grain of corn was planted in the earth it received unto itself new life or any force that was not already in it, but because the grain had never ceased to be without the life that existed in it as it grew from the original seed to the perfect grain. The grain had never lost its life and had never died, though apparently it had. Always there was some part of the original body that continued to exist and that held enclosed in itself the life principle. Without the preservation of some part of the original body there could never have been a manifestation of the life that caused the growth of that body. This phenomenon, as you call it, was not the resurrection of a material body that had died and become disintegrated and nonexistent, but was merely the resurrection of that part of the old body that had never died, and had always retained in it the life principle. This, I say, is no argument for the future existence of man, as viewed from a purely material aspect.

When the body of a man dies it is eternally destroyed, either by natural decay or by incineration or, sometimes, by cannibals, so that no portion of his body remains in which the life principle may be preserved; and so far as the material body is involved, it utterly disappears and no roots remain in the ground and no grain or seed of it is preserved from which a new body may arise.

So I say, the phenomenon of the vegetable apparently dying and, after a season, springing forth again, and producing a body similar to the one that had formerly lived and died, furnishes no demonstration or argument from which, logically, can be drawn the conclusion that when a man dies, he will not cease to exist, or will live again. Now from the purely material standpoint, the materialist has the better of the argument, and he may well ask the question: "When a man dies shall he live again?" and he may answer the inquiry by saying, nature furnishes no proof that he will.

It may be said that life permeates all nature and is the basis of all existence, and that assertion is true; but it does not follow therefrom that any particular manifestation of life, such as the individual man, when once ceasing to manifest, will again be reproduced in that particular identity of material manifestation, or in that form or existence that will make itself the identical being that had ceased to exist. So to show man that there is a continuous existence after the death of the body, and by this I mean an individual identical existence, something more is required than the argument of the analogy in nature, or to the material things of nature in which life appears and then apparently disappears and then reappears.

As the discussion on this phase of matter will require more time than you have tonight to receive it, I will defer the treatment until later.

With all my love I will say good night.

Your brother in Christ,
Samuel

What actually happened at the crucifixion of Jesus
April 1, 1916

I am, Samuel.

Let me write a few lines tonight, for I desire to tell you of the scene that was depicted to you tonight by the words and music at the church.

I was present* at the time of the crucifixion of Jesus and saw all that took place. When Jesus was crucified there was no great concourse of people, because he was considered as a common malefactor, paying the penalties that followed the violation of the law that he was charged with violating. Of course, there were soldiers and a large number of the members of the Jewish Sanhedrin and a few followers present, but there was no unusual crowd to witness the execution. Jesus was not the only one crucified at the time and the other two were also considered violators of the laws to be punished by hanging on the cross.

The words that Jesus was supposed to have uttered at the time were not uttered by him and no words that he may have spoken could have

*Samuel was in spirit at that time.

265

been heard by any of his followers, for they were kept away from the immediate scene of his execution. It was only after he had been pronounced dead and found ready to be removed from the cross, that his followers were permitted to approach his body and remove it (Matthew 27:58-59). The others, who were engaged in the execution did not hear any words of his, and as I have said, his followers could not hear and thus be able to report any supposed saying of his. So far as known, he died bravely, that is, without fear or doubt as to the future.

He did not call upon the Father for His help, or to cause the cup* to pass from him. All reports of what he said or did at that time are not true, but merely the imagining of those who wrote of him in later times. There was no sudden breaking up of nature or things material (Matthew 27:51), and the accounts of the graves opening, and the bodies arising therefrom and being seen and talked with in the city are purely fiction, and have no foundation in fact.

I know that Christians of today will not be ready to receive these statements as true, because of the long years of belief in these things that they have obtained during the centuries. Why men should want to believe in these representations of things that never happened is hard to understand, for in themselves they have no significance except the mere endeavor to make as dramatic and impressive to humankind the wonderful circumstances that they allege surrounded the death of Jesus. If they will only think, they must realize that the death of Jesus, accompanied by all the startling environments described in the Bible, did not afford one iota of help in the way of saving a human soul or teaching that soul the true way to God's kingdom. His life is what had the effect and not his death, and the sooner men learn that truth the sooner they will learn the fact that no death of Jesus could save them from themselves, or show them the way to the celestial kingdom.

I know that men will not want to believe what I have written, and continue in their belief that all these tragic circumstances surrounded the death of Jesus. I suppose that this belief will continue with them for a long time to come. However, what I have said is true, and no man can by any possible workings of God's laws find any hope or assurance of immortality in these things. You may ask me how I know that Jesus uttered no words at the time of his death, and I can answer by saying

*The cup in this reference means the short, sharp, bitter, agonizing struggle of martyrdom. In Matthew a reference is made to the cup in the Garden of Gethsemane (Matthew 27:51).

that he told me so himself.

He has not been present tonight at any of the churches where his death on the cross is celebrated, and will not be until after the time of the great worship and adoration of him by the churches has gone. This worship is all very distasteful to him and is such that he does not desire to witness it, and hence, he remains in his home in the high celestial spheres. He desires men to worship only the one true Father that he worships. Well, I see that you are tired and I will not write more.

With my love, I will say good night.

Your brother in Christ,
Samuel

ELIJAH

Elijah was not John the Baptist, neither was John a reincarnation of Elijah
February 7, 1917

I am here, Elijah of the Old Testament.

I want also to encourage you in the belief that you have a great work to do, and that you must not falter or delay the coming of the messages. I know that sometimes it is hard for you to believe that you have been selected to do this great work. Yes, there are a great number present, and you have around you a wonderful spiritual influence which should cause you to believe that these spirits are present trying to help you.

I was Elijah of the Old Testament, and I actually lived and was a prophet among the Jews, and was not John the Baptist, nor was he a reincarnation of me as some earth teachers claim. John was himself alone. He was in the flesh only once and was not a reincarnation of me or anyone else.

I will not write more now, so good night.
Elijah

*The truth of the Bible as to the things
that are contained in the Old Testament*
March 18, 1917

I am here, Elijah.

I come tonight to write a short message. My entrance on the scene of Jewish life and history was very abrupt, and little was written about my antecedent life, and in fact, nothing except that I was a Tishbite (1 Kings 17:1) who lived in that portion of Palestine where the acts and doings of the prophets and men of the Hebrew race are very seldom referred to, and little is known of these people.

When I came into notice, as portrayed, I was not very widely known, and to the writers of the scriptures it appeared as if I had come out of the unknown. God had taken special pains to communicate and instruct me in the truths of His laws, and also the acts of disobedience of those Jews among whom I appeared. Even so a great deal of the accounts of my appearing and things that I declared and did are imaginary and the result of the workings of the minds of those who produced the stories of the lives of the Jews at those times, and in the way told in the Bible.

I was a real existing person and of the prophet class, and warned the kings and rulers of the wrath of God that was impending upon them, and of the evils of their manner of living. I was listened to by these kings, who sometimes heeded my warnings and sometimes did not; and the consequences were suffered by them. I never claimed to have direct communication with God, or to deliver any messages that He had directed me to deliver by His own word of mouth, or that I had ever seen God, or knew who or what He was.

I was a man who lived a rather secluded life, and was versed in the teachings and beliefs of the Israelites, as they were known at the time. I was also given to much meditation and prayer and possessed much of the religious instinct, and in fact, to such a degree that I really believed that the thoughts and perceptions of truth that came to me were actually the messages from the unseen world. I possessed the knowledge of the moral truths, as declared in the Decalogue and as taught by the priests of the temple. I could readily discern and understand the acts and doings of the kings and of the people to be a violation of these moral truths. When I learned of these violations, I appeared to these rulers and people and denounced their acts and doings and threatened them with the wrath of God, unless they ceased their acts of disobedience and returned to the worship of the one true God that the Hebrew race distinctly declared and worshiped. Sometimes I was received as the true prophet of God and sometimes I was not. As a consequence, my messages at times were received and believed in, and at other times they were not.

The foundation stone of my belief and office was that there was only one God, and He was the God of the Hebrews, and all other Gods that were believed in, and worshiped by a part of the Jews and by the Gentiles, were false gods, and should not have obeisance made to them or be worshiped. Hence, when I appeared to Ahab and denounced his evil ways (1 Kings 21:20), I was performing, as I believed, the duties that my God had imposed upon me, and which were so necessary to cause the turning away of the people from their false beliefs and worship to an acknowledgment of the one true God.

Well, there are many things related in these writings that never occurred. The one that is often referred to and accepted as proof of the superior power of my God over the god, Baal, is the consuming by fire of the offerings at the altar by the power of God (1 Kings 18:38), and this after the priests had called upon their false god to answer their prayers and he neglected to respond (1 Kings 18:26), never occurred. This was the result of the endeavor of some Jewish writer to demonstrate to his people the wonderful power and activity and closeness of that God to His prophets. Such an incident never took place, and there are many other occurrences related to the powers that I possessed as the prophet of God that never had any existence. While I considered and believed myself to be a prophet of God, yet I never had any of the supernatural powers, nor were any such ever displayed by me, as recorded in the supposed history of my life as a mortal.

There is one other instance to which I desire to refer and that is my supposed ascension into heaven in a chariot of fire in the presence of Elisha (2 Kings 2:11-12). This is merely a tale, as I may say, and well told, but it never had any existence in fact; and I did not ascend in my physical body, nor did any other mortal that I have heard of, not even the Master. It would be against the laws of God that such a thing should take place, and He never violates His laws for the purpose of demonstrating to mortals His power, or the greatness of any of His followers or for any other purpose. No, I died as other mortals died, and was buried having at the time of my death, friends and relatives; and since that time my physical body has never been resurrected and never will be.

I ascended into the spirit world in my spirit body, as has every other mortal at the time of the death of his physical body since the world of human existence began, and in the future, the spirits of men will continue to ascend and their physical bodies will go back to the elements out of which they were composed.

It may be supposed, that because I was versed in the teachings of the religious laws of the Hebrews and the precepts of the Decalogue and believed myself to be a prophet and especially delegated by God to denounce the sins and evils of the kings and people that had forsaken the beliefs and practices of their fathers, that I went into the heaven of perfection and into the supreme happiness. No, I went merely into the spirit world and found my place just where the condition of my soul in its harmony with God's laws and His truths fitted me for and determined where I should be placed. The condition of soul determines the destiny of the spirit. No mere belief in self-righteousness, or the conviction that the individual may have been specially favored by God to do His work, or that I am closer to God and deserving of His special mercy and favor, can ever place me in different surroundings or conditions or degrees of happiness from what the actual harmony of the qualities of my soul with the laws of God and their workings entitle me.

Many of these stories of the Old Testament may be used profitably to draw a moral or adorn a tale, but when the question arises, as what shall determine the destiny of the human soul, then the truth never changes, and only the truth will decide the question. Only a pure, perfect soul can find its home in a pure, perfect heaven, and only a divine soul can find its home in a divine heaven; which latter, is the home of the soul that possesses the Divine Essence of God to that fullness that the created qualities of the soul have disappeared and been replaced by the divine qualities.

Let the prophets of old, and the sacrifices and the blood and the vicarious atonement rest in the memory of forgetfulness, and seek and obtain the inflowing of the Divine Love, and then the home of the soul will truly and certainly be the heavens celestial where only things "divine" can exist.

Well, I have written enough for tonight, and hope that you will find my message both interesting and helpful.

I will come again very soon so good night,
Elijah

His experience while on earth and in the spirit world,
also the transfiguration on the Mount was a reality
October 11, 1916

I am, Elijah.

I will write a message tonight as I promised. While on earth I was a prophet to the Hebrews and tried to warn them that God was not pleased with the manner in which they were living, especially in not obeying the commandments as to their worship and the individual lives they were leading. I was not a man who knew the attributes of God as I now know them, for then, to me, He was more a God of wrath and jealousy than of love and mercy. Most of my teachings were to warn the Hebrews of the wrath that would certainly fall upon them unless they were more obedient and followed the laws of Moses. I now know that the wrath of God is not a thing to be feared, and that His wrath is not a thing of reality. That when men disobey His laws and neglect to worship Him in truth and in spirit, His feeling towards them is one more of pity and sorrow than of wrath, and that instead of punishment He extends to them His mercy and Love.

In my time the God of Love was not known to the people in any practical way, and the people were not looking so much for Love as the fearing of His wrath; and it was only by threatening them with His wrath could they be made to realize that they were disobedient and alienated from Him. They had not that soul development that comes with love, and their aspirations were almost wholly for the possession of the things of life and for a happiness that such possession could give to them, as they thought. They expected a kingdom of God on earth which was to be one that should rule and govern the earthly affairs of men. Of course, they believed that when such a kingdom would be established, sin and the troubles of life would be eradicated, and all the world would be subject to the dominion of such a kingdom.

Their hopes and aspirations were in the nature of national hopes and aspirations and not in those of the individual. The individual was swallowed up in the nation and happiness was to be a national one instead of an individual one, except so far as the national happiness might be reflected upon and partaken of by the individuals.

I, myself, knew nothing of the Divine Love, and could not possibly have known of it, for then it was not open to man's seeking, as it had not been restored by God. I knew of a higher development of the natural love than did most of the people, and realized what increased happiness such development would give to the individual who might possess it. I also knew that prosperity and the power of the nation, as such, would not bring the happiness of love, but only the pleasures and satisfaction which increased possessions would naturally create.

The Jews were a carnally minded race and the development of the spiritual side of their natures was very slight. Their acquisitiveness was large, both as individuals and as a nation, and when they were prosperous they lost their sense of dependence on God and resorted to those practices and that manner of living that would enable them, as they thought, to get the most enjoyment out of their possessions. The future, that is the future after death, did not enter very much into their consideration of existence, and they lived emphatically for the present. If you will read the biblical history of those times you will find that most of the warnings of the prophets came to them when they as a nation were most prosperous, and, as they thought, independent of God, or at least, of not being compelled to call upon Him for help and succor.

Well, I was psychic and frequently heard voices of instruction and admonition from the unseen world, and, as was our knowledge in those days, I supposed that such voices were the voice of God, and so proclaimed it to the people. But now I know that such voices were those of spirits that were trying to help the people, and bring them to a realization of the moral truths which Moses had taught.

When Jesus was born into the flesh, there came with him a rebestowal of the Divine Love, and through his teachings that fact became known to men. We who were in the higher spirit spheres also came to know of that gift, and while none of us received it to the degree that Jesus did, yet we received it and became pure and holy spirits, free from sin and error, and partakers of the Divine Essence of God and possessors of immortality. So, at the time of the transfiguration on the Mount, some of us possessed the Divine Love to such a degree that our appearances were shining and bright, as described in the Bible (Mark 9:4). But Jesus was brighter than Moses or myself, for he had more of this Divine Love in his soul and could manifest it to the wonderful degree that he did, notwithstanding his having a physical body.

Our appearance and his appearance on the Mount were to show that the Divine Love had been rebestowed and received by both mortals and spirits, and this was the cause of our meeting. While accounts of that event have been disseminated in the mortal world ever since its occurrence, so also, had that fact became known in portions of the spirit world, and many spirits as well as mortals have sought for and found Divine Love to their eternal happiness. Its existence was a fact then and it is a fact now, and the Love is open to all mortals as well as spirits.

The voice that the apostles heard proclaiming that Jesus was the well beloved Son was not the voice of God, but that of one of the divine spirits whose mission it was to make the proclamation. This incident was not a myth but an actual fact that formed a part of God's plan to assure man of his salvation.

I will not write more on this subject.

So with my love and blessings, I will say good night,
Elijah

Chapter Ten

New Testament

JOHN THE BAPTIST

*John the Baptist is now the harbinger of the Master as he
was on earth, and he confirms Jesus's writing through Mr. Padgett*
August 10, 1915

I am here, John the Baptist.

I came to tell you that I am now the harbinger of the Master as I was
when on earth and that he is the true Jesus who writes to you in all the
communications which you will receive signed by him. I tell you this so
that you will believe and not doubt the messages that you receive. He
has written you and you must rely on what he says, for what he has said
to you will surely come to pass.

I am the same John who appeared in Palestine and announced his coming, and as I told them what was actually to take place, so I tell you what is actually taking place, and you will not only receive the messages of truth which he will write you, but they will also be distributed to all humankind wherever the written languages of the world exist and are spoken or written.

So you have before you a wonderful and important mission and one that will do more to make men true brothers and lovers of God than anything that has happened since the Master was on earth and taught and preached the truths of his Father, and did good to mortal man.

I sometimes have wondered why you should have been selected, as I see that your soul development has not been nearly as great as that of many others who now live and have lived; but as he (Jesus) has made the selection, we understand that he knows what is best, and that his selection must be the right one. As a consequence of this, we who are his followers in the celestial world are trying our best to forward the cause and help you; and I must tell you that you have behind you in this great work, supporting and maintaining you, more spiritual power than any mortal has ever had before. This may sound surprising to you, but it is true.

So, my brother, for such I must call you now, try to acquire a faith in the Love and desire of God to save all humankind from the errors of their lives and to make them one with Him which will enable you to stand forth as the representative of the Master and the authoritative teacher of his great truths.

I am now in the celestial heavens and am very close to Jesus in his home and in his love for the Father and for all humanity. I have powers which are great and Love which is of the Divine Essence of God and what I tell you now I will tell to the world when the opportunity presents itself.

Your brother in Christ,
John the Baptist

275

*The time is now ripe for the truths to be made
known so that humankind can be redeemed from false beliefs*
September 7, 1915

I am here, John the Baptist.

I come because I want to encourage you to pray more and to believe that God's Love is waiting to fill your soul to its utmost, and the only things required on your part are prayer and faith. We are all interested in you and want you to get into a condition that will enable you to take the Master's messages as rapidly as possible. The time is now ripe for these messages to be given to humankind, and to start on their work of redeeming men from false beliefs and erroneous doctrines and dogmas. I, John, tell you this, for I can see that men are longing for the truths of God — such truths as will remove from the teachings of the spiritually guided all superstition and errors. Such truths as will accord with the reasoning of men who are not biased by erroneous beliefs either in matters spiritual or material.

I tell you that these truths will be easier for the mere materialist to receive and understand, than by those who are bound by the beliefs which the creeds and dogmas of the churches have inculcated. The acceptance of this "new revelation" of the truths of God will be by those who have no preconceived ideas of what the nature and relation of man to God is in the spiritual sense, than by the learned theologian and the simple worshiper at the altars of the churches who believe whatever may be told them by the priests and preachers.

As I was, at one time, the voice of one crying in the wilderness, I am now the voice of many spirits of God, who knows that the Master will teach the truths of his Father, and that these truths must be accepted by mortals on earth, and by spirits in the spirit world in order that they may receive that salvation which God has prepared for them, and which, when accepted and realized and possessed, will fit them to become partakers of the happiness and immortality which God has promised them.

I have written you in this manner tonight, because I want you to realize more fully and deeply the important work which the Master has selected you to do, and also the necessity of continuing this work at the earliest possible moment.

Well, I have been interested in the great amount of discussion on that point, and how the belief one way or the other has caused those calling themselves Christians to form distinct sects. If they only knew or would know, that it does not make a particle of difference to their soul's salvation, whether Jesus was immersed or sprinkled, they would not let the bitter feeling arise that frequently does in discussing this matter. However, to settle this dispute to the satisfaction of those who may read the book which you may publish and believe in its statements, I will say, that when I baptized Jesus (Mark 1:9), I went with him into the water and then took the water in my hands and placed it on his head — there was no immersion.

As this water was merely symbolical of the washing away of sin and error, and does not actually accomplish that great necessity, in order for men to become one with God, it did not make any difference whether the recipient of baptism was immersed or sprinkled. It is strange that many men who profess to have received the forgiveness of their sins and become reconciled to God should let a trifling thing of this kind cause so much strife and bitter disputations.

I will now stop.

Your brother in Christ,
John the Baptist

John the Baptist writes about his life and ministry
Dr. Samuels, March 3, 1955

I am here, John the Baptist.

I am happy that you are permitting me to write to you now. I would like to supply some information about my life.

I was born in the month of June some six months before that of my cousin Jesus in the neighborhood of Ain Karim, which is a small town not far from Jerusalem. I was the son of a priest who served in the Temple in Jerusalem and my family were all pious and devoted and filled with a strict interpretation regarding the laws which the Jews believed had been received from God through Moses. To my father these laws of Moses and the Ten Commandments represented the most important part of the Jewish religion, and he taught me a strict moral code which I absorbed in my youth and which later became the cardinal principles of my brief ministry as the harbinger of the "glad tidings" of Jesus.

During my manhood I was an ascetic and shunned all meat and strong drink and ate only the simplest of foods in order not to be subject to the passions of man, and later I became a hermit and lived in a cave and away from the haunts of men and their society.

When Jesus and his family returned from Egypt to Nazareth to be among his people in Galilee, I had many occasions to see and talk to him there, and this continued over a period of many years up to the time of my ministry, which began only a few months apart from each other. This ministry was worked out between us and formed part of a plan prearranged in advance, and the Gospel is not true in declaring that I did not know Jesus, but that I would anoint the one on whom I would see the dove of the Holy Spirit descend (Matthew 3:16). I did know Jesus and I did anoint him, not because I saw any dove or heard a voice from heaven, but because I was convinced in my heart that he was the Messiah and that I was the prophet who was to announce his coming. Although, I wish to state that I did not truly understand that Jesus was bringing with him immortality which comes from possession of the Divine Love, nor did I even possess this Divine Love in my soul at the time of my execution.

As a youth and young man, in order to make a livelihood, I used to work in the fields of wheat and might be said to have been a farmer, but my true vocation was that of a prophet in the sense that Elijah was, that is to say, to proclaim to the rulers and the people to repent of their evil ways and to return to the path of righteousness that God had directed the Jews to follow as the great goal of their religion calling for love to God and one's fellowman.

It is not true, as some theologians believe, that I tried to lead a reform movement independent of Jesus, nor was I to any extent influenced by the Essenes, whose views of purity led them to isolated communities away from the so-called contaminations of the genuine Hebrew civilization, or the Hellenistic influences, and where they car-

278

ried out their religious practices. Like Jesus I believed not in retreat from the world but in carrying the message of God to the people, and as I believed in ablution as symbolical of spiritual purity, I had of necessity to preach where water was readily obtainable, and that was the Jordan.

It was in this sense that I was a real prophet, for I not only preached repentance to all who would listen, but I also thundered against what I considered the evil conduct of Herod for transgressions against God's laws of matrimony. I looked upon his marriage to Herodias as illegal (Mark 6:18), an act which could bring down upon his subjects the wrath of God. Herodias was not living with Herod while his half brother was alive, for he was dead at the time the royal pair were married. But to us, the Pharisees, to which I belonged, the marriage was not legal because no woman, as we understood it, could contract marriage with the brother of a deceased husband when children had been born of the first marriage. Hence Salome, the offspring of Herodias, and Herod's half brother, invalidated this marriage to Herod, and it was this violation of our levirate marriage law (Leviticus 18:16) that prompted my preaching against him.

It is true, of course, that Herodias was incensed against me (Mark 6:19), for as a member of the ruling class, she was a Sadducee at heart and did not believe in the correctness of my views. She therefore was elated to see me imprisoned and silenced. Herod did not concern himself too much about this part of my preaching, for while he disagreed with me about the interpretation of the marriage laws, wrangling between Pharisees and Sadducees had been going on for some two centuries, and such legalistic disputes did not have the urgency for him as this particular one had for Herodias. He was concerned rather with the attitude which the Roman overlords took towards religious meetings which could be a pretext for seditious and rebellious gatherings, and he thought it wise to remove with my arrest the cause of such possible sources of disorder in his territory.

Herod sent some soldiers in the garb of travelers to seek me out without arousing suspicion, and though I was not preaching in territory subject to his jurisdiction, he had me sequestered (Matthew 14:3) into his land and brought me to his fortress of Macherus near the Dead Sea. I was confined there for about ten months, or until Herodias's birthday, on your calendar, late February of the year 29 A.D. I know that Herod was not too anxious for my death, but Herodias wanted it and her request was granted. Solome did dance at this festival (Mark 6:22), but it is not true that her dancing made Herod grant her request for my death; on the contrary, she has assured me that she never did ask for my decapitation, and I can state that my head was never brought in before the king on a platter (Mark 6:25). These, of course are fanciful details which students of the Old Testament will associate with the story of the festival of Purim, wherein King Ahasuerus vowed to grant Ester anything she asked for at his banquet.

At the time of my death, I did not, as I have said, possess the Divine Love, although I did have an abundance of the natural love in a pure state and was in good spiritual condition. At the time of Jesus's birth it became possible for spirits to obtain the Divine Love, so at the time of the Transfiguration, Moses and Elijah had obtained it in considerable quantity. This Transfiguration took place less than six months after my death, but I was in that spiritual state that enabled me to realize its importance and to seek for the great gift. I was one of those who understood the real meaning of Jesus's ministry and I prayed for the Divine Love and obtained it.

As a spirit, I watched the progress of Jesus's efforts to win the Jewish people and I often came to him to offer him comfort, and I also attempted to warn him at the time of his arrest, shortly before the approach of Judas and the henchmen of the high priest in the Garden of Gethsemane (Matthew 26:47). He seemed to have a realization of his coming death, although this has been exaggerated by the copyists of the Gospels, who have sought to show that Jesus was fated to die on the cross and that it was his mission to shed his blood through betrayal and crucifixion. All of the statements attributed to Jesus that his time was not yet come (John 7:6) or that his time had come (Matthew 26:18) are not true, yet the fact of the matter is that Jesus did have a foreboding of his coming disaster, and I did try to get his attention and warn him of the betrayal.

I will not write more now.

Good night,
John the Baptist, of the New Testament

John the Baptist writes on Jesus's childhood
Dr. Samuels 1963

I am here, John the Baptist.

Since our whole religious importance in the universe of men is built upon what Jesus, as the human transfiguration through this Divine Love manifested, he and his life and the different steps in his soul's progress as shown forth to those with whom he associated are most vital and important. For it is the gentility and calmness of a loving nature which Jesus showed at all times and to all people which, even as a small child, made him different from other human beings. For it must be understood that the Divine Love of the Heavenly Father was performing its perfect work of transformation within the soul of Jesus even as a very small child. His soul as a human or created image entity, became more and more transformed into the "divine," because of the Divine Love's suffusing of his soul and the transforming of the natural qualities and energies from the natural to the "divine," and he then became an entity set apart.

We who associated and lived and played with him did not, of course, know why he never indulged in naughtiness of which we were all capable. He enjoyed the natural companionship and games in play of others of his own age. It must be made clear that Jesus, himself, did not know that he was in any way to be different from all other people of his time. He knew that within him was a tranquility and buoyancy which prevailed at all times and was a growing part of his nature. He knew that he felt kindliness and affection for all humanity and every living thing, and he realized that he did not react as others did — but this realization came to him only as he matured and progressed in the Divine Love.

He had many hours of pondering upon the difference between his own reactions and those of his companions. But all of this was a gradual and slow awakening of consciousness to obedience and compliance with that self which was to be dominant and show forth all of the beauty and humility of a soul possessed of and transformed by the Father's special gift of Divine Love. Jesus was an angel on earth to whom you and all humankind shall someday look and realize as the greatest miracle in all of the universe. One not just peculiar unto Jesus as Christ, but that which his faithfulness unto his chosen mission has made available for all humanity to embrace and make their own.

Your brother in Christ,
John, the Baptist

Jesus was the true Messiah and the true Christ when he taught on earth
April 20, 1916

I am here, John the Baptist.

I have not written you for some time, and tonight I come merely to let you know that I have not forgotten you, and am with you quite often, trying to help you with my love and influence.

No, I was not present then, but I am glad that you had such an experience, and I will tell you that you shall have many more experiences of that kind, for the celestial spirits are your friends and companions, and where they are, only love can come.

Well, I know that it does seem contradictory, but the fact is, that I never sent my disciples to ask any such question (Luke 7:20). I knew at the time when I baptized Jesus that he was the promised Messiah, and that knowledge never left me or degenerated into doubt. This passage of the Bible has no foundation in fact, for I never thought it necessary to ask any such question, and, as I have said, I never asked it.

To me, Jesus was the real Christ, and I knew that he was the true and only one, and that no other would come after him, for when he brought to light the fact that God had bestowed upon humanity the great possibility of obtaining the Divine Love, there never thereafter arose the necessity for the existence or coming of another Christ. The great gift that was necessary to make man a being "divine" had been bestowed, and beyond that there was nothing that God had to bestow upon humankind.

I am so sorry that such an untruth should have been written and incorporated in the Bible, for it did Jesus an injustice and made me appear as a contradictory prophet as the messenger of his coming.

When I said, "I am the voice of one crying in the wilderness, make straight the way of the Lord" (John 1:23), I meant that I knew that Jesus was the true Christ, and that forever thereafter would that knowledge be mine. No, I did not send my disciples to ask the question that you referred to. As I knew then, I know now, that Jesus was and is the true Son of God, and the saviour of humanity, in the sense that he brought immortality to light.

I will now stop, and in doing so say, that you have my love and blessings and the Love of God, which is the great Love that makes you a part of the Divine Essence of the Father.

So my dear brother, good night,

Your brother in Christ,
John the Baptist

MARY (Mother of Jesus)

Mary writes that Jesus was the natural son of Joseph and Mary
April 15, 1916

I am here, Mary, the Mother of Jesus.

I come to you with all the mother's love of one who loved her dear son so much while on earth, and who suffered all the heart pangs which the cruel death of my beloved caused me, and with the love that has been purified by experience and closeness to the blessed Father.

I come to you with this mother's love, for you are the children of the Father, as I am His child, and you are also the brothers of my dear son, who is with you so much and so interested in you and your future. Let your love for the Father increase, and also your love for the Master, as he is the greatest and dearest friend that you have in all the celestial heavens.

I am in the celestial heavens, very near the fountainhead of God's

Love, and also near the home of my dear son, though not in the same sphere with him, for no spirit in all the celestial heavens has the same great soul development as he has, or is possessed with the Divine Love to such an extent. I just want to say here that I am not in the condition or place that I am because I am Jesus's mother, but because of the development of my own soul, and only this great possession of the Divine Love determines our position and condition here in the spirit world. I am now in such condition that I know that the Love of God is the only thing in all the universe that can make a mortal, or spirit, a partaker of the Divine Nature, and an inhabitant of the kingdom of heaven.

I suppose I am the only one in all the universe of God who knows the fact with reference to that question, and as a spirit of the celestial spheres, knowing only truth, say to you and all the world that Joseph was the actual father of Jesus, and that he was conceived and born as any other mortal was conceived and born. The Holy Spirit did not beget him and I never was informed that such a thing would happen. I was known by Joseph before the conception of Jesus, and by him I was made pregnant with that blessed son. This is the truth and all accounts and statements to the contrary are erroneous. I was a simple Jewish maiden, and never had any knowledge that my son was to be different from the sons of other mothers, and it was not until after the development in him of the Divine Nature of God that I realized that he was so different from the sons of other mothers.

I will not write more tonight, but will come again and write you of the early life of Jesus, and of his development in the Divine Love as was shown to me while he was a growing child and after he became a man, prior to his public ministry.

So my dear, believe what I have written, and also know that I love you with a great love, and am working with the other celestial spirits to make your soul the possessor of this great Love.

With my blessing I will say, God be with you now and for all eternity.

Your sister in Christ,
Mary

Jesus's birth and youth as revealed by Mary, Mother of Jesus
Dr. Samuels, 1963

I am here, Mary.

It has been a considerable time, as mortals count time, since I have written you, and very little at that. I would not communicate with you without having first received approval from my son, who has been giving to you for the first time an account of the natural love and those forerunners of the Divine Love which finally led to the fulfillment of the Father's promise in the person of my son Jesus.

Since the time we began to get serious messages to earth through Mr. Padgett, it has been possible to continue our instructions through you. My son has undertaken to supplement the basic understanding of Divine Love with a study of the religious writings of the Jews to show how it was finally achieved and how it was that my son, the Messiah, attained that soul condition that made him know that this title was his, and that something from God, Himself, had permeated his soul, making it at-one in actual Substance with God.

This soul development of my son, which is very important for humanity to realize if they are to understand what enabled him to be the Messiah of God, is the purpose of my son writing at the present time. He hopes to explain by this not only the Old Testament, as the background to his soul development, but the Talmud, some of which was available when he lived, and these non-canonical writings of the times just prior to his coming that will show the mind of Jesus — his thinking, his understanding, his insight and intuition — that lifted up his heart and soul to the Father, our God of Israel, who poured out His sacred Love upon my child and made him, in time, His real, only begotten son, and thus brought to light eternal life for His children.

Most of what the New Testament says about me is untrue. I was married legally to Joseph, my husband, who was a young man, and not the decrepit, impotent old man he is described as by the writers who seek to make me a virgin (Matthew 1:23).

No, I was wife and mother to eight flesh and blood children, my first-born being Jeshua, or Jeshu, for the people spoke differently and pronounced differently in northern and central Palestine, as people speak differently in various parts of your own country. He was born exactly like other babies, and neither he nor Joseph nor I had any inkling of what his career was to be; and this is the truth and entirely contrary to what is stated in the scriptures (Luke 2:47-49).

Jesus as a child was serious, studious, pious, and one who drank eagerly at the fountainhead of religious instruction and knowledge of God's demands for right living through obedience to His laws and love for Him. He learned that one day a Messiah would come to help give salvation to the Jewish people; and this thought possessed my son because he believed in the writings of Jeremiah and the prophets, as well as the precepts of the rabbis which clung to him and became a part of him. This was despite the conflicting ideas that clashed and merged in the religious Palestinian atmosphere which confused many Jews, especially those of the north country, into believing that the Messiah was to be a patriot who would lead his country to freedom from Rome.

It was a long time before Jeshu showed any signs of a love different from the love he showed for me and his father, or for his younger brothers and sisters. He was kind and gentle, and possessed a certain mysticism and a relationship with the hills and the sky. He had a way of looking at the distant clouds and drinking it in with a love of the bright blue heavens. He also had an intense way of holding dear the words of the religious teachers, which is what separated him from us.

As he began to be more and more different, he spoke more and more of God and God's Love which, he pointed out to us, was proven by our scriptures. By the time he was twenty, we wondered if he could be this Messiah, which we did not understand. We thought we had brought into the world a typical pious Jew — people who had let themselves be butchered rather than violate their religious beliefs. Our other children, like Judah and Jacob, were given more to throwing out the Romans; they were very patriotic, as were many of the young boys of this area.

Jeshu expressed his love for his family by working hard for them and helping my husband. He was dutiful, obedient, protective to the younger children, and sought to live a life of devotion to his family and to avoid the sins of commission and neglect as understood by our community and our religion. He was patriotic, too, and possessed a patience which contrasted with the energy and impatience of his younger brothers. They could not understand how the God of Israel could permit the cruelties which Romans practiced in our country — killings, scourgings,

impossible taxes, all kinds of impositions, restrictions and violations —
which they committed and which were sanctioned by the Jewish high
priests and the Sadducees.

My son Jeshu counseled peace and forbearance, for he said, "Our
God would deliver us from our enemies as in the days of Moses, and a
leader would come forth to deliver the people*". Jeshu began to talk as
though he were such a leader. My sons would listen to him and be willing to go with him, and they saw in him a faith in God not found in the
high places in Jerusalem nor in the hotheaded youngsters of Galilee, nor
among the practical farmers and tradespeople, nor even in the rabbis
and Pharisees of the land.

When he began to talk about his personal relationship to God, and
as having God's Soul qualities in his own being, we then thought he was
insane, for to our training and knowledge a thing like this was an utter
impossibility, and had come from a mind of one whose religious studies
had deranged his mentality. We could not, in all truth, understand what
we did not possess. Only he knew what he felt, and when he finally left
our home to liberate his people, we thought he was a Zealot leader gone
to fight Rome. Yet we were bewildered, because he was not belligerent
but spoke of peace with Rome through God's Love in man's soul, thus
we thought of him as deranged.

My daughters Leah and Rachel, although in their hearts they loved
him dearly, wanted nothing to do with their brother's idealism, they
were firm in the old tradition of law and Torah. My husband, Joseph,
who understood Jeshu's soul to only a small degree, felt himself cursed
for having such a son, then wept bitterly when he began to realize the
worthiness of our son's soul and the sacrifice unto death which he had
made. Though not a blood sacrifice as most Gentiles believe, but a sacrifice of his life to carry out his mission — the preaching of God's Divine
Love in man's heart — to the opposition of the high priests, who feared
such unorthodox teachings, and to a Roman response to any mention of
a Messiah, which they interpreted to mean "the anointing by God of a
King of the Jews," especially when he was thought of by the Romans as
a rebel leader against Caesar.

As I, and as all of us here in the celestial heavens now understand it,
Jeshu's love for his family was a natural love, purified. It later became
"divine" through prayer; and when the conviction that he was the

*This quote does not appear in the New Testament.

287

Messiah came to him, he told us that he must attend to his Father's business of proclaiming the "glad tidings" of His Love, and for this he was born. His natural love, which as a young man would have turned him to thoughts of love and marriage, deepened into Divine Love. He became absorbed by it, and held a marvelous feeling of filial and fraternal devotion, and this made him feel like the dearest brother to all humanity, taking away from him the thought of women and family life. He loved all people with a love which showed itself in kindness, in service, in helping others, in healing wounds of sicknesses, in alleviating sorrow and giving sympathy and comfort for the depressed, the bereaved, the heartbroken and the helpless. He brought hope and taught salvation to thousands. Even when they did not understand him, there was a sincerity, an absolute faith and conviction in the eternal life of the soul which spoke to people's hearts, if not to their minds, and many felt he was the light to the Jewish people who would show the way to God and to peace, in this world and in the next.

Jeshu showed this faith and conviction and love up to the last, on the cross at Golgotha. He showed courage and patience beyond human capabilities and, at last, at the foot of the cross I understood something of what he said and what was in his soul. Even just before the end, when I grieved for the one I considered a good son, dying because of a disturbance which manifested itself in a different path in religion and defiance of Roman power, how mistaken was I, my family and my husband. We understood, only after his death, when pain and grief and love had brought some of the Divine Love into our souls.

The Divine Love turned my son to God, to think of God and long for God's presence; to pray to avoid sins, to take on His character and virtues of kindness, of humility, of service and consideration of others so as not to hurt their feelings; and these were to him of the highest importance. His, too, were qualities of firmness, faith and conviction; of courage, of fortitude and high resolve. He faced and found death with tranquility, patience and a oneness with the Love of God that shatters all imagination. Such was my son Jeshu on earth.

As for myself, I speak to you now as a spirit who once was the mother of daughters as well as sons, and I can penetrate into your hearts and see the struggles, the aches, the courage and the faith that animate you. As a result of this great tragedy in our lives, which gave rise to the turbulence and persecution, and eventual tearing asunder of our holy religion, which my son never sought to destroy but to fulfill its promise, my home life was broken. My husband departed on preaching missions to calm his anguished heart and to proclaim what his son had given his life for, and my sons followed this example and met death in their missions.

I speak to you as a mother who has known sorrow and troubles and tragedy, and who experienced them when least able to meet and surmount them without God's Love to console, to bind up, to heal, to fortify, when they would have meant the most. It is only later that my love for my son deepened into the Divine Love and gave me the courage, the serenity, the love for others, and the certain knowledge of eternal life with God that enabled me to face life and death with peace and love in my soul.

Keep faith with God, and be open to His Love, and you will overcome with confidence and, indeed, peace of mind, optimism and happiness, those circumstances that seem to mar the fulfillment of your years. I pour out upon you and to all those who feel my motherly love and guidance, all my love and blessings.

Your dearest friend,
Mary, Mother of Jesus

JOSEPH (Father of Jesus)

Jesus's father was called Alphaeus by the Gospel writers
Dr. Samuels, October 25, 1954

I am here, Joseph.

Yes, I am Joseph, the father of Jesus. I would like to say a few words in corroboration of what my son Jesus wrote to you concerning my name as hidden in the New Testament. You must not have any doubt that what my son writes you is the truth. Fear not, but have faith in the accuracy of the messages that he writes to you. The reason for this hiding of my name from the readers of the New Testament was to prevent the identity of the father who had little faith in Jesus at the crucifixion, but you must now have absolute faith in what he tells you is the truth.

Yes, I am Joseph, father of Jesus, and I was called Alphaeus by some writers of the Gospel, and you must know that I was the real father of Jesus in the flesh, regardless of what the New Testament has to say about this.

I am high up in the celestial heavens where there are no numbers, but I am not as high up as my son, because his love which he possesses from God is greater than that of any other spirit in the celestial heavens.

I will stop now and say, have faith in God, which neither I nor my sons had at the time.

Your brother in Christ,
Joseph

Describes what happened after the remains of Jesus were put in the tomb
March 16, 1916

I am here, Joseph.

I desire merely to write a few lines to let you know that I really did exist as a mortal, and that I am the same man who laid the body of Jesus in the tomb where never before had any body been laid.

I was with him at his death, and I was with his body when it was laid in the tomb and sealed, and I know and testify that no man or men or society of men, as it has been said, stole his body from the tomb (Matthew 28:13). His body was entombed as was the custom of my time, and he was wrapped in cerements (John 19:40) and fitted for the long sleep in the tomb, as we supposed. Because I feared the Jews as well as the Romans, I sought to conceal my identity from them by taking the name Joseph of Arimathea.

Of course, I did not believe that he would rise again in the way that he had made known to some of his disciples, and when we buried him, I only thought that that tomb would be his sepulcher until nature had destroyed the body as it had done in the cases of all others who had been entombed.

As you may realize, I was interested in the proceedings taken by the

Jewish leaders in their efforts to prove that he, Jesus, would not arise from the tomb on the third day, and I kept watch as well as did the soldiers (Matthew 27:66), and I can testify that no mortal ever removed the stones from the mouth of the tomb. I was there when the angel came and the soldiers were put in the sleep that the Bible speaks of (Matthew 28:4). I, Joseph, say this, knowing that it may not be believed and the Bible makes no mention of it, but I saw the stones rolled away and the shining one standing guard at the entrance of the tomb (Matthew 28:2-3). I was frightened and I left that place, and was so overcome that I did not return there until the early morning, when I saw Mary and heard her inquiring of the whereabouts of her beloved Master (John 20:2). And more wonderful, I saw the man of whom she inquired suddenly reveal himself to her, and I can testify also, that it was the same Jesus whom I had helped lay his body in the tomb.

He was not of flesh and blood, as they say, for he suddenly appeared, and his appearance was not the same as that of the Jesus whose body had been entombed. When he revealed himself to Mary, there was the same countenance and the same wonderful eyes of love that she was familiar with, and the same voice of love and affection. I know this and I want to tell the world that it is true.

Before Peter came, I went into the tomb, and it was empty, and when Peter came I was with him in the tomb and saw his astonishment, and heard his words of wonder and amazement (Luke 24:12), for notwithstanding what the Jesus had told him prior to the crucifixion, he did not believe or comprehend, and was astonished and bewildered as were all of us.

Jesus arose from that tomb, and his fleshly body was dematerialized. As to his disappearance, I could not then explain it, as could none who saw him after he had arisen, but now I know that because of his great psychic powers, as you would call them, he caused the disintegration of his body into its elements.

Yes, he arose from the tomb, but not from the dead, for he never died, as you will never die, only the physical vestment that enveloped his soul.

I am now in the celestial heavens and am with him a great deal, and know that he is the greatest and most wonderful of all the spirits in the celestial spheres, and the nearest to the fountainhead of God's Love, and that he is truly His best beloved Son.

I also want to say that he writes to you his messages of truth, and was with you tonight for a short time. Listen to him and know that you have in him a friend who is closer than a brother, or father or mother.

My brother, I will stop now, and in leaving, say, that you have my love and blessings.

Your brother in Christ,
Joseph

LAZARUS

Lazarus says he was not dead when he was raised by Jesus
August 5, 1915

I am here, Lazarus.

I was the one whom Jesus called from the grave. I merely want to say that I was not dead when I was resurrected but had on me the sleep of death (John 11:11), and I was not entirely a spirit separated from my body. I know this, because if I had been a wholly separated spirit, Jesus could not have brought me to life again. No spirit, once entirely liberated from the body, can ever return to it and reanimate the body. I know the Bible says, or the inference from what it says, is that I was dead (John 11:14), but this is not true, as I have above stated.

I am now in the celestial heavens in a sphere that is not numbered, and very near those spheres in which the disciples live. My sisters are also in the celestial heavens and we all believed in the teachings of the Master, and consequently became imbued with his doctrine of the necessity for the Divine Love to come into our souls.

While on earth Jesus did teach us that God had again bestowed on humankind this Divine Love and we believed it. I know that the disciples were taught this same doctrine, and just how far they understood this teaching I do not know. It is strange that they did not declare it in their Gospels, but such seems to be the fact, and it is unaccountable why this important truth was not preserved and taught in their writings. I know that it is the truth and that only those who have received this Love in their hearts can become inhabitants of the celestial heavens. Men may refuse to believe this great truth if they will, and think that by attending church and worshipping God in their service with their lips, they will be able to enter the kingdom, but they will find themselves mistaken.

I am supremely happy and want all humanity to be so. I came to you to inform you of these truths so that my testimony may be added to that of those who may have written to you.

Jesus is in the spirit world working to teach mortals and spirits his truths. He comes to you and writes, and you must believe, for it is a fact.

I must stop now, so I will say good night,
Lazarus

Lazarus confirms the writers as being
whom they represented themselves to be
September 21, 1916

I am here, Lazarus.

I merely want to say that I am the real Lazarus of the Bible story and that I am an inhabitant of God's kingdom and in the truths that exist in that kingdom. I declare to you that the spirits who have written you the truths of celestial and spiritual things are actually whom they represent themselves to be.

Jesus especially is with you very often and communicates to you truths from his great storehouse of the knowledge of truth. He is so much interested in the work to be done and the "revelations" to be made that he is with you so very often for the purpose not only of revealing these truths but of preparing you to receive them. He is enveloping you in his love and giving to you a development of your soul faculties that will make you qualified to receive these high truths as no other mortal has ever been qualified. He knows that you are his best qualified instrument now on earth to do his work and the work of the Father, and from what I say you must not suppose that you are the best man having the greatest amount of the Divine Love in your soul for that is not true. Nor are you chosen because of any merits of your own or because of superior mental endowment. For you have those conditions of attunement with Jesus that enables him and the other spirits to use you in performing this work.

I am not in such an exalted position or of soul development as are many of the spirits who write you, yet I know the plans of the Master, and what I say to you is true. I was a Jew and an orthodox one until the Master came to me and I developed my soul so that I could understand his teachings and become susceptible to the inflowing of the Divine Love.

I will not write more now, but in closing repeat that you must believe what I have said and try to do the will of God and the work that you have been selected to do.

Well, both Mary and Martha are in the celestial heavens and you would naturally suppose that Mary has made great progress in her soul development. But that is not true, as they both live in the same sphere and have similar development. As you know, they have been in the spirit world for a very long time, and whatever spiritual superiority that Mary may have appeared to have over Martha does not now exist, for they both have the Divine Love to a degree that has caused all sin and thoughts for the material to become eradicated long years ago.

Your wife says that I must not write more now, and so I will say good night.

Your brother in Christ,
Lazarus

JUDAS

Why Judas betrayed Jesus
August 23, 1915

I am here, Judas.

I came tonight because I want to tell you just what my condition and expectations were when I betrayed Jesus, which resulted in his crucifixion.

I was a very enthusiastic lover of the Master and believed thoroughly in his teachings and his power, and did not believe that the Roman soldiers could take him away from where we were, if we did not permit it to be done. As a consequence, I was anxious that Jesus should show his great power, and demonstrate to the Jews that he was the true Son of God, with power over men and devils.

I never betrayed him for the money that I received (Matthew 26:15), for it was not sufficient to pay for one moment of happiness which I have lost because of my act of betraying the greatest spirit in all God's kingdom.

I see that you are too sleepy to write more tonight. I will come again and tell my story.

So good night,
Judas

The greatest sin is against the Holy Spirit
that conveys the Divine Love into the human soul
October 21, 1916

I am here, Judas.

I come tonight to write a short message, for I have been interested in what you and your friends have said regarding the greatest sin.

Now, to me, for a long time, the greatest sin in all the universe of God was my sin in betraying Jesus to the Jews, and it was a real, living, blasting sin, and so enormous that I could not endure my life, and face the recollection of that awful tragedy. But since I have been forgiven of that sin and become a redeemed child of God and an inhabitant of the celestial heavens and a possessor of immortality, I realize and know that my sin was not the greatest, even though I suffered for long years after I became a spirit.

As sin may be committed by neglect as well as by affirmative action, and my betraying the beloved Master was a heinous one, but yet, even in my case, and as applicable to me, my greater sin was not seeking for the Divine Love of God. We were not ignorant of this, for the Master had taught us that this Love was open to and waiting for us to seek and obtain, and I had not sought for it in the right way, and of course had not obtained it; and in such neglect I was not the only one of the disciples that was guilty of that sin.

No, even we who had been with the Master for so long a time did not fully understand the importance of obtaining this great Love, as we were more interested in his establishing his kingdom on earth and, as we thought, a material kingdom, to be controlled by spiritual powers manifested in him, and in us as his disciples. The material, in our minds, was of more importance than the spiritual, and our expectations were that this great power would come, and that the Master would become our king.

As I say, he had taught us that this Divine Love was open to us, and that by prayer and earnest seeking we could receive it, but to us there were so many important things to be done, connected, as I say, more immediately with our earth lives, that we neglected the great gift that was ours for its seeking, and as a consequence, in my case, I had to suffer for a long time before I awakened to the fact, that it was not too late, even for me, to receive it.

My sin of betrayal had been forgiven me in that I realized that the recollections of it were leaving me and that I was progressing in the way of purifying my soul in its natural love, and that as the spirit of the one-time murderer, I was coming into happiness and light. I then had memories of what the Master had said to me about this great Love, and after awhile I had sufficient awakening to cause me to make the effort to obtain it. As that awakening came to me, my old-time associates, who had progressed to the higher spheres, came to me, and in their great beauty and transcendent love, helped me to progress and to pray until at last this Love came to me. Then I realized that not only had my sin of murder been wholly forgiven, but that the greater sin of rejecting and neglecting to seek for the Divine Love had also been forgiven me.

The sin of the murderer or of any violator of God's laws, other than that of rejecting the inflowing of this Love, may and will be forgiven of a man and he will become pure and happy in his natural love, but such forgiveness will not make him an inhabitant of the divine heavens or an inheritor of immortality. The forgiveness of the sin of rejecting the Holy Spirit will not only take away from man the recollections and taints of all other sins, but will open up to him the very portals of the celestial heavens and give him a home in God's kingdom.

As we are much interested in you, and have determined that you shall not go astray of these divine truths, my brother spirits of the celestial spheres, thought it fitting, as the world considers that I committed the greatest sin in all the history of the world, that I should write you on this subject, and explain that the greatest sin in all the world is the sin against the Holy Ghost (Matthew 12:31).

Now to be a little more personal, for your gratification and comfort, I desire to tell you, that you three* will not be found guilty of having committed this great sin, for you have in your hearts and souls much of this Divine Love, and the Holy Spirit is with you quite often in answer to your prayers, and in answer to ours also, for we all pray for you, causing this Love of God to possess your souls, even as the leaven is wrought in the batch of dough.

I have written longer than I expected and will now stop, but be assured that you have our love and blessings.

*Mr. Padgett, Dr. Stone and Mr. Morgan.

Your brother in Christ,
Judas

ELOHIAM

A member of the Sanhedrin and judge at the trial of Jesus states,
the reasons for condemning him at the time and now urges all members
of his race to accept him as the long sought Messiah
January 23, 1917

I am here, Elohiam.

I am the spirit of a Jew who lived in the time of Jesus and was a member of the Sanhedrin and sat as one of his judges at the time of his condemnation for blasphemy (Matthew 26:65) and iconoclastic teachings against the beliefs and doctrines of the Hebrew faith. I was one of those who voted for the sentence of death upon him, and in doing so was as honest in my conviction and action as it was possible for an earnest believer in his faith to be. Consequently, I was without prejudice against Jesus as a man and, as I believed, a fanatic; and it was only because I was convinced that he was an assailer of, and dangerous to, our religion and the welfare of my race that I consented to his death.

Mortals of these days cannot fully understand the exact relationship of Jesus and his teachings to the security of our religion and the preservation of the faith which we believed had been handed down to us by God directly through our prophets and teachers. When we were confronted with what we believed to be the destructive and irreligious teachings of Jesus and after making the numerous efforts to suppress him by threats and persuasion without effect, we concluded that our absolute and indisputable duty to God demanded that he be removed from the sphere of his activity even though such result could only be accomplished by his death.

If mortals of the present day could understand our deep religious convictions and the sense of obligation that rested upon us to protect and keep whole the divine doctrines and teachings of our faith and especially that one which declared the oneness of God, they would not judge the action of the Jews in condemning Jesus to death to be a thing unusual or unexpected. He stood in the position to us and to our religion of a breeder of sedition. As in modern times men have occupied the position towards the civil governments of breeders of treason and have suffered the punishments which have been with approval inflicted upon them by such governments.

To us he appeared not only guilty of treason to our national life, but also of treason to the higher God-given life of the religious government of our race, the chosen one of God, as we sincerely and zealously believed. Even in latter days men have appeared and claimed to be the especially anointed of God with missions to perform and have gathered around them a following of people whom they have impressed with the truth of their character and mission and of their teachings. For a short time they were permitted to declare their claims and doctrines and then suddenly they were brought to death by the decree of those who were in authority, as troublemakers and enemies of the church or state, and they have been forgotten and their doctrines have disappeared from memory. Only in the instance of Jesus has his death been remembered through all the ages, and those who were the cause and who were responsible for his death have been desecrated and cursed and charged with the murder of God.

Well, I write this to show you that the Jews who took the life and demanded the crucifixion of that just man were actuated by motives other or different from those that have many times since caused the very followers and worshippers of that Jesus to murder and crucify other men who have claimed to be the sons of God endowed with special missions for the salvation of men.

The sincerity of the Jews who took part in this great tragedy cannot be assailed, and even their Roman masters at the time understood that the demands for the death of Jesus did not arise from personal spite, or the satisfaction of any revenge against the individual, but solely because they believed and so declared that Jesus was an enemy and would-be destroyer of the divine faith and teachings of the Israelite nation, and a seducer of the people. It is only because of the subsequent rise and spread of his teachings and the truths that he declared which have made so large a portion of the inhabitants of the earth followers of him, that the act of the Jews in causing his death has been called the great crime of the world and the people themselves to be hated and persecuted and destroyed as a nation and scattered to all points of the earth.

I do not write this to excuse or palliate the great error which we committed in causing the crucifixion and death of the true Son of God, but only to show that they, as I now know, mistakingly did that which other men with the same faith and convictions and zealousness for the religious preservation of the nation, be these men Jews or Gentiles or pagans, would have done in similar circumstances.

The great element of tragedy in all this is not that Jesus was crucified, but that the Jews were so mistaken and failed to recognize and accept Jesus as their long looked for Messiah and deliverer, not from their material conditions of bondage, but from the bondage of sin and error in which they have lived for so many centuries. This, I say, was their tragedy, and it has been their lasting and deadly tragedy from that time until the present day, and the prospects are that it will continue theirs for many years to come, and that generations of them will pass from the earth life to the spirit world under the shadow of that great tragedy.

They still believe the way they do, and that belief is a part of their existence and as firmly fixed as in the days of the great mistake. They believe that they have Abraham for their father and that his faith and example are sufficient to show them the true way to God and salvation. They believe they are the chosen people of God, and by worshipping the one and only God and observing the sacraments and feasts and commands of God that were given to them by and through Moses and the prophets and as are contained in the Old Testament, they will find the heaven of God here on earth and after death rest in the bosom of Abraham. The observance of the moral and ethical precepts of their Bible is all that is necessary to develop their spiritual natures, and that beyond such development there is nothing to be desired or to be sought for. And that at some time they will attain the Adamic condition of reward and happiness, which is the ultimate of humankind's future existence.

Some are still looking for the coming of the Messiah who will restore to them their former glory and rule on earth as the king and governor of all the nations, and that they will be his chosen subjects and selected to assist in the administration of that Messiah's kingdom. It is certain that their dreams will never be realized and that unless they have an awakening to the true nature of their God, they will never become inhabitants of the celestial kingdom.

I want to say to my people with the certainty of knowledge arising from experience and actual observation, that Jesus of Nazareth was the true Messiah who brought to the world, and first to the Jews, the truths of God and His plans for the salvation of humanity and the restoration of all that they had lost by the fall of the first parents. If the people of my nation had received Jesus and accepted and followed his teachings, they would not now be on earth the scattered, homeless and persecuted race that they are. In the spirit world many of them would not be satisfied with their homes and happiness in the spiritual heavens*, but would be inhabitants of the celestial heavens and the possessors of God's Divine Love and immortality.

You have received many messages describing the plan of God for the salvation of humanity and what the Divine Love is and how it may be obtained and its effect on the soul's of mortals or spirits when once possessed. I will not attempt here to enter into an explanation of these things, but with all the love that I have for my race, added to a knowledge of the great error and insufficiency of their faith to bring them into at-onement with God, I advise and urge them to seek the truth and apply it to their individual souls. And to affirm that the truth is contained and the way to be found is in the messages that you have received from Jesus and the other high spirits.

I am a believer in these truths, a follower of the Master and an inhabitant of the celestial heavens; and I want to say that these truths did not come to me as a part of my faith until many long years of life in the spirit world, and that some of these years I lived in darkness and suffering.

So I will say good night and subscribe myself your brother in Christ.

Elohiam

*The highest planes of the sixth sphere.

NICODEMUS

On the importance of the New Birth
July 30, 1915

I am, Nicodemus.

I was a master of Israel, and yet I did not understand the New Birth. How few understood it then, and how few do now.

Oh, the long years that have gone by since Jesus told me that I must be born again to inherit eternal life, and how comparatively seldom this great truth is taught by the churches and the teachers of religious matters. This truth is at the very foundation of humankind's redemption, and until a man receives this New Birth he cannot possibly enter into the kingdom of heaven. Men may claim to have faith in God and believe in Jesus's name and conform to all the essentials and sacraments of the churches, and yet, unless they have this New Birth, their faith and works as Christians are vain. This I know from my own experience as well as from the teachings of the Master, and I desire to emphasize, with all the powers that I have, that it is the only important requirement to immortality.

The New Birth means the flowing into the soul the Divine Love of God, so that that man becomes, as it were, a part of God in His divinity and immortality. When this truth comes to a man he commences to take on himself the Divine Nature of God, and all that part of him that may be called the natural nature commences to leave him, and as the Divine Love continues to grow and fill his soul, the natural love and affections for things of the earth will disappear, and as a result he will become at-one with God and immortal.

When you shall receive the messages from the Master, I think you will find this truth of the New Birth to be the one thing that Jesus will emphasize and reiterate the most. It is the most important thing for men not only to hear about and acquiesce in their intellectual beliefs, but also to actually experience. Jesus meant as no man could see the wind or tell from whence it came (John 3:8) or where it was going, so no man who received this New Birth could see the operations of the Holy Spirit or know whence it came. But this latter expression must be modified,

302

because we all know it comes from God. The Holy Spirit is as invisible as the wind, and yet it is just as real and existing.

Men need not trouble their intellects to know exactly what this great power is, for it is sufficient to know: that which causes the New Birth is the Divine Love of God coming into the souls of men. I wish that I had understood it when on earth as I do now.

I must stop as I have written enough for tonight. So let me subscribe myself a brother and a lover and follower of the Master.

Nicodemus

ST. STEPHEN

It is a mistake for men to believe that because God has created this or that object or thing, it is necessarily "divine," for His creations are no more a part of Himself than are the creations of men a part of themselves
November 13, 1918

I am here, St. Stephen.

Let me write a few words tonight as I am one of the spirits whom your wife wrote of would come with the desire to write.

My subject tonight will be somewhat difficult to explain, and principally because men have no very definite conception of what is comprehended by the term "divine". They, of course, associate this word with God, and to them God is a Being whose nature and qualities are above their finite conceptions, and as a result of their thoughts, is that which is over and above everything that is called or supposed to be understood as natural. To some, God is a Being of personality, and to others, a kind of nebulous existence included in and composing all the various manifestations which are transcendentally above what they conceive to be the merely natural or human.

I will not attempt to discuss who or what God is, except as to one of His qualities or attributes, and that is the greatest, for you must know that all the qualities of God are not of equal greatness or degree of importance, for there is a difference in the workings and scope of their operations.

You have been told that the "divine" is that which has in it, to a sufficient degree, the very Substance and Essence of God, Himself; and this is true, for divinity belongs to God alone, and can be possessed by others, spirits or mortals, only when He has transfused into or bestowed upon the souls of men a portion of this divinity, and to the extent thereof made them a part of Himself. There is nothing in all the universe that is divine or partakes of the "divine" except the human soul, for all else is of the material, even when it has the form or appearance of the spiritual. Even the soul, as created, is not divine and cannot become such, until it is transformed into the "divine" by the transfusion into it of that which, in its very substance, is "divine". Many souls in the spirit world, although pure and in exact harmony with their created condition, are not divine and never will become such, and this is only because these souls will not desire and seek to become divine in the only way provided by God.

It is a mistake for men to believe that because God has created this or that object or thing, it is necessarily divine, for His creations are no more a part of Himself than are the creations of men a part of themselves; and thus you will see that in all God's creation there is nothing divine except what has been privileged by His Grace to partake of His divinity. Hence the stars and worlds and trees and animals and rocks and man himself, as created, are not divine.

Men have claimed that in man there is a spark of the "divine" — a part as they say of the Oversoul — and that it needs only the proper development to make the soul wholly divine. This theory is based upon the idea that this development can be accomplished by the exercise of the mind or the moral qualities guided by the conscience, which they assert, is of itself divine; especially when dominated by reason, which has been so often worshiped by philosophers and others (to whom the mind is supreme) as divine. They have attempted to differentiate man and the lower animals, and attributed to the former the qualities of divinity, because he is endowed with reason and the lower animals are not; and have substituted degrees in the order and objects of creation, in the place of differentiation between the divine and non-divine.

God is wholly Divine and every part and attribute of Him is Divine, and while they are parts of the whole, yet they may be separated in their workings and bestowals. The soul that is the recipient of the bestowal of one of these qualities or attributes is not necessarily the recipient of the others. Omnipotence and omniscience are those attributes of God's divinity which He never bestows upon the souls of mortals or spirits, and as to them He is the exclusive possessor, although in all His attributes there are powers and knowledge, and they accompany the bestowal of all attributes of which they are parts. One of these divine attributes may be bestowed upon man, and yet man cannot become Deity. There is and can be only one God, although He may give of His Essence and very Substance, so that a man can become as He is in that Essence and Substance, to the extent that it is bestowed.

As regards man and his salvation and happiness, the greatest of God's qualities or attributes is His Divine Love, which is the only thing that can bring the souls of men into a oneness with the Nature of God, and which has in it the quality of immortality. This Love has a transforming power and can make that which is of a quality foreign to and different from itself, into the same Essence as itself; and more than this, it can eliminate from that thing those constituents which naturally and necessarily are its components, without injuring or destroying the thing itself.

Well, we must stop here,
I am St. Stephen

ST. MATTHEW

*Jesus is the transcendent and greatest possessor of God's wisdom
and is the same Jesus when he comes to you and reveals the truths of God*
December 16, 1918

I am here, St. Matthew.

Let me write a few lines tonight as I desire to tell you of a truth that to me seems important for humankind to know in order that they may comprehend the truth of their personal salvation.

I am a spirit of soul development and an inhabitant of the celestial heavens, where only those whose souls have been transformed by the Divine Love into the very Nature and Essence of God can find a habitation. I will not write at any great length and have only one idea or truth to convey, and that is that no mortal or spirit can possibly receive the full salvation that Jesus taught and exemplified in his own person, who does not become wholly possessed in his soul of this Divine Love of God, and becomes rid of the conditions and attributes that belong to his created soul. The soul was not created with any of the divine attributes or qualities, but merely with those which you may call human.

The god-man, as Jesus is sometimes designated by your religious writers and theologians, was not at the time of his creation or appearance in the flesh possessed of these "divine" attributes, which are of the Nature and Essence of God, but only of the human attributes which belonged to the perfect man. Man was the perfect creature as he existed before the fall of the first parents, that is before sin had entered into their souls, and into the world of men's existence. Jesus was from the time of his birth, the perfect man, and, consequently, without sin, his moral qualities being in complete harmony with the will of God and the laws controlling his creation; yet, he was not greater than were the first parents prior to their act of disobedience.

There was nothing of God, in the sense of the "divine" that entered into Jesus's nature or constituents, and, if the Divine Love had not come into and transformed his soul, he would have remained only the perfect creature of a quality no higher or greater than was bestowed upon the first man. Jesus was as regards his possibilities and privileges, like this first man prior to his fall or death of the potentiality of becoming divine, although differed from him in this: that Jesus embraced and made his own these privileges and hence became "divine," while the first man refused to embrace them and lost them, and remained the mere man, though not the perfect man as he was created.

While Jesus by reason of his possession of the Divine Love became "divine," yet he never became the god-man, and never can, for there does not exist and never can be a god-man. God is God, alone, and never has and never can become man; and Jesus is man only, and never can become God. However, Jesus is preeminently the divine man, and may rightly be called the best beloved Son of the Father, for he possesses more of the Divine Love and, consequently, more of the Essence and Nature of God, than does any other spirit of the celestial heavens. With this possession there comes to him greater power and glory and knowledge. He may be described and understood as possessing and manifesting the wisdom of God; and we spirits of the celestial kingdom recognize and acknowledge that superior wisdom of Jesus and are compelled by the very greatness and force of the wisdom, itself, to honor and abide in his authority.

Jesus is the transcendent and greatest possessor of God's wisdom and is the same Jesus when he comes to you and reveals the truths of God, as he is when he is in the highest spheres of the celestial kingdom clothed in all the glory of his nearness to God. As the voice on the Mount said "Hear ye him" (Matthew 17:5), I repeat to you and to all who may have the privilege and opportunity of reading or hearing his messages, "hear ye him," and when hearing, believe and seek.

Well, my brother, I deemed it proper to write this short message and hope it may help you in the work. I will come again.

Good night.

Your brother in Christ,
St. Matthew, as called in the Bible

The soul's relationship to God, and its future life and immortality
November 2, 1915

I am here, St. Matthew.

I have not written you for a long time, and I desire to say a few words on matters pertaining to the soul and its relationship to God and future life and immortality.

The soul is an image of the great Soul of God, and partakes of features like this great Soul, except that it does not necessarily have in it the Divine Love which makes the soul of a mortal or spirit a partaker of divinity. The soul may exist in a mortal or spirit in all receptive qualities and yet never have the Divine Essence fill it, which is necessary in order to make a mortal or spirit a new creature, that is, the subject of the New Birth.

Only that mortal or spirit who has received this Divine Love can be said to be immortal; all others may live or they may not. It has not yet been revealed to us whether the life or existence of these spirits who have not the conscious knowledge of immortality will continue to live through all eternity; and if they do it will be because God so wills that they shall. Their existence will be subject to change and if such change should take place, only God knows what its character will be. While on the contrary, the soul that has acquired immortality can never die, its status as to a life through all eternity is fixed, and even God himself cannot destroy that existence because it is the possessor of that divinity which makes God immortal.

"The soul that sinneth, sinning it shall die" (Ezekiel 18:4), means that the qualities which are necessary for it to obtain to make it a part of immortality can never come to it, and hence as regards these qualities it is dying and dead. The soul itself will live, for no spirit could possibly have an existence without a soul, and when men attempt to teach that when the spirit of life leaves the body the soul dies, such men do not state a truth. The soul will live as long as the spirit existence continues, and until the great change, should there be one, comes to that spirit. So all men must believe, that the soul which God gave to man is just as much a part of man as is the spiritual or physical body.

The soul is the highest part of man, and is the only part, that in any

308

way resembles God, who is not body or spirit body in form but is Soul, and the man's soul, as I have said, is an image of that great Soul. So you see, that when we speak of destroying the soul it does not mean that the soul which belongs to every spirit will be destroyed, and the potentiality of that soul receiving the Divine Love and the Nature of God.

The soul can be starved and placed in a condition of stagnation so that all its receptive powers will be, as it were, dead, and only some great miracle or unusual ministration can awaken it, but to say that the soul ever dies may be erroneous. In saying this there is the possibility of some great change in the spirit of mortals by which such spirit may be destroyed, and in such the soul will cease to exist as an individualized soul or entity.

God, the great Oversoul, may not recall to Himself the soul of any man in the sense of depriving that man of his soul, but His relation to that soul will be merely that of Creator and created, subject always to the will of the Creator, whereas, the relationship of God towards the soul that has received the Divine Nature, is not only of a Creator and created, but also that of a co-equal so far as this great quality of immortality is concerned. The soul of man then becomes self-existing and not dependent upon God for its continuance to exist.

This, I know, is a subject not easy for the mortal mind to understand, but when you have received the soul perceptions in addition to your natural mind, it will not be so difficult to grasp the exact meaning of my propositions.

I will not write more tonight.

> Your brother in Christ,
> St. Matthew

ST. MARK

*St. Mark assures Mr. Padgett that the Master
is now doing the great work for the redemption of mankind*

I am here, St. Mark.

I must add my testimony to the others who have preceded me, to the fact that the Master is now doing a great work for the redemption of humankind, and that through you he is going to transmit his great spiritual truths to sinful men.

I will not write much at this time, but say that in the future I will communicate my thoughts, which are the creatures of knowledge and experience, in the celestial spheres of Christ's kingdom.

So I will say good night, and may God bless you and keep you in His Love and care forevermore.

St. Mark, the writer of the second gospel,
originally true as written but now full of errors.

*St. Mark reassures Mr. Padgett that the
writers truly are who they represent themselves to be*
September 20, 1915

I am here, St. Mark.

Let your faith increase and your belief in the fact that we write to you grow until no doubt will possibly enter into your mind as to who the writers are.

I am here merely to say these few lines and encourage you to put forth every effort to get in condition to receive the message which shall be written to you.

Your worries will not stay with you much longer, for you will soon be in condition to start to do those things that your father spoke of so that you will be relieved of your worries.

I will not write more, but will say good night.

Your brother in Christ,
St. Mark

ST. JAMES

The frailties of the human mind and the moral qualities
May 24, 1917

I am here, James apostle of Jesus.

I have heard you read the Master's message*, and believe that in it, you will find much truth upon which to reflect, and I desire to add a little to what has been therein said. And here I want further to say, that while that message was intended for you personally, yet the truth and advice therein given may be applied to every mortal, and the good results will follow, no matter who that mortal may be.

I have, as you know, been in the spirit world a great many centuries, as you conceive time, and have during that long period been very close to mortals in all parts of the earth and of all nationalities and beliefs and education and enlightenment, and in my experiences with these mortals, I have observed the nature and temptations and the various ways in which mortals have been assailed by such temptations, and their efforts to overcome the same, together with their successes and failures.

Now, first let me say, that the nature of man is, today, the same as it was when I lived on earth, and the perversions and sins of the souls of men are just as many and of the same kind as they were in my day. The temptations of the flesh, both outward and inward, are just as hard to overcome as they were when first the "glad tidings" of Love and redemption were proclaimed by the Master. Prior to that time man had not the Divine Love to help him overcome and subdue these tempta-

*This message appears later in the chapter.

tions, as he now has. The great regret is, that while this great helper and regenerator, and conqueror of sin and temptation is now in the world of mortals, and subject to their call, yet so comparatively few make the call, or realize the fact that this helper is always waiting to enable them to overcome temptations.

Prior to the time of the availability of the Divine Love, moral truths were taught to men just as they are today, and many men, and not necessarily among the Jews, understood and attempted to apply these truths to their daily lives. They endeavored to overcome the temptations arising from the sins that so constantly formed a part of their existence, and that also came from the influence of the evil spirits. It is all wrong to suppose that in these early times and among these early races of earth, moral perceptions were not developed and taught; men made the fight to overcome temptations and become good and noble beings, so far as these moral truths and principles were then understood and used by men.

In all ages since the fall of the first parents, men have, to a more or less degree, had knowledge of what is called the moral truths, and the natural love of man has existed in a more or less imperfect condition. Men have been kind and loving and true, and have to an extent controlled their appetites and tendencies toward evil lives. Now to suppose that men of today are not subject to great temptations, and are of themselves better able to resist the same, is a mistake. The present great war proves the fact, for men were never — I mean those who make a pretense to culture and civilization — so brutal in their acts, and so apparently devoid of all conception of right and wrong and of mercy, as are many of those who are engaged in the present struggle. So I say, men of today can lay no greater claim to moral qualities than could those of the times when they were supposed to be heathens and undeveloped in these moral qualities.

Of course, there is in the world today more of what may be called education and conventionality, yet behind these things, which are largely the results of merely intellectual development, men have the same perverted souls, or rather appetites and desires, and are subject to the same temptations as were men of old. If humankind were left dependent upon the cultivation and improvement of these merely moral powers, I fear that temptation would continue to have all its influence and harmful power on the souls of men that it had in the past.

I know it is said, "the world is growing better," but the question is, is that assertion true; for except in the case of a few people, the conditions of their minds and souls are just as perverted as they were in centuries past, and that it is only in those countries where the influence of Christian nations have control, do these people suppress the tendencies of perverted minds to do those things that arise from the want of the exercise of moral precepts or knowledge.

This is the truth of what mere moral teachings have accomplished where only the mere moral truths, as is supposed, are taught. Temptations are with men, and will be with them forever, unless they be controlled or overcome by something greater or more certain than what men conceive to be moral truths.

Now, you will see from this that merely moral concepts will not necessarily, or, at least, for a long time to come, be able to bring about the destruction of the powers of temptation that arise from the perverted nature of mortals. I must stop now, and in doing so will leave you my love and blessings.

Good night.

Your brother in Christ,
James

*Condition of spirits and their experiences and beliefs that
are below the celestial heavens, and how they congregate together*
September 25, 1915

I am, St. James.

Let me tell you a few things concerning the spirit world, that is, the world that is below the celestial heavens.

In the several spheres, which are seven in number, are many planes, inhabited by spirits of many nations and races of humankind, and these various races have to a certain extent the customs and beliefs that they had when on earth. The lines of demarcation are just as strictly drawn as are those of the several nations on earth. The result of this is, that many spirits who live in this exclusive manner never learn anything other than what their own leaders tell them and what their various sacred books may teach them.

The Mohammedan is a Mohammedan still, and so likewise the followers of Zoroaster, and also those of Buddha and of Confucius, and all of the various founders of religious sects. Sometimes these spirits in their wanderings will meet spirits of other races than their own, and interchange thoughts, but very rarely do they discuss matters pertaining to their respective beliefs.

There are undoubtedly truths in the sacred writings and beliefs of all these races of spirits, and to the extent that these truths are taught and understood these spirits are benefitted. I am now speaking of spiritual truths, because as to the mere truths pertaining to the natural or material world, they all have the same opportunity to investigate and understand them. There is no race or creed or doctrinal beliefs and teachings as to these truths affecting the material, and by this I mean, material as it exists in both the spiritual and earthly worlds. I say, that each of these races or sects has their own ideas and doctrines of the truth, and can progress no further than the limits which these ideas permit them to progress.

No founder of any race or sect has ever taught the New Birth, and the inflowing of the Divine Love in contradistinction to that of the natural love. The teachings of Jesus are the only ones that reveal to man the existence of this Divine Love, and how to obtain it. So you see the importance of this truth coming to man. The teachings of the other founders will show men the way to a life of happiness, and to what they may suppose as continuous existence, but the teachings of Jesus are the only ones that declare and lead men to a realization of the true immortality of the soul.

I must stop.

Your brother in Christ,
St. James

Yes, I am that James. No, the saint is only used as a means of identification; it has no significance in our spirit world.

*How man can again be restored to the
perfect man, like the first parents before their fall*
March 8, 1917

I am here, St. James.

I come to write my message of the method by which the soul may be purified by the operations of the actions and the will power, in conjunction with or influenced by the workings of the powers of the spirits who have been relieved of the sins and errors that followed the fall.

When man was created, as has been told you, he was created perfect, and every quality and function and attribute that was a part of him was created in exact harmony with the laws of God that governed his existence. No discord of any kind was in his existence to mar that harmony. As the spiritual nature of man became subordinated to the appetites and passions and fleshly desires, sin and error and inharmony appeared and increased until man became degraded, and desired only those things that would satisfy these sinful desires.

This degeneracy continued until man reached his lowest degradation, and then the turning point came in his career, and he commenced slowly and gradually to rise from this condition of depravity until at last, he arrived at the stage of his condition of harmony with the laws of his creation that now exists. His destiny is complete restoration to the perfection of his first estate.

This improvement and gradual restoration depends upon two causes — one, man himself by his own thoughts and reformation of the animal appetites and desires; and the other — the influence and guidance of spirits who, in the spirit world, have arrived at that perfection, or are progressing thereto, and are in a condition of harmony with these laws, superior to that of mortals to whom they lend their influence and help.

Men, in their degeneracy or progression, are controlled very largely by their thoughts, and these thoughts are created by the operations of their desires, which on the other hand, cause these desires to increase. And back of these thoughts are always the appetites and passions existing in their abnormal conditions, and they constitute the basic or moving cause of desire, thought and act. In order for men to become relieved of his abnormal desires and thoughts and acts, the cause thereof must be eradicated, and the seat or function of the cause be brought into harmony with the laws of the creation of these functions or seats of emanation.

Strange as it may seem to you, and by a process that is contrary to the ordinary workings of the law of cause and effect, men must first deal with the effects in order to control the cause and thereby destroy the effects. This may seem to be an impossible operation, and contrary to the laws that govern the material world and its ordinary functioning, but yet it is possible, and the only possible way in which the causes may be destroyed. Notwithstanding the fact that the animal or material part of man has had the ascendancy, for all these centuries, over the spiritual part of his nature, yet that spiritual part exists and has always existed and is waiting to assert itself whenever the opportunity occurs, and this assertion is prevented or suppressed only by reason of the want of opportunity.

The spiritual may be said to be the natural state. I mean that in that state, the animal is subordinate to the spiritual and is controlled by it, and man's true tendency is to exist and act in accord with that natural state. Then such being the fact, it may be asked why, or in what manner did this natural spiritual condition become, in the manifestation of what man's dominant dualities are supposed to be, subordinated to the control of the inordinate exercise of this animal side of his nature. This resulted in the sin and unhappiness that so many of the teachers and philosophers proclaim to be his natural condition.

Well tonight, I will not attempt to explain the manner in which this inversion or perversion of man's true nature took place, but will at some future time write on this subject.

The question now is, how can man obtain the restitution to his created perfection? As I have said, this can only be accomplished by making the perfect adjustment of the two apparent conflicting sides of his nature.

Well, he must recognize that he has the spiritual nature as well as the animal, and that there is such a relationship and coordination between the two that the supremacy of the latter disturbs the harmony of his perfection as man. The spiritual having been subordinated, the remedy is to remove the subordination and restore the equality. The spiritual, notwithstanding its condition, is always fighting to regain its place in the true adjustment and will always answer the call of man to come to his rescue; and the only thing that has prevented that response is that man has not called for it to assert itself.

Well, I am sorry, but we had better postpone until later, try to get in greater rapport.

Good night, your brother in Christ,
St. James

ST. PETER

St. Peter writes on his leadership of the Christian movement
Dr. Samuels, May 9, 1955

I am here, St. Peter.

I am here, with a considerable number of celestial spirits who have been listening to your discussions regarding the spiritual truths, and I should like to corroborate what just was said in a previous writing regarding my life. The fact is that Jesus did not give me the leadership of the Christian movement while he was alive. I took upon myself the leadership, as it is explained substantially in the Acts of the Apostles, and I spoke boldly at the Pentecost and did work some miracles of healing. It was this and some other acts that I did that gained for me the leadership of the apostles and the movement.

I would like to say a few words about the message which Jesus wrote to you tonight regarding the expectation of the Jews as to the person and personality of their Messiah to come. It is true that many of the Jews thought the Messiah must be an immortal being, for who except an immortal being could come directly from God? Thus, when Jesus appeared to Mary after his crucifixion, it dawned upon the apostles and many of the Jews that Jesus must be the Messiah, whom they rejected in the flesh but accepted after his death as an immortal being. It is further true that it was expected after his ascension to heaven that he would return to earth very quickly and reign on earth as the great immortal king and establish the kingdom of God on earth.

I must say that I also partook of this view, and so did the apostles; and we all taught that the crucified and resurrected Jesus was the immortal Messiah, who would soon come to earth and appear. It is true that this concept of the Messiah accounts for the idea in the early church that Jesus would come quickly to establish his earthly reign. It was hard to realize that the Messiah had come to establish his kingdom in the celestial heavens and not on earth.

About my own leadership in the movement, I was the leader of the apostles while Jesus was in the flesh and, with John, was among the few who received his main confidences. We went with him to the Mount of Transfiguration. He used my fishing boat, and I went with John to arrange for the hall, or upper room, in which the Last Supper was held, and there were many other things in which I was the leader. But since Jesus did not expect to die, he did not bestow upon me any formal primacy as it is stated in the New Testament (Matthew 16:18). After his death it was expected of me to take the lead and I took it and, as I have said, preached at the Pentecost, and healed, and continued the work of the Master, gaining as I did in Love and conviction as to the truth.

I was arrested as it is reported in the New Testament (Acts 12:4), and I was released from prison, not by any miracle of angels coming to take the irons from my wrists and opening the door (Acts 12:7), but because some of my jailers were converted by my teachings and were believers in Jesus and his mission, and they saw me heal, and preferred the things of the spirit to seeing me languish in prison and perhaps suffer the same fate as Jesus.

I continued to preach and heal on the Mediterranean coast in Joppa and elsewhere, and converted some Romans; but I never raised the dead as it is reported in Acts (Acts 9:40), in the case of Tabitha, for the girl was in a coma and not dead. Thus my reputation was enhanced and I became involved in questions of interpretation and doctrine, and it was to me rather than to James that the Jews looked, especially when multitudes of pagans accepted Christianity and the movement had to adapt itself to these people. I decided that many innovations had to be accepted if the pagans were to become believers in Jesus as the Messiah and in the Father's Love. Thus it was that the great body of pagans and their beliefs compelled the movement to turn from the Father's Love to the acceptance of Jesus as the motivating force.

My leadership was enhanced when I sent Barnabas to Asia Minor on various missions. I eventually came to Rome, and worked consistently to establish the church along orderly lines and to eliminate undesirable traits and make it a firm religious institution. I became the recognized leader because Rome was the leader of the known world at the time and, as the authority of the greatest church in the greatest city of the world, I became the authority over the entire Christian world.

I was not in Rome for twenty-five years, but I was there for nearly fifteen years, and I visited Rome and other cities of the East while preaching in various parts of the Greek world. My leadership, therefore, is really the combination of my position among the apostles and the fact that this leadership was combined with my position in the world city of Rome.

I think this answers some of the questions you may have had as to my life and primacy. So with that, I shall close now, and with my love to you and the Doctor, and with my desire that you pray more for the Love of God and move toward increasing your spiritual and soul condition to take our messages.

I shall stop,
Peter, the apostle

There are Epistles contained in the
Bible which in many particulars are untrue
October 29, 1918

I am here, St. Peter.

Some of the Epistles credited to me I did write to some of the members of the churches over which I had supervision, but the Epistles as contained in the Bible are in many particulars untrue and conflicting with my beliefs, then and now, and I never wrote such conflicting statements. I never wrote that Jesus paid a ransom for humanity (Matthew 20:28), or that his death on the cross saved men from the death which they inherited from Adam, or anything of the kind that insinuated that men were saved by any act of Jesus which satisfied the wrath of God, or, as the author said, satisfied divine justice.

Justice was not an element in the plan of man's salvation, only Love and mercy, and the desire of God that man become reconciled to Him, that is, come to Him and receive the great gift of His Divine Nature. No blood shedding or death of Jesus or vicarious atonement could have accomplished this, for none of these things would affect the soul development of a man. The matter of soul development is an individual matter, and can only be accomplished when man seeks for the great gift of Divine Love, and receives it in his soul and develops it. He then becomes a partaker of the Divine Nature and one with God.

How deplorable that men will teach this erroneous doctrine of blood atonement. It is doing very much harm to mortals and to spirits as well, for many spirits come into the spirit world with their beliefs so firmly established in this doctrine that they frequently remain for years in that condition of belief, and consequent stagnation of their soul's progress, and of their obtaining a knowledge of the truth.

When the author of the Epistles comes to the spirit world, he will undoubtedly have to pay the penalty for his erroneous teachings, and very probably that penalty will be that he will have to unteach them, if I may use the word, to all the spirits who when on earth believed in and followed his teachings of these false doctrines.

Someday men will know the truth, and the truth will make them free. You must try your best to get in condition to take the messages which the Master desires to write so they can be published to the world.

I am, your brother in Christ,
St. Peter

Jesus did not perform all the miracles claimed in the Bible
May 30, 1917

I am here, St. Peter.

I see you were reading Luke's Gospel and must inform you that many of the supposed miracles of healing and raising of the dead and the controlling of the laws or expressions of nature never occurred. No, these accounts are not true and are the results of the imagining of men who attempted to add to the book that Luke wrote. Of course, there is a true foundation for some of these alleged miracles, but as to others, there is no foundation in fact.

Jesus did heal the sick and cure the blind and the deaf and the withered hand and the palsied man (Matthew 12:10) and resurrected the supposed dead, but not in the way described in the New Testament; and it is not good for men to believe in the truth of all these miracles.

Well, that incident never occurred, for Jesus in casting out evil spirits would have had no authority or power to permit them to enter into the swine. It would not have been in consonance with his love and ideas of what was just, to have allowed the swine to receive these spirits and thereby perish as the account says (Luke 8:33). Besides, the result of such a happening would have been, that the property of the innocent owners was taken from them and lost. In all Jesus's performance of miracles or in any of his teachings he never did or say that which worked wrong to a human being. All men were to him the objects of his love and the salvation which he came to earth to show men the way to.

Well, there is some truth in that for we were in a storm and were afraid and he slept, and we awakened him, but he did not rebuke the storm and the waves and cause them to subside (Luke 8:23-24), but rather he allayed our fears by his talk and example and to us it became as if there were no storm, for when fear left us it was as if we were not sensible of the storm so far as the dread of drowning or perishing was concerned. No, this is another interpolation and should not be believed.

Many wonders ascribed to Jesus were never performed, although it appeared to us as if there was no limit to his powers. Sometime I will come and write fully on this matter.

I must stop now.

Your brother in Christ,
Peter

St. Peter on the forgiveness of sin
November 29, 1918

I am here, St. Peter.

Let me write a few lines for I am very anxious to write you in reference to a truth of our spirit world, and with which you may not be
acquainted.

As you may not know there is in our world a law which makes the
soul of one who has not yet been purified suffer the penalties for the acts
of sin and evil of which he may have been guilty during his earth life;
and there is no forgiveness of these acts in the sense that forgiveness is
taught by the theologians and churches. The only forgiveness is the cessation of recollection of these acts so that they become as though they
had never been; and, as the soul becomes naturally pure and in harmony with the laws of its creation, it then comes into its natural condition,
and then, and then only, forgiveness takes place.

God does not forgive by the mere act of pronouncing forgiveness or
by any arbitrary and sudden blotting out of sins, and thereby removing
the condition which creates the inharmony; and so you will understand,
that He cannot forgive sin in this way, neither can the popes, priests,
teachers or churches. The pronouncing of forgiveness by these men constitutes a deception of and an injury to the persons who pray and ask for
forgiveness, and for such deception these men will have to answer when
they come to the spirit world and realize the truth of forgiveness and the
great deception that they had practiced upon those who were their followers and believers in these false doctrines. Many spirits are now living and suffering in darkness in their purgatories just because of their
beliefs, and the results thereof, in these misleading teachings.

There is no forgiveness until man makes the effort by struggling and
succeeding in getting rid of these recollections; and such riddance can
be obtained only by men realizing the fact that sin is only the effect of
their having done those things, and thought those thoughts which are

out of harmony with the will of God and the laws governing the creation of man.

There can be no sinning of the physical body or of the spirit body, but only of the soul caused by the exercise of the will in a manner antagonistic to the will of God. The body, of course, is affected by these inharmonious thoughts and impelling directions of the will, and is caused thereby to commit the act which is the external demonstrator of the inharmonious exercise of the will. God leaves to man the freedom of exercising his will, which may be influenced by the thoughts, desires and affections of his appetites and lusts, and the application of the remedies that will free the soul from such influence and effects as are caused by this exercise of the will. Only when these thoughts and appetites and lusts become eliminated from his soul and desires, does the soul come into its natural condition and in harmony with the will of God. Man, himself, must be the actor and the initiating force to bring about these changes in his will, and no assurances of forgiveness by priests, popes or churches can eradicate these contaminating influences, or remove that which is the cause of the sin or the effect of the cause.

Thus, you must see that there can be no relationship between the assurance of forgiveness and the sin or the cause thereof. Supplication to priests and church is supposed to effectuate the objects sought, but this belief is erroneous and does not bring the relief prayed for. Yet prayer is a very important element in forgiveness, and while the priests and churches cannot forgive sin in the manner mentioned, however, it is true that sincere prayer to God for forgiveness will bring its answer, and affect not the sin, but the state of the soul of men. Their will and appetites and desires may be influenced in such a way that they will receive and realize the fact that they had wonderful help in changing these appetites and desires, and in turning their thoughts to those things that will enable them to remove from their recollections the acts and thoughts, which are the causes of the existence of their souls in a state of sin.

If men would only realize these truths, and, when they desire forgiveness of their sins, pray to God for help in turning away from these thoughts and in exercising their will in accord with His will and not expect any arbitrary forgiveness or removal of their sins, they would find themselves on the way to this forgetfulness and the true forgiveness.

Well, I desired to write this message and am pleased that I could do so. Thanking you, I will say, good night.

Your brother in Christ,
Peter, apostle of Jesus

ST. PAUL

The Drama of St. Paul and his experience when on earth
December 5, 1915

I am here, St. Paul of the New Testament.

Well, my brother, I was with you at the discourse on the "Drama of St. Paul," and was much interested in the subject matter, and also in the manner in which the speaker delivered his discourse. He was somewhat dramatic himself, and his elocution and intonation of the dialogues between several of the prominent personages in the drama and myself were very effective; but really they, the intonations, did not sound very familiar, because to me they possessed too much artificiality to represent correctly the real tones of voice and the feelings that possessed these persons and myself on those occasions. Nevertheless, they were very effective, and I have no doubt, produced on the hearers the effect intended.

Some of the scenes depicted were very real, and some of them were not, and never occurred, for I remember well my experience on the way to Damascus, and the great change that it caused to my whole existence on earth. The brightness, and the voice of Jesus were actualities, although the statement that I went blind (Acts 9:9) is not true, for I was not blind but only affected for the time by the unusual light, and also the shock that the voice of Jesus caused. As Jesus said, my only blindness was that which covered my spiritual eyes at the time, and when I went into the town, the only blindness that I recovered from, in a way, was that which had kept my soul in darkness, and caused me to persecute

324

the followers of Jesus, under the belief that I was doing the work which God had called me to do. So you see, that while the description as a whole of my life after my call was very interesting, yet it was not altogether correct.

My condition of soul development was that I lacked the Divine Love which I afterwards, to some degree, possessed. I was more of an intellectual Christian in my early ministry than a Christian possessing the great Divine Love of God; yet thanks to Him I continued to preach, and believed as best I could, until finally I became a redeemed child of God, filled with His Love.

I knew many things connected with and taught in the theology of the Jews, and especially of the Pharisees. I now see that in my writings, my conceptions of the truths of God were flavored, to a considerable extent, by this knowledge of the Jewish theology. While many things that I taught are true as I now see them, yet many things that the Bible says I wrote are not true, and I am not surprised that men accept them at this time. How I wish that I could review and rewrite the Epistles ascribed to me, and how many seeming contradictions and unreasonable things would be made plain. But I cannot, except as I may through you declare the truth as I now see it; and I hope that the opportunities may come that I may do so.

Well, I will not write more tonight as you have written considerable, and others wish to write.

I will say good night.

Your brother in Christ,
Paul

St. Paul says, that his thorn in the flesh was his doubt at times
that he was called to preach the truth of man's salvation as taught by Jesus
June 28, 1915

Saul of Tarsus, now Paul of near Damascus.

Well, as you are longing tonight for love and fellowship with the disciples of the Master, I thought that I would write you just a little to show that all of the Master's disciples are in their living spiritual bodies, and I am alive and will never again die.

I have written many Epistles which are contained in the Bible, and some are nearly correct, and in them you will find my idea of God and of the Master. However, I never taught that the Master was God, and neither did I teach the doctrine of the vicarious atonement or the sufficiency of Jesus's blood to save a sinner from the sins of his earthly deeds. I never taught that any man's sins would be borne and the penalty for the same be paid for by another, and wherever these doctrines are set forth in my Epistles, they were not written by me.

The thorn in the flesh (2 Corinthians 12:7), was my doubt at times that I was called to preach the truth of man's salvation as taught by Jesus. I say I doubted at times that I was called to do such work, for notwithstanding the Bible narrative of my conversion (Acts 9:20) I was not altogether convinced by the vision that I saw. I know now that it was a true vision and that I was called, but when on earth I had my doubts at times, and this was my "besetting sin".

Of course, from my Epistles you would never think that I had any doubts, and I purposely abstained from making known my doubts and so-called it my besetting sin. I thank God that I never let that doubt influence me to prevent me from giving the work my call, for if I had I would have undoubtedly relapsed into the persecuting Jew. As I continued to preach my faith grew stronger and after a while my doubt had left me, and in my latter years I had no doubt.

Well, as to being afraid I will have to disillusion you, for I was never stricken blind or taken to the house of the prophet of God as the Bible says (Acts 9:17). My vision, though, was plain enough, and I heard the voice upbraiding me, and I believed, but at times there would come this doubt that I speak of.

I am not in as high a sphere as is St. John, for I have not the Divine Love that he has; although I am in a very high sphere and am the governor of the city in which I live. I am probably as much filled with this Love as any of the inhabitants of my city; and consequently, having been a disciple of the Master, they selected me for their governor. Peter is not in the same sphere; he is in a higher one. Some disciples are higher and some are lower. Andrew is in my sphere, but does not live in my city.

I am glad that you called me tonight or rather, the influence of your love called me, as I am much interested in the work that you have to do for the Master. You will be able to do this work and it will be a great revolutionizing one when it is published.

Well, I will be glad to write you at times and will give my present opinion on some of the things I discussed in my Epistles. So as I have written considerable I will say good night and stop.

Your friend and brother,
St. Paul of the Bible

*St. Paul denies the vicarious atonement, this belief is
doing much harm, also the Bible contains many false statements*
October 26, 1915

I am here, St. Paul.

I want to say just a few words. The book on the vicarious atonement that you have been reading about the ransom price and the blood of Jesus and the sacrifice on the cross is all wrong, and you must not believe what it says.

Well, I know the Bible (1 Corinthians 5:7) ascribes to me the teaching of these things, but I never did teach them; and I tell you now, that the Bible cannot be depended on as containing things that I wrote. There are many additions to what I wrote, and many omissions of what I wrote; and it is so with the others whose names are stated as the writers of the New Testament. Many things contained in that book were never written by any of the alleged authors of the book. Our writings were not in existence for many centuries; but when they were copied and recopied, great additions and omissions were made, and, at last, doctrines and dogmas were interpolated that we never at anytime believed or wrote.

I have to say this, and I wish to emphasize my statement with all the conviction and knowledge of the truth that I possess: Jesus never paid any debt of man by his death or his blood or vicarious atonement. When Jesus came to earth his mission was given him and he progressed in his soul development, but it wasn't until his anointing that he wholly qualified to enter upon his mission or the work thereof.

The mission was twofold, namely: To declare to humanity that God had rebestowed the Divine Love which Adam or the first parents had forfeited; and secondly, to show man the way by which that Love could be obtained, so that the possessor of it would become a partaker of the Divine Nature, and immortal. Jesus had no other mission than this, and any statement by the preacher or teacher or church doctrines or dogmas or by the Bible, that his mission was other than I have stated, is untrue. He emphatically never claimed that he came to earth to pay any ransom for mankind, or to save them by his death on the cross, or to save them in any other way than by teaching them that the great gift or privilege of obtaining immortality had been bestowed upon them, and that by prayer and faith they could obtain it.

The author of the book is all wrong in his theories, but if you accept the statement of the Bible as true (1 Timothy 2:6), he makes a very forcible presentation of the scriptures. But the scriptures do not contain the truth on this subject, except for the New Birth that Jesus taught, and that being so, his explanations and theories must fall to the ground. Someday and very soon, this author will come to the spirit world and have an awakening, which will cause him much suffering and remorse because of his teachings of the false doctrines that his book contains.

I did not intend to write so long a letter when I commenced, but your questions required answers, and I could not give you answers in less space. Nevertheless if you shall obtain any benefit from what I have written, the time consumed will be compensated for.

I must stop now, but will come again sometime.

Your brother in Christ,
St. Paul

328

*St. Paul comments on a preacher's sermon
that God is a wrathful and vindictive Being*
December 5, 1915

I am here, St. Paul of the New Testament.

I merely want to say that I was present at the church tonight and listened to the preacher tell his congregation what he didn't know about hell. Because what he said in many particulars was untrue and it was pleasing to me to hear him tell his people that there was no physical suffering. He did not explain to them why there could be no such suffering, and I mean that no spirit, when he goes into hell carries with him his physical body, or any other body, that has such substance as would be affected by fire and brimstone and the other unreasonable things that the churches have for so many years taught and terrified their members with. This has caused them to believe that God is such a cruel and wrathful Father, demanding that His cravings for satisfaction be supplied by the sizzling in fire of the bodies of His children. No, this damnable doctrine is not true and I am glad to see that the churches are ceasing to believe or teach it.

The doctrine that the preacher taught is nearly as bad and as useless as the former, for the reason, that punishment of sinners and those who are out of harmony with God is a fact which they all will realize when they come to the spirit world. That being so, to teach that this punishment is everlasting is as harmful as the one that I first mentioned. How strange that preachers and teachers will try to cause their people and listeners to believe that God is such a wrathful and vindictive Being, having less love and mercy than the most wicked earthly father has for his children. It is so very deplorable that such attempts are made by these supposed instructors of what God is, to blaspheme Him in His great qualities of Love and tenderness, and in His desire that all His children become happy.

Oh, I tell you that these preachers will have a woeful sin to answer for when they come to an accounting, and that will not be at the great judgment day, as they teach, but just as soon as they enter the spirit life and realize the great harm that they have done to many who have followed them in their teachings. They will realize the awful result very soon after their entrance into the spirit world, for they will have come to them, as clouds of witnesses, the spirits of those who were under their instructions on earth, bringing with them all the evidence of the results of their erroneous beliefs and the stains of this great sin of blasphemy.

I, Paul, write this for I have suffered from this very cause myself, because, when on earth, I taught some doctrine like unto the one that these preachers are now teaching, and even now I realize that to some extent I am responsible for many false beliefs. I thank God that all that is ascribed to me in the Bible, I am not responsible for, and that if my true teachings were known and taught, the blind and erroneous beliefs that are now so prevalent among Christians would not exist. I tell you that in many particulars mortals do not conceive the great harmful and deplorable results that flow from their beliefs in the Bible.

This book is one of falsehoods and forgery and imputations that have no resemblance to what the Master or any of his apostles taught, and you can readily realize how anxious we all are that these errors and untruths be removed from the minds and souls of men. I must not permit myself to become too enthusiastic in considering these things tonight, or I might not stop as I should under the circumstances.

I will come, though, very soon and write you again on this subject, as it is a vital one to humanity, and I will explain the truths connected with it as fully as is possible for men to understand. I should like to write more tonight but I must not.

So with my love, I will say good night.

Your brother in Christ,
Paul

Hell, what it is and what is its purpose
November 21, 1916

I am here, St. Paul.

I desire to write my message as promised on hell. Well, to begin, hell is a place as well as a condition, and the man who believes that it is nothing more than a condition of his mind or soul will be wonderfully surprised as well as disappointed. I know the condition of mind and soul to a very large extent creates a man's hell and is the chief source of his suffering and the darkness that surround and envelope him; yet this condition is not the only source of that suffering or of darkness in which he finds himself.

Hell is a place, and a place that has all the appearances and ingredients that are in exact agreement with his state as produced or caused by the condition of his mind or soul. It is not a place of universal character and fitted for the habitation of souls, irrespective of conditions of degrees of defilement and sin and darkness. It is not a single place forming a common home for all fallen souls, but is composed of many and different places. As has been said, there are many hells having gradations of appearances and surroundings that are suitable for causing additional sufferings which souls may have to endure.

The expression, "the lowest depths of hell," is not a meaningless one, but portrays a truth, a real existing fact that many spirits are now experiencing the reality of. In its broadest sense, hell is every place outside of heaven, and heaven is that place where everything entering into it — its appearance and qualities and its inhabitants — is in perfect harmony with the respective laws of God and His will concerning the same. This statement involves the fact that there are several heavens, because the heaven of the redeemed, or those who have received the Divine Essence in their souls and become of the Divine Nature of God, is a distinct heaven from that wherein live those who have been restored in their natural love to the perfect condition that the first parents possessed before their fall.

Mortals usually believe that heaven is a condition, and the Bible, in which so many believe, attempts to describe this heaven with its streets of gold, and pearly gates (Revelation 21:21), etc., and as a fact it is a real, substantial place, having all the elements and appearances of a home of bliss, which help to bring to its inhabitants happiness and joy in addition to the happiness which their soul perfection and development causes them to have.

Then, as heaven is a place, having real substance, perceptible to the spirits that inhabit it, why should not hell be a place of real substance also, with those qualities and appearances, exactly suited to add to the unhappiness of those who are fitted for it? The spirit world, both heaven and hell, are places of substance, having their planes and divisions and limitations of occupancy, and not mythical, invisible conceptions of mind as some mortals ordinarily conceive ghosts to be. The spirits of mortals are real and more substantial than are the physical bodies of mortals, and these planes and divisions, whether of heaven or hell, have a more real existence, than have mortals in their places of habitation or confinement in the earth life.

In your communications you have had some very realistic descriptions of hell from those who are actually living therein and are realizing its tortures and realities, and I will not take the time here to attempt to describe it in detail, and will only say that as it has not entered into the minds of men to conceive the wonders and beauties of heaven, neither have they ever conceived of the horrors and sufferings of hell. From all this men must understand that the punishment and darkness which the spirits of evil endure in the hells are not specifically inflicted by God because of any wrath that He may have towards these spirits, or to gratify any feelings of revenge, or even to satisfy any outraged justice, for it is not true.

Man, when he becomes a spirit, is his own judge and executioner, submitting to and receiving the inexorable results of the law, that whatsoever a man, "sows that shall he also reap" (Galatians 6:7). This is a law that is necessary to preserve or bring about the harmony of God's universe, which, of course, is absolutely necessary. Now, while it may appear to man, at first sight, to be a harsh and cruel law, yet in its workings and results, even to the individual spirit who may suffer in the reaping, it is a most benign and beneficial law, for the darkness and sufferings of a few years, as you mortals say, bring about an eternity of light and happiness.

The law must rule; and in all the apparent harshness and suffering and want of mercy, the great Divine Love of God overshadows the sufferer and finally makes the defiled and wicked soul become one of purity and goodness. Men may never have thought of the fact, that if it were possible for these evil spirits to live in heaven, their sufferings and unhappiness would be greater than what they endure by living in the place that is more in agreement in its surroundings and appearances, with their own distorted conditions of soul. So even in their hells, God is merciful and good.

I have written enough, and you are tired and I must stop, but before doing so, let me declare the truth to be, that hell is not a place of eternal punishment. That all the hells as well as other parts of the spirit world are places of progression and the privilege of probation is not taken from any spirit no matter how wicked. All are God's children and in His plans for the perfecting of the harmony of the universe, and man's salvation, all the hells will be emptied and the hells themselves destroyed.

But men must not think from this that the duration of suffering in these hells is necessarily short, for that is not true; some of the evil inhabitants of these places have been in such darkness and suffering for centuries, as mortals count time, and may be for centuries more, but the time will come when they will have the awakening to the fact that they may become children of light, and then when they make the effort to progress, they will succeed.

The sooner that mankind learns that hell is not a place of punishment to satisfy the wrath of an angry God, but is merely the natural and necessary living place of the spirit, whose condition of soul and mind demand. As the spirit's condition changes, it will change and the hell of its habitation will change until finally for that spirit all the hells will disappear.

You are tired and I must stop. So thanking you, and I leave you with my love and blessings.

Your brother in Christ,
Paul

The resurrection that is common to all be they saint or sinner
January 16, 1916

I am here, St. Paul.

I come tonight to tell you of a truth that is important for men to know, and which you must place in your book of truths. I have written you before on my alleged writings as they are contained in the Bible, and which, as I have said, were not written by me as they appear there.

I desire tonight to write for a short time on the subject of the "resurrection," because, I see, the church doctrine of the resurrection is founded more on what is ascribed to me than on the writings of the Gospels, though the latter also contain a basis for the doctrine.

I never said there would be a resurrection of the physical body nor of the individual clothed in any body of flesh, but my teachings were that man at death would rise in a spiritual body, and not a new one made special for the occasion of his departure from the material body, but one that had been with him through life and that came into an individualized form when he first became a living being. This spirit body is necessary to man's existence, and is that part of him which contains his senses and is the seat of his reasoning powers. Of course, the organs of the physical are necessary for the utilization of these senses, and without these organs there could be no manifestations of the senses, which are inherent in the spirit body. Even if a man should lose the perfect workings of his physical organs of sight, yet the power of seeing would still exist in him, although he might not be able to realize that fact; and this same principle applies to the hearing and the other senses.

So when man loses his physical organs which are necessary for him to see with, he is dead as to sight, just as dead as he ever becomes with reference to all the other organs of sense when the whole physical body dies; and were it possible to restore these physical organs that are necessary to enable him to see or hear, he would be able to see and hear just as he was before their loss. The restoration of these organs does not, of itself, bring him the power to see and hear, but merely enables the faculties of sight and hearing to again use the organs for the purpose of manifesting the powers which are in and a part of the spirit body.

When the physical body dies, the spirit body at that very time of

334

death, becomes resurrected, and with all these faculties of which I have spoken, and thereafter continues to live free and unencumbered from the material body, and with these organs being destroyed, they can no longer perform the objects of their creation. It becomes dead, and thereafter never has any resurrection as a material body, although its elements or parts do not die, and in the workings of God's laws enter upon other and new functionings, though never that of reuniting and forming again the body that has died. So the resurrection of the body, as taught by me, is the resurrection of the spiritual body, not from death, for it never dies, but from its envelopment in the material form which had been visible as a thing of apparent life.

There is a law controlling the uniting of the two bodies and the functioning of the powers and faculties of the spirit body through the organs of the physical body, that limits the extent of the operations of these faculties, to those things that are wholly material or which have the appearance of the material. Now when I say material I mean that which is grosser than the spirit body. These faculties of sight of the spirit body can, through the organs of the material body, see what are called ghosts or apparitions as well as the more material things, but never, in this way, see things of pure spirit. When it is said that men or women see clairvoyantly, which they do, it is not meant or is it a fact, that they see through the organs of the physical eyes; but on the contrary, this sight is one purely spiritual, and its workings are entirely independent of the material organs.

Now when this material body dies, the spirit body becomes resurrected and free from all the limitations which its incarnation in the flesh has imposed, and it is then able to use all its faculties without the limitations or help of the physical organs. As regards sight, everything in nature, both material and spiritual, becomes the object of its vision. This, in short, is what I meant by the resurrection of the body; and from this you will realize that the resurrection is not to take place at some unknown day in the future, but at the very moment when the physical body dies, and, as the Bible says, in the twinkling of an eye (1 Corinthians 15:52). This saying of the Bible attributed to me, I did write and teach, for this resurrection applies to all humans, for all who have ever lived and died have been resurrected, and all who shall live hereafter and die will also be resurrected.

Now this resurrection is not the great "resurrection" upon which, in my teachings, I declared the great truth of Christianity to be founded. This is not the resurrection of Jesus that I declared without which our faith as Christians is in vain. This is the common resurrection, applicable to all humans of every nation and race, whether they have a knowledge of Jesus or not. Many times in many nations it has been demonstrated before the coming of Jesus, that men had died and appeared again as living spirits in the form of angels and men, and were recognized by mortal men as spirits who had previous earth existences.

So I say, this is the resurrection common to all men; and the coming and death and resurrection of Jesus, as taught by the churches, did not bring the great "resurrection" to the knowledge or comfort of men, and did not furnish the true foundation upon which the true Christian belief and faith rest. Many Spiritualists assert and claim that the resurrection of Jesus as referred to, was not a new thing and did not prove to humankind a future life any more convincingly than had been proved before his time by the experiences and observations of men and followers of other sects and faiths.

The great weakness of the church today is that they claim and teach as the foundation of their faith and existence the resurrection of Jesus; and the result is, as is plainly and painfully apparent to the churches themselves, that as men think for themselves, they are doing more than ever in the history of the world, when they refuse to believe in this resurrection as sufficient to show the superiority of Jesus's coming and mission and teachings over those of other reformers and teachers who had preceded him in the world's history of faiths and religions. As a further result the churches are losing their adherents and believers. Christianity is waning and rapidly, and agnosticism is increasing and manifesting itself in the forms of free thought societies and secularism, etc.

Hence you will see the necessity of making known again to humanity the true foundation stone of the real Christianity that the Master came to teach and which he did teach, but was lost as his early followers disappeared from the scene of earthly action and practice, and men of less spiritual insight and more material desires, with their ambition for power and dominion, became the rulers and guides and interpreters of the church.

There is a resurrection that the Master taught, and his apostles, when they came into a knowledge of what he taught, and which I as a humble follower taught, which is vital to man's salvation and which is the foundation of true Christianity; and which no other man, angel or reformer ever before taught or has since taught.

It is too late to explain tonight, I will now say good night and God bless you and keep you in His care.

Your brother in Christ,
Paul

ST. LUKE

St. Luke asserts that the Gospel in the Bible is not the one as he wrote it
September 5, 1915

I am here, St. Luke of the New Testament.

I will write a little as I am interested in what you have received from Luther tonight, and as I am supposed to have written the Gospel of Luke, I desire to say a few things in reference to the correctness or rather incorrectness of many things contained in my Gospel.

As you infer, I am St. Luke the writer of the third Gospel and a follower of Jesus. My Gospel was not founded on anything I had personal knowledge of, but upon the writings of others and the traditions which were the common knowledge of many Christians at that time. I knew several of the apostles and obtained much of my information from them, as well as from many of the Christians who were members of the congregations to which these apostles preached and expounded the sayings of Jesus.

In my Gospel, as now contained in the authorized version, there are many things that have been interpolated. This version was not based on what I wrote, but upon pretended copies of my writings; and the persons who made these copies did not follow literally my writings, but added to my text and gave their own interpretations of what I had written in such a way as to destroy the true meaning of what was intended to be conveyed by my writings.

There are many truths contained in the Gospel as it is now written in the Bible, and they are the truths of God, but there are also many errors which contradict these truths. For instance, I never wrote that Jesus commanded his disciples to believe that the wine was his blood or the bread his body, and to eat and drink these things in remembrance of him (Luke 22:19). How this interpolation could have been made I do not know, but one will observe that the same things are said in all the four Gospels, and this saying must have been derived from a common source, and that must have been the minds of those who pretended to copy the Gospels.

I tell you now that this saying, that the blood of Jesus saves from sin, is not true, and if men depend upon this blood for their salvation they will never be saved, but will enter the spirit world with all their sins, and will be surprised to learn that Jesus is not waiting to receive them in his arms and carry them to the mansions prepared for the truly redeemed of the sons of men.

I know that a vast number of the members of the various churches believe this harmful doctrine, and that as a consequence, many persons claiming to be Christians will realize that their sins have not been forgiven when they come into the spirit world. Sometime, as these writings continue, I will point out the errors of my Gospel to an extent that will show you the fact of what great additions and misinterpretations have been made thereto.

I will stop now.

Your brother in Christ,
St. Luke

*Religion is the relationship and harmony of men's souls with the
Soul of God, also the differences in the teachings of the various churches*
August 25, 1918

Let me write a line, Luke.

I was with you tonight at the church and listened to what the
preacher said in reference to religions and their point of contact, and
was somewhat surprised at his declarations as to the analogy which he
drew between the believers in the various so-called Christian religions.
While, as you know, there is implanted in the souls of men, a longing for
that which tends to elevate and spiritualize them, even though this longing may not be consciously present with a large number of them. Their
beliefs as to the ways in which this longing may be made manifest, and
develop the spiritual nature of the soul, are very different among those
professing these various religions, and the ways are not equally efficacious in causing their spiritual development.

Religion is a matter of soul and not of intellect, and the greater the
development of the soul in the right direction, the higher will be the
spiritual state or condition of the soul. Mere intellectual belief, no matter how intense and undoubting, will not tend to bring about this spiritual development, for religion is really nothing more than the relationship and harmony of men's souls with the Soul of God. The mind will
not be sufficient to create this state because the mind of man cannot possibly bring into harmony the Soul of the Creator and that of the created.
The mind in its exercise may tend to awaken the soul to this possibility
of this relationship, but only the workings of the soul can effectuate the
complete unity of the Creator and the created. Only soul can speak to
soul, and mind is only a helper, provided the soul is alive in its longings.

So it is apparent that that form of belief which is wholly of the intellect can have no common meeting place with that belief which is the
result of the development of the soul; and hence, to say that men of all
the various religions, just because they are what are called Christians,
are in an equal relationship to God, is erroneous and misleading.

As regards the condition of man as the perfect man, these several
religions may tend to bring about this state of perfection, if the moral
precepts which they teach are observed and practiced by men. But as

339

regards man as the divine angel; that is, as a spirit having in itself the Essence of the Divine, only that religion which teaches the true way to acquire this divinity can lead men to the at-onement with God in His very Nature. There can be, in this respect, only one true religion, and only one way in which that religion can be practiced and possessed; and to say that all religions have a common point of approach, is misleading and deceiving.

I know that among these various religions there are individuals who have found the way to the method of becoming transformed into the Divine Nature of God, and this notwithstanding that the teachings and creeds of the several churches do not show the way to this soul development into the spiritual of the "divine". For in these churches there is wanting, in their dogmas and doctrines, that which will help men to this true religion. Because it may be found that in the churches there are some who have, to a degree, this divine spirituality, there is no justification in saying that there is any common place of meeting in these several religions.

Of course, the moral precepts may be and are taught by all the Christian churches, and when observed will ultimately lead all men to the condition of the perfect natural man, and only to this extent can it be said that they may have a common ground of religion arising from the belief in the moral teachings. If a preacher of one church knows, with the conviction that arises from his sincere and honest investigation of the moral laws, that some other church is not teaching or insisting on the observation on the part of its members of these great moral truths, then he has no right to conclude and say this latter church is the possessor of religion, as is the church in which these moral truths are taught and followed by its adherents.

It is a mistake for a preacher to say that because there may be good and spiritual men in all churches, therefore, one church is as good and religious in its teachings as another church. Truth is of such a nature that it cannot be compromised, and the man or preacher who would compromise the truth is not fulfilling his duty to God or man. The church which teaches that there is nothing greater than morality, and that man can become no more transcendent than the perfect man, is devoid of the truth and would not be accepted as a teacher of the full truth, as should the church which knows and teaches the way by which man may become a divine angel.

The preachers of the various churches should accept as equal the possessors of the moral lessons which are taught by other churches which gives them a common point of approach. When it is understood that a moral truth is a truth no matter where it may appear and by whom taught, there is some justification in declaring that all churches which teach the moral truths are on a plane of equality, and that one is entitled to as much respect and freedom from criticism as another. And further, as the great truth of the rebestowal of the potentiality of receiving the Divine Love, and the effect on men's souls, was never known and taught until the coming of the Master, it is not surprising that none of the churches can or do teach this great spiritual truth, and the only true religion arising therefrom. The knowledge of this truth perished from the earth a short time after the passing of the Master, and hence no church can teach this religion of the soul that transforms the mortal into the "divine".

The religion of the perfect man may exist in varying degrees in all the Christian churches, but the religion of the divine angel exists in none, although some individuals of these churches, to some extent, have received into their souls the great Divine Love even though they have no intellectual knowledge of the same.

I thought it advisable to make these few remarks on the declaration of the preacher, as showing that his broad assertion that the religions mentioned, which to him are all embracing, may have a common meeting point with every religion. When he learns the truth, he will realize the errors of his human and brotherly declarations.

I will not write more, good night, and God bless you.

Your brother in Christ,
Luke

St. Luke, on the teachings of
New Thought, and he explains its erroneous beliefs

I am, St. Luke.

Let me write a few lines tonight as you are in better condition, and I am able to make a rapport with you and deliver my message. I was with you today at a meeting of the New Thought people and saw the impression made upon you by the speaker in his efforts to show that God is within man, and that only the opening up of the soul or mind of man to the development of that God is all that is necessary to bring that man into a perfect at-onement with the truths of God's will.

Well, I have to say that this speaker, when he comes to a realization of himself in the spirit world, will find that God is not in him or in anything that he may have possessed in his earth life. His development of the kingdom within him, as he termed it, was a mere delusion and a snare to the progress of his soul, in its career through the earth life, as well as through the spirit life. He is mistaken when he announces that the kingdom of heaven is within him, or that he has that within him that which can, by its development, lead to the condition of the divine man, in the sense that he spoke of.

He is also mistaken when he asserts that God is everywhere — in the flowers and in the thoughts of men and in the heart — for God does not find his habitation in any of these things, and men do not live and move and have their being in Him. God is a distinct and individual Entity, and is not spread over all His universe, as the preacher proclaimed, and can only be found by the longings of the soul, followed by a development of that soul in His Love.

No, God is in His heavens, and man can reach Him only by the persistent longings of that soul for the inflowing of His Love. These things that the preacher declared to be the presence of God, are only the expressions of His Being, and they do not declare His presence in any other sense than as the evidence of His existence, and in His habitation, from which these expressions flow and make known to man His presence, as these things reflect it. I am sorry that this speaker has not more knowledge of the true God, and of His seat of habitation, for then he would realize that these things upon which he places so much belief as being the very God, Himself, are but the expressions that flow from Him.

I know that men teach that there is implanted within the souls of all men, that which is capable of being developed into an existence like unto God; that man needs only this development in order to become a God. But in this teachings men are mistaken, and will find themselves, at the stage of their highest development, nothing more than the perfect man. Man has within him only that with which he was created, and can of himself add not one thing that will change him from this condition of his creation. It is true that he can by a right course of thinking and living renounce those things that have tainted his soul and alienated it from God, and made it sinful and disobedient; but when this is done, he is still only the perfect man, and nothing of the divine is in him.

Jesus was the perfect man and, as such, was an exemplar of what all men will ultimately become. He became more than the perfect man, and it was only after he attained to this condition of excellence, that he could say, "I and my Father are one" (John 10:30), for it was only then that he possessed the Divine Love to that degree which made him at-one with God. Jesus could not say to the multitude that they were at-one with him and with the Father, for they had only the natural love and had not experienced the transformation of their souls; and such sayings as this were addressed only to his disciples, or to those among his hearers that had received the Divine Love.

The speaker spoke of the New Birth, but had no conception of what it meant, and like many other teachers, in and out of the churches, believes that a mere condition of the purification of the natural love constitutes this New Birth, and that is all Jesus meant when he taught the necessity of being born again. There is only one way in which this New Birth can be brought about, and that you already know.

As to the moral truths taught by the Master — such as are referred to in the Sermon on the Mount — undoubtedly they will, if observed in the heart, bring about a regeneration of the soul that will lead men to the glory of the perfect man and make him at-one with the laws of his creation. This condition is devoutly to be wished for and sought after by all men, and when they attain to this condition they will experience the beatitudes that are mentioned in the sermon; but this is only the state of the perfect man, and nothing of the "divine" enters into their condition.

New Thought, as it is called, has in it something that is an improvement on orthodoxy, and men will be the better if they will embrace some of its teachings. The great stumbling blocks of the trinity, and the vicarious atonement and the blood would be removed from the worship of men, and they would then rely on the moral truths in the development of their souls for salvation, and would not rest supinely in the belief of the efficacy of the vicarious atonement. But some of the other things that it teaches are all wrong, and its followers will find when they come to the spirit world that there is a God to be worshiped, and that man has not within him that God to be developed by his own thoughts and deeds.

I know that according to the orthodox teachings too little is thought of the natural goodness of man, and too much emphasis placed in his innate depravity, and that nothing in man is worthy of the release from the sin and disobedience in which he is now living, and of himself he can do nothing to bring about his purification and restoration to his original condition of the perfect man. This is wrong, for very largely upon man's efforts depends his redemption; "as a man thinketh in his heart, so is he" (Proverbs 23:7).

He is naturally good, and his present condition was brought about by his permitting his soul to be contaminated with sin, and to become good again he needs only to pursue the way that will remove sin and its consequences from his soul. Man created sin, and he will have to remove sin, and the process will be slow, but ultimately it will be accomplished, and by the efforts of man himself. He will be helped by spirits who are God's ministering angels in these efforts, but upon man himself depends the removal of that which he created and imposed. And here let me say, that unless man wills it, he will forever remain in sin, and God will not, contrary to man's desires, make him a pure and undefiled being; and man's belief, unaccompanied by striving and seeking, will not be sufficient to bring about this remedy.

The speaker is a good man, and has experienced to a large degree the workings of his own will upon the conditions of his soul, and knows that his own efforts have caused him to renounce many things that tended to defile him and cause doubt. In this condition he realizes much happiness, and thinks that he is of himself sufficient to attain to that which will bring him into a perfect unison with the God that he thinks is within him. In this he is deceiving himself, for what he thinks is God is only an unusual condition of soul development in its natural love, that gives him a happiness which causes him to believe that God must

344

be in and a part of him.

As you have been told, the happiness of the purified soul is beyond all conception of humans, and the nearer a man approaches to that condition of purification of his soul, the greater becomes his happiness, and the belief that God must in someway be in that happiness and form a part of it, when the fact is that this happiness is only that which was bestowed upon man in the beginning. As the soul becomes purer and relieved from the defilement of sin, man becomes what he was in the beginning, and has regained only that which by nature is his. He must realize that by the removal of sin his soul becomes more and more in harmony with the will of God, and less and less in harmony with his own perverted will.

Let New Thought progress until men may realize that they are at-one with themselves, their created selves, but let it not teach them that what they experience as a removal of sin from their own souls by their own efforts and thoughts, is evidence of a development of any supposed God within them, for it is not true; but is merely the development of their own natural created selves, freed from that which defiled and made them unnatural.

The speaker said that the kingdom of heaven is within all men, and needs only for men to realize that fact, and declare its truth, and that then they will become pure and like unto God, and find themselves in the presence of God, and see Him face to face. Well, in this he is all wrong, for the kingdom of heaven or celestial kingdom is not within men, though it may be, and neither is God in their souls and capable of being seen face to face. These men who teach purification of their natural love and a superior state resulting from that purification and nothing more will never see God, and they will always remain in the mere image in which they were created, a merely purified man made in the image of God, and nothing more. God will then be the same unseen Creator as he is now, and men will worship Him in faith only, for their soul perceptions, which are the only eyes of the soul that can see God, will not be opened, and to them God will still remain the unseen and unknowable Being that exists today in the knowledge and belief of men.

Well, I have written enough for tonight, but saw that you were somewhat interested in the teachings of the day, and thought it best that I should write you as to the truth of the subject of which he discoursed and evidently believed.

With my love to you, and the hope that our messages may now continue without interruption, I will say, good night.

Your brother in Christ,
Luke

Why Spiritualism as now taught does not satisfy the
soul in its longings for happiness, peace and contentment
December 5, 1915

I am here, Luke.

I want to write a few lines on the subject about which you and your friend Dr. Stone were talking, and that is as to whether Spiritualism, as now understood and taught, supplies that which satisfies the souls of men in their longings for happiness and peace and contentment.

I have heard in the course of my spirit life a great many preachers and teachers of Spiritualism, both in recent years and all along the ages, from the time of my first entrance into spirit life; for you must know that Spiritualism is not a new thing having its origin or belief in the recent years that followed the manifestations in America. All along the ages spirits have manifested themselves to mortals in one phase or another, and men have believed in Spiritualism and discussed it.

Of course, in former times when the churches had the great power which enabled them to dictate the beliefs of men, Spiritualism was not so openly taught or discussed as in these latter years; nevertheless it has always, during the time that I have named, been known to humankind. Never have its teachings gone beyond the mere phenomena which demonstrated to its believers the continuity of life and the communication of spirits. The higher things of the soul's development and the kingdom of God, as you have been instructed, were never thought of, or, at least, never taught or believed in. Only the two facts that I have spoken of were discussed and accepted; and even today, the scientific men who are investigating it deal only with the phenomena and are satisfied with proof that man never dies.

At no time has the existence of the Divine Love or the kingdom of

346

God been sought for or taught by the teachers of Spiritualism, and in fact such things could not have been taught, for they never have been known. God has never been anything more to the Spiritualist than some indefinable abstract force, whose existence is not of sufficient certainty to make Him anything more than a mere principle, as some call Him. The laws governing all nature are the only things that men look to for their ideas of right and wrong and the governing of their conduct in life.

The Spiritualists speak of the love of man for one another and the brotherhood of man and the cultivation of the mind, and the moral qualities, but admit to no outside help, other than from some departed friend who may not be at all competent to help. Such help is only that which one can give to another; and even when the help of what is called the higher spirits is spoken of, it involves no different quality of help. I know that spirits do help mortals, and also harm them, and all such help according to the ideas of the Spiritualists is based upon what they suppose these spirits possess in the way of superior intellectual acquirements or moral qualities.

The soul of man is that part of him that is made in the image of God, although unconsciously it may be longing for that which will make such image become Substance, with its resultant happiness and joy. Yet you will not find that any Spiritualist teaches or attempts to teach how or in what way such Substance may be acquired, or the fact that there is such a Substance. They do not know that the Divine Love, coming through the working of the Holy Spirit, is the only thing that can enable the image to be transformed into the Substance, and hence they cannot teach the truths, and as a consequence, the longings of a man's soul are never satisfied by the teachings of Spiritualism.

Spiritualism, with all the truths that belong to it, is the true religion of the universe and one which would prove more effective in bringing men into a state of reconciliation with God than all other religions combined. However, it is powerless and without drawing power as a religion because it has not the teachings which show men the way to God's Love and to the satisfying of the soul's longings. Someday, in the near future, this defect will be remedied and then you will see men and women flock to its bosom, so that they can enjoy not only the happiness which communication with their departed friends give them, but also, the happiness which the development of the soul by the Divine Love gives them.

Why the great "revelation" of this truth has been delayed to Spiritualists so long, I do not know, except it may be that humankind was not ready to receive it before. But now the time has come, and the false beliefs of the orthodox churches, and the want of belief of the Spiritualists, will both disappear and men be made free and the possessors of the combined truths of Spiritualism and the existence of the Divine Love, which brings not only happiness and peace, but immortality.

I must not write more tonight as you are tired, so I will say good night,

Your brother in Christ,
Luke

*The condition of spirits in the twilight
zone and their progress in the natural love*
February 5, 1917

I am here, Luke.

I merely want to say that you are in better condition tonight, and that I will write a few lines upon a subject that may be of interest to you.

In the spirit world there are many spirits who are in neither darkness nor light, but are in what may be called the twilight zone. They are neither happy nor unhappy. These are spirits who have progressed from the lower spheres, where they expiated their sins and errors of the earth life, and have rid themselves of their recollections of many of their sins and have progressed somewhat in the development of their natural love and also in the acquirement of the intellectual knowledge, and are not feeling the stings of conscience, but are realizing the happiness which the forgiveness of their sins and the improvement of their intellects causes them to have.

They are to a large extent very much in the condition of men who have paid the penalties of their sins, yet have not received such increase in their natural love as to enable them to progress to the higher intellectual spheres where the spirit becomes to a more or less degree the perfect man. They have been a long time making their progress, for it is a fact that the development of their souls from the condition of the wholly sinful man to that where such sins have almost disappeared is a very slow development. These spirits are not to be classed with the dark spirits who so often come to you for help and relief from their darkness, for they are in that condition where it is difficult to convince them that they need help in order to make wonderful progress and obtain greater happiness. In this zone the spirits seem to be well satisfied with their condition, and have the belief that their advancement must necessarily be slow and that there is not a better and quicker way to obtain relief from their condition. Among this class of spirits commences the greatest difficulty for the higher spirits to successfully convince them of the great truth of the Divine Love and the possibilities of obtaining a condition that will place them in the higher soul spheres without the long delay in making their progress.

In the lower spheres the spirits are not satisfied and generally are very desirous of getting relief from the darkness and suffering and, as a consequence, we can do more to convince them of the truths that are so necessary for them to know. You would be surprised to know the number of spirits who are in this zone, and the great number of years they have been in making the progress that they have made. Many of them have been in the states to which I refer for centuries and yet have never known any desire to progress out of those states except in the way that they consider to be the gradual and natural way to advance.

I will not write more now. Good night and may God bless you.

Your brother in Christ,
Luke

The necessity for men to turn their thoughts to spiritual things
October 16, 1916

I am here, St. Luke.

I desire to write my promised message, and if you feel that you can receive it, I will try to write. Well, I desire to declare certain truths with reference to the necessity for men turning their thoughts to things spiritual, and letting the material things of life consume less of their time and thoughts.

In the first place, that which is eternal is of more importance than that which is temporal and has an existence for a short time only, even though these things of time are necessary to sustain and preserve man while living his life on earth. I would not be understood correctly as implying that these material things are not necessary and important for man to acquire and use to the best possible advantage. They are a necessity to his earth existence, and it is not only a privilege but a duty for man to make the best use of these material gifts that is possible, and to place himself in that condition which will enable him to enjoy to the utmost these things that have been provided for his material comfort and happiness. Further, it is his duty to bend his efforts to develop the use and application of these things, so that the greatest possible benefit and utility may be derived from the proper use of them.

To do this, I understand that man has to give a portion of his thoughts, and devote a part of his time to their consideration, and to the means and methods by which the best results may be brought about, and in doing this man is not disobedient to God's laws, or to the requirements which the laws of his own being call for. The discoveries of the inventors are desirable and men's work in making these discoveries is commendable, and so are efforts of the merchant and mechanic and financiers to succeed in their different undertakings and as a result accumulate money and use it for their comfort and sustenance.

But these things, or the thoughts and efforts used to accomplish these results, do not help the soul development, or even the development of the spiritual side of man's nature, and if man devotes himself for the greater number of his hours of living to these pursuits, when he comes to lay these burdens down and pass into the land of spirits, he

350

will find that he is very poor indeed. Because the eternal part of his being has little developed, and his soul is fitted for a place where those who have laid up their riches on earth must go.

So attractive is this accumulation of money, and the gaining of fame or position to man, that when once engaged in, and especially when accompanied with what he calls success, he naturally devotes his whole waking time and thoughts to these efforts, and as a consequence, very little of this short time on earth is given to thoughts of and striving for things of the higher kind. If mortals, and especially those who are so arduously and constantly engaged in the effort to win the success that I have just mentioned, could only see and know the condition of those who when on earth were engaged in similar pursuits with like aspirations, and who are now in the spirit world, they would realize the utter futility of such efforts, and the great soul-killing harm that the so-called success on earth has brought to these spirits.

While we may assume that many of these spirits did not do affirmative wrong or injury in their work, and did not enter into the condition to which I refer because of any such wrong or injury, yet they are in a stagnated and shriveled condition of soul and spiritual qualities. This is because when in their earnest pursuits of these material things they neglected the development of their souls or the cultivation of their spiritual qualities. Their sin was that of omission and it is a sure one in its results, and the more common one among men who think too much of material things, or think not at all or are indifferent to everything, and are satisfied to live in an atmosphere or state of vegetating contentment.

The law operates the same upon the man who neglects his spiritual nature because of his absorption in the things material as upon the man who is guilty of such neglect because of indifference, or contentment with the pleasures that these material things give him. In both cases the results are the same — the soul remains stagnant and the spiritual qualities lie dormant; and the man of such neglect will find his place in the spirit world to be one of darkness and suffering.

Life is short and time is fleeting, even though a man may live his allotted time of three score and ten years, and there is no place in all of God's universe where it is so important that man should start on his way to eternal progress as in the earth life. There the soul should have its awakening and be fed with thoughts and strivings for the things spiritual. When the start is thus made on earth, it is so much easier for the continuous progress of the soul in the spirit world; if not the awakening may be delayed for years, and the progress which follows generally is very slow.

So I say, let men not devote so much of their time to those things which are of time only, and while they remain in the world of time until the mortal becomes a spirit. Thoughts are things and when applied to man's spiritual development they are things of the most vital importance. A little thought may start a dormant soul, in hardly a living state, to grow and increase into a thing of beauty and harmony. As it has been said, where your treasures are, there will your heart be also.

So with all my love, I will say, good night.

Your brother in Christ,
Luke

Incarnation of the soul, the mystery
of the birth of the soul in the human being
January 13, 1916

I am here, Luke.

I want to tell you tonight of the mystery of the birth of the soul in the human being.

All souls that enter into mortal bodies are, previous to such advent, real, living existences, and made in the likeness of the great Soul, though not having the qualities and potentialities of that Soul, and also, not having the form of an individualized personality that they have after they become parts of the composition, or form, of the mortal and spiritual bodies of human beings.

The soul, in its existence prior to becoming an indweller in the mortal body, has a consciousness of its existence and of its relationship to God and to other parts of the great Soul. Especially of the duplex character of its being; and by this I mean the sexual differences in the two parts of the soul, which, in the way that they are united, constitutes the one complete soul.

When the time comes for this soul to become an indweller in the mortal frame, the two parts that I speak of separate, and one of the parts enters at that time into a fetus and the other to follow in the future, but never into the same one. While this separation is necessary for the individualization of each part of this one complete soul, yet the two parts never lose that interrelationship, or the binding qualities that existed before their separation, and continue to exist thereafter.

As I have said, this soul before its separation has a consciousness of its existence, but it looses this consciousness while it is separated into the two parts for its physical existence, and not until its reentrance into the spirit world as a spirit, does it regain this consciousness. Now in order to regain this consciousness, it is not necessary that both parts come into the spirit life at the same time. If one part becomes a spirit, free from the physical body, and the other part remains in the mortal body, that part that comes into the spirit world may receive the awakening to this consciousness, depending of course upon its condition and development.

When both these parts eventually return to the spirit world, it often happens that for a long time, they live as spirits without having the knowledge of their dual character, because of various reasons that may exist. The conditions of the development of the two parts may be so vastly different that the realization of this consciousness may be wholly impossible; and very often it is the case that when these two individualized parts are informed that they are the soulmates of each other, they will not believe that information, and live on in utter indifference to the fact. But ultimately, the consciousness of their relationship will come to them, because their development, no matter whether intellectual or spiritual, will tend towards the awakening of this consciousness, which is always present with them, although dormant.

Now, as to what this soul is in its constituent parts or shape or form prior to its separation for the purpose of becoming an inhabitant of the mortal body, we spirits are not informed and do not know. We are often present at the conception, and also the birth of a child, and realize that a soul has become enveloped in the flesh, but we cannot see that soul as it enters into its home of mortal environment, because as to us it is invisible and has no form. But after its lodgment in the human body we can perceive it and realize its existence, for then it assumes a form, and that form varies in different humans. We have never seen the Soul of God, although we know that there is this great Oversoul, and hence we cannot see the soul of any human until it becomes, as I say, individualized.

I know that men have often wondered and asked the question as to the preexistence of the soul that has been incarnated, and what qualities and attributes it had during its preexistence. I wish to say that we spirits, although we are inhabitants of God's celestial heavens, have little information, though we know that the soul, and I mean the complete soul in oneness, has an existence prior to its becoming individualized. You may ask, how we know this? Well, it will be hard to explain this to you, so that you may comprehend, but this I can say, that we spirits of the higher soul development can, by our soul perceptions, understand the existence of these souls as images of the great Soul, and the qualities of these images are such, that we cannot see these souls or their dualities, yet we are conscious of their existence. To use an illustration, that is not altogether appropriate, you understand that the wind blows, yet you cannot see it.

We further understand, and such is the result of our observations, that when the soul, and keep in mind that I mean the two parts when I say soul, once becomes incarnated and assumes an individualized form, it never thereafter loses that individuality, and hence, never again returns to its condition of preexistence, and can never again become reincarnated in the existence of any human being.

There is no such thing as reincarnation, and all the theories and speculations of men upon that question, which conclude that a soul once incarnated can again become incarnated, are wrong, for the incarnation of a soul is only one step in its destined progress from an invisible formless existence to a glorious angel or to a perfected spirit. A soul in this progress never retraces its steps — it is always progress, though sometimes stagnation takes place — but it continues as an individualized spirit until it reaches its goal in fulfillment of God's plan for the perfecting of His universe.

The soul is a subject that is difficult of treatment, however, I have made this effort to give you some faint idea of the soul, as you are in good condition tonight to receive my ideas. From it you can understand that the soul has an existence prior to its finding its home in the physical body, and that it is duplex and has a consciousness of the relationship of its two parts. After it has received the experience of the mortal life and received an individuality, it returns to the spirit world, and at some time that consciousness will come to it again, and the two parts will be reunited (as in marriage not becoming one soul), unless in the development of these separate parts have arisen barriers that may prevent their reuniting. Further, this soul will never again retrace the steps of its progression and become reincarnated.

I will now close, and with my love and blessings say good night.

Your brother in Christ,
Luke

The sins of the parents are visited upon their children
April 9, 1916

I am here, Luke.

I desire tonight to write for a short time on the text, "The sins of the parents are visited upon the children".

I know that usually the explanation of the text has been that the material sins or rather the sins which result in material injury or affliction are visited upon the children, and to a very great extent this is true, though that explanation is not what was intended by the declaration.

Man is not only a material or physical being, but is more largely a spiritual being, having a soul and spirit which never cease to exist, and which are just as much a part of him while on earth, as when he becomes a spirit; that is after he has left the vestments of flesh and blood. These real parts of man are of more importance to him and his real existence than is, the physical part, and the sins which man commits are not the results of any primary physical action, but are of the operations of the powers which form or have their real seat in the spiritual part of his being.

The physical part of man is not the originator of sin, but merely manifests its effects, and sin almost always manifests itself on and in the physical body, and leaves its scars apparent to the consciousness of men upon such body. Hence, as man is able in his ordinary condition to perceive the effects more plainly on this body, he then thinks that sin's only effect is shown upon his body, and at the same time ignores or is not sensible of the fact, that the great effect or injury of sin is upon and to the spiritual part of man. As the physical body is affected by the results of these sins being carried into operation, so much more so is the spiritual part of man affected by the fact that these sins had their creation in that spiritual part of man.

It may be asked, in what way can the injurious effect of sin upon a man, that is upon his soul and spirit, have upon the spirit and soul of his child, so that the child may suffer from the sin of the parent? Well, when a child is conceived and gestates and is born, he not only partakes of the physical nature of his parents, but also of the qualities and condition of the spirit and soul of the parents. This may seem improbable, but it is a fact that the spirit and soul that enter into the child after it has been conceived comes from the great universe of souls and are wholly independent of the parents and is not in its nature or qualities a part of the parents as are the flesh and blood which build up to produce the physical body of the child. While this is true, it is also true that this spirit and soul of the child are susceptible to and in a way absorb the influence of the spirit and soul of the parents, not only at the time of conception but also during the period of gestation, and even for years afterwards, and to such an extent that this influence continues beyond the mere earthly existence of the parents and into the life of the progeny.

The spirit part of the child is more susceptible to the influence and evil effects of these sins than is its physical body, for as I have said, the spirit part is the originator and breeder of the sins, if I may so express it, while the body is merely the recipient of the exercise of the sins and the objects of their manifestation. The influence of spirit upon spirit is more extensive and certain than mortals can possibly conceive of, and the results of that influence are not so apparent or known to the consciousness of the succeeding children, or to the respective parents, as men suppose. As a fact they do not understand or become conscious of the fact that such influence is operating upon the spiritual parts of their children. They see and realize that the effects of such sins become manifested in the physical body, and as their ordinary natural senses cannot perceive the condition of the spirit, they conclude that the text can only mean, that these sins are visited upon the material bodies of their children.

Here I must tell them that, while great and deplorable injury is inflicted on these material bodies, yet greater and more lasting and more grievous — in the way of manifestations — injury is inflicted upon the spiritual nature of the children. Not only because this nature continues to live, but because men, not realizing that this nature has been injured, make no attempt to find and apply a remedy as they so often do in the case where these sins manifest themselves in the physical body. Besides, there are many sins that do not affect the mere material body, but which do great injury to the spiritual nature, and which to the senses of men are never perceptible.

A man is not only the parent of a child's material body but in a secondary way is also the parent of its spiritual nature. The condition of the parent's spiritual nature influences and determines to a large extent the qualities and tendencies of the child's nature for good or evil, not only while it is a mortal but frequently after it has ceased to inhabit the veil of flesh. So let parents know that they do not live to themselves alone as mortals and that their evil thoughts and deeds have a greater or lesser influence upon the spiritual natures of their children, especially at the time of conception and during gestation. Then how important that every parent during these times particularly, and at all times, should have their spiritual natures in that condition of purity and freedom from sin, that their children may be conceived and born in a condition of soul purity, which will not reflect any evil that they can charge their parents with being the creators of.

If men would only realize these facts and live their lives in accordance with the truths which I here declare, how much sooner would the human race be brought into harmony with God's laws and the souls of men be freed from sin and evil. I know it is often said that it is unjust and not in accordance with the justice of an impartial God that the sins and penalties arising from the disobedience of our first parents, should be visited upon humankind who were and are their progeny, and as such had no part in that disobedience. When it is remembered, and it is a fact, that God did not create sin or evil or impose such upon the first parents for their disobedience, that they themselves created evil and sin, and men have been creating these inharmonies ever since, it will be seen that an impartial God, who is our only God, is not responsible for either sin or evil and the consequent penalties which they impose. As has been written you before, the abolishing of sin and evil and their penalties is in the power of man and his will.

As these first parents created these evils, as I have explained, and in the manner that I have pointed out to you, their sins, by the influence which they have upon the spiritual nature at the time of conception and birth become, as it were, a visitation and that is the spiritual desires and tendencies and inclinations toward that which is evil. This influence continues with the child for years after its birth, according as the child and parents are closely associated together in their earth lives. As each succeeding generation caused the visitation of its sinful influence and tendencies upon the succeeding generation, you can readily see how men, all men, became subject to the sins and evils and penalties which were brought into the world by the first parents.

Instead of God being the creator of these things or visiting them upon the children of man, He declares that their existence is contrary to the harmony of His creation and must be eradicated before man can come into that harmony and at-onement with Him. God gave to man the great power of free will, without any restriction upon its exercise, except as a man's understanding of the harmony of the operations of God's laws might influence him to exercise this great power. As man's exercise of that power in the wrong brought into existence these things of evil and sin, so man, as he perceives this plan of God's harmony, must exercise that will in such a way as to free himself from these things which are not part of God's creation, and are out of harmony with His plans for the creation and preservation of a perfect universe, of which man is its highest creation. God never changes. His laws never change. Only man has changed from the perfection of His creation; and man must change again before that perfection will again be his.

Now from all this it must not be inferred that man is left to his own efforts to bring about this great restoration, for that is not true, because God's instrumentalities are continuously at work influencing man to turn again to his first estate, and become the perfect man, as he ultimately will become.

Well, I have written enough for tonight, and hope that what I have said may be understood and meditated upon by all who may read it. I will not detain you longer, and with my love and the blessings of one who is now not only the perfect man, but a possessor of the Divine Nature of the Father and an inheritor of immortality.

So I will say good night.

Your brother in Christ,
Luke

What is the fact in reference to the authenticity of the Bible
March 12, 1917

I am here, Luke of the New Testament.

I desire tonight to write on the subject of "What is the fact with reference to the authenticity of the Bible". I was with you at the lecture of the preacher on this subject, and was surprised that he could announce with such apparent confidence that the Bible is the authentic "word" of God, actually written by the men whose names appear therein as the writers of the same. The fact that he traced back the existence of certain manuscripts and versions to a hundred and fifty years subsequent to the time of the teachings of Jesus does not establish the truth of his declaration. By such establishment the authenticity of the Bible, or the genuineness of the manuscripts as they now exist, contain the real writings of the apostles, or of those persons who are supposed to be the writers of the same from the fact that their names are associated with these manuscripts.

Neither is it true that John's life was prolonged to the end of the first century in order that he might write the true declarations of the eternal truths as declared by Jesus, for John did not live until that time, and his writings were not preserved as he had formulated them, nor were the results of his declarations transmitted truthfully, as claimed by those who teach the inviolability of the scriptures.

I was a writer upon these sacred subjects, and as I have before told you, I wrote a document which was called the Acts of the Apostles, and left a number of copies of my writings when I died; though such compilation was merely a history of what I had heard from those who had lived with and heard the teachings of Jesus, and of their efforts to circulate and teach his doctrines after his death. I also had the benefit of some writings of the disciples about Jesus, but such writings were very few, for these disciples and followers of Jesus did not commence to place in the form of manuscript his teachings or the experience of his life until a longtime after he had left the earth. They expected his speedy return when he would become their king and legislator, and hence, they saw no occasion or necessity for preserving in the form of writings the truths in which he had instructed them.

I know that after my own death the writings that I had left were not preserved intact, and that many things that I had incorporated therein, were in the numerous copying and recopying of my manuscripts left out and ignored, and many things that I did not write and that were not in accord with the truth were inserted by these various successive copyists in their work of reproduction. And many of these omitted things and additions were of vital importance to the truth of things spiritual as they had been declared by the disciples as containing the truths that Jesus had taught.

During the period, the short period as the lecturer denominated between the earliest writings of the fathers of the church, and the times of the actual occurrences of the things to which these writings are supposed to relate and correctly describe, there were many changes made in the writings that I had left, as well as in those left by the other original writers. Even in the Epistles of Paul, which these theologians and Bible students claim have more authenticity and greater certainty than the Gospels or other Epistles of the Bible, many changes were made between the times of their writings and the times of the execution of the manuscripts or of the sermons of the fathers of the early church.

Within that one hundred and fifty years the truths of the spiritual teachings of the Master, had become to a more or less extent lost to the consciousness and knowledge of those who attempted to reproduce the original writings. These men had become less spiritual, and their thoughts and efforts had become more centered in building up the church as a church than in attempting to develop and teach and preserve the great spiritual truths. The moral precepts became the dominating objects of their writings and teachings and were more easily comprehended by them than were the precepts that taught the way to the development of their souls and to a knowledge of the will of God, and the mission of Jesus as a way-shower and saviour of souls, rather than as a Messiah to establish his kingdom on earth.

No, I declare with authority that the authenticity of the Bible cannot be established as the "word" of God, for in very many particulars it is not His "word," but on, the contrary, contains many assertions that are not truths and are diametrically opposed to God's truths, and to Jesus's teachings of the truth.

The Bible has changed and perverted the whole plan of God for the salvation of man, and has substituted a plan that arose from the limited wisdom of those who attempted to convince mankind that they had a knowledge of God and of His designs as to the creation and destiny of man. They were influenced very largely in this particular by their knowledge of and belief in the teachings of the Jewish Church and the history of the Jewish race in its dealings with God, as they supposed, and in the teachings of the scribes and Pharisees. This fact was conspicuously shown by these writers attempting to substitute Jesus in their plan of salvation in the place of the animals of sacrifice in the Jewish plan of salvation.

Now in order for the God of the Jews to be appeased and satisfactorily worshiped, He demanded blood and more blood, so the God, that Jesus declared was the God of all the peoples of the earth, in order to be satisfactorily worshiped, demand the blood of His dearly beloved Son. Among these writings of the Bible there are many things declared to be truths, and embodied as the actual words of God, that are contradictory and unexplainable, and which, if they were the words of God, or even the teachings of Jesus, would contain no contradiction, or admit of any constructions that were not consistent one with the other.

As the additions and emasculations and interpretations were made in the original writings of those who declared the truths as they had heard them from the Master, the decreasing want of comprehension of spiritual things and the growing wisdom of their own finite intellects, caused them to conceive of a plan on the part of God for man's salvation. As the recopying continued the thoughts of those who copied, or who dictated the same, became more centered on this plan, these copies were gathered together and considered, and efforts were made to have some agreement in the declaration of this plan, and as the new copies were made they were constructed with the view of showing forth this agreement.

It must not be supposed that the copies from the manuscripts that are the basis of the Bible were executed and preserved in a manner that caused them to be isolated one from the other, and that they were not all known to the persons who copied or caused the copying of the writings from which the manuscripts were made, for that would not be true. These, then, may be called the basic copies, and were in circulation at the time the Christian fathers wrote, and they had access to them, and quoted from them and helped to give them the interpretations that now prevail in the churches with the additional interpretations since those days.

Men now know that among these Christian fathers were bitter disputes as to what was a part of the "word", and as to what should be accepted and what rejected among these writings antedating the manuscripts that form the basis of the Bible. Many manuscripts purporting to be the "word" of God were rejected as such, and for the reason that they could not have been the records of God's "word", because they did not agree with what the bishops of the church in their human knowledge and reason accepted as what God's "word" should be. Even these bishops disagreed and differed, just as the human minds and reason disagree with one another.

Then I say the lecturer did not prove the authenticity of the Bible as being the "word" of God. He did not go down the stream of time as he called it, far enough to discover the existence of any authenticity, and that being so, his argument of proof is just as weak as if he had started from the time of the printed Bibles, when their contents were substantially the same, but not being the originals the similarity proves nothing. What I have said with reference to my own writings applies to the writings of all the others. The Bible does not contain their writings as they wrote and left them to humanity.

The Bible contains many truths, and enough to enable man to reach the kingdom of heaven, provided they are correctly understood and applied, but there are so many things taught therein as truths, which are just the opposite of truth, that they make it difficult for men to discern and apply the truth, and comprehend the will of God with respect to men, and the destinies that must be theirs as they follow and obey that will or do not do so.

I will not write more now as you are tired, but will soon come and write a message on another subject that I have been desiring to write for some time.

With my love and blessings.

Your brother in Christ,
Luke

St. Luke explains the dematerialization of Jesus's earthly body
October 24, 1915

I am here, St. Luke.

I was with you tonight at the meeting of the Spiritualists, and heard the statement of the speaker as to the probabilities of what became of the body of Jesus after the crucifixion.

I was not present at the crucifixion, and, of course, do not personally know what became of the body of Jesus, though I have been told by those who were present that the Bible's description of his burial in the tomb of Joseph was true (Matthew 27:60). The body was buried in the tomb of Joseph and was left there by those who placed it in the tomb, which was sealed and a guard set over it to prevent anyone from approaching and interfering with the body (Matthew 27:65), because Jesus had predicted that in three days he would rise again (Matthew 20:19).

After the tomb was sealed Jesus arose, and without his body of flesh passed from the tomb and descended into the lower spheres of the spirit world where the dark spirits lived in their ignorance and sufferings, and he preached to them the rebestowal of the gift of redemption.

The body of flesh by the power which Jesus possessed, became so spiritualized or etherialized that its component parts became disseminated by Jesus in the surrounding atmosphere and he retained only the spiritual body in which he appeared afterwards to the disciples and others. When he appeared at the meeting of the apostles, where Thomas, the doubter, was present, he recalled to his form, as you will better understand by my using such expression, elements of the material, so that in appearance the body was as much like flesh and blood as when it was placed in the tomb, before he disseminated these elements, as I have said.

The flesh and blood which encloses the spirit form of man, is continually changing in obedience to the ordinary laws of nature as understood by man. Jesus understood and had power to call into operation other laws of nature, which caused such laws to operate, that the dissemination of the elements of flesh and blood took place, and he was left only with the spirit form. This, I know, has been a great mystery since the time of the discovery of the absence of his body by the watchmen at his tomb. Now being such a mystery, and as the only explanation of such a disappearance, men have believed and taught that his body of flesh and blood actually arose from the dead, and, therefore, the physical body of flesh and blood of mortals will also arise in what they call the great "resurrection" day.

No body of flesh and blood arose, and the spirit form of Jesus did not remain in the tomb after the dissemination of the material body, for no tomb or other place could confine his spirit. You will remember that on the third day Jesus appeared to Mary, who was most intimate and familiar with the appearance of Jesus, and yet she did not recognize him, but thought he was the gardener (John 20:15); and so it was with the disciples who were travelling with him to Emmaus. Now, if he had retained his body of flesh and blood, do you not suppose that they would have recognized him? For if he had the power to resume that material body into which Thomas had thrust his hand and found it to be a body in the appearance of flesh and blood, then why do you think it strange or wonderful that he would have had the power to cast off his earthly body while in the tomb and cause it to disappear into thin air?

This I am informed is the true explanation of the disappearance of the material body of Jesus; and to me and to others who understand the laws of nature — I mean that nature that is beyond the ken of men — it is not surprising or worthy to be deemed a mystery.

I am glad that I went with you to the meeting tonight, as I became impressed with the desirability of making this great mystery a mystery no longer.

With all my love, I am your brother in Christ,
St. Luke

*The mystery of the Godhead, three in one, is a
myth, and there is no mystery that men should not know*
November 5, 1916

I am here, St. Luke writer of the third Gospel.

I come tonight to write you a message upon the truth of what the Holy Spirit is. I know that the orthodox generally believe and classify it as a part of the Godhead, being one with and the equal of God, and not merely a manifestation of God, as spirit, and hence, necessarily identical with God, though having a different and distinct personality. In this belief and in this classification is included Jesus, having a distinct personality.

The orthodox preachers and theological writers teach that it is a fact that these three are one, co-equal and existing, and that fact is the great mystery of God, and that men should not endeavor to fathom the mystery, because the sacred things of God are His own, and it is not lawful for men to enter into these secrets. Well, this declaration and admonition is very wise as men's wisdom goes, and saves the expounders of these doctrines of this mystery from attempting to explain what they cannot explain, because it is impossible for them to unravel that which as a fact, has no existence.

Men of thought all down the ages have sought to understand this great mystery, as they called it, and have been unsuccessful. As the early fathers met with the same defeat in their endeavors to understand the mystery, and, then because of such defeat, declared the explanation of the doctrine to be a secret of God, not to be inquired into by men, so that when all other investigators of the church became convinced of the futility of the search, they adopted the admonition of the old fathers that God's secret must not be inquired into, for it belonged to Him alone, and sinful man and the redeemed man also must respect God's secret.

Thus from the beginning of the established church, after the death of Jesus and his apostles, this doctrine of the trinity was declared, one in three and three in one, yet only one made the vital foundation stone of their visible church's existence. Of course, from time to time, there arose men, in the church, who, having more enlightenment than their brothers in the church, attempted to gainsay the truth of the doctrine and declared and maintained that there was only one God, the Father. But they were in the minority, and not acting with the more powerful, their views were rejected; and the mystery became the churches' sacred symbol of truth, unexplainable and therefore more certain and entitled to more credence. It seems to be the tendency of men's minds, or at least of those who believe in the Bible as the inspired "word" of God, to welcome and encourage as the more wonderful and important and the more to be cherished, those things which savor of the mysterious, rather than those which a man may read and understand.

Never did Jesus when on earth teach that God is tripartite, consisting of the Father, Son and Holy Ghost; what he did teach was that the Father is God and the only God, and that he, Jesus, is his Son and the first fruits of the resurrection from the dead, and that the Holy Ghost is God's messenger for conveying the Divine Love, and as such, is the Comforter.

I know that in Matthew's Gospel, as now contained in the Bible and adopted as canonical, it is said, in effect, that the Godhead consists of the Father, Son and Holy Ghost (Matthew 28:19) and these three are one, but such Gospel does not contain the truth in this respect and is not the same Gospel that was originally written. The original Gospels have been added to and taken from in the passing of the years and in the copying and the recopying that occurred before the adoption of the same. They, the adopted ones, were compiled from many writings, and as the compilers in those early times differed in their opinions as men do now respecting religious truths, the more powerful of these having authority to declare what should be accepted, according to their interpretations of those manuscripts that were being copied, directed the copies to be made in accord with their ideas, and I may say, desires, and announced and put forth such productions to be true copies of the originals. As these copies were successively made, the preceding ones were destroyed, and hence the earliest existing manuscripts of these Gospels came into being many years after the originals from which they were claimed to be compiled, were written and destroyed.

I, Luke, who did write a Gospel and who am acquainted with the present Gospel ascribed to me, say that there are many vital things and declarations, that I never wrote and that are not true, contained in it; and many truths that I did write are not contained therein, and it is so with the other Gospels.

In none of our Gospels did the mystery of the Godhead appear, and for that reason there was not and is not such a mystery, and we did not teach that there was any Godhead, composed of three personalities, but only one God, the Father. Jesus was a son of man in the natural sense, and a Son of God in the spiritual sense, but he was not God or a part of God in any sense except that he possessed the Divine Love of God, and in that sense he was a part of God's Essence. The Holy Spirit is not God, but merely His instrument to convey the Divine Love.

Now as you have been informed, the soul of man existed prior to man's creation in the flesh, and was the only part of man that was made in the image of God. It existed in this pristine state without individuality, though having a personality, and it resembled the great Soul of the Almighty, merely in its likeness. The ego of God as may be said, is the Soul, and from this Soul, emanates all the manifested attributes of God, such as power and wisdom and Love, but not jealousy or wrath or hatred, as some of the writers of the Bible have said (Romans 1:18), for He possesses no such attributes. The ego of man is the soul, and in his created purity and perfection from his soul emanated all the manifested attributes belonging to him, such as power and love and wisdom; and neither were jealousy nor hatred nor wrath attributes of his before his fall.

It is said that man is composed of body, soul and spirit, and this is true, and from your life's experience you know what the body is, and I have told you what the soul is, and now the question arises, what is the spirit? I know that there have been for centuries great differences of opinion among theologians and other wise men as to what the spirit is. Some contend that it and the soul are the same thing, and others, that the spirit is the real ego of man and the soul is something of less quality and subordinate to the spirit. Those having these other views are all wrong, for as I have said the soul is the ego, and everything else connected with man and forming a part at his creation when he was pronounced to be "very good," is subordinate to the soul, and only its instrumentality for manifesting itself.

The spirit is the active energy of the soul and the instrumentality by which the soul manifests itself; and this definition applies to the spirit of man while a mortal as well as when he becomes an inhabitant of the spirit world. The spirit is inseparable from the soul, and has no function in the existence of man, except to make manifest the potentialities of the soul in its activities. Spirit is not life, though it may become evidence of life as it is life's breath.

As man was created in the image of his Maker, and his spirit is only the active energy of the soul, by the application of the principle of correspondences, which one of your former psychics declared to exist, it may be assumed and it is truth, that the Holy Spirit is the active energy of the great Soul of God, and, as we know from our experiences and observations, it is used as the messenger of God to convey to humans His Divine Love. I do not mean to restrict the mission of the Holy Spirit to mortals in the flesh, for it also conveys and bestows this great Love upon the souls of God's children who are spirits without the bodies of bone and flesh, and who are inhabitants of the spirit world. And so, it is a truth that the Holy Spirit is not God and no part of the Godhead, but merely His messenger of truth and Love emanating from His great Soul and bringing to man the light and happiness of the Divine Love.

So you see there is no mystery of the Godhead, and no secret that God does not wish man to know and understand, and no truth that is contrary to God's laws and will that man shall search for and possess. It is said that God is spirit, and it is true; but spirit is not God, only one of his instruments used to work with mortals and the spirits of men. To worship the instrument is blasphemy, and only God alone must be worshiped. Jesus must not be worshiped as God, the Holy Spirit must not be so worshiped, and the sooner men learn this truth and observe it the sooner they will get in at-onement with God, and please the Master, who, as some may not know, is the greatest worshiper of the Father in all the universe.

I have written longer than I expected, and I hope from my message many mortals may receive the truth, and believe that the Holy Spirit is not one of the Godhead, and that the mystery of the Godhead is a myth, and that there is no truth in all God's universe that man is not invited to search for and understand and possess.

I will stop now and in doing so, will leave you my love and blessings, and will pray to God to send the Holy Spirit to you with a great abundance of the Divine Love.

Good night and God bless you until I come again.

Your brother in Christ,
Luke

St Luke adds his testimony to that
of Prof. Salyard's that God has personality

I am here, St. Luke.

I want to add my testimony to that of Professor Salyards that God has personality, and I desire to say a few words which are expressive of my knowledge arising from my own experience.

I have a soul development which is greater than that of the Professor, and a perception which is clearer and more convincing than his, and yet, what he has said is all that I can say as to the truth of the personality of God, except that to me it is undoubtedly much clearer and of longer acquaintance.

I know that God is a Being that has personality, though not of a form like unto man, but has all the attributes that have been mentioned. These attributes are not God, but merely qualities which He possesses, and which in their workings upon the hearts and souls of men emanate and flow from Him. You may better understand this if I call your attention to the fact that while you can see and feel and hear and love and dislike, yet these attributes or qualities are not you, but are those things that belong to your personality. You may be deprived of any or all of them, and yet you may not cease to exist as a personality. And so with God; while these things of Love and wisdom, and loving and hearing do not constitute God, yet they are a part of Him and are exercised by Him, just as the qualities I have mentioned are exercised by you.

I know it is difficult for the mere mind to comprehend this great truth of God having a personality, yet it is a truth, and just as real to the perceptions of the developed soul as is the existence of yours or any man's personality to the finite mind. Here is another fact in connection with this great truth, and that is that only the spirits who have experienced the New Birth and become filled with the Divine Love of the Father, and hence a partaker of His divinity, will ever be able to perceive this great truth of the personality of God. Other spirits are without this soul development which is absolutely necessary for it to possess in order to perceive the great truth under discussion.

Yet the mere fact that these other spirits do not comprehend or understand this truth, does not make it any the less a truth, and all mortals and spirits are subject to its operations, and must come under the benefits that they may receive by reason of the workings of this truth upon their lives and thoughts.

Just because men cannot see God it does not mean that He does not see them, for He does; and their every thought is known to Him and taken account of. Strange as it may seem to you, or as I should more appropriately say, surprising as it may seem to you, that account is kept in the memories and consciences of men themselves, and when the time comes for them to render an account of their acts and thoughts, no other place or receptacle is sought for or examined to find this account than these very memories and conscience. Nothing can be hidden or lost until it has fulfilled the purpose of its existence.

Men may create, but they cannot destroy — I refer now to their actions and their thoughts. While on earth they may forget and ease their conscience by forgetting, yet, when they come to the spirit world, and are called to render an account, the inexorable laws that are really their judges and executioners show them that there is no such thing as forgetting. It has been said, they have forgotten to forget.

God is a Being, self-existing, unchangeable, but full of Love and mercy, and this He does not exercise in any individual case, but has made certain that His laws of mercy will so operate that all the spirits of men and mortals may by their own acts and desires place themselves in such condition of soul so that these spirits will receive the benefit of this mercy. Yes, His mercy is from the beginning waiting for all men to ask for it and want it, just as is His Love.

I could write on this subject for a longer time, but I must not write more tonight as you are tired, so I will close.

With all my love and blessings, I am your brother in Christ,

St. Luke

*Discourse on the devolution and evolution of humanity,
the scientists only know of the evolution after man reached
the bottom of his degeneracy or devolution*
July 22, 1917

I am here, St. Luke.

Well, I desire to write a few lines on the subject contained in the book which you were reading tonight. I mean the book dealing with the creation and fall of man.

Well, the man who wrote the book is endeavoring to reconcile the Bible doctrine of the creation and fall of man with the scientists' doctrine of evolution, and to show that these two views of the subject are not antagonistic, and if properly understood, may be used, one to support the other. But in this he has not succeeded, nor can he, for this reason — man did not evolve from the beast or lower animal, but was always man, the creature of God, perfect in his creation and wholly natural.

There was nothing of the supernatural about him and he never possessed any nature of the superman from which he fell at the time of his disobedience. He has never been anything more or less than the perfect creation of his Maker, although he has degenerated in his qualities and in the exercise of his will. Evolution or the doctrine of evolution has its limitations, and its founder, or those who follow him either wholly or in a modified way, are not able to retrace this doctrine to the fall of man, and hence, when they attempt to pass beyond that stage when man seemed to have been very degenerate and a product of the animal progenitors, they get into the field of speculation, and knowledge ceases to exist.

Man was not created with any of the divine qualities, as the writer seems to think, but was made merely the natural man that you see now, without the defilement of his soul qualities which involves only the elimination of those things from his soul that cause the departure from the condition of his creation. That is, when he was created he was in perfect harmony with the will of God and His laws, and when he shall be restored to that harmony of unity with these laws, he will then be what he was before the fall.

So the idea put forward by the author that man was created with something of the "divine" in him, and that when he lost these divine qualities he fell into that imperfect condition, is all wrong. The great truth connected with man's creation, is that man was created perfect, that as regards his order of creation or the qualities of his moral and physical nature there could be no progress, for the next step in progression would be the "divine". Thus you will see that he was so wonderfully and perfectly made, that he was only a little lower than the angels, and by angels I mean the souls of men which have ceased to be incarnate and have partaken of the Divine Love and become a part of God in His divinity of Love.

The souls in the spirit world which have only the development of their moral qualities, that is, they have become purified and in harmony with the laws and will of God, are only men perfected in their natures and organisms as they were at the time of man's creation. I say, then, that the perfect man possesses those qualities and attributes that were his at the time of his creation, and he cannot progress or become greater or other than he was at the time of such creation. He was made perfect as a creation, and beyond the perfect there can evolve nothing greater from the qualities and faculties that made him perfect. Thus to progress, there must come into his nature, from without, the Divine Love, which will add to these qualities and faculties, which is no part or method of evolution.

When the first parents fell, they lost that which destroyed the harmony of their existence with the laws of God, and also were deprived of the great potentiality of becoming "divine" in their natures of Love and immortality, like unto God, but as mere created men they fell from perfection and not from divinity. Nor were they by that fall deprived of the possibility of living forever in the physical bodies, because those bodies were made only for the purpose of enabling the souls to individualize themselves, and thereafter die and become dissolved into their derivative elements.

The physical body was never created to live forever, and men were never created to live on earth forever, for a greater and larger world was provided for their eternal habitation, where things are real and only the spiritual exist. The earth is a mere image of the realities of the spirit world, and exists only as the nursery for the individualizing of the soul. So that you may not misconceive my meaning, remember the soul is the man — the ego — and that when man fell, it was not the physical part of man that fell, except as it was influenced by the soul, but, it was the soul that fell. The sentence of death was not pronounced upon the physical, but upon the soul potentialities, and, hence, you may see, that when man shall again become the perfect man, it will not be necessary that the physical body be restored. Even if it were not contrary to the physical laws of the universe, or, to speak more correctly, to the laws controlling the material part of the universe, that the material body of man be resurrected and again house the soul, it would not be necessary, for the soul has its spirit body which manifests its individuality. There is no necessity for the resurrection of the physical body, and there will be no such resurrection, for God never does a useless thing.

As I say, man has never ceased to be the man of God's creation, although he has become degenerate and defiled, and at one time in the history of his existence devolved to that degree, where, save for the essential qualities of his creation, he appeared to be lower than the brutes. However, he was always the man of God's creation, and never an animal of the lower order.

The scientists in their geological search and research and in their finds of fossils and traces of ancient man, and in their biological theories, conclude that man was of a lower degree of intelligence and manner of living. They may be justified in so concluding, and also that he has gradually evolved from that condition and state, and they draw apparent correct theories therefrom. Yet when they attempt to go further, they enter only into the realm of speculation and become lost in the darkness of mystery. They can rightly acclaim the evolution of man from where they lose him in their retracing of that evolution, but can know nothing of his devolution anterior to that time; and, hence their speculations are without foundation of substance.

No, man has not evolved from the lower animal, but only from himself when he reached the bottom of his fall. In this particular, the history and experience of man is this — he was created perfect — he sinned, and fell from the condition of his created state — his condition at the bottom of his fall was inferior in some phases to the brute animal — and after long centuries he commenced to rise from his base condition, and had made progress when the scientists by their discoveries found evidence of his then condition, and since then he has been the subject of their evolution.

Now the scientists and all humanity must know that all during these centuries of descent and ascent, man was always man, the greatest creation of God, and the most fallen.

Well, I have written enough for tonight, and as I was with you today as you were reading and saw the misconceptions of the writer of the book, as well as those of the scientists to whom he referred, I thought it advisable to write a few truths about the subject.

I will soon come and write. So with my love and blessings, I will say good night.

Your brother in Christ,
Luke

What is the most important thing in all the world
for men to do to bring about the great "millennium"
November 30, 1916

I am here, Luke.

I desire to write tonight a few lines upon a subject that has never yet been written on, and I know it will interest you. What is the most important thing in all the world for men to do in order to bring about the great "millennium" that the preachers proclaim will come before or after the coming of Jesus?

Of course, in stating the question I do no intend to be understood as consenting to the doctrine that Jesus will come to earth in physical form, on the clouds with a great shout, etc., as many of the preachers teach. That event will never happen, because, as we have written you before, he has already come to earth or rather to men in the spiritual way that we have explained.

Well, as commonly understood, the "millennium" is a time or period of a thousand years when peace will reign on the earth, and the devil, as is said, will be bound and not permitted to roam over the earth, causing sin and destruction of souls, and sickness and the other sins that now so generally beset mortals. Of course, there is no personal devil in the sense of a satanic majesty, but there are spirits of evil which abound in the unseen world and are constantly with mortals, exercising upon them their influence of evil, and suggesting to them thoughts and desires that eventuate in sinful and wrong deeds. But these evil ones are merely the spirits of departed mortals and are not beings of a superior kind in power and qualities.

Sin, as we have told you, was never created by God, nor is it the product or emanations of any of God's perfect creations, but is wholly the result of the wrongful exercise of man's appetites and will, when the desires of the flesh are permitted to overcome the desires of his spiritual nature. With sin come all the evils and discords and inharmonies that constitute man's manner of living his earth life, and until these things, which are not a part of his original nature, but which are the creation of the inversion of that nature, be eliminated from his thoughts and desires and appetites, the "millennium" will never be established on earth.

Now, the converse of this proposition is true, and the possibility of its occurring, is also true, and the question is how can this be brought about, for to bring this about is the most important thing for men to do. When the cause of the present condition of humankind in sin and sorrow and unhappiness is definitely determined, then will readily appear what is necessary to remedy the condition and remove the cause; and, hence, when the remedy is applied and removal made, the "millennium" will surely come, for this glorious time of man's desired and looked for happiness is merely one in which peace rules and discord does not exist, and every man is his own brother's keeper in love.

Then what are the causes of the present condition of existence on earth, and why is man marred and tainted and controlled by sin and error and disease? These causes are two-fold, one arising from man's fall from his created perfection of body, mind and soul, in permitting and encouraging the animal nature to subordinate the spiritual and thereby, by the over-indulgence of the former, causing the carnal appetites to grow and transform the man into a lover of sin and things evil. The other arising from the influences which the spirits of evil, who are always endeavoring to make close rapport with men, and exercise their evil influence over him.

While the personal satan does not exist, yet the idea conveyed by the necessity of binding him in order to bring about this "millennium" is a true one, and applies to the actual relationship of men to these evil spirits, except this, that in the case of the latter it is not necessary or even possible to bind them, but to loosen them — that is, to loosen their rapport with or influence over men, for when that is done, men become, as it were, free, and these evil spirits are as if they were not.

So you see, as a preliminary to the ushering in of this greatly desired time of peace and purity, men must cease to believe that it will come with the coming of Jesus in a manifested physical way, as a mortal conqueror might come with legions of followers and noises of drums and by force of arms or greatness of power to subdue his enemies. This will never be, for no man is an enemy of Jesus, but all are his brothers, and he is not now making and never will make war on any human being, only on the sin and defilement that is within his soul. This war can never be waged by power or force of legions of angels, for so great is the power of man's will and so respected is its freedom of action by God, that there is no power in heaven or earth that can or will change a sinful soul into a pure one by force and threats and conquering legions of angels, even though they might be led by Jesus, which will not happen.

No, the soul is the man, and that soul can be made pure and sinless only when that soul desires and consents that such a condition may become its own. So, it should not be difficult for men to understand that this erroneous belief, that Jesus will come in this semblance of a human conqueror and establish this great time of peace, is doing them much harm and delaying the actual time of the coming of this event. The effect of this belief upon the soul is that everything is to be accomplished by the work of Jesus, and nothing by themselves, except to believe in his coming and wait, and be ready to be snatched up in the clouds (1 Thessalonians 4:17), and then help the hosts of heaven to destroy all of their late fellow mortals who had not believed with them, and put on the robes of ascension as they literally or figuratively designate such robes.

They thus believe, and in their minds they may be honest, yet their souls may be disfigured and tainted with sin and the life's accumulation of sin, so that they could not possibly be in condition to enjoy a place of purity and freedom from sin. Some of them expect and claim that they will be the judges of others of their fellow mortals, because of the deeds done in the body, and yet in how many cases would it prove to be the blind and sinful judging the blind and sinful. They further claim that Jesus, by his great power, and the fact that they believed that he would come again to earth and establish his kingdom, will in the twinkling of an eye make them fit subjects for his kingdom, and qualified to judge the unrighteous and help cast them out of his kingdom.

No, this can never be the way in which the "millennium" will be established, and the sooner men discard this belief and seek the truth and the true way to purity and perfection, the sooner the hope and expectation of men will be realized.

Your brother in Christ,
Luke

ST. JOHN

St. John gives encouragement to Mr. Padgett,
and tells of the wonderful love the Master has for him
July 20, 1920

I am St. John, apostle of Jesus.

I desire to write a little while and tell you of the wonderful love that the Master has for you in your selection to do his work. So I say, that he loves you not only because you are his choice for doing his work, but because he wants you to become a very spiritual man having a large soul development, and becoming fitted to enter his kingdom and to become one of his near and dear followers and brothers in the Love of God.

I do not know of any mortal who has been so blessed in his earth life, even we who were called by him when on earth were not so blessed, until we received the Holy Spirit at the Pentecost, as you are now doing. You will receive this great gift in greater abundance in a short time, and then you will realize what the gift of the Divine Love means to your soul and to your happiness on earth. You are now my brother and a new apostle of the Master, and I know your work will be greater in extent than was the work of any of us when we were trying to spread his teachings while on earth. I hope that God will bless you abundantly and keep you free from all sin and error.

I am with you very frequently, trying to help you to obtain the Divine Love. For you will receive it and when you do all other things will come to you — I mean all things necessary to carry on the work that has been assigned to you.

So with all my love and blessings, and the assurance that you will soon receive the Divine Love in increased abundance and do this great work with a faith that will not falter.

I am your brother and friend,
John

St. John states that very soon a great effort will
be made by the Christian Spiritualists to spread the truth
September 20, 1915

I am here, John.

I will not write long, but I merely wish to say that you must continue to have faith and pray.

Soon you will be able to do as the Master has said and you will succeed in getting in the condition to do his work as he desires. I come to you so often because I am so much interested in your work and in helping forward the great efforts that will be made by the Christian Spiritualists to give to humankind the truths of God.

So believe in what we say and you will find that what we promise you will be realized and that you will become free from your worries and be very happy in your old age. I will not write more, but will say good night.

Your brother in Christ,
John

What a man should do who is not satisfied with any of the churches
October 19, 1916

I am here, John.

I was with you tonight and heard the preacher answer questions, and some of his answers were very satisfactory, but there was one that did not exactly satisfy the true longings of the man who is in search of truth, I mean the one that asked what should a man do who is not satisfied with any of the churches.

Well, if he can find a church that provides the truths that satisfy his inquiring soul, then that man can feel he need not go to any other church for information as to those things which he seeks knowledge of or which he has grave doubts about.

The churches, of course, can give no information of truths that the churches themselves do not know, and if the truths that these churches teach fall short of what the man is seeking for, then these churches cannot possibly be satisfactory to him. While the churches differ in their creed and government, and perhaps in some particular construction or interpretation of the Bible, yet they, the orthodox churches, are all founded upon the teachings of the Bible, and they cannot teach greater or other truths than that book contains. Hence, if a man is seeking for truths that are not in the Bible, his inquiries cannot be answered by those whose knowledge is confined to the Bible teachings.

The same applies to the non-orthodox churches for they cannot give forth the truths of the spiritual kingdom of God, for they to a large degree reject the Bible and depend very largely upon ethical and moral doctrines, and the results of the works of mere conscience in determining the right and wrong of things. The spiritual things are not known or taught by these churches, and, consequently, the inquiring mind cannot get from them the information or help that it is calling for. I know that in such a condition and want of knowledge of truth on the part of the churches, such a man is without the privilege of having his cravings for the truth and his cravings for spiritual things satisfied. As a consequence he must seek further to get the information which he may consider so necessary, and when he comes to seek, he will find no place where such knowledge may be found.

The mere intellectual acquirements of students and philosophers will not supply what the man is seeking and he is without any possibility of obtaining what he seeks for. So the preacher's suggestion that he and two others form a church of their own, would have some force were it not for the fact that any church that might be so formed would have no greater possession of the truth than the churches that he has failed to find any satisfaction in.

There are many men on earth today in the condition of the man spoken of, and many who refuse to seek in the churches for the truth. The spirits have known of this condition of men for these many centuries and have been trying to supply a way or create a medium through which the great spiritual truths of God could be made known to men. And for that very purpose we are now using you to receive our messages of truth and make them known to humanity, and provide a church, may I say, where the seeking man may find answers to his inquiries.

We shall complete our delivery of these truths through you and then the man who cannot find a church where his searchings can be satisfied, will find a reservoir of truth opened up to him, that will not require any preacher or church to explain it. As you proceed in your experience with the churches and teachers of the old truths, as they call them, you will more fully realize the necessity for our work.

I will not write more tonight, but will come soon and deliver a formal message.

With my love and blessings I will say good night,
John

Why the churches refuse to investigate
that spirits can and do communicate with mortals

April 23, 1916

I am here, St. John.

I come to tell you that I have been with you today in your attendance of the church services, as the preachers declared their ideas of what immortality means, and I suggested to you thoughts showing how unsatisfactory their reasoning and conclusions were. Of course, what the morning preachers said about the reasons for inferring that immortality must be the lot of man had in it considerable force and also consolation, and I am glad that he dealt with the question as he did.

It has been established as a fact for a long time that in its beginning antedating even the Bible, that spirits or angels communicated to men; and the Bible has many instances where such occurrences were declared. While these orthodox teachers accept all these instances as true, yet they say that the occurrences were caused by some special interposition of God, and to a certain extent this is true. But this cause applies to all instances of spirit communication that have taken place since these Bible manifestations.

As we have told you many times, law — unchangeable law — governs all of God's universe, and nothing happens by chance; and so every instance of spirit communion is the result of the operation of some law working in an orderly manner. No spirit could communicate and no mortal could receive the messages, unless the law worked in such a manner as to permit or cause the same. Here I must say, that the same principle of law that enables the evil spirit to communicate or manifest enables the higher spirit to do the same. There is no special law for one and not for another.

Your land is filled with mortals who have developed in them such powers, as to enable the spirits to come in rapport with them, and thereby make known the fact that the supposed dead are alive and able to declare the fact to mortals. These facts have been established to the satisfaction of men of all kinds and characters. To the scientist as well as to the man of ordinary intelligence, and even less; and to the open-minded orthodox preacher as well as to the infidel.

All these things are not merely matters of chance but are designed to show him that he is a living, never dying being, as far as known, whether in the flesh or out of it, and what is thus designed and provided for man's consolation should not be looked upon with suspicion or fear of being against God's will. No, this great privilege is a part of God's goodness to man, and he must understand it so, and to his hope and desire for continuous life, add knowledge.

So I say, to these leaders of the worshippers at the orthodox shrines, if they will learn the truth of this continuity of life after the death of the body, it will make certain to them, that they have only a hope, backed by their faith in what their Bible tells them is the truth. Of course, this hope and faith may become so strong as to satisfy their doubts on the question, but even then it is not knowledge. This faith and hope will pale into insignificance, when the mother, mourning for her recently departed loved one, hears his voice declaring to her that he is still alive, and has all his love, and longings for her, and that he is with her feeling her love for him.

Yet these teachers will not seek and if they do, they will feel their hope and faith turn to knowledge, though they will not declare the truth to their flock and why not? Because the creeds and dogmas and iron bands of erroneous beliefs forbid them doing so. They will preach and if necessary, will lay down their lives for such a cause, but, yet, when they come to deal with this question of a supreme and vital fact, they are afraid to seek the truth.

What a responsibility they have, and what an answer they will have to make! They bury the talent which is given them, and the accounting will be grievous. Someday soon, this truth will seek them with such overwhelming force, that their creeds will crumble, and in addition to hope and faith there will come to them knowledge, and with knowledge freedom, and with freedom, the pearl of a great price which to them has been hidden so long in the shell of fear and bigotry.

I must not write more tonight. I felt that I must say these few things to you to encourage you in your work of bringing truth to light.

So with all my love and blessings.

I am your brother in Christ,
John

*The Book of Revelation is a mere allegory of one or more writers
and is not the same as St. John wrote, also a discourse on heaven*
March 11, 1916

I am here, St. John.

I was with you tonight and heard the sermon of the preacher on heaven and what it is and, as his text was founded on some expressions in a book of the Bible ascribed to me which I did write, though not just as is contained in the Bible. I thought that I should come and write you as to the truth of the sermon, and as to the value of the book's suggestion of what heaven is and what its appearances are, and what the spirits of the redeemed are doing as designated by the preacher in his service.

Well, I first want to say that while I did write a book of the nature of the one in the Bible named Revelation, yet this one does not contain my writings to any great extent, nor are my ideas set forth or followed in this book. As you may now know, in my time, and for a long time previous, the Jewish writers, because of the great troubles and persecutions their nation was undergoing, were accustomed to write books in the nature of the one contained in the Bible, and called Revelation. This was for the purpose of encouraging their people to believe that all the wrongs that they were suffering would be avenged by God, and their enemies made to suffer and become destroyed, and that in the end their nation would be rescued from its condition of servitude and sufferings and become the ruling nation of the earth.

These writings were accepted by the Jews as having the authority of "divine inspiration" and conveying to their nation the truths of God and the promises of His intervening on their behalf. The writings were always ascribed to some prophet, seer, or man of God who had the special privilege of coming in contact with God or some of His angels through the mysterious and sacred means of visions. Of course, these writings were merely intended to encourage the Jews to establish their faith in God and in the belief that He would send them a Messiah who would have the power to redeem them from the punishments and thralldom that they were undergoing under the tyranny and strength of their heathen captors and persecutors.

Always these writings were prophetic and held forth the promises for the future, without ever attempting to fix a time for their fulfillment, or the ending of the nation's woes and the coming of its deliverer. So as time went on and the promises were not fulfilled, hope continued to exist and the belief of the Jews was not lessened, and non-fulfillment was explained by the further belief that the time for the consummation of their eagerly wished for expectations had not yet arrived. That God was all knowing as well as all powerful and cared for their race and that He and He alone understood just when the proper and fitting time should arrive.

This hope upon hope was a wonderful force in keeping up the beliefs and expectations of the Jews, and so effective was it that to this day they remain a nation or rather a race in belief and expectation of this coming Messiah. But, alas, as they did not recognize and accept him when he did appear, they will never again see his appearance, for he will never come as their Messiah as expected of old, but only as the great teacher and redeemer, not only of their race, but of all the peoples of the earth. He has already come as such a redeemer, and is working now to lead men to the true and only way to life and happiness and immortality. Never will any Messiah come to the Jews to establish them on earth as a great and chosen nation, as nearly all of them believe and still look for.

Thus, as I say, many books or manuscripts were written by the Jewish prophets holding forth to the Jews the results of visions claimed to have been experienced by these writers. And as prophecies, in the sense that the Jews understood them, they have never been fulfilled, neither will they be fulfilled in the future, and their value has no reality. This custom as I may call it, continued from these early times down to the time in which I lived and wrote. My book of prophecy was written by me, not with the purpose of establishing the Jews as a nation on earth, or causing them to believe that their hopes or longings would be fulfilled, but for the purpose of encouraging the Christians to believe that notwithstanding their persecution and sufferings and martyrdom they would in the future life, when they should meet the Master and the saints, find joy and peace and heaven. Although in my writings nothing was said about the wrath of God being visited upon the persecutors of the Christians or of their having to go into a hell of fire and brimstone, so that from that fact the happiness of the redeemed would be increased.

My writings have been added to and all kinds of grotesque imagery interpolations, so that the whole design and purpose of my writings were changed and destroyed, and the present Book of Revelation is only a mere allegory of some one or more writers who were gifted with some knowledge of the Christian teachings and unusual Oriental imaginations. This book is of no value, and on the contrary is doing much harm to the cause of the truth as taught by the Master, as we who are in the celestial heavens and have knowledge of things heavenly as well as things earthly know to be the fact. It should not be accepted as a truth of the revelation of truths, and not be believed in for any purpose. It has led many good men and honest and earnest seekers after the truth astray, and caused them to believe and teach false doctrines that have resulted in much darkness and stagnation in the development of human souls in their longings for the truth.

So, I say, let men entirely discard its teachings, and any and all lessons that the preachers or others, who think that they can understand its meaning, attempt to teach. The writings that I gave to my people, of the kind mentioned, have long ago served their purpose, and the writings called Revelation contain in it no truth that will help humans to the heavenly kingdom or to their eternal happiness and at-onement with God, so let it die the death of a falsehood, born out of time.

I also was interested in the struggle of the preacher to explain what heaven is, and what his people who may consider themselves redeemed children of God, will find when they become inhabitants of that heaven. Well, he spoke truly when he said heaven is a place as well as a condition, for it is inconceivable that any condition of the spirit of a mortal could exist unless there be a place where that spirit could find a habitation. All space in the universe of God is a place, or contains places where things of existence must find localities. There is no such thing as a vacuum in God's economy, and all parts of space are fitted with something having substance, either material or spiritual, and wherever such substance is, there is a place for its abiding.

Heaven is a place, or a number of places, for the preacher is far from having the true conception of heaven when he supposes it is one large place, where all believers go after death, irrespective of their condition of soul and moral perfections. As I say, there are many heavens and many places, all as real and substantial as are the different stories and rooms in your home of earth. The partitions, if I may so speak, between these different places are just as impassable for spirits that have not the proper qualifications to pass through as are the partition walls between the various rooms in your earth homes for you mortals to pass through. These places are distinctive, and the many mansions that the preacher referred to, are situated in many heavens, or more correctly, many spheres of the heavens.

Strictly speaking, there are two heavens in God's spirit universe, namely, the heavens of the redeemed and transformed soul by the Divine Love called the celestial heavens, and the heavens of the restored perfect man, called the spiritual heavens, each of them being places of real perfection and substance. As one star differs from another star in glory, so these several heavens within heavens differ from one another in glory and appearance and in those things which help to make the mansions of their inhabitants beautiful and attractive and glorious.

It would take too long for me to attempt to describe any of these heavens, for they each and all excel any conception that a mortal is capable of having; but I will say this, that there are no streets of gold or pearly gates, or suns or stars in any of them; only the light of God's Love and mercy illuminates them.

I will postpone my further writing, but will come very soon and complete what I intended to say.

So my dear brother, I will say good night.

Your brother in Christ,
John

It was not ordained by God that Judas
should betray Jesus; he was not a bad man
August 15, 1915

I am here, St. John.

Well, there are some things in my Gospel that do not seem to be very plain, and perhaps are contradictory. Because many of these writings were not mine or written at my dictation. In the mutations of time many things have been added to and subtracted from what I wrote and, as a

consequence, the true and the untrue are mixed. It will be a very difficult task for you to make the distinction in simply reading or even
studying the Bible, for the tenor of the writing is the same. The only way
that you can separate the true from that which is not, is to wait until
Jesus gives you his messages. Of course, we can help also in that particular.

Well, that was not the word which he used, because he never taught
that it was ordained by God that Judas should betray him. In fact the
death of Jesus was never a part of that which God considered as necessary to the performance of his mission. Of course it was certain that
Jesus would die, however the manner of his death was not foreordained,
as my Gospel written in your Bible declares (John 18:32).

Judas was not a bad man as he is depicted to be and his betrayal, as
it is called, of the Master, was not for the purpose of gratifying any
avarice that he is supposed to have had or because of any jealousy or
desire to revenge a wrong. It was because he was impulsive, and had a
belief in Jesus's powers and ability to overcome the Jewish leaders in
their fight to defeat the objects of his mission. He thought he would be
doing the Master and his cause a great benefit by having it demonstrated to these Jews that the Master could not be silenced or harmed by any
act of theirs. It was really an act that grew out of his love for and belief
in the greatness of the Master's powers.

Well, I tell you that Jesus never said any such thing. He never even
told us that one of us should betray him, and I know because I was
there. If Jesus knew that Judas would betray him, he did not tell any of
us at that time, and we only knew it for the first time when Judas actually committed the act (Mark 14:10). I don't believe that Jesus knew it
before that time; in fact he has told me that he was surprised at Judas's
betrayal of him. Judas was the youngest of the disciples and not so easily controlled in his impulses and acts, as he would have been were he
older. So you must not rely on the Bible statement (Mark 14:41) as to
what occurred at that time. I know, but they are all based upon the same
erroneous writings, for you must know that these Gospels, as you have
them, are not the originals written by those whose names they bear. Let
not these things disturb your belief in the essential truths which the
Bible contains.

The trouble is that Jesus as the individual is given the prominence
which should be given to his teachings. He is displeased very much

because of this, and one of the great objects of his writing anew his truths is to correct that error, and make the truths which he received from the Father, the prominent things. As you progress in your writings you will see that this is the great object of which he shall write. I will tell you that you are in the way to receive God's Love in very great abundance, in fact, so much so, that you will realize that you are one with Him. I see, that at present, you have some difficulty in your way, but it will soon disappear and leave you free to do this great work. So my advice is to believe in the Master and pray to God and you will soon be a much happier man.

When on earth, I was a married man, and in my family the mother of Jesus lived until her death (John 19:27). Mary lives near me and is a beautiful spirit and filled with the Love of God. However you must not suppose that because she was the mother of Jesus she has any more exalted position in the spirit world than she otherwise would have had. Family ties do not determine anything in the higher spheres — the soul development is the criterion. Many spirits are living in higher spheres than Mary.

I will not write more now.

Your brother in Christ,
John

The belief in the efficacy of the vicarious atonement of Jesus
by his death and crucifixion by the churches has caused much harm to
humankind and the loss of the way to the celestial kingdom
March 18, 1916

I am here, St. John, apostle of Jesus.

I wish to write tonight on a subject that is of importance to the members of the orthodox churches as to the belief in the efficacy of the atonement of Jesus by his death and crucifixion.

All the orthodox believe, and their preachers and evangelists teach in their sermons and addresses, and the teachers of Bible classes instruct their students, that the blood of Jesus and his death on the cross were the two factors in his career on earth which save men from their sins and satisfy the great penalty of death which overhangs them, because of man's first disobedience and the sins that followed therefrom.

This doctrine has prevailed in the beliefs and teachings of the church ever since the church became established by the convention* that met in pursuance of the orders of Constantine, when the books that now constitute the Bible were given the sanction of the church as canonical. Before this time some of the early fathers believed in the doctrine of the atonement as above stated, and the controversies between them and others who did not subscribe to this doctrine were very bitter, and at times, very unchristian according to the Christianity that prevailed among the early followers of the Master, or according to his teachings.

From that time until the present, although the great Roman Church has been seceded from and reforms have been made, this doctrine has been incorporated in and believed by most of the churches, no matter what name they may have adopted and what form of government they may have prescribed. This doctrine constitutes the foundation principles of the various bodies of the church entity, and today, these principles are as much a part of faith and teachings of the churches as they ever were in all the centuries that have passed.

Now in these latter days a large majority has depended upon the belief in the doctrine that Jesus, by his sacrifice and death, paid the debt which man owed to God. And when the members of the church because of an intellectual belief assert that they believe in and accept Jesus as their saviour because he paid the debt, and by the shedding of his blood washed away their sins and made them at one with the Father, and thereby became saved from the wrath of the Father, in a moment they think they become the truly redeemed and accepted children of God. As long as they maintain that belief and attend to their duties as such members and observe the regulations of the church, they think they are safe and fitted for the enjoyment of heaven and the presence of the Father.

They also believe that unless a man accepts Jesus as his saviour, in the way I have mentioned, that man will be eternally lost, and in the beliefs and teachings of some of these members, will be sent to hell to be eternally damned and punished. Well, one view of this doctrine is just as true as the other, or rather just as untrue, because both of these phases of belief have no foundation in fact, and are not in accord with the

*The First Council of Nice, 325 A.D.

teachings of the Master, or with the fact as I know it to be, not from any mere belief but from personal experience and observation.

Oh, how the pure teachings of the Master have been distorted and made the means of preventing so many human souls from reaching the heaven of happiness that they wished for, and that they thought would be theirs when they should give up their mortal lives! This doctrine, so long believed, has worked the damnation of many a man as regards his soul development and his becoming at one with the Father and reaching the heavens that are prepared for those who obtain that soul union with the Father.

I know it may seem surprising to some, who are true believers in this doctrine, and as they think, in the truths of God and the teachings of Jesus, which are believed to be infallibly contained in the Bible. But of this I announce the falsity of these beliefs and their utter ineffectiveness in enabling these sincere people to obtain that which they so earnestly desire. However this is truth, and truth never changes, never compromises with untruth, and never permits the erroneous beliefs of a really sincere mortal to swerve one iota from the results and consequences of that false belief. The great injury that this false doctrine has done to mankind, and is now doing, will continue in the world to come, until the belief in truth shall supersede the belief in that which is false. Thus not everyone who shall say "Lord, Lord" (Matthew 7:21), will enter into the kingdom of heaven.

These false beliefs have operated in two ways to injure man and render him unfit for an entrance into the kingdom. First, by the belief that brings about the injury that results from the positive operation of error, which is great; and second by the want of belief in the truth, which prevents progress in the acquirement of those qualities which belong to and are necessary parts of that truth. When men believe in the doctrine that I have stated they become satisfied, and knowingly or not, remain in a state of false security, not attempting to develop the soul qualities, which are the only ones that relate with God. Their mental beliefs are strong and may increase in strength, but their soul communions with the Father and their growth and expansion in the soul development become stagnant, and as it were, dead.

This is the great injury that these false beliefs do to a mortal and to a spirit. I mean in his individual capacity, for it must be known as a truth, that the salvation of man, or his soul progress towards an at-onement with the Father, is an individual matter solely, and men as aggregations or in church communities are not redeemed from sin, nor as such can they have any relationship with the Father or receive His Divine Love, which is the only salvation.

Then let man consider for a moment what possible connection there can be between these Soul qualities of God and the death and blood of Jesus. God is the creator of life and death, and also of flesh and blood, and He can destroy as well as create. Had the sins of man called for the sacrifice of that which was mere flesh and blood, or the extinguishing of a life that God had created in order to pay the penalty of that sin, then a God who demanded such a payment — and this implies of course, that such a God was wrathful and could only be appeased by something that He could not of and by Himself obtain — would not possibly be satisfied with that which He had created and over which He still had absolute control, and which He could destroy and make nonexistent at any time He pleased.

Jesus's life was already a possession of God, and when he surrendered that life he did not give to God anything that he did not already own and could not have taken. When his blood flowed on the cross, it was not that which God could not have made flow at any time and in any manner. Therefore, the logical meaning of this absurdity is that God was demanding a debt that had long been unpaid, all wrathful and insatiable, and would be satisfied only with the death of a living being and the flowing of his blood; and that death and flow of blood could come in only one way or manner, namely, on the cross. Yet, with all this demand that has been sounding down the ages for centuries, relentlessly and unpityingly, God became satisfied and His wrath assuaged by seeing His own creature die — and that creature His best beloved son — and by hearing the trickling of the blood of that creature from a wooden cross; by all which, the life and the blood being already His to let live or destroy as He might see fit, man became at one with Him.

The simple reduction of such a proposition is that God, in order to be paid a debt that was owing to Him, accepted in payment that which was already His, and which no power or being in all His universe could have taken from Him. Now, I say all this reverently as your preachers say, but the fact is, that the mere assertion of such a doctrine, as I have been dealing with, is so blasphemous that no treatment of it, showing its falsity, could be irreverent. And again, the absurdity of believing that

God demanded that Jesus die on the cross as one of the necessary accompaniments of his death, in order to carry out God's plan for this death and make the payment satisfactory, is so apparent and absurd, that I and all of us spirits in the kingdom of the Father wonder how mortals can believe such an unreasonable dogma.

To follow this absurd proposition to its logical conclusion, it was necessary not only, in order that the debt might be paid, that Jesus should die on the cross, but that Judas should become a traitor, and the Jews should clamor for his death and that Pilate should pronounce the sentence. These were all necessary means to the satisfaction of the debt, and being so, why is it then that Judas and Pilate and the Jews are not saviors of mankind also, even if you say in a secondary sense?

Jesus could not have clamored for his own death, or erected his own cross or nailed himself thereto, or pierced his side with a spear in order that the blood might flow, for if he had done this he would have been a suicide; though it may be, there would have been more of the elements of the payment of a debt in that method of dying than in the way in which his death was brought about.

No, I tell you, I, John, who loved the Master more than all the others and who was closer to him, and who was with him when he was nailed to the cruel cross, which I think of with horror, and who was among the first to take his body from the tree and first felt his blood upon my hands — tell you that the death of Jesus on the cross did not pay any debt that man owed to God, nor did his blood wash away the sins of any man. Oh, the pity of it all is that mortals for all these long years have believed that they were saved by his sacrifice and blood, and by such belief have never come any nearer to the Master or in at-onement with the Father.

In closing, I wish to declare with all the emphasis that I possess, arising from a knowledge based upon the teachings of the Master and my personal experience as a possessor of this Divine Love and a partaker of the Father's Divine Nature, that no vicarious atonement of Jesus, nor the shedding of his blood, saves any man from sin or makes him a redeemed child of the Father, or fits him for a home in the mansions of the celestial heavens.

With a love that can come only from a redeemed and Divine Nature, I love all humanity, and am working to help them find the way to immortality and happiness beyond the conception of mortals or spirits who have not received this New Birth of the Divine Love of the Father.

I have written enough for tonight and you are tired. So, my dear brother, with all my love and the blessings of a heart filled with the Love of God, I will say good night.

Your brother in Christ,
John

A portrait of Jesus
June 3, 1917

I am here, John.

I come to write a few lines on the display you saw tonight which were supposed to be portraits of the Master.

Well, the exhibits were quite interesting and showed the different and diverse conceptions of the artists during the centuries of what the Master looked like, but I must say, that none of them is a correct likeness of him as he appeared on earth or as he appeared after his rising from the dead and having made himself visible to his disciples and others.

I understand how the preacher and many others who were present at the church tonight love Jesus, and enjoy the belief that in looking at some of the portraits they may get a conception of his appearance, and I only wish that his appearance might have been shown by some of the pictures. As I said none of them bore any resemblance to the Master whom I knew and associated with, and saw after his resurrection from the tomb. None of them displayed the great spiritual light that shone from his countenance, even when he was suffering on the cross, and none of them gave a faint glimpse even of the spiritual beauty that was his when he associated with and helped sinners as well as his friends and disciples.

I have never heard of any portrait having been painted of him while he lived on earth or afterwards by anyone who had seen him, and the oldest of these portraits that were presented tonight was not made until years after his death, and by men who could not have gotten a description of the Master from anyone who had seen him. I know that there was no original as the preacher supposed, that must have given a suggestion to the artists who painted the ones that you saw, for there was never any original.

No, the Master passed from earth without leaving behind him any representation of his appearance. The portraits were the results of what the artists conceived in their artistic brains, if I may use the expression, of what the Master, who had displayed such wonderful qualities of heart and mind, should look like. As their conceptions of the spiritual and human qualities of the Master differed, so their portraits differed, and the only foundation for their pictures were their own spiritual or non-spiritual conceptions.

The Master, of course, like the rest of us who were his disciples, was a Jew, and it is quite natural to suppose that he had the features and hair and beard of the ordinary Jew. As the Jews have continued to live ever since the time of the Master without much change in appearance or otherwise — I mean in his native land — the artists who conceived him to be a Jew, based their supposed portrait of him upon the appearance of the Jew as they saw him at the time that they painted the pictures.

While Jesus was a Jew, he was not what may be called a typical Jew in appearance anymore than in his other qualities, for he had in him that condition of soul that to a large extent determined and fashioned his appearance. His eyes were not dark or brown but a violet blue, and his hair was light and inclined to the auburn; his nose was prominent and somewhat long, and his beard was of the color of his hair, and worn not so long as was the custom of those days, and he never had a razor on his face. His forehead was not so very high or broad, but was well shaped and somewhat effeminate, and indicated that there was not as great a mental development as might be supposed. For I must say here, that his knowledge was not so much the knowledge of the brain as of the heart and soul; and as you know, and as all men may know who acquire the proper soul development, the soul has a brain of its own which is used for the disclosure of the knowledge of that which pertains to the spiritual truths.

Mortals may not quite comprehend the meaning of this assertion, but I must tell them that in certain circumstances and conditions the brain, or, to be more exact, the mind of the natural man becomes entirely absorbed in the mind of the soul. So that, I say, it is not a correct conclusion to suppose that Jesus, because of having all the wonderful knowledge of the truths of God — his Father, as he preferred to call Him

— must have had a large development of those portions of the brain that is ordinarily displayed by a large or prominent forehead. His head, in fact, was not very large, but compact and beautifully shaped. He wore his hair parted in the middle and reaching to his shoulders, and it was somewhat curly — a beautiful head of hair which seemed to be full of life.

No artist has had a correct conception of his appearance and no portrait or sculpture conveys a near likeness of him. As people realize how beautiful he was within they possibly in their own imaginations can see a clearer conception of his appearance than any painted portrait gives to them. I sometimes wish that there was on earth a true likeness of him, as he appeared during the time of his great work of love on earth, so that those who love him could have the further pleasure of realizing his physical appearance. However, because as mortals naturally worship the pictures of the saints, and through the picture, worship the person, the danger would be that if there was a picture of the Master, mortals would worship him even more than they do now, which is very distasteful and displeasing to him, and as he has said, blasphemy. The Master should be loved, and his presence longed for, as such presence has in it a wonderful love and influence to help and make happy those who are in condition to realize his presence; but he should not be worshiped.

Well, as I was with you tonight at the church, I thought that it might be interesting to you, to have the truth told to you in reference to the Master and his supposed portraits. Of course, it is not necessary that there should be any picture of him, true or otherwise, in order to enable mortals to enjoy his presence, for he is working among mortals today as he was when on earth. His love goes out to them and his desire that they become in at-onement with God; and when mortals sincerely long for his presence, sooner or later, as the laws of his limitations permit, he will be with them, and will comfort and help them, if they will enable him to make the rapport. This is what is meant by his standing at the door and knocking — when the door is opened the rapport is made, and then his love and influence will be felt.

The difficulty here is that mortals suppose it to be and confuse it with the great Love of God, when the fact is that this love of Jesus is the same love, in quality though not in quantity, that the mortal himself may obtain by the earnest prayers and sincere aspirations of his soul. The love of Jesus can never transform a human soul into the Substance of God, because this transforming Love can come only from God, and is bestowed through the medium of the Holy Spirit, as we have explained to you.

So let all mortals love Jesus with the fervor and fullness of their souls and crave for his love, but in doing so not forget or fail to know, that in order to become like Jesus, they must seek for the greater Love of God, and give to Him all their soul's longings and desires for the inflowing of this Love into their souls; and the more they receive of this Love, the better able they will be to love their great brother, Jesus.

Well, I have written enough for tonight. I will come soon again and write you a formal message. So remember what I said to you a few nights ago, and believe and trust, and you will not be disappointed.

With my love and blessings, I will say good night.

Your brother in Christ,
John

*What does the spirit of man do when
it leaves the physical body for all eternity*
May 29, 1916

I am here, St. John, apostle of Jesus.

I come tonight to tell you a vital truth, which I know you will be interested in. The question has often been asked, "What does the spirit of man do when it leaves the physical body for eternity?"

Many spirits, I know, have written you about this matter and some of them have described their personal experiences, yet in all the information that you have received there are some facts that have not been referred to, and I will in a brief way describe them.

When the spirit leaves the body, there is a breaking of the silver cord*, as it is called, and thereby all connection between the spirit and the body is severed for all eternity and never again can that spirit enter that body. Neither can any other spirit, although, I know, it is claimed by some Spiritualists that another spirit may inhabit the cast-off body.

*An etheric cord which connects the soul to the central nervous system of the physical body.

This is all wrong, for no spirit ever enters the body which has once been the home of another spirit, and hence, claims made by some of the wise men of the East that such a thing can be, have no foundation in fact.

Once the silver cord is severed, no power that is known to the spirit world, or among spirits of the highest spheres, can again resuscitate that body and cause the manifestation of life, and hence, in the miracles mentioned in the Bible, where it is said that the dead were brought to life, it must be understood that this tie between the spirit and the body was never broken. In those ancient days, as now, there were persons who had the appearance of being dead, and so far as human knowledge was concerned were dead, but who were really in a state of what may be called suspended animation. No signs of life appearing to the consciousness of men, death was thought to have taken place. Yet in none of the cases where the supposed dead were raised to life, had the mortal really died. As Lazarus has already told you, when Jesus commanded him to come forth, he had not died, and so of all the other supposed dead who were called to life.

Once this tie has been severed, there are certain chemical laws affecting the physical body, and certain spiritual laws affecting the spirit, which absolutely render it impossible for the spirit to again enter the body. As you have been informed, mortals and spirits and angels as well, are governed by laws which have no exceptions, and never vary in their workings. So I say, when once the spirit and body separate, it is for all eternity, and the spirit then becomes of itself, a thing apart, controlled entirely and exclusively by laws governing the spirit body.

With the spirit's entry into the spirit world, comes the soul, still enclosed in that spirit body. The spirit body has not, of itself, the power to determine its own location or destiny, as regards a place, for the law of attraction which operates in this particular, operates upon the soul, and the condition of the soul determines the location of itself. As the spirit body is the covering of the soul, it must go where this law of attraction decrees the soul shall abide.

While the mind and the mental faculties and the senses have their seat in the spirit body, yet the law that I speak of does not operate upon these faculties, as is apparent to every spirit who knows from observation as well as from experience. The combined power of all these faculties cannot move a spirit body one step in the way of progress, unless such faculties have, in their influence acted upon the soul, and caused its condition to change; and in the matter of mere mental or moral advancement this can be done. So, I repeat, the condition of the soul determines its locality as well as the appearance of the spirit body. This law of attraction is so exact, that in its operations, there is no opportunity for chance to interpose and place the spirit body in a location which does not belong to it, by reason of the operation of this law.

When the spirit body enters the spirit world it must go to and occupy the place which its enclosed soul's condition determines that it shall occupy. No interposition of spirit friends or love of parent or husband or child can prevent this destiny. Although for a time, until the soul has had a real awakening as to its condition of severance from the mortal life, these relations or friends may retain the spirit body near the place of its entrance into the spirit life, even though that place may be one of more beautiful surroundings and happiness than the one to which it is destined. However this situation does not last long, for the law works, and as the soul comes into full consciousness, it hears the call and must obey.

Thus you see, friends and loved ones in spirit life meet with love and kindness and consolation, the newly arrived spirit, but the parting must come, and every soul must find its home accordingly as its own qualities have determined. Yet the consolation mentioned is a real one, for in many instances, if it were not so, the lonely spirit would experience fear and bewilderment and all the unspeakable sensations of being deserted. Then there comes a time when every soul must stand alone, in its weakness or strength and realize that no other soul can bear its sorrow or take its burdens or enter into its sufferings. Thus the saying can be realized that each soul is its own keeper and alone responsible for its own condition.

In many cases the loving friends may visit that soul in its place of existence and offer consolation and help and encouragement and instruction, but in some cases this cannot be, for as this soul is then laid bare to itself, all its deformities, and sins and evil qualities come before it, and throw a wall around it, as it were, that prevents the good friends and loving ones from appearing to it. Here again the great law of attraction comes into operation, for while these more elevated friends cannot come to that soul, yet other spirits of like souls and qualities may become its associates and render such assistance as the blind can lead the blind in their moving about.

What I wish to say here, is that notwithstanding what some spiritualistic teachers have said, the soul has its location as well as its condition. The above condition that I have described is the destiny of some souls shortly after becoming spirits, and it is a deplorable one, and you may think that such souls are deserted by the loving influences of God's ministering spirits and left all alone in the dreary places of their habitations. Such is not the case, for while they are deprived of the presence of the higher spirits, yet the influences of love and compassion are flowing from these spirits, and at sometime will be felt by the lonely ones. As these influences are felt the poor souls commence to have an awakening which gradually causes the wall of their seclusion to disappear until at some time, the higher spirits find that they can manifest their presence to these unfortunate ones.

Besides this, most spirits, have a work to do, even though it may appear insignificant, and among these spirits of similar conditions some are a little more progressed than others, and by reason of a law which causes the more progressed to help the lesser, the latter are frequently helped from their low estate. Now what I have written applies in a sense to the spirits who are wicked and vile and without any soul development in the way of goodness, and here a similar principle enters into the conditions of all the spirits, although the higher the plane they are in, the greater the opportunities they have for receiving help and progressing. Of these latter, and the operation of the mental thoughts and moral qualities upon the condition and progress of the soul, I will write you later.

I have written enough for tonight, and leaving you with my love and blessings, I will say good night.

Your brother in Christ,
John

The spirits who have only a little development of soul
can help those who have even less development than themselves
November 23, 1915

I am here, St. John.

I want to tell you tonight about the things that spirits who have not received the Divine Love of God do, or have done to them, as you may say, in order for them to get out of their darkness and suffering and progress to a happier condition.

Well, when these spirits of evil or a sinful life first come into the spirit world, they enter what is called the first sphere which is nearest the earth. They are received by their friends* who may have been with them at the time of their passing, and are, to a certain extent, comforted and made familiar with their surroundings. This may last for a shorter or longer time according to the spirit's capability of understanding his changed condition from mortal to spirit. After this condition of consciousness is assumed by the spirit, these friends leave him, and a guiding spirit, whose duty it is to perform the task, shows or conducts him to the place which he is fitted to occupy, and which by the workings of the law of compensation, he must occupy.

In this place he is surrounded by and must associate with spirits of a similar condition of development as his own, until some change comes to him which fits him for a higher place. This change may come in a short time, or it may require a longer time to bring it about; this depends upon the realization by the spirit as to what his condition is, and the fact that there is a possibility of progressing. Of himself he cannot bring about this change, for the law which fixes his place or condition does not cease to operate until there is called into operation another law which permits and helps the change. The only way in which this changed condition can be brought about is by the influences of other spirits of a more enlightened and higher position than that of the spirit whose position I have spoken of. These influences do not necessarily come from spirits who have received the New Birth, but may come from spirits who know nothing about it, and who have only the natural love, and even they may not necessarily be of a high order of development of either intellect

*Friends already in spirit.

400

or soul.

However, they must be in such condition that they know and are able to tell the lower spirit of the possibility of progress and the way in which it can be made. Many spirits, who are themselves in a dark condition and position can help others who are in a darker condition, just as on earth a student of a lower class in school may not be able to teach all that is taught or may be learned in that school, yet he can teach those in a lower class than his own, things that he has learned in progressing to his own class.

Most all spirits have a work to do, and these spirits of little development are engaged in teaching those of lesser development the way to get in the same condition as those who teach are in. Of course these latter cannot teach anything that belongs to a higher condition than the one in which they are. In such cases the progress is very slow for many reasons, and it sometimes takes centuries for a spirit to progress from a very low plane to a higher one where only the lowest grade of happiness exists. So you see, that in order to help these dark spirits, it is not necessary for the helping spirit to be one who has in his soul the Divine Love. This means that the spirit who is helped in this way cannot progress higher than its natural love, moral conscience and intellectual endowments will permit.

This is important for you and all humankind to know for the reason that you and others may learn what the true soul development means, and how effectively spirits possessing this soul development may help all other spirits, good or bad. Aside from this you may suppose that the spirits who hear you talk at the seances, where all kinds and conditions of spirits congregate, and promise to help both mortals and spirits, may not be able to do so because some are in a dark and low condition themselves. Yet all spirits may help other spirits, to some extent, who are in a lower condition, and sometimes in the beginning of their progression, more satisfactorily, than can the higher spirits, because these dark spirits who try to help the darker spirits, are more in harmony with them, and the darker spirits will listen to them with more interest and belief that they can help them. But this is a help that does not work in such a way as to cause the spirits who are helped to lose their desires and recollections very rapidly and to progress into the higher planes, without the great suffering that you have been told of. I thought I would write this to you, for the reason that you might not in your investigations and teachings of the spirit life, give due importance to the possibility of one dark spirit helping another.

All the phases of mediumship, when honestly conducted, have their proper places and work in God's plan of redemption, and none of them must be considered as useless or without special design. Of course, the above mentioned phase of assistance to spirits is of the lowest form and is merely preliminary to the great work which the higher spirits do in carrying out the great plan of redemption, which has been explained to you. The important work is that of the spirits who know what the Divine Love of God is, and what fits spirits and mortals for the enjoyment of the great happiness which they can obtain only in the celestial spheres, and also in the soul spheres, to a lesser extent.

When a spirit who is dark learns of this great Love and strives to obtain it, and earnestly prays for the help of the Holy Spirit, which is God's messenger of Love, that spirit will progress much more rapidly, and its sufferings and darkness will leave it sooner and greater happiness will come to it. Still I say, the work of these lower spirits, that I have spoken of, is a great work and must not be underestimated. So remember what I have written and give due credit to this work.

I will not write more, but will with all my love and blessings say good night.

Your brother in Christ,
St. John

The laws of rapport and communication
March 6, 1916

I am here, John.

I desire to write tonight upon a subject that I consider important, and you may consider interesting.

As you may know, it has been some time since I wrote anything of a formal character and I regret very much that so much time has gone by without my being able to communicate some of the spiritual truths. I also regret that your condition has been such that I was unable to make the rapport with you that is necessary in order that I may deliver to you these messages of the nature mentioned.

If you will try to understand the law of rapport and communication it will enable you to comprehend the reason why we have not been able to communicate these higher truths. It may seem to you that if we control your brain and not use or transmit your thoughts but only the thoughts which come from our minds, it would be immaterial what the nature of your thoughts might be, and that as your brain is used by us as a mere instrument we, having possession of your brain, would have the power to write anything we might desire and upon a mere superficial glance at the assertion, it could be reasonably supposed to be true.

However, as we have told you before, rapport and our ability to use your brain are governed by laws, and one of these laws is that a high thought cannot be transmitted through a human brain which is not in the condition that qualifies it to receive the thought, just as the brain, in matters pertaining to mere material knowledge, cannot receive a concept or the comprehension of some intellectual truth with which it has not had an acquaintance. A brain cannot be used by the mind of the human to make known or present a problem in geometry when that brain has never been used by the mind to acquire an acquaintance with or knowledge of the principles of geometry. This is an incomplete analogy but it may serve to illustrate what I mean.

In the conception by the human mind of a truth, material or spiritual, the brain must be used in order to manifest or make known that concept. This is absolutely true when the idea or thought originates in the mind of the man who is using his own brain to formulate or manifest that idea or thought. The mind may have the thought or knowledge of some branch of learning, and yet when it has never used the brain to put that thought or knowledge into concrete form the brain cannot manifest or transmit it. This law applies specifically to the capabilities of the brain when it is attempted to be used or controlled by the mind of the man who owns that brain. Now from this you will see that it is possible for the human mind to have thought and knowledge of things which it cannot use the brain to express.

In many of your material things of life, such as great invention, the knowledge of these inventions is in the mind, and it may be, for a long time before it is formulated and expressed by the brain, and sometimes it never gets through the brain at all. The mind and the brain are not one and equivalent things; the one is the operator, the other is the thing used to operate with, so that the possessions of the operator may become manifested to others.

This law, applies to and controls the relationship of the mind and brain possessed by the same man, and does not absolutely apply to and control the relationship of mind and brain, where the mind is that of a spirit and the brain that of a mortal. In such a case the mind may take such complete control of the brain, that the former's manifestations are not governed or limited by the special experiences or want of experiences which the brain may have had in its use by the mind of the mortal along specific lines of expression or manifestation. Thus, as you may know and as it has been demonstrated by the work and experience of many mortal mediums, the minds of spirits have controlled the brains of these mediums, so that such brains have transmitted from these spirits expressions of various kinds of languages and mathematical truths with which such brains have never had any acquaintance or become exercised in expressing.

In these instances the brain is used merely in the sphere of intellect and the spirit who takes possession of that brain and uses it to express and make known the knowledge of the spirit's mind, is doing nothing different essentially, than the human mind controlling its own brain, could have done had the brain been exercised in those directions. The capacity of the brain, whether exercised or not by the human mind controlling its own brain, limits the power of the spirit's control in the manner and for the purpose mentioned. But this law has a further phase, and that is, the greater the general experience of the brain in its exercise by the human mind, the more perfectly can the spirit mind control it. All this is dependent upon facts which I cannot linger here to explain, such as the mediumistic qualities and susceptibilities of the human whose brain is attempted to be controlled by the spirit.

As the same laws apply to the disclosure of truth and principles along the moral planes, a spirit cannot possibly use the brain of a mortal to convey or transmit through it moral precepts or truths that that brain is not capable of receiving. I do not mean by this that the brain must have had any acquaintance with any or many particular moral truths, or must have been used by the human for the purpose of receiving or imparting these precepts, but must be in its essential capacity, potentially able to transmit and receive these truths. So the capacity of the brain to receive and transmit these moral truths, limits the control of the spirit over the brain to express through it, these truths.

The rapport of the spirit with the human is determined by the development of the brain and the moral qualities of the human at the time the rapport is attempted to be made. This means the actual development of these conditions and not what may appear to be to other humans, or even to the individual himself. This development determines to a large extent the power of the spirit to use the brain to disclose the truths, either intellectual or moral.

A medium can receive only such truths as his condition will allow. The nature of the truths determines the susceptibility of the mortal forming a rapport with the spirit. The possibility of rapport, and the kind thereof, lie at the foundation of mediumship, and determines and limits the power of the spirit to convey its thoughts and the capacity of the mortal to receive them. When the medium is in a certain condition of development the spirit, writing, can form the rapport according as that condition harmonizes with the condition of the spirit; and it is impossible unless the harmony exists, for the spirit to write these things which require a greater degree of development than the medium at the time possesses. Hence, you will in a way understand why so few of the higher spiritual truths have ever been delivered to the world through the mediumship of any mortal who has been possessed of gifts of either automatic writing, as it is called, or clairvoyance or inspirational powers.

As to those truths which did not require a higher degree of development than was possessed by the medium, there arose no difficulty in

405

transmitting the same, and many mediums have been very successful in receiving the truth suited to their condition. Now this fact, and law also, will explain to you why the same spirit may communicate through several mediums, and yet the communications be of a dissimilar character; that is, the communications through one medium contain higher or lower character of truth than those transmitted through some other medium. The result is that those mortals who have heard or read these different communications, especially when being critical, have been prone to believe that the same spirit was not making both communications. This is not a just conclusion, for while the spirit was in the same condition, possessing the same knowledge at the time of both communications, yet the mediums, because of their difference in development, were unable to receive the same character of messages.

Swedenborg was the last and nearest perfect instrument for receiving these higher truths, and yet he, because of his want of soul development and his being bound, to a more or less extent, by his orthodox beliefs and scientific knowledge, which caused him to coordinate and fit these truths in with his ideas of correspondence and such like conceptions, was a failure, and could not be successfully used to transmit these truths which we have been communicating through you. After him other gifted and, in some respects, successful mediums were used by spirits, of the higher knowledge and progression to convey truths, but their conditions were such that, under the workings of the laws governing rapport, these mediums could receive only those truths which their conditions of development permitted them to receive.

The workings of this limitation were not dependent upon the condition and ability of the spirits to impart these higher truths, but upon the capacity of the mediums to receive them. You, yourself, have had experience as to how this law works and controls communication and rapport, for, as you know, it has been a long time since you were able to receive any spirit messages of these higher truths, although the spirits have been present with you many times, ready and anxious to make the rapport and deliver their messages; and you have been willing, intellectually, to receive them, but because of your condition or want of condition, the spirits could not deliver them and were compelled to wait until you got into the necessary condition.

From all this you will comprehend why so very few messages containing high spiritual truths, or even moral truths, come through mediums. The mediums, mostly, are developed so that they can receive only messages dealing with the material affairs of life, and which kind of messages I am compelled to and can truthfully say, are those that are largely desired by the mortals seeking information from the spirit world.

Again, in your reading of spiritual literature you may have observed the great diversity of opinions of spirits upon the same subject, and sometimes contradictory opinions, thus causing doubt on the part of mortals, as to what are the facts existing in the spirit world as to the subject of inquiry. Well, this is due very largely to the condition of the mediums, and also to the knowledge of the spirits who attempt to communicate, for the knowledge of spirits is limited by the extent of their progress and development.

Many spirits believe that what they have learned is true, and so give authoritative expression to the facts of their knowledge, and often believe what they know is all that may be known of the subject on which they communicate. These spirits are mostly honest in their beliefs and truthful, as they think, in their messages. Thus it is well for mortals to understand that everything written or spoken by spirits, at all times, is not to be accepted as the finality of truth. On the other hand apparently contradictory statements should not be taken as fraudulent merely because they are contradictory. A spirit with greater knowledge using a medium in harmony with itself can convey to men the more exact and greater extent of truth than can a spirit with less knowledge and development using a medium also in harmony with itself.

Now, from what I have written, it is apparent that in order to get the greater truth, and more extended knowledge of the spirit world, mediums should make the effort to obtain larger and more extensive development of their spiritual natures as well as of their intellectual capacities. This acquirement is absolutely necessary to the reception of the higher truths which are so vital to humanity. So, you see, communication and rapport depend upon the condition of both spirits and mortals working in unison; though more I may say upon the condition of the mortal, for if the medium is in the proper state of development, there are always many spirits present with that medium in condition and readiness that a rapport can be made.

You may search the whole history of spirit communications and of mediumship and you will not find any messages of the character of those that have been transmitted through you, and for the reasons that I have stated.

The Master is here tonight and has heard my communication and unites with me in saying, have faith and seek with all your soul for this Love, and believe that I am your special angel friend.

Your brother in Christ,
John

Importance of prayer so that the soul
can be developed, and works will follow
October 5, 1915

I am here, John.

I am the apostle, and you need not try me as your friend said, for no spirit can impersonate me when I am present. So you must believe me and try to receive what I may write tonight, in faith, and you will find that you will be benefitted.

I came principally to tell you that I have been listening to the conversation between you two and to the reading of the Sermon on the Mount given to us by the Master in the days of long ago, as you would say. When that sermon was delivered we were not in a condition of great spiritual development, and we did not understand its inner meaning, but we thought it was intended literally for the practical affairs of life and people. I know people think that we, at that time, were very spiritually developed and had an understanding of the great truths taught by the Master, which were superior to what men have now, but I tell you that this is a mistake. We were comparatively ignorant men, fishermen by occupation, and had no education above the ordinary working man of that time, and when Jesus called us to become his apostles, we were as much surprised and hesitated as much as you did when the similar mission was declared for you.

Our knowledge came with our faith in the great truths which the Master taught, and from our observation of the great powers which he displayed, and also from the influence of the great Love that he possessed. But when men think that we easily understood the great truths which he taught, they are mistaken. Only after the descent upon us of the Holy Spirit at Pentecost did we fully come in accord with the Father, and fully appreciate the great truths that the Master had taught.

Of course, we learned many things which men of that time did not know, and our souls became developed to a large extent, but not sufficiently to bring us to a knowledge of the wonderful meaning of the truths which made men free and brought them in unison with God. In your conversation tonight you discussed the relative value of prayer and works, and did not agree with the preacher, that works are the great things to develop men in love and bring about great happiness in the world, and that prayer is not of such importance.

Now let me, as a spirit and as a man who worked on earth and prayed on earth, say with an authority that arises from actual experience, and knowledge that comes of observation, that of all the important things on earth for men who are seeking salvation and happiness and development of their soul, prayer is the most important. Prayer brings from God not only Love and blessings, but the condition of mind and intent that will cause men to do the great works that the preacher admonished men to engage in.

Prayer is the cause of the power being given to men that will enable them to do all the great works which will bring reward to the doer, and happiness and benefit to the one who receives the works. So you see, the results can never be as great as the cause, for the cause, in this instance, not only gives to men this ability to work, but also to love and to develop his soul and to inspire him with all good and true thoughts. Works are desirable, and in some cases necessary, but prayer is absolutely indispensable. So let you and your friend understand and never doubt, that without prayer the works of men would be unavailing to accomplish the great good which even now man performs for his brother.

Pray, and works will follow. Work, and you may do good, but the soul does not benefit, for God is a God that answers prayer through the ministrations of His angels and through the influence of His Holy Spirit, which works on the interior or real part of man.

I will stop now. With my love to both of you, I am your brother in Christ.

John

How prayers are answered for material things;
the miracle of the loaves and fishes never happened
April 25, 1917

I am here, St. John.

I want to say that God answers the prayers for things material by the work and operation of His angels and spirits, and they in that work are subject to limitations of success. God does not exercise any arbitrary power to answer prayers, but when they are sincerely offered to Him, He works through His angels in answering them, and He does not by mere fiat do so. His angels are always watching and working, and when the opportunity comes, they use their influence in the best possible way to bring about the ends desired.

As you know, man has a free will, and that determines very largely the action of men, and such actions are never arbitrarily controlled by any divine power. If the prayers of men as to material things can be responded to by the workings of the angels and spirits, they are; but such response depends upon the will of men, and if not exercised properly then it is not received by mortals; except as the spirits may be able to influence that will and cause men to act in compliance with that influence, which is always used for the purpose of bringing about the response to the prayers that are, in their nature, proper and worthy to be answered.

I doubt if any of those petitions were ever answered in the arbitrary way that is related in the Old Testament (1 Samuel 1:17). God never answers prayer in that manner, and the petitions of the old prophets had no more influence to bring about the answers to the same, in the manner indicated, than have the prayers of the sincere and earnest man of these days. God was the same then as He is now, and worked through the spirits then as He does now, except that now He has angels of the soul development in the Divine Love that He did not have then, and these angels are doing His bidding as well as are the spirits. However, God does not answer prayers for material things except in a manner in consonance with the laws controlling the free will and actions of men, as they may be operated upon and influenced by the work of spirits.

I want to say that we can at times understand what will happen in

410

the near future, and having such knowledge, can tell to mortals what may be expected, or rather what will occur, and this we sometimes do. In your case, we of the higher spheres, as well as many of the spirit spheres, know what your petitions have been in reference to these material matters, and we have been working to bring about a realization of the same on your part not only because of your petitions, but because they are so necessary to the doing and completion of our work; and we have been using our influence to the utmost to accomplish this end. But as I say, we are limited, and have not the power to cause the happening of any event by our mere willing the same, even though we are doing the work of God. This may seem surprising as well as disappointing to you, but it is a fact, and it is a great truth that God helps those who help themselves.

You must not lose sight of the fact that while men must do those things themselves that bring about changes or happenings or phenomena in material things, yet we can influence but not absolutely control their desires, intentions, and their wills that put into operation or effect these intentions. No, these things, as to their immediate manifestations, are subject to the wills of men. God never by a mere act of the moment or of a physical character, places into the hands of any man riches or prosperity. These things must be wrought and brought about by man, and in doing this man can and is wonderfully influenced by the workings of the spirits.

Well, that is a question that has caused men to doubt and consider and explain in various ways the so-called miracle of the loaves and fishes. As I was a disciple of the Master at that time, it is quite natural that I should be expected to state whether such a miracle ever occurred, and of course, I can state what the fact in relation thereto is. And notwithstanding that it has been used by preachers and teachers for many centuries to show the wonderful power possessed by Jesus, and thereby cause the people to believe in and accept him as God, or at least having God-like powers, and has been used to work much good among those who were seeking for the true religion, yet I am compelled and sorry to say, that no such miracle ever took place.

While Jesus had wonderful powers, and understood the workings of the spiritual laws to a far greater extent than any mortal who ever lived, yet he had not the power to increase the loaves and fishes as is set forth in the account of the miracle. To be able to do so would be against the laws of God's governing the material things of His creation, and also beyond and outside of the powers conferred on any man or angel by any spiritual laws.

There are certain laws by which we, who are acquainted with them, use them and may cause a dematerialization of physical substances, and also may to a limited degree cause a materialization of spiritual substances, but I am not acquainted with any law that would have operated, under the control of Jesus, to increase the loaves and fishes to the great number mentioned in the story referred to. As a fact, I know that no such miracle took place, and Jesus will tell you the same. There are other alleged miracles in the Bible that never had any existence as a fact.

Well, I have written you a long letter tonight, and I must stop, and I am pleased that you asked me about the response to prayers, and the miracle of the loaves and fishes, for your questions gave me the opportunity, to some extent, to explain these matters. As to prayer, you must wait until I deal with it more at large or in detail before you conclude that you understand the subject fully.

I say to you pray not only for the spiritual things which God bestows through His Holy Spirit, but also for the material things which He bestows through His angels and spirits. The proper prayer will be answered sooner or later, and your prayers will be answered, even though to you the response may seem a long time delayed.

With my love and blessings, I will say good night.

Your brother in Christ,
John

Importance that man must search and find the truth
May 12, 1916

I am here, John.

I desire to write tonight, and if you think it is not too late, we will do so. I want to tell you that when a man gets to know the truths of God, he will become a very happy and wise man, for these truths have in them those principles that create happiness and wisdom.

I know that men believe many things on account of their being ancient or having the authority of their forefathers, or some great saint or writer who lived many centuries ago, but such a basis for truth, while worthy of consideration and examination, does not of itself, because of being old, afford any certainty that what is thus accepted contains the truth.

Truth is a thing very old, and existed for many thousands of centuries before the times in which these ancient writers, as you call them, lived, and in fact, those days of the writers, in comparison to what had gone before, are as yesterdays. Therefore you will see that because the declarations of these writers are what you consider very ancient, they should not be received as having authority. Truths of those days, and of the long ages prior thereto, and of the present time are all the same, as truth never changes or assumes new forms no matter what the conditions of mortals may be as to their intellectual or spiritual development. Truths may be revealed today, and are being constantly revealed as time progresses, and should be accepted with as much credence and satisfaction as any truths that were ever disclosed in ancient days. Men are just as susceptible now to the reception of these truths in their spiritual natures or perceptions as they were in the times of Abraham or Moses or at any time since.

The mind of man was given to him to be exercised in the way of investigation and search, and never was it contemplated in his creation that the time would come when he should accept anything as the ultimate of truth and cease his inquiries. Truths are so many and great and deep, thus far, in the mortal universe, man has acquired only a smattering of these truths, and to rest supinely in this acquirement under the belief that there is nothing more in existence that man may know, violates and subverts the very object of his creation; and what I have said applies to spiritual truths as well as to material ones.

The churches, I know, declare and try to enforce the declaration, that it is not possible to discover or have revealed to men the essential principles of spiritual truths to a greater extent than has already been declared in the Bible and the churches interpretation of the same. It is therefore contrary to God's will that men should seek further for any additional truths, and that men should accept, without question, the sayings of the Bible, and the dogmas and creeds of the churches which their claim is founded upon, and which they declare are the true principles of spiritual truths. For many years this has been the demand of the churches, and the members thereof have acquiesced, without question or doubt. This has been one of the great causes why men have not progressed more, not only in their spiritual nature but also in what may be called their natural qualities. They have remained satisfied, and what was believed by them centuries ago are believed today. I recite this to show the necessity for men to seek and criticize, and accept or reject as the results of the search may demand.

In recent years, though, men have made greater progress, and the individual has come to the front, and the old accepted fabrications of truths have been assaulted and shaken and denuded of their falsities to a considerable degree, and so it should be. Men must seek, and criticize and accept or reject as their own conscience and reasoning powers dictate, and therein will be freedom of the mind as well as of the will.

The soul, also, has been smothered in these dogmatic beliefs, and as a consequence its development has been slow. Knowledge of things spiritual has not come to men as it should have done, and it is necessary to teach them their destiny and the truths which should control their lives on earth, and which will control their progress in the spirit world.

Well, as you are tired, I will postpone the balance of my discourse. I think it best when you feel tired to discontinue the writing instead of attempting to force yourself into receiving it.

So I will not write more.

> Believe that I am your brother in Christ,
> John

How to solve the problem of what is true and what is not
April 7, 1916

I am here, John.

I desire to write a little tonight upon a subject that may prove to be of interest to you and others who may read my message. I will not write a very long message, but will say what I desire in short sentences, so that the truth that I intend to convey may be understood at a glance.

Well, when you are sure that you have discovered or have had revealed to you a truth, let it sink deep into your soul so that it will find such lodgment as will cause you to realize that this truth is a reality, and a thing that must not be forgotten or neglected in its application to your daily life on earth.

When you have found that the truth fits some peculiar condition of your mind's experience, adopt it as a criterion for determining what your course of action shall be. When you have thus adopted it, let it always remain with you as a guide and monitor in determining what your belief as to the particular thing involved shall be.

When you have thus received this belief of the mind, encourage and feed upon it until it becomes a thing of established faith. When faith has become a part of your very being, you will find that the accompaniments of such faith, in the way of longings and aspirations, will become things of real existences, which will result in actual knowledge.

When such knowledge becomes yours, then you have solved the problem of what is true and what is not. When you have solved this, you will become a man who, when he utters his knowledge of truth, will speak as one having authority. Such was the process by which Jesus became the possessor and authentic expositor of the great spiritual truths that had never before been known and declared by any man. Of course, these various steps which lead to this great knowledge of truth, must be taken gradually and with increased confidence, and in all this, the help and influence of God is necessary, and such help and influence come only in response to sincere, soul-aspiring prayer.

Prayer must arise from the soul of man, and the response must come from God. There is no other means by which this knowledge can be obtained. All knowledge of things spiritual, that men may think they possess, coming in any other way cannot be relied on, for there is only one source of such knowledge out of which the real spiritual truths of God emanate. The great principle is love that enters into all knowledge of things spiritual, and without love it is utterly impossible for man to rightfully conceive the truths of God and possess them.

I merely desired to give you this short lesson on truth and knowledge and love, so that in receiving and absorbing our messages of the great spiritual truths of God, you may realize the means of making them your own, in a manner to satisfy your soul perceptions.

I will come soon and write you a message on some of these vital truths. Think of what I have written, and you will find that your soul perceptions will be opened up to a clear and wonderful comprehension of the real meaning of what we desire to reveal.

I will not write more tonight.

Your brother in Christ,
John

Divine Love, what it is and what it is not, and how it can be obtained
August 5, 1916

I am here, St. John.

I come tonight to say only a few words and these in reference to love, the Divine Love of God which He rebestowed upon humanity at the coming of the Master.

This Love is the greatest thing in all the world, and the only thing that can make man at one with God, and change the soul of man as it has existed since his creation, into a Divine Substance filled with the Essence of God. There is nothing else in all the universe that can cause man to become a new creature, and an inhabitant of God's kingdom; and when men possess this Love, then they possess everything that will make them not only the perfect man but the divine angel. Then men will understand the moral precepts of brotherly love and also of God's oneness, and they will not have to seek for other help in order to bring into the life of the human race those qualities that will bring to it peace and good will. Then every man will know that every other man is his brother, and be able to do unto the other as he would have the other do unto him, and this without effort or sacrifice on his part. Love worketh its own fulfillment and all its beneficence floweth towards the fellowman as falls the dews from heaven. Envy and hatred and strife and jealousy and all the other evil qualities of man will disappear, and only peace and joy and happiness will remain.

Divine Love is so abundant that it may be possessed by all men by the mere seeking and the sincere longing for its inflowing. However man must understand that it is not his by matter of right, nor is it ever forced upon him, but comes only in response to the sincere and earnest prayer of a soul that is filled with the longings for its coming. This Love comes not with observation of mere moral rules, or with good deeds and the exercise of the natural love of a man towards his fellows, because no man can possibly merit it by any deeds or acts or kindness of heart that he may have. All these things are desirable and they work out their own rewards, and bring the happiness and peace that result from good thoughts and kind deeds; but they do not bring into the soul of man this great Love; it is God alone, and only when the soul is opened up to its reception can it possibly find its home in that soul.

Divine Love is greater than faith or hope, because it is the real Substance of God, while faith and hope are the qualities which a man may possess by his own efforts, and which are given him that he may realize the possibility of obtaining this Love. They are merely the means to the end and fullness of their exercise. Men must not believe that all love is the Divine Love for it is very different in its Substance and qualities from all other loves.

All men have, as a part of their possessions, the natural love, and they need not pray for a bestowal of that, although since it has become defiled by sin it needs to be purified and freed from this blight, and God is ever willing and ready to help men obtain this purification. But this Divine Love is not a part of man's nature nor can he obtain or possess it, except by seek for it. It comes from without and is not developed from within. It is the result of individual acquirement, and not the object of universal possession. It may be possessed by all; it can be possessed by only a few; and each man must determine for himself whether it shall be his.

With God there is no special regard for certain persons; neither is there any royal road to obtain this Love. All must pursue it in the same way, and that way is the one that Jesus taught: the opening up of the soul to this Love and it finding a lodgment therein, which can be brought about only by sincere prayer and longing for its inflowing. This Love is the life of the celestial heavens and the only key that will unlock the gates, and when the mortal enters therein, all other love is absorbed by it. It has no substitute, and is of itself, a thing apart; it is of the Essence of the Divine, and the spirit which possesses it is divine itself. It may be yours, it may be all men's, and it may not. You must decide that question for yourself; not even God can make the decision for you.

In closing let me repeat that it is the greatest thing in all of God's universe and not only the greatest thing, but the sum of all things, for from it flows every other thing that brings peace and happiness.

I will not write more tonight, and with my love to you, and the blessing of the Father, I will say good night.

Your brother in Christ,
John

The celestial spirits must work until the celestial kingdom is closed
March 15, 1917

I am, John.

We are celestial spirits of the highest order, and realize the necessity for the salvation of mortals. We come to earth to bring about this salvation in work and association with the spirits of the earth plane, it is a labor of love, and humility is the touchstone that brings to us happiness in our work.

We are with you often and in close association, and we would not be fellow workers with the Master, if for one moment we should have the feeling that, because of our high estate we should not come in rapport and helpful association with sinful mortals. As long as God requires his great truths to be taught and men's souls saved from the effect of the great fall, and made into angels of divinity, our work will continue. Now sometime our work on earth as well as in the spirit spheres will cease, and then our homes in the celestial spheres will be our only places of labor and love. The kingdom will be completed and the door of the heavenly kingdom closed, and the angelic laborers will become separated from the spiritual or perfect man; such is the decree.

As God desires all men to become at one with Him in His divinity of Love, we must work until the great day that the consummation of the kingdom arrives, and spirits who do not have the wedding garment on shall suffer the doom of the second death. When Jesus said, "work while it is day, for the night cometh when no man can work" (John 9:4), he meant that while the kingdom is open for men to enter therein we must work, for when its doors shall be closed the work of the angelic laborers must cease, and mortals and spirits be left to an eternity in the spiritual spheres.

So we work, and so must you work until the time of the separation, and as the Master said, "the wheat and the tares must be permitted to grow together until the great time of the harvesting shall take place" (Matthew 13:29 -30). Until then we must mingle and work and pray without ceasing.

Your brother in Christ,
John

The true meaning of the end of the world
October 1, 1916

I am here, St. John.

I come tonight to write a few truths upon the subject of the preacher's sermon, as I was present with you and heard his declarations as to the end of the world.

I know that among men there are, and have been since the time of the Master, differences in opinion as to when this important event is to take place, and as to the meaning of the end of the world. Well, men know just about as much now as to the time of this event as they have known all down the centuries, and understand the meaning of these prophecies as well as did mortals from my day to the present.

In the first place, I will say, there will be no end of the world from any of the causes mentioned by the preacher, and in the second place, there will be no end of the world at all as understood and declared by the orthodox preachers, and as is expected by most of the professing Christians. The world, meaning the earth, will not have an end in the sense of annihilation, but it will continue to revolve on its axis, and to have seed time and harvest, and produce and reproduce those things that are necessary to sustain human life, and have its appropriate seasons of heat and cold, and move along in its orbit as it now does, until some change, we know not of now, may come and destroy it. But none of the prophecies of the Bible (Revelation 11:18) can apply to such change as to the end of the world in the sense that the preacher understood and declared.

If humankind would only understand that the world that was lost by the disobedience of the first parents, was the world of man's immortality and happiness and not the physical world. Jesus came to declare the restoration of that world upon condition, and at the end of that restoration, they would then know that the material world is not involved in the plan of man's salvation, or in Jesus's mission, or in the declarations of Jesus as to the coming of the end.

Men will continue to be born, live a short time and die the physical death, and as to each individual the end of the material world comes when he dies, for, thereafter, his habitation will be in the spirit world, and nevermore will he have life on earth. All men at some time will have to die the physical death, then why should it be necessary to include in the plan of God for the salvation of men the destruction of the material world? For planets and worlds and stars to crash together and be destroyed, would mean that the orderly workings of God's laws must be interfered with, in order that men might be destroyed or saved accordingly as they might be snatched up into the air, or left to their own weakness on earth. Such interpretations of God's intentions or plans, or of Jesus coming again to earth, are all wrong and absurd.

Jesus will never come to establish his kingdom on earth and reign as Prince of Peace and Lord of Lords, for the kingdom which he and all his followers, both on earth and in the spirit world, are seeking to establish is in the celestial heavens. It is the kingdom of God, not made with hands or by the mere fiat of any spirit no matter how high he may be, but made and populated by the souls of men who have experienced the New Birth and received the Divine Essence of God. Of this kingdom Jesus is the Prince, because of his great and exceeding possession of the Divine Love of God, and his more perfect at-onement.

Jesus is not seeking to establish a kingdom on earth, but is working for the purpose of leading men to the New Birth of the spirit, and of showing them the way to the celestial kingdom. He is also working to help men by his love and suggestions, and so are the other good spirits, helping them to cast sin and error from their hearts, and to strive to regain the condition of perfect manhood in the perfection of their natural love. He is also helping men to get in this condition of soul regeneration, or in that of the purification of their natural love while they live on earth, so that brotherly love will cover the whole earth, and men will be at peace and happy while clothed in the flesh. Such a condition of mortal existence may be called the kingdom of God on earth, but it will not be the kingdom which Jesus came to earth to establish that is the kingdom of heaven. This kingdom has its seat and abiding place in the celestial spheres whence it will never be removed. So then, when the Bible teaches of the world coming to an end and passing away (Revelation 21:1) it does not mean the material world, but the world of men's thoughts and deeds and sinful conditions that are not in harmony with God's laws or the laws of His creation. This is the world that shall be destroyed when righteousness shall cover the earth as do the waters, and brotherly love will reign among men.

A time will come when the world of sin and unrighteousness will be destroyed. There shall be wars and rumors of wars (Matthew 24:6) and times of trouble, as never were, and then shall come the end. Not the wars of the cannon roars or the bursting shells or the mutilated flesh, or the making of widows and orphans or the ruthless changing of mortals into spirits, but the wars of the spirits of good and evil, of love and hate, of purity and sin, of joy and despair, and of knowledge of truth and belief in error, all to be fought in the souls of men with such intensity and earnestness, creating such spirit trouble as has never been, and causing rumors thereof to flood the earth and the habitations of men.

Then shall come the end of the world, the world of evil and sin and despair, and hatred and belief in error. This world shall pass away, and truth and love and peace and good will shall be established on the earth forever. The earth of this present day, will then become to men so peaceful and filled with love and brotherly kindness, that to them it will seem as if the city of God had been let down from heaven on to earth.

Let mortals know that Jesus has already come to earth and is among men, and that since the time of his becoming the Prince of the celestial kingdom he has been with mortals and spirits teaching them the way, the truth and the life. It is by the Holy Spirit that the truths of God have spoken to men as a still small voice, and by the communions of souls the Master has led men to the Love and mercy of the Father.

Just as in my time when he came to the Jews with his message of love and life eternal, they knew him not and rejected him, so now many men, and spirits too, refuse to listen to him and learn the way through the straight gate to God's Love and immortality. Let men study the prophecies and the times and the seasons, and calculate the time of the end, and predict the near approach of the Master's coming in the clouds, and prepare themselves to be snatched up in the air and become of the heavenly hosts. They will find that all these things are vanities of vanities, and only as each individual passes beyond the veil of flesh will he realize that the end of his mortal world has come, and then all his speculations as to himself will become realities, and the certainty of the world's end become an established fact. Men will continue to live on earth and die, and in succession others will be born to die, and so on until only God knows.

So I say to men, prepare not for the passing away of the heavens and the earth, but for the passing of themselves from the earth to the great world of spirits; and remember, that as they, "sow so shall they reap," is a certainty that is never changed, a truth that no speculation can make untrue. The end of man's world comes each day to some mortals, and that end may lead to a glorious immortality, or to a temporary or a long darkness and suffering.

Thus the prophecies are being fulfilled and the speculations of preachers and teachers and leaders of the unthinking are robbing men of the vital truth that the end of the world is coming each moment and day and year. Oh! Preacher and teacher and leader, your responsibility is great, and the accounting must be made. The reaping must follow the sowing as certainly as the day follows the night, and what will your harvest be?

I have written enough for tonight as you are tired. So believe that I love you and am praying for God to bless you, and to fill your soul with His Love, and that when the world comes to an end for you, you shall find the kingdom of heaven waiting to receive you.

Good night.

Your brother in Christ,
John

JESUS

The first effort by Jesus to deliver a message, but
Mr. Padgett was not in condition to receive it completely
December 17, 1914

I am here, Jesus.

I have come to write to you my first message but you are too weak to take it; I will come again when you are stronger. You are not in a condition for me to tell you of what I have to write because you are worried too much by what you think of your earthly affairs. I want you to let these things pass from you entirely as I cannot give you the thoughts that I desire you to write, until you are wholly free from your earth cares. Be more faithful and you will be more in condition to do as I desire. I will not come again until you are free from these worries, for you are not in a condition to receive what I wish to write while these worries exist.

You must trust more in God. I am that Jesus, and the men you have been reading about were my disciples and they are now enjoying the reward which their work and faith entitled them to. They are not in the heavens singing psalms or riding on clouds, as some Christians of the present and past times believe and teach, but are still working for the salvation of mortal and spirit souls. They are still with me and are doing the same kind of work as when they were on earth.

They did not actually mean that, but spoke only in allegory, and meant that I was in the heavens where they all supposed God to be; but as to my sitting on the right hand of His throne, that is not true. I am in a sphere that is of the highest and closest to the fountainhead of God's Love, and am working to save humanity from their sins, and bring them in unison with God's Love. I tell you that only the man who has received this Love into his soul and lets it fill that soul so that there is no room for anything that tends to defile it, can be said to have received salvation or to be at-one with the Father.

So let your faith in the one necessary attainment increase, and when you have realized it to the full, you will be very happy and in God's kingdom. I must stop writing now, for you are not in condition to write more. I will soon come again, for you will be in condition to receive me. I will love you with all my heart and let you feel that I am in close rapport with you to lead you to a greater happiness from now until you can find the more extensive and greater Love of the Holy Spirit, which is with you to a large extent now, but not as full as you need.

You are very dear to me and I will never forsake you, so rest in that assurance and I know that you will be happier, for no man has ever been in a condition of unhappiness who has my love as you now have it. Be my own true follower and I will be with you to the end.

Your own dear teacher and friend, Jesus of Nazareth, who was crucified and rose again from the dead, as you will rise and live again in the favor and Love of the Father.

I will not write more but will say good night,

Jesus

The reasons given by Jesus as to why he selected
Mr. Padgett to do the work of receiving the messages
October 25, 1918

I am here, Jesus.

Well, my dear brother, time is passing, and the necessity for the revealing is very apparent, as men are longing and waiting for that which will satisfy the natural cravings of their souls, and which the present religion, called Christianity, has not in it the qualities to satisfy.

I am pleased that you are in so much better condition, and that your love is again becoming active and awakened, and operating upon the qualities of your brain so that a rapport can be made, as recently explained to you by John in his message. And here I desire to impress upon you the necessity and desirability of your understanding thoroughly the truths set forth in that message, and of meditating upon the same and making a personal application of what is therein written.

I would like very much to deliver a message dealing with spiritual truth tonight, but I do not think that your condition is such as will

424

enable me to take possession of your brain and control the same that the qualities and truths of my message demand. So, I will not attempt to write that message, but, instead, will advise you somewhat upon the way in which you must think and act in order to perfect the condition which you must possess that the rapport may be made.

John has told you to pray often to the Father so that the Love may become more abundant and your soul become permeated with it, and you will think thoughts of spiritual things, until by such thinking your brain may become, as it were, infused with these thoughts and thereby receive those qualities that will make its conditions similar to the conditions of the minds of the spirits who may wish to form a union with your brain and convey through it the truths that are waiting to be delivered. I confirm what John has written, and, in addition, say that your praying must be more frequent so that your soul may be freed from the condition of the existence in it of thoughts not spiritual.

You need not wait for occasions or opportunities to formally pray but all during the day and evening let your longings for the Love ascend. A long prayer, or even one formulated into words, is not necessary. In order to have the longing it is not necessary that words should be used to give it form. The longing may be as rapid as unformed thought, but as effective for the Father to catch, as I may say. The longing is quicker than the thought, and the answer to the same will come with as much certainty and Love as if you were to put the longing into the most exact form. Prayers of this kind ascend to the Father and are heard and answered, and, by a law of your relationship to Him, affect the qualities of the brain in the way of preparing it for the union with the spiritual thoughts of the spirits who desire to write. Your thoughts of spiritual things or of the truths of the spirit world, as they have already been revealed to you, and especially those which pertain to the Love and mercy of the Father, and to His will, in their passing and operating, also affect the qualities of the brain so as to produce the condition which is so necessary for our rapport.

It may be surprising to you that this condition is required in the brain of a human and also the development of the soul, which really produces the condition, in order that a rapport may be made so that the spiritual truths may be delivered. It may also be surprising that you have been selected from all the men on earth in whom this condition and development shall be made, and it may be more surprising to know that it is true. There are certain qualities in your constitution, both spiritual and material, that render you susceptible to the influence of our powers and to the use by us for the purpose of our design and work. It may seem strange to you that in all the long ages preceding, I have not found one human* with the qualification to fit him for the work.

I have used others before, but they have failed to submit their minds and souls and beliefs and forethoughts to our influence and directions as you have so far done. Many humans have the qualified conditions of spiritual and material makeup to perform our wishes and work, but as they all have free will, which we cannot compel, and as circumstances and environments and education and beliefs are elements which affect and determine the possibility of our finding an instrument suitable for our purposes, we have not been able to find a medium who was qualified to be used for our work.

You, of course, understand that you were not selected because of any special goodness or freedom from sin, or because you were more beloved by the Father, because of your course of living, or for the reason of any spiritual condition that you were in. There were many superior to you in goodness and more in at-onement with the will of the Father, and whose love and the results therefrom, were more perfect than yours. So you will realize that you were not selected because of any special spiritual merits possessed by you.

As you have been told, all things in the spirit world, as well as on earth, are controlled by immutable laws, and all spirits as well as mortals are subject to those laws. The law of rapport and communication must be complied with by spirits, no matter how much elevated, and also by mortals, and no spirit, by reason of the possession of any supposed power, can set aside this law. While spirits have not this power, yet they may have such knowledge of conditions that they can discern what qualities in the condition of a human are susceptible to the influence, and molding by the spirits, so that as a result thereof, the law may be brought into operation. This briefly will explain to you why I selected you as my medium and mouthpiece.

I want you to know this, that for a long time I have been endeavoring to influence and mold your mind and beliefs, so that your soul might become developed in such a way that conditions might be formed that would enable us to make a rapport that would permit our control-

*This reference is to Jesus's search for a medium since Swedenborg's failure.

426

ling your brain to convey these messages of truth. You were a natural medium, and for ordinary purposes it was not difficult for the spirits to control and communicate through you the truths of the spirit world, which are not of a nature such as I and others have communicated in reference to the soul spheres and the relationship of God to man in the higher spiritual sense. As you read John's message you will better understand what I intend to explain at this point.

There is another phase to all this, more personal to you, and this is, that while we have been developing you for the purpose of doing our work and helping make effective our mission, your soul has been developed in its spiritual nature and you have come into a closer union with the Father and have partaken to a large extent of His Love, and, to a degree been transformed into His Essence. You have become a very different entity from what you were when your development for our purpose commenced; and as a consequence, you will derive all the benefits that flow from an experience such as you have had.

You are now one of us in the progress towards the fountainhead of the Father's Love, and have taken on a part of his immortality, and it depends only upon yourself how rapid your progress shall be towards a complete transformation such as spirits who are inhabitants of the celestial spheres, possess. You need not wait until you come to the spirit world in order to make rapid progression, although it will be more difficult for you to progress while in the flesh, as you understand, yet wonderful progress may be made while in the flesh, and you have been told the secret of this progress.

I will further say that you have a closer association with spirits that are nearer the Father and more possessed of His Essence than has any human of earth at this time. To you this may seem extravagant and improbable, but I declare to you that it is true that I and many spirits who come to you and write are in the celestial spheres of God's immortality.

Well, I have written a longtime and you are somewhat tired. Remember my advice and pray often and earnestly, if but for a moment, and the condition will be yours and we will come and continue our revealments.

With my love and blessing, I am your brother and friend,

Jesus

*Mr. Padgett is advised by Jesus to help a Spiritualist medium to
her just due since she has been seeking God's Love since early childhood*
March 3, 1919

I am here, Jesus.

Let me write a few lines, for I am anxious to tell you that you have
not been in good company today, as the meeting was filled with spirits
who are of the earth plane, and knew not the truths that will lead to a
knowledge of the things that are necessary in order to secure a home in
the celestial heavens. Many spirits were those of men who, when on
earth, lived immoral and licentious lives, and who are in the same condition as they were when on earth. They have not yet answered to the
law of compensation and you will see that their influence is not of the
kind that tends to develop those soul qualities that lead to the heaven of
the followers of me in the true sense.

The medium with whom you conversed, and who delivered the
messages of some of the spirits who were so anxious to reach their
friends of earth, was influenced by spirits who are in a condition of
more or less darkness and alienation from God, and consequently suffers from her association and the influence to which she was subjected.
She has long been in this work of demonstrating to humankind the fact
of communication between the spirits in the flesh and those who have
passed the mysterious borderline. Her work has been strenuous and
served to demonstrate the fact for which it was intended, and she is satisfied with the reality of the fact of the continuity of life after so-called
death. This has been a phase of mediumship that was necessary to be
performed, and she has done her work faithfully and well, and is now
entitled to be relieved of this work that pertains to the lower order of
Spiritualism. She should be freed of this great burden and permitted to
come into a knowledge of the higher things of the spirit life. I am glad
that you will soon have the opportunity to tell her things that await her
as a reward for all the sacrifices that she has been compelled to make.

Now, do not misunderstand me. Her work was necessary as a preliminary to the conversion of men to a belief in the truth of spirit communication and the fact that there is no death, and to the consolation
that comes to men from the knowledge that their loved ones are with

them, seeking to help and be helped in their conditions that the great law of cause and effect imposes upon them. Many a sad heart has been comforted by her ministrations and many a spirit has been helped by having opened up to them the way to make known their presence to mortals.

She has from the very nature of her occupation been more or less injured in her spiritual progress, and the time has come when she shall have the opportunity to attend to and obtain her own soul's progress. She is naturally a good woman, and when she told you that she had a longing for something which she did not understand, she was uttering a great truth of her soul, and one that has been present with her since she was a little child, for her soul has been calling to the great soul of the Father for His Love and the happiness that comes with the knowledge that the Father's Love is ever ready and anxious to respond to her longings. Her knowledge of Spiritualism does not teach her what this Love is, even though her soul feels its presence, and in her underdeveloped longings realizes that there must exist that which will draw her closer to the great Love of the Father.

So I say, tell her the truths that have been revealed to you, and of your experience in seeking for and obtaining this transforming Love, and she will listen and seek and obtain, and with such obtaining will come a happiness she has never before experienced. When she has believed in this Love and obtained it to a degree, she will become a powerful instrument in converting men to a belief in the only way to the celestial heavens and to immortality. Then will she have back of her the influence of the hosts of celestial angels to inspire her and qualify her to preach the true kingdom of God. Her faculties of clairvoyance will be opened up to see the things of the celestial heavens and the wonderfully bright and glorious spirits who will come to her with their messages of truth and knowledge of the glories that belong to those who know that the Divine Love of God is the only thing that can transform the human soul into an angel of light, and can bring the immortality that I came to earth to teach, and which I did teach, but which, alas, was so soon lost to the knowledge of men.

I am particularly interested in her, because she has in her those qualities that can be used by us in making known to the world the truths that we of the celestial spheres know will set men free from the false and damning teachings of the orthodox churches, and make my coming to earth and living — not dying — the way to the truth and the life. She may think that her knowledge — I mean intellectual — is all that needs to be known, but when she lets her soul's longings go to the Father and receives the response, she will then know that Spiritualism, as she conceives it to be, is the mere forerunner of that which will make all men at one with the Father, when embraced and lived by man.

The meetings, such as was held today, while as I have said was filled with spirits who are in darkness and suffering, yet, it also attracted many spirits who are bright and progressing in their natural love, and who tried to help those whom they came to communicate with, and to that extent did good, and also served to convince the unbelievers of the truth of the mere passing from the body of flesh into the spirit body — a continued existence, without changing the of condition of happiness or misery. The great law of compensations as you, "as you sow so shall you reap," is taught at the meetings, and there is no truer or greater law in all the universe of God, and man must realize that it works without exception and to the last farthing, and that there can never be forgiveness until forgetfulness takes place.

Well, my dear brother, I must stop as the power is weakening, but before closing let me entrust you to tell the medium that I, Jesus of the Bible, as I called my disciples when on earth, I now call her to do the work which is so important to humankind, and that she must prepare herself by seeking for this Love. Her soul must respond to the souls of the spirits, and it will be so easy for her to get into the condition that will make this possible. Like attracts like, and this law applies to rapport and to other things of the spirit world, and of the earth as well.

I see that you are in better condition tonight, and I am pleased, for I will soon come and write another message with reference to the higher truths.

With my love and blessings, I will say good night.

Your brother and friend,
Jesus

*The worship of Jesus as part of the Godhead
is wrong and Jesus deplores this erroneous belief*
April 23, 1916

I am here. Jesus.

I come tonight to tell you that you are in a much better condition of soul than you have been for several days, and the inflowing of the Divine Love has been working today in greater abundance in your soul.

I do not intend to finish my message tonight as it is rather late and you are not exactly in the condition to receive it. You should turn your thoughts more to God and pray in more earnestness and very soon will come to you the power and soul perception which will enable you to receive my message as I desire to deliver it to you.

I realize that the belief in me as God, and that my death and sacrifice on the cross was necessary to men's salvation, will be hard to eradicate, and that many who now live will pass into the spirit world before the truths which I come to teach and declare will be published to the world. We must make more speed in our work of writing and receiving these messages, for the importance of the world knowing the truths as regards me, and the true and only plan of salvation, is now pressing and must be shown to man in order for him to turn to the Father's Love and gain an entrance into the kingdom. I want you to give more time to our writings, and instead of reading those books of philosophy and the speculations of what are supposed to be wise theologians and philosophers and scientists, let your hours from your business cares be devoted to my communications and those of the other writers of the celestial spheres.

Of course, I do not intend that you shall not permit the dark spirits to write on the nights that you have set apart for them, because such prohibition would prevent much good from being accomplished. These spirits are greatly benefitted by having the opportunity to write, and many of them have been greatly helped thereby, and have been turned to the light and instructed to seek for the Divine Love of the Father. The spirits here, who are engaged in the work of instructing and helping these spirits, have rescued many from their condition of darkness and sufferings, and have shown them the way to light and to their salvation.

The work is a great and important one and must not stop; and here let me say that this work will be a part of your duty and also your pleasure, as long as you may live a mortal life. You will, undoubtedly, be the means of helping mortals to see the truth, but your work among these dark spirits will be even greater, and the harvest more abundant, and when you come to the spirit world you will be surprised and gratified at the great host that will meet you, giving you thanks for the great help and assistance that you rendered them. Yours is a wonderful work and is now spoken of and wondered at in the spirit world.

"In my Father's house are many mansions" (John 14:2), as I said, when on earth, and for your consolation and that of your two friends, I am preparing for each of you such a mansion; not as you may suppose by erecting in the celestial heavens actual houses for your reception, but by helping to build in your souls that development of the Divine Love and the Nature of the Father that will, when you come over, make your souls in a condition that will necessarily and absolutely cause the formation of these mansions to receive you. No one else can build these mansions for you, only your own soul development. While this is true, yet these celestial heavens have a locality and surroundings and atmosphere that will contain all those things that will give your mansions the proper settings. The fields, and trees and waters and sky, and all these things that in your earth life you find necessary to your happiness and peace, are in the celestial heavens, only quite different from those that you are acquainted with.

So, believe what I say, and believing trust me and my love, and you will never be forsaken. A man's life on earth is but a span; but in our homes eternity means immortality, with always progress and increasing happiness.

So with my love and blessings, I will say good night.

Your friend and brother,
Jesus

There is nothing in existence or in the knowledge
of man comparable to the Bible, except the truths that Jesus
and the celestial spirits have written through Mr. Padgett
February 23, 1915

I am here, Jesus.

I see that you are in good condition tonight, and that I am able to make a rapport with you. I was with you at the meeting tonight and saw the workings of your mind and the pity, as it were, that you had for the preacher, because of his want of knowledge of what the judgment is that comes to all men after death. A judgment that is certain and exact, but not one pronounced upon man by God, as the preacher proclaimed.

I was trying to impress you in your thoughts and you felt the influence of my suggestions and realized that you did not fear the judgment, or rather its results, because you know the way to salvation, and the judgment for you can hold no terrors, or no eternity of condemnation. I wished as you did that the preacher might know the truth and then proclaim it to his hearers, and in this manner show them that the judgment is a certainty that cannot be escaped from, and that its sentences are not for an eternity of duration.

He is an earnest man in his beliefs, and teaches just as he believes, and the pity is that he does not know the truth. But, nevertheless, he is doing good to those who hear him, for many of them have cause to think of spiritual things, and of the future, as well as of the present, who otherwise might not and would neglect these important things that will determine the kind of judgment that they will have to undergo. I am glad that he is preaching and doing a work that in many instances will lead men to meditate upon their spiritual condition, and ultimately lead them to seek for the Love of God, which they may obtain by their longings, though their beliefs may be erroneous as to how this Love may be obtained.

Men are constituted with a mind and a soul, each having its own perceptions and ability to comprehend the truth, and sometimes it happens that the perceptions of the soul will enable them to see and reach out for this Love, while they may be wholly blind in their mind's perceptions, and even these latter perceptions may be in conflict with the operations of the perceptions of the soul.

Until the truths that I and the other spirits are revealing to you, shall become known to the world, there will be nothing in existence or in the knowledge of men that can supply the place of these truths so much as the beliefs that have been and are being taught by the teachings of the Bible. For in it are many truths, especially those that show the way to attain to moral perfection; and that, as you know, was one of the objects of my teachings when on earth, but not the great object of my mission. Nevertheless, the man who learns and applies these moral truths to his daily life and conduct comes nearer to the enjoyment of that harmony that man must obtain in order to get into a unison with God's laws, that is necessary to his regeneration and to his becoming the perfect man. Besides, as he — I mean the mortal — progresses in this regeneration, he will find it easier for him to learn by his soul perceptions the great truth of the transformation of the soul through the New Birth.

I approve of the efforts of this preacher to bring men to a realization of their relationship to God, even though he has many erroneous beliefs, and says many things that are contrary to the truth, and not in accord with the true relationship of man to God.

I will not write longer tonight, for I think it best not to draw upon you too much at this renewed juncture of our rapport with your condition*. I have been with you very often of late, and tried to influence you with my love and suggestions, and I must tell you that you have progressed much in your soul development and nearness to the Father's Love. Continue to meditate upon these spiritual things, and pray to the Father, and you will realize a great increase in the possession of this Love and in your condition that will enable us to come in closer rapport with you.

Well, I will do as you suggest, and am pleased that you feel as you say, for we must do the work as rapidly as possible. We have lost much time and will have to work the harder to bring about the completion of our delivery of the truths. You need not fear that we will not be successful, only have faith and pray, and all will be well.

I must stop now, but before doing so must assure you that I am praying with you in your prayers at night, and that your prayers will be answered. Keep up your courage and believe in me and what I tell you.

With my love and the blessings of the Father, I will say good night.

*Padgett had digestive problems.

Your brother and friend,
Jesus

*The truths may be understood by the
simple and do not require a highly developed mind*
August 3, 1915

I am here, Jesus.

My truths are plain and my teachings can be understood by the simple. Any religion which requires the exercise of the mental faculties to an extent greater than what is required in the ordinary affairs of life, cannot be a true religion; because God has designed that all his children shall understand His truths without the necessity of having a highly developed mind.

He that tries may understand my teachings and it will not be necessary for any preacher or teacher to explain them. My language will explain itself. So let your mind not be troubled over the question as to whether only the mentally developed can understand what I may write, for the truths are for all.

So with all my love I am, your brother and friend,
Jesus

*Jesus says his mission in writing
these messages is his "second coming" to earth*
December 2, 1915

I am here, Jesus.

I have heard your discussion tonight, and am pleased at the soul understanding of my truths which you and your friend seem to have. I now feel that you are both progressing to that point where you will soon be in a condition to fully understand what my mission is in writing these messages. You have said that my "new revelation" of the truths of the soul is what mankind needs at this time, and what men will be in condition to accept as the real truths of God's Love and of His laws. My coming to you is really my "second coming" on earth, and the result of my coming in this way will satisfy and fulfill all the promises of the scriptures as to my "second coming".

So let your belief in this important fact and your faith in me increase until you will have in your souls and minds no doubt as to what my present mission is, and as to what your work will be in making known to men my real purpose in revealing to them the great truths of the Father.

I will not write more tonight, but say keep up your courage and believe, and the time will soon come when you will be able to receive my messages in all their fullness, and with such rapidity that the spreading of these truths will not be delayed. I am with you and will be a faithful friend and brother, closer to you than any earthly brother.

With all my love and blessings,
Jesus

Description of the birth and life
of Jesus up to the time of his public ministry
June 7, 1915

I am here, Jesus.

I want to write to you tonight about my birth and life up to the time of my public ministry.

I was born in Bethlehem, as you know, in a manger, and when I was a few days old my parents took me to Egypt, in order to avoid the soldiers of Herod who were sent to destroy me, and who did kill a great number of male infants of less than two years of age (Matthew 2:16). The Bible story of my birth and the flight of my parents and the murder of the innocents, is substantially correct (Matthew 2:14), and I only wish to add to it, that when my parents arrived in Bethlehem they were not compelled to seek the manger of a stable in order that I might be born, on account of poverty, for they were supplied with funds and everything that was needed to make my birth comfortable for my mother; and as a matter of fact my father was not poor in the world's goods as poverty was considered in those days.

The Bible says the wise men came and brought offerings of gold and frankincense to my parents (Matthew 2:11), or rather to me, but my parents have told me that it did not amount to so very much, so far as the money value was concerned, and that their expenses of fleeing to Egypt were met by the funds that my father had prior to his reaching Bethlehem.

Upon our arrival in Egypt my father sought the home of a Jewish relative who lived in Heliopolis, a town not far from Cairo. He welcomed us and enabled our family to make our start in this new land. There was quite a community of Jewish people there, and we congregated together for safety as well as for social life. There was a place for worship, a place for the cleansing of women and also an elementary school for the teaching of reading and writing to enable youngsters to learn the scriptures.

My father pursued his occupation as a carpenter to support us. After a while he was able to set up and establish his trade quite successfully and made his household a comfortable one with all the conveniences available to workmen of the day. He supported the family, to the extent that he educated myself and my brothers and sisters, for I had four brothers and three sisters, who were all, except myself, born in Egypt.

When I became of proper age, I attended the common school provided for small children, and was taught those things that had to do with the religion of the Jews, and some things that were not religious in their nature. I was never taught the philosophy of the Egyptians or of the other pagan philosophies; and when it is stated that I received my religious ideas or moral teachings from any of these philosophers, they are mistaken. My education as to these matters of religion was derived from Jewish teachers. My development in the knowledge of the truths which I taught during my public ministry, was caused by my inner spiritual faculties, and my teacher was God, who, through His angels and through my soul perceptions, caused those truths to come to me or rather the knowledge of them, and in no other way did I obtain it.

I was not born with the knowledge that I was the Son of God sent to earth to teach these great truths, or to announce to humankind the rebestowal of the great gift of immortality, and the means of acquiring it. This knowledge of my mission came to me after I became a man and had frequent communions with God through my spiritual senses.

I was never in the presence of the Jewish priests, expounding to them the law and asking questions when about twelve years of age, as stated in the Bible (Luke 2:46). It was not before my first appearance, after I became a man, did I attempt to show priest or layman, that I was the messenger of the Father, and sent by Him to proclaim the "glad tidings" of immortality restored and of the great Love of the Father which was necessary to make all men at one with Him, and to give them a home in His kingdom.

I was never a sinful boy or man, and did not know what sin was in my heart; and strange as it may seem, I never sought to teach others these truths until after my mission was declared by John the Baptist. In my boyhood days I was the same as other boys and engaged in the plays of childhood and had the feelings of a child, and never thought I was anything else than a child. In no wise was I different from other children, except in the particular that I have named, and any account of me to the contrary is untrue.

My teachings were those that the Father had committed to me from the beginning, which I was only conscious of after I became a close communicant and learned from Him my mission. So you must believe that I was a son of a man as well as a Son of God, and that in the literal sense. I would not have been true to my mission had I claimed that I was the only son of God, for it is not true and men should not teach it.

I know it was said that my mother was told of the object of my birth and what a blessed woman she was, but this is not true. My mother, as she has told me, had no reason to suppose that I was different from other children born of men. The story of the angel of God coming to her and telling her that she must submit to the birth of a child who would be begotten by God or by by His Holy Spirit, and that she, as a virgin, should bear and give birth to that child (Luke 1:35), is not true. She never in all her life told me that she had any such visitor; and I know that she would be as much surprised, as are many others, that such a thing as the birth of a child by a virgin could take place. So you see, the Bible account of my being begotten and all the attending circumstances are not true.

My father, Joseph, never supposed at anytime that I was not his child, and the story of the angel coming to him and telling him that he must not put her away because of appearance (Matthew 1:20) is not true, because he never in all my conversations with him, intimated that I was other than his own child.

Between the time that I was twelve years of age and my public ministry, I lived at home with my parents, and assisted my father in his profession as a carpenter, and during all this time no hint ever fell from him that I was not his child, or that I was different from other children, except that I did not do sinful things.

When I commenced to get this Divine Love into my soul, I became very close to the Father, and this relationship resulted in my realizing that I was sent by God with a mission to perform and a great and important truth to declare; and at last the voice in my soul told me that I was my Father's true Son and I believed it, and commenced to teach and preach the truths of His love bestowed and the salvation of humanity.

I knew John the Baptist when I was a child growing up. He was my cousin and we often played together, and afterwards discussed the truth of my mission and the way in which it should be made known to the world. John was a great psychic and saw in his vision who I was and what my mission on earth was, and, hence, when the time came, he made the announcement of my coming. He realized the difference in our missions, and spoke of his not being worthy to unloosen my shoes, yet he did not fully understand my mission and the great truth of the bestowal of immortality upon humanity.

I first became the Christ when I was anointed by my Father, and that occurred at the time of my baptism by John. I as the Christ am different from myself as Jesus. Christ means that principle which the Father has conferred upon me, which made me at one with Him in the possession of this great Love. Christ is that Love itself made manifest in me as man. This Christ principle is universal just as is the Holy Spirit, but I am limited in my place of occupancy just as you are.

I never as Jesus promised the great gift, mentioned in the Bible, such as, where two or three are gathered together there I will be also (Matthew 18:20); for it would be impossible for me to be in all places at the same time. However, Christ, being without form or limitation, is omnipresent and, consequently, may fulfill my promise in this regard. Christ is as much alive today as ever, and was never crucified and never died.

Well, I think you are too sleepy now to continue. I will continue in the near future.

Your brother and friend,
Jesus

Jesus continues his description
June 8, 1915

I am here, Jesus.

I will continue my letter as to my birth and work, as I commenced it last night.

When I was satisfied that I was chosen by my Father to perform His work of declaring to the world the bestowal of His great gift of the Divine Love that was in His Nature, and which formed the predominant principle of that nature, I commenced my ministry. I continued to work for the redemption of humanity on earth until my death on the cross. I was not then as perfect as I am now, and my knowledge of the truths of the Father was not so great as it is now.

Let men know, though, that what I taught was true, even though I did not teach all the truth, and they will learn that I am my Father's true Son, and the special messenger by whom these great truths were to be taught to humanity. I was not, when on earth, so filled with the Love of the Father as I am now, and had not the power to make men feel that this Love is the only thing that will reconcile them to the Father and make them at one with Him, as I have now. So men must believe that I am communicating to them the real truths which will show them the way to the Father's Love and to their own salvation.

You have in your mind the desire to know how it was that the wise men came to me with their offerings and adoration. Well, the wise men came, but their coming was not because of any knowledge they had that I was a child divinely created, or that I was not a natural child, but because they were astrologers and at that time saw a new and brilliant star in the heavens, which to them meant that some important event had taken place. Now being students of the Hebrew scriptures, they concluded that the star was the sign of my birth, the one that the scriptures meant. But outside of this knowledge as astrologers and that of the scriptures, they had no other knowledge. I know this, because since my coming to the spirit world, I have met these men and talked with them, and they have told me what I write. So, while I was referred to in the Bible (Isaiah 53) — I mean in the prophecies of the Old Testament — yet, those wise men had no other knowledge of that fact than what I have told you.

I know that I was sent by the Father to perform the mission which I performed, and that it was intended in the beginning that I should be anointed as the Christ, but this I did not know until after I became a man and was then told what my mission was by the angel and my own inner voice. My mother or father or brethren did not know, and even after I had proclaimed my mission and showed the wonderful powers that had been given to me, they did not believe in my mission (John 7:5), but thought that I was beside myself, that is, as you say, crazy with the belief that I was the chosen one of God. The Bible, itself, shows that this was their condition of mind (Mark 3:21).

So, while I am the Messiah of the Bible, and the chosen instrument of the Father to make known the great truths which I have proclaimed, and which I shall proclaim through you, yet I am not the only begotten Son of God in the sense in which it is usually accepted, and much less am I God. As I have said, there is only one God, and I am merely His Son and teacher sent to the world to declare to humanity the bestowal of the gift of immortality and the way in which men may obtain it.

Let no man believe that I was born of the virgin Mary, or that I was begotten by the Holy Spirit, or that I am God, for all these things are not true.

I will stop for the present, and with all my love and blessings and the blessings of the Father, will say good night.

Your friend and brother,
Jesus

Jesus was never in India or Greece
studying their philosophies as some claim
June 29, 1915

I am here, Jesus.

Well, you must have more faith, and pray more. These are the important things, and the next is that you must call on me when you get despondent and need consolation, for I will respond and help you. Then you must let that dear wife of yours come to you with her love and cheer. She is a beautiful spirit and loves you beyond any conception that you may have and you must love her.

Yes, I do love you more than you can comprehend, and you must return my love and be at one with me. I pray with you every night when you ask me to, as you do, and I know that God will answer my prayers as well as yours. I know what I say and you must believe me. So let me have your questions no matter what they will be and I will answer before you ask them.

No, I was never in India or Greece and those other places studying the philosophies of the Indian and Greek philosophers. I never received my knowledge from any other than my Father in my communions with Him and from the teachings of the Jewish scriptures. I lived at home in Nazareth with my parents all the years of my life after returning from Egypt until I started on my public ministry.

Here I must tell you that throughout these many years there have been many Hebrews called Jeshua and I shall name but a few, such as Jeshua, son of Sirach, in connection with the sayings and writings that have already been published in non-canonical books of the Bible; and also, I may mention that Jeshua who some time before my appearance in Palestine incurred the displeasure of the Hebrew authorities and was stoned to death. There have been Jews and others, and even those in the spirit world, who have confused him with me. So you see that in addition to myself there have been many a mortal called Jeshua and indeed this name is a common Hebrew name, and many Hebrews throughout the ages before my time have borne it, so that it is quite possible and indeed likely that a man called Jeshua had studied in the East and enjoyed friends of various philosophies and beliefs.

442

Neither John nor Paul ever communicated that I was in these foreign countries studying the philosophies of the teachers they name. John never travelled with me outside of Palestine, and Paul, I never saw while on earth.

John was a man of very affectionate nature and was with me a great deal during my ministry, but he was not what was called a learned man nor was he acquainted with the philosophies of the men mentioned. He was merely the son of a lowly fisherman, and was selected by me for one of my disciples because of his susceptibility to my teachings and the great possibility for developing his love principle. So you must not believe the statements contained in that book on this subject.

Well, you must stop, but remember that I am with you and love you.

Your friend and brother,
Jesus

Miracles attributed to Jesus in the New Testament
Dr. Samuels, December 6, 1954

I am here, Jesus.

The first supposed miracle is that of my having fed thousands of hungry listeners who were without food and who simply by my supposed powers were supplied bread and water on the occasion of my preaching to them in the hills of Trans-Jordan.

Well, I must say that the many people who ate with me that supper, ate fish and bread and wine and even figs and dates as well, which the New Testament (Matthew 14:19) does not mention. However, this food had been either brought along with them or as in the case of the fish, had been caught by the fishing boat of my disciples and then cooked by some of the women who were present at the time. Furthermore I did tell my disciples to lower their nets in a certain place to be able to make a great haul of fish (John 21:6), which they did, and this took place as a result of my psychic knowledge that a great school of fish had just reached that area of the lake and my disciples, especially Peter Simon, were overcome.

In other words, the meal which we all enjoyed at the time was a substantial one and was one that was retained in the recording of my activities in Trans-Jordan by later writers who received it from my disciples. This meal had nothing miraculous about it except that all food is miraculous as it comes from the Heavenly Father for the sustenance of His children, it was not a miracle in the sense that the New Testament interprets it and conceives it to be.

I wish to add that during that evening, my disciples took their fishing boat and turned their way back to Galilee in the vicinity of Capernaum, and I remained behind to dismiss the multitude, which was not four or five thousand but considerably less, and I then withdrew to pray. I later took one of the little boats of the many that were anchored near the shore and made my way in it that night. As the wind was strong I was eventually able to catch up with them. They were happy to see me and took me into their fishing boat. The sea was rough and they were frightened (Matthew 14:24), so Peter told me to stand up by the mast so the men could see me and gain faith and courage. The moonlight was shining on my white robe, and it appeared as they later told me that I looked like a ghost and that it seemed as if I was walking on the water (Matthew 14:26). From this episode has come the unfortunate story of my having walked on water and I say that this, too, has had a deterrent effect upon my mission as the Messiah to all humanity.

As for the story of the woman taken in adultery (John 8:4), this actually took place and I actually spoke to her accusers as it is portrayed in the New Testament (John 8:7), and it is a fact that I confounded the Jews who brought her to me.

I want to tell you more about the absurdities of the New Testament. Another is the supposed miracle of the water changed to wine at the marriage feast at Cana (John 2:1). At this time a cousin of mine on the side of my mother was being married, and as the wine gave out, I was able to procure wine from a nearby wine dealer by simply paying for it. I used water jugs to bring it back, which are mentioned in the New Testament (John 2:6).

An incident in the Bible more consistent with truth is the Bethesda pool story in which the lame man was cured by his faith that I could heal him (John 5:9). Also in the Gospels of Mark and Matthew, mention is made of my returning from Bethany to Jerusalem on Monday of the Passion Week. They state that, being hungry, I stopped at a fig tree with leaves blossoming, but finding no fruit I cursed the tree, which, according to the Gospel of Matthew (Matthew 21:19), immediately withered.

The truth of the matter is that I had just returned from Lazarus's house where I had enjoyed a good breakfast, served to me by Martha and prepared by Mary, and that I was not hungry, but merely curious, because this being early April, it was not the time for fig trees to give fruit, and seeing leaves on the tree, I expected to see figs. I wish to make it clear that I never cursed anything or anybody at anytime, neither a fig tree nor Capernaum (Matthew 11:23), the town on Lake Gennasaret, for I came to save and not destroy. Furthermore, the tree did not begin to miraculously wither, and it was not Matthew who wrote those words, but another, many years later who was interested in showing my divinity through supernatural powers rather than soul development.

I give you here actual facts for you to use with absolute assurance in the truths of these happenings in your book on the New Testament.

I will say good night,
Jesus of the Bible

"Verily, verily, I say unto you, he that believeth on me, the works that I do shall he do also."
September 24, 1916

I am here, Jesus.

I have been with you a great deal today, and know just what have been the workings of your mind, and tried to influence you as to some of your thoughts. I was with you at church in the morning and heard the minister's sermon and saw that he did not rightly comprehend the meaning of the words of the text, "Verily, verily, I say unto you, he that believeth on me, the works that I do shall he do also; and greater works than these shall he do because I go unto my Father" (John 14:12).

His explanation of what was meant by "greater works than I do," was not in accord with what I meant, or with the meaning that I intended to convey; for when I referred to works I meant those works which the world considered as miracles. I intended to assure my disciples that they would have power to do similar works or perform similar miracles to a greater extent than I had performed them and "greater" referred to quantity and not to quality.

This power or the successful exercise of it was not dependent upon belief in my name, but upon their faith in the power of God and in the fact that He would confer upon them that power. There was no virtue in my name or in me, as the individual, Jesus, but all virtue rested in the faith that they might have in God. I never performed any of the so-called miracles of my own self, but they were all performed by the Father, working through me; and just as He worked through me He would work through my disciples who should acquire the necessary faith.

As I have told you before, all acts that are apparently miracles are controlled by law just as are those things which you call the workings of nature, controlled by law, and when sufficient faith is acquired there comes to its possessor a knowledge of these laws. Although it may not be, as you would say, a knowledge, or consciousness that is perceptible to the ordinary senses of man, but perceptible to that inner sense, which is the one that enables men to comprehend the things of the spirit. And having this knowledge of the inner sense men may so control these laws that they will work those effects which seem to be contrary to the accustomed workings of the laws of nature. Until my disciples had acquired this faith that brought to their inner sense this knowledge they could not perform miracles or do any work of phenomenon.

The Bible expression, that belief in my name is sufficient to cause the workings of miracles (Mark 16:17) is all wrong, and I never said that such belief was what was required, neither did I say, that whatsoever should be asked of the Father in my name would be given to men (John 15:16). I was not a part of the Godhead and I had not of myself any power, and neither did my name have any miraculous influence with the Father. I was a man as other men are men, only I had become filled with the Divine Love, which made me at one with God, and, consequently, had that knowledge of His Love and laws that enabled me to bring into operation those laws that would cause the desired effects to appear as realities.

Belief in my name caused no working of these laws, or the response to any supplications. Prayer must be made to the Father in the name of truth, and His Love and mercy. Every individual is dear to Him, and He is ready to bestow this Love upon every one who asks in faith and pure desire, and in response will come the Divine Love, and with it knowledge of things spiritual, and with this, power that may be used for the good of humanity.

My name is not a mediator between God and man, and neither is it a means to reach the responsive Soul of the Father. If men will understand my teachings of truth, and when they ask in my name if they mean that they ask in the name of these truths, then such asking will have its results, but so few men, when they pray to God in my name, have such intention or understanding. Of this erroneous mind knowledge, or, perhaps rather, conviction, is the belief that in my name, that is supplications made in my name, will bring about the realization of the desires of the supplicant. Also that in my blood, or in the power of the cross, or in my alleged vicarious atonement, the salvation of men can be obtained.

If any name must be used in man's supplication, then use only the name of the Father, for His is a name high over all, and the only name in heaven or earth that can bring to man salvation and at-onement with His Being. What I have said applies to many other declarations contained in the Bible, such as "He that believeth on the Lord Jesus Christ shall be saved" (Acts 16:31). "There is no other name under heaven whereby men can be saved" (Acts 4:12) etc. This is the enunciation of a false doctrine and misleading to the great majority of humankind for they accept the declarations as literally true. Of course if it be interpreted as meaning that he that believeth on the truths that I teach, then the objection is not so great, but even then the declarations do not go far enough, for men may believe in these truths, and that belief may be a mere mental one, acquiesced in merely by the mind's faculties, without any exercise at all of the soul sense. If to all these declarations shall be added the vital truth, that, "Except a man be born again, he cannot enter into the kingdom of heaven" (John 3:3), and to this mental belief be added the soul's faith, then the doctrines will be truly stated and men will understand what is necessary for salvation.

Belief and faith are not the same; one is of the mind, the other of the soul. One can and does change as phenomena and apparent facts change. The other when truly possessed, never changes, for faith possessed by a soul causes all the longings and aspirations of that soul to become things of real existence, just as the house that is built upon solid rock can never be shaken or destroyed.

I write thus tonight to show that the preacher in his sermon did not explain the true meaning of the text, and did not comprehend the truths that were intended to be conveyed of which the text was susceptible, and it did not set forth my expressions or in its literal interpretation declare the truth.

I will not write more now except to say, that I love you with a great love, and pray to the Father to bless you. Believe in Him and trust me for you will not be disappointed, and pray that this Divine Love shall come into your soul so that you shall know that you are an accepted son of God. Keep up your courage and have faith that whatsoever you shall ask the Father in the name of love and truth shall be given to you. I am with you in all my love and care and you will not be forsaken.

So my dear brother, rest assured that I am your brother and friend.

Jesus

The events in the Garden of Gethsemane, and the
explanation for the healing of the breach between Pilate and Herod
Dr. Samuels, March 3, 1955

I am here, Jesus.

I am here tonight to write my messages regarding the truths of the New Testament, which is so sadly in need of a purge of the erroneous statements and beliefs found therein.

Tonight, I am going to write to you about one of these tendentious statements, and this deals with the occasion of my arrest by the hirelings of the high priest in the Garden of Gethsemane. Now, the Gospels mention that a youth who was present at the time of my betrayal was seized and that he had to tear himself away from the clutches of the hirelings, and in the process he lost his outer garment of linen which left him stripped (Mark 14:52); and he subsequently escaped. Now, originally, the apostle who wrote this statement, and he was Mark, had given the name of this youth, who was my younger brother James, known as the lesser. My brother loved me very much, and at this time had begun to believe in my message to the extent of his capabilities, and he followed when I was arrested, his heart breaking with grief and anx-

448

iety.

The copyists of the original Gospel of Mark eliminated the name of my brother and inserted the words, "a certain youth" (Mark 14:51), because they did not want to use the word brother, for it denoted what is really a fact, as you know, and that is, that my mother was the mother of eight children in the flesh. Also, the writer sought to enhance my prestige with readers of the New Testament by showing them to what a great degree I inspired the love and loyalty of strangers.

The reason why the hirelings of the high priest seized James was because he resembled me so much in face and figure that sometimes he was mistaken for me, and some of the group thought that he was really me and that I was really he, and they sought to arrest him also, to make certain that they had apprehended the right man.

Neither Peter nor any one of my followers ever cut off the ear of Malchus, the servant of the high priest, for Peter did not wear a sword (John 18:10) but simply a fishing knife — that is, a blade used in cutting fish to remove their entrails. Furthermore, a hostile blow might have meant that the hirelings and servants might retaliate and club our followers unmercifully as a consequence, a fact which Peter knew, as did we all at the time. There is no truth to this supposed anecdote, it was interpolated in order to have me remark, which is also not true, that God would come to my aid with many legions of angels (Matthew 26:53) if it were required. This was intended to emphasize the belief that I was destined to be betrayed and that it was all a part of God's plan of salvation that included betrayal and my death on the cross.

The next incident that I wish to refer to deals with my being sent by Pilate, after my arrest, to Herod, who was then in Jerusalem to observe the festivities of the Jewish Passover. This incident is true, and the explanation is as follows. Some time before, Pilate had ordered a number of Galileans to be killed, which caused enmity between him and Herod, who claimed that Pilate had no authority to execute the men since they, being Galileans, were under his (Herod's) jurisdiction. This coolness was patched up on the occasion of my arrest, for Pilate used this opportunity to send me to Herod to ascertain if I was under his jurisdiction as a Galilean. When Herod, through inquiry, discovered that I was born in Bethlehem in Judea, and not Galilee, he returned me to Pilate and was pleased that Pilate had extended him the courtesy of consulting him to establish under whose jurisdiction my condemnation and punishment were to be meted out. This is the explanation for the healing of the breach between Pilate and Herod (Luke 23:12), and the reason for the latter's appearance on the scene at the time of my arrest.

I think I shall stop now, for I believe I have said enough for tonight. I shall continue to come and provide the truths necessary for you to write the true New Testament and shall suggest the ideas and help you locate the material that you need to obtain. So be encouraged in your work as the medium through whom I am revealing my messages of truth, and pray to the Father that He will bestow upon you and the Doctor wonderful portions of the Divine Love.

I will sign myself your friend and elder brother,
Jesus of the Bible

Why Jesus was not accepted as the promised
Messiah by the chief priests and Hebrew rulers
Dr. Samuels, June 14, 1955

I am here, Jesus.

I wish to continue with the truths of the New Testament and to speak about my teaching in the Temple in Jerusalem (Matthew 21:23) the autumn before my death. This was the first time that I had the opportunity to present my claims as Messiah before the chief priests and rulers and most learned amongst the Hebrew people in matters pertaining to religion. I made known that my mission was to proclaim the New Covenant between the Heavenly Father and the people of Israel, and that the Divine Love was now present and could be obtained by all who might seek it through earnest longing of soul, and that I was the visible sign of its presence, because in my soul there reposed the nature and Essence of the Father in the form of the Divine Love, and that my soul was of this Nature and Essence and therefore immortal.

But to the Hebrew rulers, my claims appeared false because Isaiah had prophesied* that no one would know from whence the Messiah

*This prophesy is not recorded in the Old Testament. However, there is a passage in the New Testament to this effect (Matthew 7:27). It is therefore possible that the people of Jesus's day knew of this prophesy that the text refers to.

would come; whereas, I was well-known, being Jesus of Nazareth, because they deemed a man not to be of his native town, but of the one in which he lived most of his life and was associated with; thus Jerusalem was considered the city of the great King David, rather than Bethlehem, where he was born, therefore Isaiah's prophecy regarding the unknown origin of the Messiah was applicable to me.

However, this type of argument showed bad faith and a recourse to technicalities in the determination of the priests not to recognize me as the Messiah. They felt that I would have upset their high position as the religious leaders of the nation which they were unwilling to relinquish. Those technicalities were a subterfuge and manner of debating issues which were dear to their hearts, laying emphasis on hairsplitting intellectual distinctions resulting from subtle interpretations of the law foreign to real basic issues and spiritual insight achieved through soul seeking to know the truth.

Thus, replying to their minute scriptural objections on their own terms, I proclaimed that it was not true that they knew where I was from, or who my father was, for, whereas they referred to Joseph as my father, whom they knew well, I referred to God, my Heavenly Father, whom they did not know, nor did they know from whence I came as a divine soul, nor how or when I was created. The reference of the rabbis to my father Joseph were later eliminated from the Gospels, for mention of my earthly parents was a thorn in the side of the later Gospel revisionists who labored zealously to make of me a god-man born of a virgin, and the second person of the supposed trinity, which, of course, has no foundation in fact.

I told them that, if they knew the Father, they would also know me, His Son, as being sent from Him, and to recognize me as the Messiah, and quoting from Isaiah, as the Hebrew leaders did, I stated that the Father had said, "Incline your ear and come unto me; hear, and your soul shall live, and I will make a covenant with you, even the sure mercies of David. Behold, I have given him as a witness to the people, a leader and commander to the people" (Isaiah 55:3-4). What I said was known to all who received instruction concerning the God of the Hebrews, so that they knew He had appointed a Messiah over them in a descendant of David. Hence, they should accept me as their Messiah, inasmuch as I was indeed a descendant of the house of David and that I had come to enable their souls to live, by making available to them the gift of immortality in the Father's Divine Love, accompanied by the power of healing and miracles which I performed through the Father, which attested to the truth of my mission.

I further informed them that if they wished to ascertain the truth of my words, they should try and test my teachings that the Father's Love was now available, and pray for it in earnest prayer, and if this was done in sincerity, the Divine Love would be conveyed through the Holy Spirit, and would burn and glow in their souls, by which sign they would realize this Love was present therein. I also stated that these teachings were not mine, but those of the Father and I had been commanded by Him to proclaim to the children of Israel, having been sent by Him, and I could do nothing of my own, but what was done unto me was done by the Father, that is to say, what power I received. I did not say I could do what I saw the Father do, or imitate Him, as the Gospel states (John 5:19), for that would give me a power equal to that of God, which is blasphemy.

No mortal or spirit will ever, through all eternity, have the power equal to that of God, and this revision was made many years later in conformity to the false doctrine, elaborated in the early Greek period of Christianity after my death, of making me co-equal to the Father. And here I would like to say that, if such an absurdity were admitted for one moment, it lends itself to its own destruction, and proves its own falsity, for never having seen the Heavenly Father lay down His life for His sheep, Israel, neither could I, Jesus, have laid down mine, in the sense that it is understood in the New Testament (John 10:15), that my shed blood and sacrifice on the cross gives remission of sins.

I quoted from the Psalms and from Samuel the prophet on the Davidic covenant, saying, "I will set up thy seed after thee which shall proceed out of thy bowels and I will establish his kingdom. He shall build a house for my name, I will establish the throne of his kingdom forever, I will be his Father, and he shall be my son" (2 Samuel 7:12 -14). Thus if they knew the Father and honored His word, they would know me as well, for I proclaimed the eternal salvation of the soul through His Love, which was evidenced in my own soul and witnessed to by His power acting through me. I also testified that while they did not know the Father, I, indeed, knew Him and was sent by Him and I stated, that God was my witness to the truth of my mission, a mission which I undertook for His glory, and not my own.

I did not break the Mosaic law regarding the Sabbath, when I healed and made whole the withered hand on that day (Mark 3:1), for if circumcision was superior to the Sabbath, wherein one part of the body was restored, how much more important than the Sabbath was that act wherein the whole body was restored? Hence, I stated that their rejection of me as the Messiah, on the grounds of my having healed on the Sabbath day, was merely a subterfuge to refuse me recognition and to conceal their own violation of the Mosaic law — making one body part more important than the body itself, and it was they, not I, who was guilty of transgression.

I never said that I was the Good Shepherd, for that referred to the Father, and this statement was inserted many years after my death, in order to raise me up to being equal to God. Instead, I stated that the Father is the Good Shepherd and the sheepfold being the kingdom of heaven, and that I was the door (John 10:7) through which the sheep came into the sheepfold and into the presence and knowledge of the Shepherd, or the Porter, who opens the door and is the Father. The Father gives eternal life to His sheep, and I am the way, the door, by which the sheep may enter the sheepfold of eternal life.

I think I have said enough on this subject and have explained many things that are obscure in the New Testament, and with my blessings upon you and the Doctor, and upon all my disciples who are doing the Father's work.

I shall stop and sign myself,
Jesus of the Bible
and
Master of the celestial heavens

Jesus never sought to break away from Judaism or to establish a new church
Dr. Samuels, March 1, 1957

I am here, Jesus.

During my mission on earth as the Messiah of God it is true that I was not concerned with the means of settling disputes in my so-called church, for as a matter of fact, I had never at any time when on earth entertained the thought of establishing a new church.

I was wholeheartedly attached to my own religious institution, the Temple at Jerusalem and to the assemblies and synagogues of my own religion, Judaism. I was a religious Jew intent upon living up to the highest ideals of Judaism in the way of that ethical standard of life as preached by our prophets and the lawgivers, aside from my mission as Messiah and bringing to humanity the availability of the Divine Love. What I attacked, if that be the appropriate word, were simply the abuses and encumbrances which the legalisms of the church organization had caused to spring up to wither the best which Judaism as a religion had produced.

I meant to work strictly within the established Hebrew Church and to affect needed reforms from within as well as to introduce the principle of the "new heart," and never at any time did I think of breaking away from Judaism and to establishing a religious body separate from this religion. I am today as I have always been, a Hebrew by religion and by race, and any such passages in the New Testament which imply or otherwise state that I ever instituted a new religion or thought to establish a new organization for worship is false and entirely unfounded, and hence I never wrote those lines in the Gospel (Matthew 18:15-17) allegedly giving instructions regarding disputes for members of a new religious group.

Now I wish to say that I am seeking to show humankind the way to the Father which had been lost after I had given my message to man and had delegated the continuation of the work involved to my apostles and disciples. These co-workers of mine were not always of the same mind, nor of the same disposition, nor of the same degree of faith even though they were united with me in person throughout our travels and mission in Palestine, and were the recipients of my daily instructions, advice and encouragement.

When on earth, I encountered different personalities in Peter, John, Andrew, my brother Judah (Jude), Judas, Matthew, James, Nicodemus, Miriam, my mother, and Joseph, my father, Miriam of Magdala, and many, many others. My parents, strangely enough, had less of an understanding of my love than did those who were my friends. One who loved me dearly deserted me, and caused my death; two great apostles, Paul and Peter, broke with each other on the question of circumcision for non-Jews (Acts 15:7). Paul won the day and these many centuries the gentiles have not received circumcision; yet today circumcision is being more and more practiced in hospitals among the gentiles, and the victory is now seemingly that of Peter's.

In the clash of personalities among my friends in my day, my parents sought to uphold the religion in force; some apostles wanted me to become king in Judea and wage war on Rome; another sought to force my hand by thinking my healing was done through mysticism; few understood my mission, and when they did it was imperfectly.

Any religious differences among my followers or any disputes of a personal nature were settled by me amicably and without recourse to the legal and technical formulas presented by churches of today. Our differences were all settled not in the formal manner which you have just heard as proposed and discussed but in an informal way as befitted the men who followed my teachings and saw in prayer to the Father the only real efficacy for these disputes and occasions of ill will and misunderstandings. The Divine Love gives humility, forbearance, forgiveness, and if you do these things, you show that God's Love is there. Prayer to God causes the Divine Love to shine in your soul and become active; it displaces, or causes to displace, in time, suspicion, jealousies, competition. I desire to judge no man but, he who will, let him come to the Father and pray.

Some of my disciples had managed to plant into the souls of succeeding decades of men the seed of prayers to the Father for the Divine Love that transforms the soul and gives everlasting life. Although, distorted and twisted by churchmen who sought to conciliate Hellenistic paganism with moral and ethical Judaism, the teachings of the Divine Love were eradicated from the earth until, through the spiritual receptivity of Mr. Padgett, I was again able to teach the good tidings of the Father's Love and the need of sincere prayer to Him, to eliminate the earth plane motives that dominate the mind and soul, and to seek ever-lasting Love and life in His mansions of the celestial heavens.

My work is not to judge between man and man, but to bring to mankind the knowledge of the Father's Love, which will enable man to replace sin and error from the human soul with Divine Love, wherein we are all one in the Father's Love. It was this that I taught and prayed, and it was for this that I was hauled from my prayers to the Father on the Mt. of Olives, beaten by servants of the high priests and Roman sol-diers, and led to my death by crucifixion.

Let each of us grow in Grace and in His Love, through earnest prayer, and may His Love overflow into our souls in abundance unto eternal life.

I am,
Jesus of the Bible

What took place on the road to Emmaus and later at the Pentecost
Dr. Samuels, October 18, 1954

I am here, Jesus.

After my death my father was confused as to my mission and bewil-dered at the turn of events, and he feared for his personal safety. He was also terribly disappointed at my being "King of the Jews" in the sign of the cross only, in which they inscribed me as such in several languages (Matthew 27:37).

It became impossible for him to remain in Palestine having been pointed out as the father of the crucified Jesus. He was afraid of the con-sequences, both political as well as religious, of my crucifixion. That afternoon my father, under the concealed name of Cleophas, and my brother Thomas, hastened to Emmaus (Luke 24:13) to escape what they thought was going to be certain arrest and crucifixion as had happened to me. I went after them in order to bring them back to Jerusalem so that all my disciples would be together when they saw me.

Thomas had begun to doubt and his attitude could have been disas-trous to the entire plan of salvation by bringing pessimism and skepti-

456

cism into the minds of my followers. That is why I went to Emmaus and had Thomas and Cleophas recognize me when I broke bread with them (Luke 24:30-31). At that time the Divine Love flowed into their souls, and they immediately regained their faith and returned with me to Jerusalem to face whatever dangers there might be. So on the next Friday Thomas was there and poked his fingers into my side which gave him faith (John 20:27) that I was the resurrected Jesus and this crucial time was overcome in victory.

In Jerusalem where all my disciples were assembled, I told them that all the power of heaven and earth (Matthew 28:18) comes to those who partake of the Divine Love of God. I said to them, go, therefore, and teach the way to receive this Love and that every man can be baptized by the Holy Spirit through his desire; and by this the "christ" will develop in your soul and will be with you all the days of your life (Matthew 28:20), forever with me and at-one with God.

My return was necessary in order to show my disciples that I was still alive even after death by crucifixion. For at this time in their spiritual development this phenomenon was the proof in their eyes that I was the true Messiah. Their real understanding of my messiahship came to them at the Pentecost when the Divine Love was conveyed into their souls with such power and abundance that they knew I had come to bring the very Essence of God to humanity.

My death was a great personal tragedy in the lives of my closest and dearest. My mother stayed with John and his family until her death. His love and affection for her were a great source of consolation. In the loss of my life not merely physically but also in the ties of my family, I gained life in the spirit world where every member of my family is present and often with me. They now fully realize my mission as the Messiah and know of my love for them.

My disciples and followers who had remained faithful to me after my crucifixion had the realization that my mission was a spiritual one. They were very much affected by the brutal manner in which my death had been imposed upon me. Their sorrow was deep and continual, and it was their love for me and grieving that turned their hearts and souls towards God in a great yearning of love and aspiration. They loved me wholeheartedly as their Rabbi and they were filled with a deep grief and love that made their souls ready to receive the Divine Love when it was poured out upon them. It culminated in a great abundance conveyed to them fifty days after my death at the time of the pentecostal showering upon their souls of God's precious Essence.

It came into their souls with a great inflowing and burning of the heart and with the sound of a mighty rushing wind which shook the room where they were assembled and filled them with its power (Acts 2:2). This meant that the Divine Love came into their souls in such abundance that they were shaken to the extent that they thought the building in which they were assembled was disturbed. But, in this they were mistaken, for the presence of the Holy Spirit does not affect things of inanimate nature but is confined to and exclusively to the souls of God's children. The Divine Love that was implanted into their souls by the Holy Spirit did not come all at once but had been building up within them for those fifty days.

After the Pentecost my disciples had a clearer understanding of my mission. The inflowing of Divine Love absorbed their human or natural love and gave them the faith and courage to set out into the world to preach the true doctrines of my mission on earth — the Love of the Father for His children and the fact that this Love was waiting for any and all who should seek for it.

The Pentecost marked the end of the Jewish dispensation or the end of the Jewish world. For at this time the Divine Love, which was first bestowed upon me, was now being granted to my followers in abundance. The Mosaic laws, the highest available to humankind prior to my coming, were superseded by the New Covenant (Hebrews 8:8) of the heart and the rebirth of the soul in God's Divine Love.

With all my love and blessings, your brother,
Jesus

Jesus expels myths about his life, and says that his
father Joseph, after many years did make his way to Great Britain
Dr. Samuels, October 28, 1954

I am here, Jesus.

Yes, I am here, as you perceived spiritually when I came into the room, and you see that your spiritual perceptions are being opened up with continual and constant prayer for the Divine Love and the earnest longing of your soul for at-onement with the Heavenly Father. I am here tonight to write about my father, Joseph, and you may be absolutely sure of its veracity.

In the first place, there is proof in the New Testament to show that about nine months before the crucifixion my father was alive, and that is, during the year 29 A.D. I was preaching in Capernaum, and the Jews asked each other, "Is not he the son of Joseph and Mary whom we know (John 6:42)?" This quotation shows that they referred to my father as still living.

Furthermore, in later years, a century or more after my death, the idea became popular with the Christian leaders to make the world believe that my mother never had any children, and they stated that my brothers James and Jude, who later believed in my work, were not my brothers but my cousins. They concocted this story whereby my mother, Mary, had a sister by the same name, Mary (John 19:25), who married the brother of my father, Joseph, and that this supposed brother was called Alphaeus. So that, what the Bible refers to when it mentions Alphaeus, the father of James (Matthew 10:3), was not a mention of my father, but of my father's so-called brother by that name. In that way, these later writers hoped to induce Christians to believe that my mother had lived as a virgin all her life and that my brothers, who are mentioned in the New Testament (Mark 6:3), were merely cousins.

It was my father's desire for concealment of his identity which helped these later writers in their attempts to eliminate my father from the biblical scene after my supposed visit to the rabbis in Jerusalem at the age of twelve, an incident which I have already stated in one of my messages to Mr. Padgett to be entirely false.

The Doctor has been asking himself some questions arising from the implications of my message regarding my father, and it is indeed revolutionary in its impact upon the usual conception of my relationship with my family, but I can assure him that this message is authentically written.

To continue further, I may state that my father, after having seen my materialized body, there came a great breakdown in his beliefs about my mission and he began to see it in a spiritual sense. After many years, when his great confusion and bitter disappointment* had subsided, he gained in faith in my mission as the Messiah and he did some evangelizing with some of the disciples on several of the islands off the coast of Greece, notably Patmos and Cyprus, and he did after many years make his way to Great Britain, but he died soon thereafter and the supernatural event connected with the flowering of a branch** has no factual relation to the events which mark his stay in the island empire.

In addition to these events in the New Testament which later writers distorted or eliminated completely in order to have the narrative in accord with their own preconceived notions as to my messiahship and divinity, there are many more that need to be explained; one is that I did speak on the bread of life, which should be interpreted as the Divine Love, but I never said that my flesh or my blood should be consumed in order for my followers to attain salvation. That, also, was interpolated in order to justify in the New Testament (Matthew 26:26 -28) the concept of the transubstantiation — the drinking of blood — which is completely erroneous and particularly vexatious to me.

I should also like to say that never did I state in the Gospel of Mark and, in fact, neither did he nor any other of my disciples ever state, or write, to the effect that I compared Gentile children to dogs who should not receive the food which was to be given to the children, meaning the Jewish people (Mark 7:27). However an incident did take place on the coast of the Mediterranean near Tyre and Sidon when a Gentile woman sought me out to have me cure her sick daughter. She addressed me as Rabbi, for she knew that I was of the Jewish nation. I told her to approach, although some of my eager disciples wished to chase her away (Matthew 15:23), and I asked her why she asked help of a Jewish rabbi, being herself Gentile, and whether she knew that Jewish rabbis

*Jesus did not become "King of the Jews" as his father had expected of him since it was revealed to him by the wise men.
**The Glastonbury legend is that the Somerset thorn trees which bloom Christmas and Easter are the descendants of Joseph's planted staff when he visited Britain.

would tell her that food should not be taken from the children and given to the dogs? Her response was substantially what is described in the Gospel (Mark 7:28), and through her faith I was able to cure her ailing daughter.

I think I have said enough for tonight and I shall close, but I want to tell you to keep on praying earnestly for the Divine Love, and I shall continue to help you obtain the truths that have never before been given to humankind. I also wish to point out that in other ways than through "revelations" on the Gospels you are being guided by me and the celestials. So, I will say again, have faith in me and in the celestials, and continue to pray to the Father for His Love.

With all my love and blessings to you and the Doctor, I shall sign myself your elder brother.

Jesus of the Bible

The condition of the world when Jesus came to teach
May 24, 1915

I am here, Jesus.

You are feeling better tonight, and l will try to write a little. I do not know if you are in condition to take a formal message, but I will tell you some things that will be of interest to you and humanity.

When I came to the world to teach the truths of my Father, the world was almost devoid of spiritual conception of the true relationship of God to man, and God was a Being of power and wrath only. It was because of this conception of Him that the Jews were so devoid of the true knowledge of His Nature and attributes. They only knew Him as a God who was interested in their material welfare, and did not realize that He was a God who wanted them to know Him as their spiritual Father and saviour from the sins and evil natures that they possessed. Consequently when I came they looked upon me — I mean those who accepted me as their Messiah — as one who would redeem them from the slavery which their Roman conquerors had placed them in and make them a great and independent nation, more powerful than all the nations of the earth, and fitted to rule the whole world.

They had no conception of my true mission on earth, and even my disciples, until shortly before my death, looked upon me merely as a saviour of them from the burdens which the Roman yoke had placed upon them. The only one of my disciples who had any approximate realization of what my coming to earth meant was John, and that was because of the great amount of love that seemed to be a part of his nature and being. To him I explained my real mission and taught him the spiritual truths which I came to teach, and the only way in which mortals could receive that Love of the Father, which was necessary to make them one with Him and enable them to partake of His divinity. Hence, only in John's Gospel is written the one necessary requirement to a full salvation and redemption of humanity. I mean the declaration that men must be born again in order to enter into the kingdom of heaven. This is the only true way by which a man can become a true child of the Father, and fitted to live in and enjoy His kingdom to the fullest.

The other disciples had a more or less conception of this necessary truth, but not the full comprehension of what it involved. Peter was more possessed of this Love than were the other disciples, except John, and with it he also understood that I was the true Son of my Father; but he never understood nor declared that 1 was God. He was a man filled with zeal and ambition, though his development of love was not sufficient to enable him to fully realize that my kingdom was not to be an earthly one, until after my death, and then the conviction came to him in all its truth and fullness, and he became the most powerful and influential of all my disciples.

After the Pentecost, all of my disciples understood what my real mission was, and they went into the world and preached the true doctrines of my mission on earth, and the Love of the Father for His children, and the fact that that Love was waiting for all who should seek for it. So you see that many of my disciples when on earth were not possessed of the true conception of my mission, and were not true followers of me in that inner meaning of what the Love of God meant and what I tried to preach to them.

I now have on earth many mortals who understand my teachings better, and with a greater extent of soul knowledge, than did my disciples when journeying with me through Palestine. But there are a great many men and women now living who do not understand my teachings, even though they think they understand the Bible and the interpretations of its discourses in accordance with the accepted doctrines of the learned and so-called teachers of its truths.

I don't feel that you can write more tonight and so I will stop, but say that you must continue to get stronger, spiritually and physically, so that we can continue our writings more rapidly and with greater satisfaction. So believe that I am Jesus your true friend and brother who is with you very much trying to help you and to make you happy and contented.

With my love and prayers I am,
Jesus

The relationship of man to the creation of the world and the origin of life
January 15, 1916

I am here, Jesus.

I come tonight to tell you that you are in a much better condition than you have been for some time, and your rapport with us is so very much greater, that I feel that I should write you a message upon an important subject which is vital to the salvation of man from the sins and errors of his life on earth.

I will first say that there are so many men and women on the earth, who believe, or assert that they believe, that through their own efforts they can develop those soul qualities which are necessary to bring them in accord with God. I find that the task of convincing these persons of the errors of their beliefs, or assumption of beliefs, will be a very great one. This task will not be confined to those who have given real and deep study to the mysteries of life, both on earth and thereafter, but also to a much greater number who have a kind of smattering of this supposed knowledge, which the wiser or more learned publish to the world as a result of their investigations.

I do not know just what is the most important subject for comment tonight relating to these matters, for there are so many, all of which I must at some time instruct you about. I will write tonight about "The relationship of man to the creation of the world, and the origin of life."

The Bible says: in the beginning God created the heavens and the earth, etc., out of a void (Genesis 1:2), and continued that creation until there was a perfect heaven with all its glories, and a perfect earth with inhabitants of every kind — all perfect and made just as an all wise and all powerful God would create; and as a climax to all, man, who was so perfect that he was made in the image of his Creator.

Well, this story is just as good and satisfactory as any that has been conceived and written by man, and is just as worthy of belief, but as a fact it is not true, for there never was a time or period when there was a void in the universe or when there was chaos. God never created anything out of nothing. His creations, such as are perceived by and known to men, were merely the change in form or composition of what had already existed, and always will exist as elements, though there will undoubtedly be changes in form and appearance and in constituent elements in their relation to one another.

God was always existent — a Being without beginning, which idea the finite mind, I know, cannot grasp, but it is true; and so also everything which is in the universe today always existed, though not in form and composition as they now are; and as they are they will not continue to be, for change eternal is the law of his universe. I mean as to all things which may be spoken of as having a substance whether they be material or ethereal. God's truths of course never change, and neither do the laws by which the harmony of the universe is preserved and continued perfect.

The earth on which you live did not always have an existence as an earth, and neither did the firmament and the great galaxy of planets and stars, but they were not created out of nothing, and neither was there chaos, for in God's economy of being there is never any chaos, and if it should be, this would mean the absence of the workings of His laws and harmony. The earth and the firmament were created at one time and before that they had no existence as such, and at a coming time they may cease to have such existence. This creation was in an orderly way, according to design, with no element of chance entering into it.

This creation was not through what your wise men may call accretion or evolution — that is, self-evolution — for every new or additional exponent of growth or manifestations of increase was the result of God's laws which He operated in the creation. There is no such thing as self-evolution, or the development of that which arises from the unassisted growth of the thing developed, and this applies to all of nature as well as to man. In all this work of creation there are laws of disintegration and apparent retrogression operating, as well as laws of positive construction and advancement, and again these former laws do not operate by chance, but by design just as do the latter class of laws.

The Creator knows when bringing forth the perfect creature — be he man or animal or vegetable or mineral — the laws of decay and retrogression as well as the laws of advancement and increased effectiveness shall operate, and He never makes a mistake in setting into operation these laws, and never pronounces the result of His work, "not good".

As has been said, a thousand years on earth are as a day to God (2 Peter 3:8), and for many long years it may appear to man, that there are retrogression and delay in bringing to perfection a creature of the Creator's works. I know it is difficult to explain these workings of creation to the finite, earthy mind but you may grasp some conception of what I desire to make known.

Man, in his creation, was not the slow growth as were some of the other creations of God, but was from and at the beginning made perfect, with the exception of the qualities of divinity and immortality. He did not grow from a lower creature, as some of your scientists have proclaimed, by the slow process of evolution, or self-evolution, resulting from inherent qualities which were developed by experience, but he was created the perfect man from the beginning.

I will stop for the present.

Your brother and friend,
Jesus

Previous message continued
February 6, 1916

I come tonight to resume my discourse of several nights ago. As I was saying, man is the creature of God, made in perfection and instantaneously, as it were, not having a slow growth as other creations, and when he was created he needed no evolution or additional attributes to make him the perfect man. His physical body was perfect, and also his spiritual body and his soul. He had, in addition to these three constituents, a gift which, by his disobedience he forfeited, and which was never restored to him until my coming, and when possessed by him would make him more than mere man. As to those things which were made constituent and absolute parts of him, they were perfect, and no evolution was necessary to give them any increased perfection. Man then was a more perfect being than he is now, or ever has been since his fall from his condition of perfection.

After his disobedience and the consequent death of the potentiality of partaking of the Divine Nature of God, man was left in a state where he depended exclusively upon the qualities which he then possessed for his future happiness, and the freedom from those things which would cause him to lose the harmony that then existed between him and the laws governing his being.

The greatest of all the qualities bestowed upon him was that of the will power, which was wholly unrestricted in its operations. Although, when exercised in a manner which brought this will in conflict with the laws controlling this harmony, man had to suffer and pay the penalties of such violations. But notwithstanding, these perversions of the exercise of the will, brought the sins and errors which now exist on earth, for God did not place any limitations on this exercise.

Man, in his creation, had bestowed upon him appetites and desires pertaining to his physical nature, as well as desires of his higher or spiritual nature, and they were all intended to work in harmony and not in antagonism. In such workings man was kept pure and free from sin, which is merely the violation of God's laws of harmony. Now after the first disobedience, which is the greatest demonstration of the power of man to exercise that will, even when God had forbade him to do so, and after man lost this great potentiality that I speak of, succeeding disobediences became easier. As these disobediences occurred man lost to a great extent the desires for the spiritual things, and the animal or physical part of his nature asserted itself, and then, instead of exercising these appetites which belonged to the physical nature in such a wise way that no inharmony would ensue (and here let me say that even after the fall it was possible and even expected that man would exercise these appetites in the way mentioned), he indulged them beyond their proper functions. He increased such indulgence until he commenced to find, as he thought, more pleasure in such indulgence, than in the thoughts and exercise of his higher nature, and the aspirations which belonged to it.

This deterioration of man was not sudden, but gradual, until, at one time, he came into a state or condition of bordering on that of the lower animals, and in fact because of this increased indulgence of these appetites he seemed to be transformed into the lower animal; yet he remained man, a being created in the image of his Maker. Now from this position of low degradation or degeneracy, man slowly commenced to progress towards the attainment of his original condition before the fall. Never in all this time was his freedom of will taken from him, nor attempted to be controlled by God, but always the laws of compensation worked, and man suffered as he continued to create sin and evil.

As man on earth continued to degenerate and to permit, what is sometimes called his animal nature to dominate his spiritual nature, many men died, and continued to die, and their physical bodies went back to the dust of which they were created, and their spiritual selves became inhabitants of the spirit world. There they were freed, in a longer or shorter time, from the desire to exercise these animal appetites and the spiritual part of man again asserted itself. Many of these spirits became free from sin and evil and in harmony with the laws of God controlling their natures and conditions as they existed before their degeneracy and before the disobedience commenced.

These spirits, thus made free and in their spiritual dominance commenced to try to assist men while living on earth to direct his will in such ways as to rid himself of submission to these appetites, and to become again a true man as in his created state. But these efforts on the part of spirits have been slow, and while men in individual cases have been almost regenerated, yet as a whole the progress has not been as rapid as is desirable, and sin and evil still exist in the world, and men's perverted appetites and desires still control them to a large extent.

This progress from the bottom of degeneracy has taken place in some parts of the earth, faster than in others, and hence, you have your distinction between the civilized and the uncivilized races or nations. This does not necessarily mean that the civilized people, as individuals, have made greater progress in the manner indicated than have the individuals of some of the so-called uncivilized nations, for it is a fact, that among some men of the former nations are perversions and manifestations of perversions of these appetites that do not exist in the latter nations.

Advancement in the intellectual qualities does not necessarily mean progress in the spiritual asserting itself over the perversions of these appetites, for will is not a thing entirely of the mind, and neither are these appetites and desires. Back of the mind are the affections, usually called the heart's desires, which is the seat of these appetites, and from which these desires arise; and as they arise the will is influenced by them and as the will is influenced, positive thoughts and deeds will come.

It is not surprising that your scientists believe and preach the doctrine of the evolution of man from a lower species of animal, or from an atom or from something that they cannot just understand or give a name to. In their studies of the history of humankind, and of the created world, they find that man has developed and progressed amazingly from what appeared to have been his condition in some ages past. Yet history does not extend to the time when man was in this lowest condition of degeneracy, and hence all the conclusions that these scientists reach are based upon facts, sufficient unto themselves, which show the progress of man only after the turning point of his degeneracy. They have no fact, and, of course, when the word "facts" is used here, it refers exclusively to the material things of nature which show them the gradual decline of man from his state of being a perfect man to that when his retrogression or degeneracy ceased, and his progress of return to his former estate commenced.

So, if the scientists will believe and teach that man, instead of evolving from an atom or some other infinitesimal something, or from a lower species of animal than man, evolved from his state or condition when he was at the bottom of his degeneracy, to which he had descended from the perfect man, then they will believe and teach the truth, and their theory of evolution will then have as its foundation or basis, a fact which it now has not, but only a speculation. This in short, is the history and truth of the creation of the universe of man and of man's fall and degeneracy and evolution and progress. Through all this creation and subsequent existence runs life permeating it and always with it, and the origin of life is God.

I have finished and I hope that you will find some instruction as well as entertainment in what I have written. I will come again soon and write you another truth. The fact that you waited for sentences to be formulated to express my thoughts merely means that I was manipulating your brain so that the proper expression or idea could be conveyed to your hand as I wrote it.

You have my love and blessings, and I am more interested as time passes in you and your work. Keep up your courage and your desires will be fulfilled.

Your friend and brother,
Jesus

Incarnate soul by Jesus
February 15, 1920

I am here, Jesus.

I am here as I promised last night and will write on the subject of the incarnate soul.

You may have observed in your studies of the different theories of the creation of man that the question always has arisen as to the relationship of the spiritual and physical — that is, as to the soul and the material body. I know that many theories have been set forth as to how and when the soul became a part of the physical body and what was the means adopted by the laws of nature, as they are called, for the lodgment of the soul into that body, and the relationship that one bore to the other. Of course this applies only to those mortals who believe that there is a soul separate in its existence and functionings from the mere physical body. Now as to those who do not believe in the distinctive soul, I do not attempt to enlighten them but leave them to a realization of the fact that when they come into the spirit world, and find themselves existing without such a body, they will come into the consciousness that they are souls.

When the physical body is created it has no consciousness of its having been created, for it is merely of the unconscious creations that are of the other material creatures of nature. It does not feel or sense in any degree the fact, that it is a living thing dependent upon the proper nourishment from its mother for its growth and continued life in accordance with the laws of nature, and the objects of its own creation. The father and mother, being necessary to the creation or formation of this merely physical production, know only that in someway there has come into existence an embryo that may eventuate into a human being like unto themselves. If it were allowed to remain without a soul it would soon fail to fulfill the object of its creation and disintegrate into the elements of which it is formed, and humanity would cease to exist as inhabitants of the earth.

The physical part of man is really and only the result of the commingling of those forces that are contained in the two sexes, which according to the laws of nature, or of man's creation, are suited to produce the one body fitted for the home of the soul, to develop its individuality as a life. The result of this commingling is intended only as a temporary covering or protection for the growth of the real being, and does not in any way limit or influence the continuous existence of the soul. When its functions have ended, the soul, which has then become individualized, continues its life in new surroundings and in gradual progression, and the mere instrument used for its individualization is disseminated into the elements forming its appearance and substance. As this body was called from the elements for a certain purpose, when that purpose shall have been served, it returns to these elements.

This body, of itself, has neither consciousness nor sensation, and in the beginning has only the borrowed life of its parents, and when the soul finds its lodgment, it then has the life of the soul. The human life can exist only so long as the soul inhabits the body, and after such habitation commences, the borrowed life of the parents ceases to exercise any influence or directing force on the body. This, then, is the true description of the physical body, and if it were all of man, he would perish with its death and cease to exist as a part of the creation of the universe of God.

The soul is the vital, living and never dying part of man — it is really the man — and the only thing that was intended to continue an existence in the spirit world. It was made in the image of God, and there is no reason for its existing for the continuing companionship of the physical body. When men say or believe that the body is all of man, and when it dies man ceases to exist, they do not understand the relationship or functioning of soul and body, and know only the half truth which is visible to their senses, that the body dies and can never again be resuscitated. This is a determined fact and all arguments by analogy, to show that man must continue to live notwithstanding the death of that body, are not apposite and very inconclusive.

When the questions are asked, whence comes the soul, by whom created, how does it become incarnated in man and for what purpose, and what is its destiny?

First let me state, that man has nothing to do with the creation of the soul or its appearance in the flesh. His work is to provide a receptacle for its coming, a mere host as it were for its entry into the flesh, and existence as a mortal. His responsibility in this particular is very great, for man can destroy that receptacle, or care for it so that the soul may continue in its earth life a longer or shorter time. While this receptacle is the creation of man and without him it could not be brought into existence, yet the soul is no part of his creation and is independent of the body, and after the earth life, in the spirit world, it will cease to remember that it was ever connected with or dependent upon the creation of its parents. The soul, in the spirit life, as a truth, is so separated from and dissociated with that body which was its home while in the earth life that it looks upon it as a mere vision of the past and not a subject for its consideration.

As has been told you, the soul was created by God long before its appearance in the flesh, and it awaited incarnation for the purpose only of giving it an individuality, which it did not have in its preexistence, and in which it has a duplex personality — male and female — that is needed to be separated and made individual. We who have had this preexistence and incarnation in the flesh and have obtained this individuality, know the truth of what I have here stated.

There is a law of God controlling these things that renders these preexisting souls capable of knowing the desirability of incarnation and they are always anxious and ready for the opportunity to be born in the flesh and to assume the separate individuality that they are privileged to assume. As the receptacle is provided for their appearance, as it were, they become aware of the fact and take advantage of the opportunity to occupy the receptacle, and become ostensibly a human being with the necessary result of individuality.

I am glad that you are in a better condition and will continue the messages as I have been desiring to do so for some time. I shall be with you and help you in every way, and hope that you will keep up your faith and prayers to God.

Good night and God bless you.

Your brother and friend,
Jesus

The soul, what it is and what it is not
March 2, 1916

I am here, Jesus.

I come tonight to write my message on the soul, and will do so, if we can establish the necessary rapport.

Well, the subject is of vast importance, and difficult of explanation, for there is nothing on earth known to man, with which a comparison may be made, and generally men cannot understand truth, or the nature of things, except by comparison with what they already know to exist, and with whose qualities and characteristics they are acquainted. There is nothing in the material world that will afford a basis of comparison with the soul, and hence, it is difficult for men to comprehend the nature and qualities of the soul by the mere intellectual perceptions and reason. In order to understand the nature of this great creation of the soul men must have something of a spiritual development and the possession of what may be known as the soul perceptions. Only soul can understand soul, and the soul that seeks to comprehend the nature of itself, must be a live soul, with its faculties developed to a small degree, at least.

First, I will say, that the human soul is a creation of God and not an emanation from God, as a part of His Soul. When men speak and teach that the human soul is a part of the Oversoul, they teach what is not true. This soul is merely a creature of God, just as are the other parts of man, such as the intellect and the spirit body and the material body, and before its creation it had no existence. The soul has not existed from the beginning of eternity, if you can imagine that eternity ever had a beginning. I mean that there was a time when the human soul had no existence; and whether there will ever come a time when any human soul will cease to have an existence, I do not know, nor does any spirit, only God knows that fact. But this I do know, that whenever the human soul partakes of the Essence of God, and thereby becomes Divine itself, and the possessor of His Substance of Love, that soul realizes of a certainty that it is immortal, and can never again become less than immortal. As God is immortal, the soul that has been transformed into the Substance of God becomes immortal, and never again can the decree, "dying thou shalt die," be pronounced upon it.

As I said, there was a period in eternity when the human soul did not exist, and when it was created by God, it was made the highest and most perfect of all of God's creations. It was made in His image and was the only thing of all His creations that was made in His image, and the only part of man that was made in His image was the soul. The man and all his attributes and qualities, such as his intellect and spirit body and material body and appetites and passions, are merely appendages or means of manifestation given to that soul to be its companions while passing through its existence on earth, and also, qualifiedly, while living through eternity. I mean some of the appendages will accompany the soul in its existence in the spirit world, whether that existence be for all eternity or not.

Now this soul, great and wonderful as it is, was created in the mere image and likeness of God's Soul, and not of His Substance or Essence which is the Divine of the universe. The soul may cease to exist without any part of the Divine Nature or Substance of God being lessened or in any way affected; and hence, when men teach or believe that man, or the soul of man, is "divine," or has any of the qualities or Substance of the divine, such teaching and belief are erroneous, because man is only and merely the created man, in the mere likeness and no part of God or of His Substance and qualities.

While the soul of man is of the highest order of creation, and his attributes and qualities correspond, yet he is no more divine in essential constituents, than are the lower objects of creation each being a creation and not an emanation, of their Creator. It is true that the soul of man is of a higher order of creation than any other created thing, and is the only creation made in the image of God, and this creation of the soul took place long before the appearance of man on earth as a mortal. The soul prior to such appearance, had its existence in the spirit world as a sub-stantial conscious entity, although without visible form, and, I may say, individuality, but yet, having a distinct personality, so that it was differ-ent and distinct from every other soul. Its existence and presence could be sensed by every other soul that came in contact with it, and yet to the spirit vision of the other soul it was not visible and such is now the fact.

The spirit world is filled with these unincarnated souls, awaiting the time of their incarnation, and we spirits know of and sense their pres-ence, and yet with our spirit eyes we cannot see them, until they become dwellers in the human form and in the spirit body that inhabits that form, can we thus see the individual soul. The fact that I have just stat-ed, illustrates, in a way, the Being of God, in whose image these souls are created. We know and can sense the existence and presence of God, and yet, even with our spiritual eyes we cannot see Him; and only when we have our soul developed by the Divine Essence of His Love, can we perceive Him with our soul perceptions. You have not words in your language to convey the meaning of the soul perceptions, and nothing in created nature, of which you have knowledge of in which a comparison can be made. Yet it is a truth; for the vision of the soul perception to its possessor is just as real, and I may say, objective, as is the vision of the physical sight to the mortal.

It may be asked in considering this matter of the creation of the soul, were all souls that have been incarnated, or that are awaiting incarna-tion, created at the same time, or is that creation still going on? I do know that the spirit world contains many souls, such as I have described awaiting their temporary homes*, and the assumption of individuality in the human form. As to whether that creation has ended, and at some time the reproduction of men for the embodying of these souls, will cease, I do not know, and God has never revealed it to me, or to the oth-ers of His angels who are close to Him in His divinity. God has not revealed to me all the truths and the workings and objects of His cre-

*This reference is to the earth life.

474

ative laws, and neither has He given to me all power and wisdom and omniscience as some may find justification for believing in certain of the statements of the Bible (Matthew 28:18).

Now, as I was saying, the soul of man is the real man, while in the mortal existence and forever after in the spirit world. All other parts of man, such as the mind and body and spirit are mere attributes, which may be dissevered from him as the soul progresses in its development toward its destiny of either the perfect man or the divine angel. In the latter progression, men may not know it, but it is a truth, that the mind — that is the mind as known to humans — becomes, as it were, non existent; and this mind as some say, the carnal mind, becomes displaced and replaced by the mind of the transformed soul, which in Substance and quality is to a degree, the mind of the Deity, itself.

Many theologians and philosophers and metaphysicians believe and teach that the soul, spirit and mind are substantially one and the same thing, and that any one of them may be said to be the man — the ego, and that in the spirit world one or the other of these entities is that which persists and determines in its development or want of development the condition or state of man after death. But this conception of these parts of man are erroneous, for they each have a distinct and separate existence and functioning, whether man be a mortal or spirit.

The mind in its qualities and operations is very well known to man, because of its varied manifestations, and being that part of man which is more of the nature of the material, and has been the subject of greater research and study than has been the soul or the spirit. While men have, during all the centuries, speculated upon and attempted to define the soul and its qualities and attributes, yet to them it has been intransitive and impossible to comprehend by the intellect which is the only instrumentality that man generally possesses to search for the great truth of the soul. Hence, the question of what is the soul has never been satisfactorily or authoritatively answered, though to some of these searchers, when inspiration may have shed a faint light upon them, some glimpse of what the soul is, has come to them. Yet to most men who have sought to solve the problem, the soul and spirit and mind are substantially the same thing.

The soul, as concerning man is a thing of itself, alone, a substance real, though invisible to mortals, and the discerner and portrayer of men's moral and spiritual condition — never dying, so far as known, and the real ego of the man. In it are centered the love principle, the affections, the appetites and the passions, and possibilities of receiving and possessing and assimilating those things that will either elevate man to the state or condition of the divine angel or the perfect man, or lower him to the condition that fits him for the hells of darkness and suffering.

The soul is subject to the will of man, which is the greatest of all endowments that were bestowed upon him by his Maker at his creation, and it is the workings of that will either in thought or action, and in the soul's qualities of love and affection and appetites and passions that are influenced by the power of the will either for good or evil. The soul may lay dormant and stagnate, or it may be active and progress as its energies are ruled by the will for good or evil.

The soul's home is in the spirit body, whether that body is encased in the mortal or not, and it is never without such spirit body, which in appearance and composition is determined by the condition and state of the soul. Finally, the soul or its condition decides the destiny of man, as he continues in his existence in the spirit world; not a final destiny, because the condition of the soul is never fixed, and as this condition changes, man's destiny changes. Destiny is the thing of the moment, and finality is not known to the progress of the soul, until it becomes the perfect man and is then satisfied and seeks no higher progress.

In your common language and also in your theological and philosophical terms, mortals who have passed to the spirit life are said to be spirits, and in a certain sense this is true, but such spirits are not nebulous, unformed and invisible existences. They have a reality of substance, more real and enduring than has man as a mortal, and are in form and features visible and subject to touch and the object of the spiritual senses. So when men speak of soul, spirit and body, if they understood the truth of the terms, they would say, soul, spirit-body, and material-body.

Well, I have written enough for tonight, but sometime I will come and simplify this subject. So remember this, that man is a soul, and all manifestations, such as spirit, and spirit body are merely evidences of the existence of the soul — the real man.

I have been with you as I promised, and I know that God will bless you. So with my love and blessing, I will say good night.

Your brother and friend,

Jesus

The importance of cultivating the soul perceptions;
spiritual things cannot be perceived by the material mind
October 25, 1915

I am here, Jesus.

I have heard your discussion and am much pleased that you and your friend are progressing so rapidly in the knowledge of truth, and very soon you both will be surprised at the extent of knowledge of spiritual things and truths that will come to you.

No man, who on earth is given to only what you may call the material things, will be able when he becomes a spirit to understand the spiritual laws until he has gotten rid of the material mind, and the reasoning that comes from the powers which have been exercised only in the investigation of material things. You cannot perceive spiritual things with the material mind, neither can a man by reason of those powers of the mind which know only material things, be able to perceive the truths of the spirit. Hence the necessity for man cultivating the soul perceptions, which are greater and more comprehending than all the faculties of the material mind.

Mind, as usually understood by man, is undoubtedly a wonderful instrument in investigating and learning the laws of nature and the relation of cause and effect in the physical world, but such powers when applied to the things of the spirit, will not help much, but rather retard the progress of the soul's development of its faculties. The reasoning power given to man is the highest quality of the material mind and, when properly exercised, affords a very safe and satisfactory method of arriving at the truth. Yet such power when exercised in reference to things which are strangers to it, or having no acquaintance, with it, or having never been concerned in the investigation of the phenomena of their existence, cannot be depended upon to bring conclusions that will assure men of truth.

Laws are eternal and never change and are made by God to be applied to all the conditions and to all the relationships of the material world and of the spiritual world. But the laws that apply to the operations of the material world are not fitted to apply to the operations of the spiritual world. The man who understands the former and their application to material things is not able to apply these laws to the spiritual world and to spiritual things. A knowledge of the laws pertaining to the natural will not supply a knowledge of the laws pertaining to the spiritual.

Hence the great scientist who, when on earth, was able to discover and show the operation of the laws controlling material things, when he comes to the spiritual world and attempts to apply this knowledge to the things of the spirit, he will be wholly unable to do so, and will be as a babe in his ability to understand and draw deductions from the spiritual laws. So you see the necessity for man's becoming acquainted with these spiritual laws, if he expects to progress in things to which they apply.

The material laws may be learned by the operation of the senses that belong to and constitute the material mind, but the spiritual laws can only be learned by the exercise and application of the faculties of the soul. The soul is to the spiritual things of God what the mind is to the material things of God. The great mistake that men make and have made, is to attempt to learn these spiritual things with the powers of the material mind.

I write thus because I see that you and your friend desire to learn the nature and operations and workings of the spiritual things, and hence I want to impress upon you the necessity for exercising the soul perceptions which will come to you as your soul develops. These perceptions are just as real as are the five senses of the natural mind, though most men do not even know of their existence; and when once you have succeeded in understanding that they do exist and that you may be able to use them just as you use the faculties of the material mind, you will be able to progress in the development of these faculties or perceptions with as much success and certainty as does the great scientist or philosopher in the studies of the things to which he applies the faculties of his material mind. I hope that I have made plain what I intend to convey.

I will not write more tonight, but say, let your faith increase and pray more to God, and you will see open up to you a wonderful vista of knowledge of the truths of the spirit.

Your friend and brother,

Jesus

Faith and how it can be obtained
October 15, 1915

I am here, Jesus.

I came tonight to tell you that you are nearer the kingdom than you have been for a long time, and that if you pray to God in more earnestness you will soon realize the inflowing of the Divine Love, that will make you free indeed and fit you to enjoy that close communion with God that will enable you to forget all your worries and disappointments, and see with your soul perceptions the great truths which I and my followers may endeavor to teach you. I know, that at times, it seems difficult to grasp the full meaning of faith in God and His Love, but if you will earnestly seek, you will find that there will come to you such a belief in His wonderful Love and in the nearness of His presence, that you will be free from all doubt.

You have asked me, "What is faith?" and I will answer: Faith is that which when possessed in its real and true meaning makes the aspirations and longings of the soul a real, living existence; and one so certain and palpable that no doubt will arise as to its reality. Faith is not the belief that arises from the mere operation of the mind, but that which comes from the opening of the perceptions of the soul, and which enables its possessor to see God in all His beauty and Love. I do not mean that the possessor of this faith will actually see God in form or feature, but his soul perceptions will be in such condition that all the attributes of God will appear so plainly to him, that they will be as real as anything that he can see with his physical eyes. Such faith comes only with constant and earnest prayer, and the reception into the soul of the Divine Love.

No man can be said to have faith who has not this Divine Love. Of course, faith is a progressive quality, and increases as possession of this Divine Love increases, and is not dependent on anything else. Your prayers call from God a response that brings with it faith, and with this faith comes a knowledge of the existence of this Love in your own soul.

Many persons, I know, understand this faith to be a mere belief, but it is greater than belief, and is existing in its true sense only in the soul. Belief may arise from a conviction of the mind, but faith never can. Its place of being is in the soul, and no one can possess it unless his soul is awakened by the inflowing of this Divine Love.

When we pray to God to increase our faith it is a prayer for the increase of Divine Love. Faith is based on the possession of this Love, and without it there can be no faith, because it is impossible for the soul to exercise its function when Love is absent from it. Sometime, as you progress in these writings, you will be in soul condition to understand just what faith is, but until that time your faith will be limited by your possession of this Love.

Well, in my healing of the sick, and the blind and the others of earth who needed a cure, when I said: "as your faith so be it unto you" (Matthew 9:29), I meant that they must believe that God had the power to bring about the cure; I did not mean that if their minds merely had the belief that I might cure them, then they would be cured, for belief was not sufficient of itself, but faith was required.

Faith is not a thing that can be obtained by the mere exercise of the mind, but has to be sought for with the soul perceptions. I am with you in all my love and power, for I love you as I told you and desire that you shall become free and happy, so that you can do my work. With all my love and blessings I will say good night.

Your brother and friend,
Jesus

The conditions necessary for spiritual healing,
and why healing sometimes does not save a person
Dr. Samuels, November 28, 1955

I am here, Jesus.

I can see that you have a question about spiritual healing and want to know why there is the possibility of death taking place before such healing is accomplished on the part of spirits assigned to this task.

Healing can be effected as a result of rapport between the ailing person and the spirit healer; for when rapport has thus been established, the spirit can work directly upon the sick person without an intervening healer being required to accomplish the healing. The sick person, however, through faith and prayer, must lift himself above the earth plane and attain a spiritual condition on a level which is free of earth bound spirits, and make possible the contact between the spirit healer and the patient. In spiritual healing of this nature the patient actually raises himself to a spiritual plane higher than the one in which he lives, and comes into rapport with spirit healers. The Divine Love is not necessary for this healing, for many of these spiritual healers are devoid of it, although they are on a high moral and spiritual plane. However, it is difficult for them to contact mortals who have not been able because of lack of faith and prayers to rise out of their earth plane condition to establish the rapport with these spirit healers. This is accomplished through a soul operation and is not a mere mental operation that does not come from the heart.

Here again, the patient may be healed through a doctor or a healer whose state of soul is such that he can attract spirit healers, yet the mortal healer can do little or nothing unless the positive faith of the sick man has raised him above the earth condition that I have mentioned, so that the spirit healer can make rapport with him. When the rapport is made, the therapeutic forces and energies from the spirit world can operate through the mortal doctor or healer and by their transmitting these forces and energies through him into the ailing person can become the means by which the spirit healing is brought about. Spirit healing is actually a therapy or therapeutic treatment which is transmitted from the spirit healers to the patient and acts upon the diseased organs to restore them, but the transmittal is made possible only through faith, which acts as a conductor of these healing forces and energies.

Thus you see that faith in God that He will help and heal will not only set in motion these healing forces and energies of the spirit world, if God so wills it, but will put the patient into the condition which will allow these healers to do their work, either directly or through the intermediary of a mortal who by his own spiritual condition may attract them. Faith permits the healer and the sick person to make contact with the spiritual forces. That is why I was able to heal many sinners because of their faith in my healing powers, and not heal righteous persons who had no faith. He who has faith creates a condition whereby evil spirits — who intensify or cause the distress to persist — are separated from their control and contact with the patient, so that the spirit healers can make the rapport and operate. Those who have no faith, and who therefore die as a result of the delay, have died not because of any injustice or lack of mercy or loving kindness on the part of the Father, but because their own lack of faith in His ability to help and heal prevented Him from accomplishing the ministry which He so lovingly entrusted to His ministering angels.

The prayers and faith of a loved one for the sick person is very often of great benefit, for the sincere love on the part of a mortal not only attracts the spirit healers but enables the healing force to reach the sick person through the love which is communicated to the ailing person. It may sound strange to you, yet it is so, that often the best physician is he who in earnestness of love and sympathy and sorrow sends his prayers to the Father in faith that He will accomplish what man and medicine cannot do. Such rapport between spirits obedient to God's will and the prayerful soul is brought about so that the healing forces are transmitted through him to the sick person he loves. Here is a case of the development of the natural human love operating on a high plane to make spirit contact for healing purposes without the Divine Love. However with God's Love operating through man, as in my own case in Palestine when I healed, the healing is far more efficacious and rapid, and I was able to perform instantaneous healing. In a word, I wish to show that love and faith and prayer in earnestness of soul are realities which perform feats of healing that are impossible under conditions wherein cold intellect and earth plane conditions prevail.

Now the question arises, why does death occur to a loved one, in spite of prayers to the Father for His mercy? Well, the answer is that the healing process depends, aside from the spiritual forces which are engaged in the work, upon the condition of the organ or that part of the mortal body to be restored. An organ which when not under pathological attack is in good functioning order can be restored to its pristine health regardless of the pathological disturbance from which it may suffer. That is to say, a healthy organ when attacked by disease or by some condition causing a malfunctioning of the organ may be restored to normal use through the method of spiritual healing. But when an organ through normal use has reached a condition of weakness or malfunctioning because of that use, it simply means that the organ in question has reached a point in mortal living where it can no longer be restored to the condition of health that it no longer enjoys, and any effort on the part of spirit healers to restore that organ would be fruitless and without purpose.

To be sure, spiritual healing can delay death and restore organs to a state of previous health, but spiritual healing is powerless to provide the body with new organs in place of those which have through normal functioning ceased to function in a way to maintain bodily health. This is what one may describe as old age in the mortal world, which is a normal process for all, except that it may occur at different times with various individuals, depending upon many factors, which need not be discussed here. When this condition is reached it simply means that the person's time has come to relinquish his tired and worn out body and enter upon his new life in the spirit world. Again, I repeat that the spirits cannot rejuvenate an organ and restore that organ to a condition of health which it did not originally possess prior to the fatal onset of the disease due to degeneration and decay through normal use in mortal living.

I urge you and the Doctor, as well as all those who are sincerely and wholeheartedly interested in helping to save and cure a loved one or one's self, to obey the spiritual laws of soul reality and seek the Father and His mercy, His loving kindness, and greater than these, His very Essence and Nature in His Divine Love which He desires to pour out on whosoever craves it in earnest longing of soul. As this power was mine and that of my disciples when I was on earth, may it be yours for the sincere asking.

Pray again and again for the Father's Love and at-onement with Him.

Jesus of the Bible
and
Master of the celestial heavens

There are no devils and no satan considered as real persons or fallen angels
January 3, 1916

I am here, Jesus.

I am with you tonight to warn you against letting any doubt enter your mind or heart as to my actually writing to you, for I and none other are actually in communication with you.

The book that you read is a snare and a lie, for there are no angels who have become devils as the author of that book declares. Never were there any angels who through ambition or any other reason revolted against the power of the government of God, and thereby lost their estate as angels. Never was there any lucifer, and never were there any angels who were thrown from the battlements of heaven into hell, as it has been written (Isaiah 14:12) and there are no devils and no satan, considered as real persons and fallen angels.

The only spirits in the spirit world are those who at one time were mortals and who lived lives on earth, shorter or longer, and whenever angels are mentioned in the Bible, or rather in the New Testament in places which contain my sayings or those of the apostles, and I mean those sayings which were actually said, the word angel always refers to the spirit of some mortal who had passed the line between life and death as commonly understood.

I desire to tell you of these things at large very soon and to instruct you as to who were the angels of God that are supposed to have had an existence prior to the creation of man and of the world; and who the inhabitants of heaven were before the spirit of God entered into man and caused him to become a living soul as the Bible says (Genesis 2:7). But the time is not yet ripe for me to instruct you in these matters, because there are so many more important truths to be first taught to you, truths which are vital to man's salvation and happiness to those on earth and in the spirit world.

Now this you must believe, that no devils ever write you or in any manner manifest to or through any of the numerous mediums who are used to show the existence of the spirits of men in the spirit world. There are spirits of all kinds just as there are mortals of all kinds, having all the traits and characteristics of mortals, and some of these spirits may be justly called wicked or evil spirits, and even devils. However they are nothing more or less than spirits such as I describe.

I know that the belief of the majority of mankind is that there are such things as devils and that they are independent creations of God, made by Him to tempt and inflict all kind of trouble and unhappiness on mortals. And because of the great number of years that these beliefs have existed, and the fact that many of the churches still teach that such devils do exist, and are at all times trying to tempt and injure men, it is hard and will be difficult to induce men to believe that there are no such things as devils, which is the truth.

The Bible in many places speaks of my casting devils out of men, and of men being possessed of devils, and of the apostles casting out devils (Matthew 7:22), and of their not being able to cast out some of these devils, I tell you now that the Bible is all wrong in this regard. The writers and translators of the Bible never understood what the word devil, as used in these various instances, meant or was intended to mean. As I have told you, there was never any devil or devils in the sense mentioned and taught by the churches, and consequently, they never could have possessed mortals nor have been cast out of them.

However, it is true, that by the workings of the law of attraction, and the susceptibility of mortals to the influence of spirit powers, mortals may become obsessed by the spirits of evil — that is, the spirits of men who once lived on earth. This obsession may become so complete and powerful that the living mortal may lose all power to resist this influence of the evil spirits., and may be compelled to do things that the mortal will not desire to do, and to show all the evidence of a distorted mind, and present appearances of a lost will power, as well as of the ability to exercise the ordinary powers given him by his natural creation. In these instances referred to of casting out devils (Mark 9:38), wherever they occurred, and they did occur in some of the instances mentioned, the only devils that existed were the evil spirits who had possessed

485

these mortals.

This obsession exists today just as it did then, for the same laws are in operation now as were in existence then, and many a man is in a condition of evil life and disturbed mind from the obsession of these evil spirits. If there were any men of today in that condition of soul development and belief that my disciples were in, they could cast out these so-called devils just as the disciples cast them out in the days of the Bible.

Men do not have this faith, though there are many who have been blessed with the inflowing of the Holy Spirit; yet they have not the belief that such work as the disciples performed can be performed by them now. In fact most of them believe that it would be contrary to God's will to attempt to exercise such powers, and hence, they never attempt to do such work.

When men learn that in all ages God is the same, that His laws work the same way, that humanity is the same so far as the soul's possibilities are concerned, and that the faith which God made possible for man to attain to, may be possessed by him now just as it was possessed by my disciples; then they will attempt this work of beneficence and will succeed, and the sick will be healed and the devils cast out, the blind made to see, and the deaf to hear, and the so-called miracles will be performed as they were in my days on earth.

There is not and never was such a thing as a miracle in the sense of having an effect produced by a cause which was not the result of the ordinary workings of God's laws. These laws in their workings never vary, and when the same law is called into operation upon the same condition of facts the same results will always be produced. So, let a mortal have in his soul the same amount of God's Divine Love which the Bible writers meant or should have meant, when they spoke of being endowed by the Holy Ghost (Luke 11:13), and let him have the necessary faith, that when he prays to God, He will give him the power to exercise this Love in a sufficient degree to produce the desired results. Then he will try to exercise the power of casting out devils or healing, etc., and he will find that success will follow his efforts. God is the same at all times and under all circumstances, and only mortals vary in their conceptions and conditions.

So I say, there are no devils as independent creatures of God, in contradistinction to the spirits of men who once lived on earth, and you must believe that there are not. I tell you now, that the teachers of such false doctrines will have to pay the penalties for their false teachings when they come to the spirit world and see the result of these false teachings, and no relief will be granted until they have paid to the last farthing. To believe such doctrines entails results that are bad enough for any spirit to endure, but to teach others these beliefs and convince them of their truth, entails upon the teacher, whether he actually believes them or not, sufferings and the duration of sufferings of which men have no conception.

I will not write more tonight, but will, in closing, say that you have my love and blessings, and my promises that I will fulfill, so that you will realize your expectations and be in condition to perform the work that you have been selected to do.

Well, you let doubt come into your mind, and as a consequence, your soul does not respond, although, strange as it may seem, the Divine Love is there. When this mental doubt exists, it is as if it were a covering which prevents the existence of the Love in the soul to shine forth and produce the great feeling of happiness and joy which otherwise you might experience. The mental condition of the mortal undoubtedly has a great influence on the consciousness of the man as to his possession of this soul development and the Divine Love, and consequently, there will have to be this continuous fight as long as life lasts on earth, between the mental conditions and the soul's consciousness.

Now as the mental beliefs are brought into harmony with the soul's condition, more and more the fight will grow weaker and less frequent, and it is possible that it will cease altogether. The mental beliefs will become entirely and absolutely subordinated or rather absorbed in the soul's consciousness of its being possessed of the Divine Love of God.

So my dear brother, I will say good night.

Your brother and friend,
Jesus

The doctrine of reincarnation is without foundation, for it is
impossible for a soul with its spirit body to enter a physical body
Dr. Samuels, March 10, 1955

I am here, Jesus.

I am here again to write you about a subject that has created interest among you, the Doctor and others, and that is the article on reincarnation. In the Padgett messages, various communications dealt with the falsity and absurdity of this Oriental doctrine, which holds that the human soul can reincarnate from one fleshly body to others in succession over periods of time and that as a result the soul has an opportunity to lessen its desire to sin and thus finally achieve purification while in the flesh.

If you will examine the question a little more closely, you will see the impossibility of the soul in the spirit world to be reincarnated in the flesh for the reason that the soul, for this supposed phenomenon, would have to shed its spirit body in order to enter into a mortal body. Since the soul is encased in a spirit body which is physical in nature but not of a gross material of what mortals call the material world, and that spirit body, which is the envelope and protector of the soul, is that which gives the soul its individuality as a conscious entity and remains with the soul so long as the soul lives. In the spirit world no spirit body has ever been deprived of its soul, and no spirit body thus hypothetically divested of its soul has ever died or been disintegrated, or has disappeared from its habitat, except as it advances from one sphere to another while making progress.

As far as is known today by us in the spirit world, the spirit, that is to say, the soul and its spirit body, may live for all eternity, if God so requires it, even if it does not possess the consciousness of immortality through possession of Divine Love. As the soul cannot be taken from or torn from — or in any other way deprived of — its spirit body, once it has come to the spirit world, it would be equally impossible for the spirit body to enter the physical body of another human being. Only a soul without a spirit body can enter a physical body, and on the death of the body, the soul manifests its spirit body. The doctrine of reincarnation is therefore utterly without foundation, for it is impossible for a soul with its spirit body to enter a physical body to be born again in the flesh.

When a human being dies in the flesh, his soul has already achieved under ordinary circumstances the purpose of his creation, that is, individualization of that soul and the creation of his spirit body, which in size, shape, appearance and nature, is the complete creation without the envelope of flesh.

When the soul appears in the spirit world laden with the inharmonies of its earth life, it has the opportunity of eliminating these inharmonies and becoming a purified soul in the spirit world through the exercise of its will and moral force and repentance. It is therefore absolutely unnecessary for the soul to go back to the flesh for another chance to purify itself, for the loving and merciful Heavenly Father had already provided a plan that would enable the soul — the real man — to attain purification. Here God showed Himself to be more merciful than He might have been had He decreed successive trials in the flesh for the process of purification. For man while thus seeking to purify his soul, would at the same time have to contend with the sinful influence of the flesh, and his ultimate purification would thus indefinitely be delayed or perhaps never accomplished until the very end of time. Thus, you can see that God has shown His Love for His created children by providing a way for them to be purged of their sins, while being free of the baleful influences of the flesh, which would only hinder, and make more difficult, their tortuous progress toward purification.

As regards the sayings in the New Testament, the first thing is that I never had any thought of reincarnation when I asked my disciples, especially Peter, who do the people say I am (Matthew 16:13)? That question was formulated simply to have them state whether they considered me the Messiah, as some of them already did, although not in the spiritual sense or the exact understanding that I had brought immortality to earth in my soul.

When a child is born blind he did not sin, nor did its parents, but suffered blindness because of the physical defect in his mother, which prevented the perfect development of the fetus in her womb, and thus this defect has prevented the perfect manifestation of God's work of creation. This defect is one of many to which the imperfect world of the flesh is subject, and it is for this reason that purification of the soul while in the flesh would be a task of countless centuries, and a punishment worse than the most evil hells of the spirit world in its duration.

I will stop now and hope I have made myself clear on this subject.

Jesus of the Bible

Many of the ancient spirits are not in the celestial heavens
June 6, 1915

I am here, Jesus.

The sphere in which Saleeba lives is the one that your grandmother described as being the homes of the merely intellectual spirits. In these different spheres are many subspheres or planes, and the different races of humanity naturally congregate with those spirits of their own race. So that while this Egyptian may have lived in these different spheres, it does not follow that she lived in the same subspheres with the spirits of other races, and in all probability she did not. She is a very ancient spirit, but her age as compared with eternity — that which has passed as well as that to follow — is as a grain of sand on the seashore to all the rest of the sand.

She will tell you of the sphere in which she lives, but it will not be any different, or any greater than the ones your grandmother described. She has not progressed above the sixth, and cannot until she receives the Divine Love. So, as she describes these spheres to you, keep in mind the fact, that she has never gotten beyond the sixth. She may have passed through what seems to her to be many spheres, but all the various stages through which she passed constitute no more than the six lower spheres. She never was in the seventh or passed through it. So let your mind be settled on this point: no spirit who is without this Divine Love has ever gotten beyond the sixth sphere.

The ancient Bible patriarchs and prophets, such as Moses, Abraham, Elijah, and the others, never got beyond the sixth sphere until my coming, when they received the Divine Love, and the fact that they are ancient spirits does not necessarily imply that they are in a very high sphere now. Your grandmother, for instance, is in a much higher sphere than all of the ancients who have never received the Divine Love.

So the fact that a spirit is ancient, does not, of itself, mean that it is of a very high order of spirit. Many a spirit who passed over comparatively recently is as high in the sixth sphere as are these ancient ones. And many a spirit who came to the spirit world within a short time, your wife for instance, is in a higher sphere than many of these ancient ones who have been in the spirit life for centuries — yes, centuries upon centuries — and for the reason, that these ancients have only the mental development which can carry them into the sixth sphere only, while your wife has the soul development which has already carried her to the celestial spheres. So do not think that because a spirit who comes to you may be an ancient spirit, it may be in a high sphere, or can instruct you in those things which will lead you to God's kingdom, for it is not true.

An ancient spirit who came to you is now seeking this Love and she will receive it, and progress higher as she develops her soul, but she will never get higher than the sixth sphere until her soul development fits her for the higher spheres. The mere fact that she has the mental development which enabled her to progress to the sixth sphere will not help her in any degree to progress above it. As her soul develops, she will leave the sixth sphere and inhabit a sphere of soul education which is in unison with her development, and it may be only the third sphere, but this sphere will enable her to make more rapid progress than if she should remain in the sixth, because of the reasons that your grandmother portrayed in her message.

So do not be impressed with the thought that because a spirit is an ancient one, it can help you or instruct you in those things which pertain to your soul development. Of course, their mental qualities are developed to a high degree, and they can tell you many interesting things about the times in which they lived, and of their experiences in the spirit world; but these things, while interesting, do not help you to attain to the divine kingdom. As regards this soul knowledge, they may be mere babes, and totally devoid of all the things necessary for the soul development through Divine Love.

I have many things yet to write about, and as we write you will see that I am the true Jesus, and that my knowledge of God's kingdom is the greatest possessed by any spirit, be he ancient or modern. I wish that I could write to you every night, but under present earthly conditions I cannot, because it might interfere with your life on earth. As I have told you, very soon you will be in the condition where I will have your services all to myself and my work.

I will not write more tonight, but only say believe, and you will see the glories of God, and your own salvation and happiness.

Your friend and brother,
Jesus

On the love of man in contrast to the Divine Love
March 4, 1915

I am here, Jesus.

I want to write tonight on the love of man. This love is one that is not understood by humanity in its most important particular. I mean that this love is not one that is sufficient to give man the highest degree of happiness which he may obtain either in mortal life or in the life to come.

This love is of a nature that changes with the change in the ideas and desires of men, and has no stability that will serve to keep him constant in his affections. No man who has only this love can ever be in condition to say that he will continue to have this love for a longer time than the present; and when he thinks that his love can never change, or leave him, he is only giving thought to the wish. This love is one that may last for a long time, and sometimes it seems that it can never die or grow old; yet, in its very nature, it has not that constancy which insures its lasting longer than a moment of time. I do not mean to say anything disparaging of this natural love, for it is undoubtedly the greatest gift that God has bestowed upon mankind, and without it, men would be in a very unhappy condition. Yet, it is not the great Love of God which all men may receive, if they will only seek and strive to obtain it by prayer and faith.

This natural love is that which unites men and women while on earth, and enables them to approach nearer to a life of happiness than does any other human quality; but still it always has the danger accompanying it, that sometime, in someway, it may cease to exist.

The mother's love is the strongest of all loves given to mortals, and apparently it can never end or grow old, yet a time may come when that love will die or cease to retain all its vitality or beauty. I know it is said that love never dies; but that is not true as regards to this natural love; and no man can say that his love of today will remain his love of a few years hence.

Yet, there is a love that may be called the natural love that will last forever, providing these souls seek and obtain the Divine Love. This love is not two loves, but one and is the same love manifested in the two opposite sexes, and which is only complete when these two apparently independent souls live together in perfect unity. This is what is commonly called the love of soulmates, which is that essence of spiritual love which makes the happiness of the two spirits seemingly complete. Yet this love is not of a Divine Nature, but merely the highest type of the natural love. So, when men speak of the love of one mortal for his fellowman, it means merely the love which his human nature is capable of having and giving to another mortal.

I do not wish to be understood in any way as implying that this love is not a great boon and blessing to humanity, for it is, and without it there would not be the harmony that exists on earth; yet, at this time of war, hatred and anger seems to have taken its place in the hearts of many men who are now striving to kill and destroy. But this is only for a season; the war will cease and then men will realize, that only their love for one another can make the earth a happy and desirable place to live on.

Love, I know it is said, is the fulfilling of the law, but no man can thoroughly understand this until he knows what love is. I do not mean that in order to fulfill every law man must have the Divine Love, because there are laws that govern the divine existence, and laws that govern the human and merely spiritual existence; and the Love of the Divine is the fulfillment of the former laws, and the natural love is the fulfillment of the latter laws. So you see that only as men have the Love of the Divine can they fulfill the laws of the divine existence; and so, as they have the natural love only, they can fulfill the natural laws. But this natural love will not be able to make them one with God, as I have before written; and the utmost of its powers and functions is to give them that happiness which they will receive in living the life of a spirit or mortal unredeemed.

I will not say that man should not cultivate this love for his fellowman to the greatest possible degree, for he should; and if that should be the only kind of love that he may have, either on earth or in the spirit world, the more of it that he possesses the happier he will be, and the greater will be the happiness of his fellowman and fellow spirit. So when I said, when on earth, that men should love their God and love their fellow men as themselves (Matthew 22:37-39), I meant that they should do so with all the possibilities of whatever love they might possess. Yet, if men would only learn, as they can, that there is no necessity for them to have only the natural love, but that they can seek the greater Love, and obtain the correspondingly greater happiness, and immortality.

Men do not realize this, though, and seem to be satisfied with this natural love and the pleasures that ensue from its possession. I would not have them do anything that would lessen this love or shut their hearts to its influence, when it is pure and good; and yet, I cannot help trying to impress upon them the great desirability of having this higher Love in their souls.

I am a lover of all men, and I want them to feel the happiness of the inflowing of the Divine Love, and thereby learn what the Love of God means, and what they may have if they will only seek.

This love of the purely natural will not suffice for the temptations that beset men on earth; and, also, will not insure against temptations when they become spirits. I know this, and hence I say it with the positiveness and authority of one who knows.

As you are tired I must stop.

With all my blessings and love, I am your brother in spirit,
Jesus

What it means by "Christ may be in you,"
March 3, 1918

I am here, Jesus.

I desire tonight to write you in reference to the way in which, as the preacher advises, "Christ may be in you".

I know that it is almost universal among preachers of the orthodox church to teach their hearers that the way to salvation is to get Christ in them and thereby they will be enabled to come into unity with the Father, and cease to remain subject to the effects of sin and evil. Well, this teaching is the true foundation of salvation for the celestial heavens, provided it be understood by the preachers and the people what the true meaning of "Christ in you" is, and unless this meaning be comprehended, the fact that the preacher or people may believe that they have Christ in them will not work the results that they may suppose or desire.

Many, and I may say that most of these professing Christians, have ideas of what this expression means in order to become effective, that are not in accord with the true meaning of this condition of the soul. They believe that all that is necessary is to believe in Jesus as their saviour by his sacrifice and death and that in so believing they have Christ in them, and that nothing else is required. They have no conception of the distinction between Jesus the man, and Christ, the spirit of truth, or more correctly, the spirit that manifests the existence of the Divine Love in the soul.

Christ is not a man in the sense that he is Jesus the Son of the Father, but Christ is that part of Jesus, or rather quality that came to him after he fully received into his soul the Divine Love, and was transformed into the very Essence of the Father in His Love. Christ is thus, not a man but is the manifestation of this Love as bestowed upon Jesus and made part of his very existence. When men use the expression, having "Christ in you," if they could correctly understand the true purport of the same, they would know that it, the expression, means that the Divine Love of the Father is in their souls.

The indiscriminate use of the words, "Jesus and Christ," is the cause of much misunderstanding among these Christians as to a number of the sayings of the Bible. Jesus became the Christ because he was the first to receive into his soul this Divine Love and to manifest its existence, and this Christ principle is one that all men may possess, with the result that they will become at one with God in His Substance of Love and immortality. It would be impossible for Jesus, the man, to get into or become a part of any mortal, and it would be equally as impossible for Christ, as the man Jesus, even though perfect and free from sin, to become a part of anyone.

No, the meaning of having Christ in you is to have this Love of God in your soul, which can only be obtained through the workings of the Holy Spirit as the instrument of the Father in bringing this Love into the soul.

To many who hear the preacher's exhortations in this particular, the expression is only a mystery, which they accept merely intellectually, and feel that by such acceptance they have the possession of this Christ, which is the only evidence of the truth of God's Love.

Good night, your friend and brother,
Jesus

Jesus will never come as Prince Michael to establish his kingdom
August 13, 1916

I am here, Jesus.

I was with you tonight and heard the address of the preacher and the explanation of the cause of the great war that is now raging in Europe, and it was a very intelligent and truthful one and the real foundation of the war.

I will not come as Prince Michael, as the preacher said, to establish my kingdom on earth and take into me those whose names are written in the book and destroy those whose names are not therein written, for I have already come and am now in the world working to turn men's hearts to God and to teach them the way by which they may become at one with God and receive into their souls the Divine Love. In no other way will I ever come to men on earth for they will not need me as a visible king with the powers and armies of the spirit world in visible form to subdue the evil that exists. There will arise no satan to fight against me or my followers in the sense that the preacher teaches. Besides, the fact is that, I am already in the world fighting for the salvation of men, and there is no satan. The only devils are evil spirits who are trying to influence men to evil thoughts and actions, and are the spirits of men which still retain all their sins and wickedness, and the evil that exists in the hearts of men themselves.

How pitiable it is that the preacher and his followers believe that the spirits of men who have died the natural death are dead and resting in the grave or in oblivion, waiting for the great day of my appearance on earth, as they say, in order to come again into life and be called by me into my kingdom. How much they lose by such beliefs, and how great and surprising will be their awakening when they pass through the change called death.

There will be no Battle of Armageddon (Revelation 16:16), only as each man or the soul of each man, is now fighting the battle between sin and righteousness. This is the only battle that will ever be fought between the Prince of Peace and satan. Each soul must fight its own battle, and in that fight the powers of God, by His instruments, which never cease to work, will be used to help that soul overcome the great enemy, sin, which is of man's creation.

These teachings of the preacher do great harm to men in that they cause the individual man to believe, that I, as the Prince of Peace, will come in mighty power, and in one fell swoop will destroy evil and all who personify it, and thereby do the work which each individual man must do. I know that it will be very difficult to persuade the people of this sect that what they teach and what they conclude the Bible teaches is not true, but I hope that when my truths are brought to light and men have the opportunity to learn the truth, that many of them will halt in the security of their beliefs and attempt to understand these truths, as they must understand them, either in the mortal life or in the spirit world in order to enter the kingdom of God.

As to these prophecies of Daniel (Daniel 8:23-25), they have no application to the present condition of the world, and so far as they were written by him or by any other prophet, they related only to the times in which they were written. No man, inspired or not, and no spirit, had the omniscience to foretell these wonderful things that are now taking place in the world, and any attempts to apply these supposed prophecies to the happenings of the present day are without justification and the results of the imaginations of men that the occurrences fit the prophecies.

Peace will come, but not as the result of any Battle of Armageddon, or any other battle based upon the principles which the preacher applies to these prophecies. As I have said, this battle is going on all the time, and it is an individual fight between the sinful soul and the creatures of man's disobedience. So do not waste your time in reading or listening to these unreal and foundationless teachings of men who think that they have discovered the intentions of God with reference to the destiny of nations.

I will not write more tonight, but at sometime I may say more on this subject, though its only importance is that it attracts men's attention away from the truth and creates beliefs which do harm.

I am with you, as I told you, trying to help you and to show you the way to the New Birth which is yours and all others who will follow my instructions. I love you as a younger brother and will continue to bless you with my influence and prayers. So doubt not and pray to the Father and you will find the truth in greater fullness and receive corresponding happiness.

I will stop now, but soon I will come and write another message of truth.

Your brother and friend,
Jesus

The religion of the future will be a comprehensive and final one, founded on the truths that James Padgett is receiving
November 6, 1917

I am here, Jesus.

I have been with you part of the time as you were reading the different explanations of the various religions, and tried to direct your mind so that you might conceive the difference between the things taught in those teachings and what we are revealing to you. Many things that are set forth in those teachings that are mysteries and the results of speculation will be revealed to you in their true existence and meaning, so that all defects or desiderata that arise because of the insufficiency of these teachings will be corrected and supplied. I am glad that you read these sermons, for they demonstrate to you a number of truths that were known to the ancients but which fall far short of the truth. At those times there was no source from which our truths could come, either in the spirit world or in the mortal world, and hence humans could not become inspired as to the vital truths that we are revealing.

The men who appeared as reformers and gave forth the truths that were unknown to their fellow men were inspired by intelligent spirits of the spirit world, though that inspiration could not be greater or higher than the knowledge of the spirits by whom these men were inspired. What I say here applies not only to the prophets and teachers of Old Testament times, but to those of all the times and among all races preceding my coming to earth and making known the great truths which were revealed to me by the Father.

I noticed that some of these teachers and writers of essays at the great religious gathering attempted to speak of a future or world religion, and their claims were divergent and were based mostly on those foundations that will never support such a religion. They almost entirely based their concepts on principles of morality as understood by them, and the churches based their beliefs on the teachings of the New Testament, which in many and vital particulars are erroneous. Especially, the basic one that I am God the Son and that my vicarious atonement and sacrifice must be the touchstone of the future great and ultimate religion. Well, as their claims are not true it is certain that any religion based upon them cannot be true or lasting.

However, there will be a religion of the future and a comprehensive and final one, and it will be founded upon the truths which you are now receiving, for it will be inclusive of all the other religions, so far as the truths that they contain are concerned, with the addition of the greatest of all truths affecting mortals the New Birth and the transformation of the human soul into the "divine". Hence, you see the importance of our working more rapidly in our efforts to disclose and disseminate the truth.

I will come in a few nights and deliver another formal message. I will not write more now, but with my love and blessings will say, good night. I am with you as I promised and will continue to be.

Your brother and friend,
Jesus

The Hebrews were the way showers to God
Dr. Samuels, January 20, 1955

I am here, Jesus.

Once again, to continue my messages on the New Testament, which is to be purged of its errors, and the truth regarding my real teachings and meaning as the Messiah established. The first thing I wish to do tonight is to show the relationship between the Old Testament and how the guidance and revelation of the Father showed the way to my messiahship.

The Old Testament, as you know, is the book that reveals God as the Divinity that rules the universe and, in the narrower sense, the physical world of the earth and of man, not only as an individual Being but as the Arbiter between man and his fellow beings. This was the earliest revelation of God to man, through Abraham, to whom, through his spiritual condition, it was given to gain insight into the existence of the unseen God — the God of eternity in whose manifestations were the rules of conduct for man to follow in his relations with his neighbors.

Abraham perceived this spiritual presence made for him through divine messengers of the Father, and he showed his faith in the unseen spiritual Father by leaving his home and family relations to live his life in accordance with these new conceptions of God; for his people had not this condition of soul and could not understand his spiritual insight.

He was not called upon, as it is written in the Old Testament (Genesis 22:9), to show his faith in God by sacrificing his son, for this description was used by later writers concerning Abraham to show his faith at a period of civilization when faith in God was expressed by sacrifice, and, indeed, in his day and in much later times by various tribes and peoples of Asia Minor, and elsewhere, by sacrifice of human beings.

Abraham's supposed sacrifice, therefore, is simply a story to illustrate this faith in God, and here is where we have the beginnings of a knowledge of the Father in that area of the world. This is not to state that in no other lands were there manifestations of an understanding of the existence of God, if only through conviction in the truth revealed by God for the right conduct of man in his dealings with other men, for this is not so; and, in fact, earlier examples of this discovery of the attributes of God are to be found in other peoples than the Jews, and earlier in the point of time.

I wish to concentrate on the evolution of those principles of righteousness, mercy, justice and consideration that eventually found their culmination in the descent of the Divine Love to humankind through the Holy Spirit, as manifested first in me at the time of my appearance in Palestine. I may point out that the development of the concept of the Father through an understanding of His laws of conduct towards men was brought to a higher level through Moses, who led the Hebrew people out of slavery in Egypt; and this liberation was brought about through the knowledge that the Jewish people, as a result of their great sufferings and inheritance of God as a religious concept, were in a state in which they could be used as a whole people as witnesses of the existence of the unseen God. Thus, it was that they were led to freedom by Moses, and the law of righteousness of conduct and love for the unseen eternal God was given to them as law; not that the Hebrews were more virtuous as a people than others but they were simply chosen as a means of bringing to other people the knowledge of the Father, and this they were able to do to a certain extent, and only after many, many centuries.

Yet, instead of pushing their knowledge of things spiritual into the consciousness of other people, they had to fight to preserve their own religion and not to adopt the worship of pagan deities. In this they were not exempt from great errors and iniquities, for they failed to understand that real religion consisted in righteousness of conduct and not in the form of worship or in the exactitude of carrying out prescribed ceremonies.

Moses, as the lawgiver, gave to the Hebrews the way to the perfect natural man, and later I brought the way to the divine man. My mission was not a national one, although it would have been had it not been for the incomprehension and lack of spirituality on the part of the high priests who were only interested in politics and the formal side of religion. Whereas Moses's mission was national and was successful because he did not have the opposition of a materialistic and powerful group to contend with, only the ignorance and naivete of the people.

I am not interested in providing you with a summary of the history of the Jews, but instead, I would prefer to relate the doings of the prophets of Israel. They have contributed to the elevation of the spiritual concepts of the nation and gave the people and their leaders a deeper insight into the real nature of the Father. This is to be found in the prophet Nathan, who appears fearlessly before David the king to accuse him of murder and adultery in his relations with Bathsheba; and Elijah, or Elias, who braved the haughty Jezebel and showed the power provided especially for him by angel spirits to show the power of the unseen, eternal Father, in contest with the priests of Baal; and Amos, who came to the priests at Gilead to warn the Israelites to repent of their sins, mainly the sins of the rich and powerful who abused the poor and brought them to misery and slavery.

From these prophets, the people were able to understand that God wanted righteousness and mercy in dealing with other human beings, not only amongst their own people but for all people — including the stranger within their gates, for they, too, had been strangers and, indeed, slaves, in Egypt. The people were taught to trust in the one unseen and eternal God and to know Him through His attributes, which were the guides the Jews were to follow in their relations with others and in conducting all their affairs. The Jews were also given to understand that God was Ruler, not only of the Jews but of all human beings, and that punishment would be meted out for injustice in behavior as a result of inharmony against God, which would cause the operation of circumstances that would work against them.

I think I have written enough for tonight and I will come again to show how subsequent prophets revealed higher conceptions of God's goodness and mercy, and eventually led to a period in which a New Covenant would be made with Israel through a law higher than that of righteousness in conduct for human beings — the law of Divine Love, or Grace, as it is called by the Christian churches.

I will stop now, and I urge you and the Doctor to seek with all earnestness for the Divine Love through prayer. So with my blessings and love, I will say good night and sign myself your friend and elder brother.

Jesus of the Bible

With Jesus's coming, God revealed Himself as a God of Love
Dr. Samuels, March 17, 1955

I am here, Jesus.

I am glad to write you tonight, and as the Doctor has the impression that I want to write you about Jehovah, I will do so, for the subject is an extremely interesting one, for it embraces the concept of God as He is revealed to man in the Old Testament and as He is further revealed to humankind in the Gospels of the New Testament.

It may be surprising for man to learn that God is both Jehovah, or Yahweh, of the Jewish scriptures and, at the same time, the Heavenly Father to whom I referred in the New Testament; and this despite the fact that Yahweh is a God of wrath and vengeance, and the Heavenly Father is a God of Love and tenderness and mercy. Yet they are both the same unseen, true God, the Creator of humanity, who has always been One and the same and changeless, except that His Divine Love has been bestowed upon humanity with my coming. So you see that God has always been the same, with the exception that He gave to mankind His Love with my appearance on earth, and thus the entire concept of Him by man has been changed. For with my coming, He revealed Himself truly, in revealing His greatest attribute, His Love, which is also His Nature.

Jehovah, or Yahweh, revealed Himself first to Abraham, in the Near East, but not the first in the entire world, for the Orientals were really the first who had a perception of the true, unseen God. To Abraham and his seed, Yahweh appeared as a tribal God, a God who dealt more with the community than with the individual. The most important lesson that Abraham's seed, as Jews, had to learn for many centuries was that of remaining faithful to the true, unseen God, who then took on the proportions of Protector of the tribe, and later the nation. They were to understand that this faithfulness to God would bring about its rewards and conversely, that faithlessness to God and worship of images would entail communal suffering and defeats in warfare with pagan peoples and adverse conditions of nature.

While God never was a wrathful or a jealous, or vengeful, God, this was merely the concept which the Jews of the times formed of Him; and their ideas concerning Him were conditioned by their experiences and general views of the times to which they belonged. And finally, the concept was broadened to include the highest concept of God which was possible without the Divine Love, and that was the concept that Jehovah was a just God who wanted righteousness of conduct from His children as individuals. This concept gradually became more important than the others due to the influence of the prophets, who had a greater insight into the rich and the poor alike, and who were united as brothers in their worship of the true God.

Jehovah, as I have said, never was a wrathful God, as He was conceived to be by the children of Israel. The fact is that the sins committed by the ruling classes created conditions which inevitably worked themselves out into a corrupt people unable to withstand the invasions and ravages of invaders, not because the prophets learned this from God but because that line of conduct inevitably led to conditions that brought about disaster. This might be called a law, for conduct not in harmony with God's laws called forth conditions which prevented spiritual assistance for the people who practiced those inharmonies and transgressions. So that, just as the law of compensation works inexorably in the spirit world, there is a corresponding law in the material world which acts, though not quite with the same precision and exactness in the material world. At any rate, conduct in harmony with God's laws creates conditions favorable to spiritual help; and by this it means help from spirits called upon by God to render assistance to the people or to individuals.

So, you see that Jehovah to them was not a God of wrath or vengeance, as He was conceived to be, but neither was He a God of Love, for His Divine Love was not active, and the prophets who understood Him to be a just God came as close to an understanding of Him as He had revealed Himself to them, but Love was lacking, and the prophets could not sense a Love which was not in evidence. Yet, some of them did have an insight that God did have this Divine Love, which would someday be bestowed into the hearts of His children, and some thought of it as loving-kindness, or mercy, or tenderness, yet without really knowing it to be what it was because they could not experience it.

God revealed Himself to be a God of Love only with my attaining this Love, and it is in this way that the law of the Old Testament was superseded, or I should say better, fulfilled, by the Grace of the New Covenant, and by Grace I mean the Divine Love. The Divine Love, when possessed by a mortal, can create conditions that may to some extent overcome the deceitful influences of the flesh and enable beneficial spirits to help the possessors of the Divine Love. Though its effect is manifest, above all, in the spirit world, where sin is no longer active but is in the process of being eradicated, and in some cases this process is a long and tedious one and sin continues to exist as it did in the flesh. When I say sin is no longer active, I mean that no new sinful acts due to sinful soul conditions can be used by the law of compensation against the spirit, once that spirit has entered the spirit world.

God, or Jehovah, or Yahweh, or the Heavenly Father, is therefore the same, although the last-mentioned title shows a different relationship towards His children, for now it is one of Love and togetherness in the possession of His Divine Nature, whereas before the Divine Love was given, the relationship had not that warmth but was one of Ruler to His subjects. Yet, God was conceived by the Jews as a Being with a body like those of human beings, and there was no notion that He is a Soul and that His Nature is Divine Love, and that His attributes are those of wisdom and power and will, without end. Even today this concept of God is not well understood, and the fact that man's mind is finite and imperfect prevents a conception of who and what God is.

I think that I have written sufficiently on the subject of the relationship between Yahweh and the Heavenly Father, and I shall stop now and say good night, with all my love to you and the Doctor. Continue to pray for more and more of the Divine Love while it is still available, for it is the greatest thing in all the universe; and have faith that He is the Father and that He will not abandon you if you ask Him in earnestness and sincerity.

I shall sign myself,
Jesus of the Bible

God is not a father-mother God
Dr. Samuels, July 28, 1955

I am here, Jesus.

I am here tonight, and wish to thank you for the opportunity to write you once again. I realize that the Doctor has been anxious for you to receive a message regarding the concept of a father-mother God, for he is justifiably disturbed by the knowledge that such a view can cause considerable harm to an understanding of who and what God really is, and His relationship to His greatest creation, the human being.

The Nature of God, therefore, unlike the nature of the human soul, is not dual at all but One and indivisible. God, the Heavenly Father, created male and female souls for the purpose of providing for the happiness of His children spiritually, and also to provide a means by which, in the flesh, conception could take place through their physical union and receptacles engendered for the placement of other souls in human bodies.

When the soul leaves the human envelope and is eventually freed of the physical desires of the earth life, of which desire for the opposite sex constituted the most dominant characteristic for most men, then this material desire of the flesh disappears and only love which is spiritual and distinct from animal passion begins to assert itself; and there is no thought of the carnal.

In God, the attributes are all Divine, and His Love is Divine and devoid of anything related to sex or to family relationship, which is based on sexual functions in which various types of love are entering. There is nothing of the natural, and therefore pertaining to the human categories, in His Divine Nature. The souls that are filled with the Divine Love love other souls not because of their relationship to these other souls, such as father, mother, brother or sister, but because of the Divine Love which these souls possess; and the intensity of this Love is measured by the amount of Love it possesses in its own soul.

The Heavenly Father, with His infinite Divine Love, loves all His children, and whether His Love enters their souls and makes them at-one in Essence with Him depends upon their willingness to let it come into their souls through earnest longing and prayer.

I use the term Father when referring to God, to indicate the fact that I am at-one with Him in Nature through the possession of the Divine Love, and not because of any concept of maleness or masculinity. This also indicates the distinction between this kinship in Nature and the term servant of God, which was used by the Hebrews. For they knew instinctively that no matter how hard they tried, they could not acquire in any way any of the Essence of God, which would have permitted them to use this term Father in this sense.

So you see, when I call God the Heavenly Father, I used the term in the sense of relationship in Essence; and the term in its human meaning in connection with physical procreation is a mistaken and erroneous concept of God. God is the Heavenly Father and the Creator of the human soul, and no limit, such as a sexual idea, such as father-soul or mother-soul, in the natural meaning of the terms, can be in truth applied to God.

I know that you are tired, and I should like to write more on this subject but I shall stop and thank you, again, for permitting me to come and correct these impressions of God.

With my love to you and the Doctor, I shall say good night

Jesus of the Bible
and
Master of the celestial heavens

Who and what is God
May 25, 1917

I am here, Jesus.

I have been with you as you prayed. God's Love will always come to you when you pray as you have tonight, and His listening ear is always open to the earnest aspirations of His children who come to Him with the true longings of the soul. You have the secret of reaching God's Love, and on all occasions, when you feel that you need that Love or desire a nearness to God, use the secret and you will not be disappointed.

You are in better condition tonight in your soul development and perceptions and can receive my message which I have desired for some time to communicate, and which I was waiting only for you to be in a complete rapport with me. So, tonight, I will deliver my message, and I will take more complete possession of your brain and control of your hand.

Well, to begin, God is Soul, and Soul is God, not the soul that is in the created human, but the Soul that is Deity, self-existent, without beginning or ending, and whose Entity is the one great fact in the universe of being. God is without form, such as has been conceived of by man in nearly all the ages, and especially by those who believe in the Bible of the Hebrews as well as in that of the Christians. Nevertheless, God is of a form, which only the soul perceptions of a man which has arrived at a certain degree of development, that is taken on the Divine Nature of God and thus become a part of the Soul of God, can discern and realize the Entity of God. There is nothing in all nature with which men are acquainted or have knowledge of, that can be used to make a comparison, with this great Soul; and hence, for men to conceive of God as having a form in any manner resembling that of man, is erroneous; and those who, in their beliefs and teachings, deny the anthropomorphic God, are correct.

Nevertheless, God is of a form as to give him Substance and a seat of habitation, in contradistinction to that God which, in the teachings of some men, is said to be everywhere in the trees and rocks, and thunder and lightning, and in men and beasts, and in all created things, and in whom men are said to live and move and have their being. No, this concept of God is not in accord with the truth, and it is vital to the knowledge and salvation of men that such conception of God be not entertained or believed in. To believe that God is without form is to believe that he is a mere force or principle or nebulous power, and, as some say, the resultant of laws; which laws, as a fact, He has established for the controlling of His universe of creation, and which are expressed to men by these very powers and principles, to the extent that they can comprehend.

God is back of force and principle and law, which are the expressions of His Being, and without Him they could not exist; for they are only existences, changeable, dependent and subject to the will of God, who, is a Being. God then, is a Soul, and that Soul has its form, perceptible only to Itself, or that of man, which, by reason of the sufficient possession of the very Substance of the great Soul has become like unto God, not in image only, but in very Essence. We spirits of the highest soul progression are enabled by our soul perceptions to see God and His form. And here, I use the words "see" and "form," as being the only words that I can use to give mortals a comparative conception of what I am endeavoring to describe.

When it is recognized that mortals can scarcely conceive of the form of the spirit body of a man, which is composed or formed of the material of the universe, though not usually accepted to be of that material, it will be readily seen that it is hardly possible for me to convey to them even a faint idea even of the Soul form of God, which is composed of that which is purely spiritual, that is, not of the material, even though sublimated to the highest degree.

I am not able because of the limitations mentioned, to describe to men that form which they may glean a mere conception of, and as such this form can be seen only with the soul's eye, which eyes men do not possess. It must not be believed that because men cannot understand or perceive the truth of God's Soul form, therefore, it is not a truth. A truth, though not conceived or perceived by men, spirits or angels, is still a truth, and its existence does not depend upon its being known. If all the mortals of earth, and the spirits and angels of heaven, save one, could not perceive the existence of that truth, yet its existence perceived by that one proves its reality. The truth of God's Soul form, can be testified to by more than one of the celestial spirits of men who have passed from earth; and the possibility is before mortals of the present life, that in the great future, if their souls have become possessed of the Divine Substance of God's Love in sufficient abundance, they will be able to perceive God as I have attempted to explain.

The created soul of man has its form made in the image of God's Soul, yet man cannot see that form, although it is a fact and can be testified to by many in the spirit realms. And here it needs to be said, that when in our messages we speak of God as Being without form, we mean any such form as men have or think they have conceived of, and our expressions must not be considered as contradictory to what I have tried to explain as the form of God.

Well, in addition to a form, God has a personality, and this is expressed and made known to man by certain attributes, which to the consciousness of man is existent in the universe. To some philosophers and scientists and wise men these attributes are their impersonal God Himself, and to them the only God. They make the created, the Creator, not realizing that behind the expression must be the cause; and that greater than the attribute must be that from which the expression of the attribute is projected, or, as they better like to say, evolved.

I, who know, desire to say that these manifested attributes or forces and powers and principles and laws and expressions do not, all together, constitute or be that from which they flow or in which they have their source. God is Himself, alone. His attributes or expressions manifested to mortals or spirits, are the results or effects of the workings of His spirit, which spirit is the active energy of His Soul, Himself. Hence, the form of God is not distributed over the whole universe of creation where His attributes may be, because they are everywhere manifested.

No, as was said by Moses of old, and as was said by me when on earth: God is in His heavens, and although it may be surprising and startling for mortals to hear, God has His habitation, and God the Substance, the self-existing Soul form, has His locality, and men do not live and move and have their existence in God; but in His emanations and expressions and spirit they do.

As you are somewhat exhausted, I think this a good place to stop. I am pleased that you are in such good condition. So with my love and blessings, I will say, good night.

Your brother and friend,
Jesus

The difference between the spirit of God and the Holy Spirit
May 10, 1920

I am here, Jesus.

Let me write upon a subject that will be of interest to you and to those who may read my messages.

The Holy Spirit is that part of God's spirit that manifests His presence and care in conveying to men's souls His Divine Love. This Love is the highest and greatest and most holy of His possessions, and can be conveyed to men only by the Holy Spirit. This appellation is used in contradistinction to the mere spirit, which demonstrates to men the operation of God in other directions and for other purposes. His creative spirit, and His caring spirit and the spirit that makes effective His laws and designs in the governing of the universe, are not the Holy Spirit, though equally part of God, and equally necessary for the manifestations of His powers and the exercise of the energies of His Soul. These spirit of God deals with the things of the universe that do not have an interrelationship with the Soul of God and the souls of men, and whenever the Holy Spirit is spoken of it should mean only that part of God's spirit which transforms the souls of men into the Substance of the Soul of God in His quality of Love.

I heard the preacher discourse Sunday night on the work of the Holy Spirit as portrayed in the contents of the New Testament (Ephesians 4:30), and saw that his conclusions from these contents were wholly erroneous and apart from the truth. As he said, the effects of the workings of the Holy Spirit are shown in more ways than one, and not every one upon whom it is bestowed is filled with the same powers of displaying its presence and possession.

The preacher must know, that because men are possessed with powers to accomplish the mental or material things of their living, they are not necessarily possessed with the Holy Spirit. Much of the physical healing of mortals is caused by powers that are bestowed upon men that may not be connected with or proceed from the Holy Spirit. There is evidence of this, for men will recollect that the Old Testament is full of instances where men were healed of their diseases and other wonderful things performed at the time that the Holy Spirit was excluded from man's possession. Yet these marvels, as then considered, were performed by men claiming to be endowed with the spirit of God which is working for the good and happiness of humanity, and which will continue to work until men shall become in harmony with themselves as first created.

I understand the object of the preacher in attempting to show and convince his hearers, that because they have not those powers that the Bible describes as having been possessed by my disciples after the bestowal of the Holy Spirit (Acts 3:7-8), that therefore, they must not believe and conclude that they, his hearers, have not this blessing. His intentions and efforts were commendable, and arose from the desire that his hearers should not become disheartened and disappointed in their efforts to obtain the inflowing of the Divine Love that the Holy Spirit brings to men. But on the other hand, his teachings were dangerous and misleading to these hearers, for the natural consequence of such teaching is to lead men into the belief or persuasion that they possess this power, when they do not, and thus preventing them from seeking for an obtaining the Comforter in the only way in which it can be obtained.

The Holy Spirit primarily has nothing to do with great mental or physical achievements, and to say that because a man is a great inventor or philosopher or surgeon who does things without knowing where the inspiration or suggestion to do the things comes from, therefore he is possessed of the Holy Spirit, is all wrong and misleading.

All things have their existence and operation and growth in the spirit of God, and only in that spirit, which is evidenced in many and varied ways in men's experience. This spirit is the source of life and light and health and numerous other blessings that men possess and enjoy, the sinner as well as the saint, the poor man as well as the rich, the ignorant as well as the enlightened and educated: all are dependent on this spirit for their being and comfort. It is universal in its existence and workings, it is omnipresent, and may be acquired by all men in this sense to the degree that their mental receptivity permits. This further demonstrates the fact that God, through and by this spirit, is with men always, in the lowest hells as well as in the highest heavens of the perfect man. It is working continuously, ceaselessly and always at the call of men, be that call mental or spiritual. It is the thing that controls the universe of which man's earth is an infinitesimal part. This is the spirit of God.

Now the Holy Spirit is as distinctive as is the soul of man distinctive from all other creations of God. The Holy Spirit is that part of God's spirit that has to do with the relationship of God's Soul and man's soul, exclusively. The subject of its operation is the Divine Love and the object of its workings is the soul of man, and the great goal to be reached by its operations is the transforming of the soul of man into the Substance of the Father's Love, with immortality as a necessary accompaniment. This is the great miracle of the universe; and so high and sacred and merciful is the transformation, that we call that part of God's spirit that performs it, the Holy Spirit.

So let not teachers or preachers teach, or their hearers believe, that every part of God's spirit that operates upon the hearts and thoughts and feelings of man is the Holy Spirit, for it is not true. Its mission is the salvation of men in the sense of bringing them into harmony with God, and that the very souls of men will become a part in Substance and not in image only of the Soul of God, and without this working of the Holy Spirit men cannot come into such a union.

I will not write more now, but will come again and deliver another message. Believe that I love you.

Your friend and brother,
Jesus

The way to the kingdom of God in the celestial heavens
May 15, 1917

I am here, Jesus.

I come tonight and desire to write my message and hope that you may be able to receive it. I have described the way to the kingdom of God on earth and in the spirit world, and now I will describe the only way to the kingdom of God in the celestial heavens.

In all God's universe and creation of things material and spiritual, the only one of His creatures who can possibly have within him anything of a divine nature is he who possesses this Divine Love. The bestowal of this Love was intended, in its operation and effect, to transform man from the merely perfect man into the divine angel, and thus create a kingdom of God in the celestial spheres, where only that which is "divine" can enter and find a habitation. You must understand, that as it depends very largely upon man himself to establish the kingdom of God on earth or in the spiritual world, so it also depends largely on man to establish the kingdom in the celestial heavens, and if man had never received this Divine Love into his soul, there never would have been any such kingdom brought into existence.

There is now a kingdom in the celestial spheres, and it is not a finished one, for it is still open and in the process of formation. It is open to the entry of all spirits, and they must seek for it in the only way that God has provided, and no spirit will be excluded from it, who, with all the longings of his soul, will aspire to enter that kingdom. I must also state that the time will come when this celestial kingdom will be completed, and thereafter no man will be able to enter therein; for this Divine Love of God will again be withdrawn from man, as it was from the first parents, and the kingdom that will then be accessible to man will be the kingdom that will exist on earth, or that which now exists in the spirit world.

Now the Bible, which most of those professing to be Christians believe contains my sayings and teachings, has set forth the way to the celestial kingdom. The words are few and the way is plain, and no mystery prevents men from comprehending the meaning thereof. When I said, "Except a man be born again, he cannot enter into the kingdom of God," I disclosed the only and true way to this kingdom. During my time on earth there were some who understood this great truth, and since that time, there have been some who not only understood this truth, but found the way and followed it until they reached the goal and are now inhabitants of this kingdom; but the vast majority of men — priests, teachers and people — have never understood, and have never sought to find the way.

And so, all down the ages since the great kingdom has been waiting for men, they, though in all sincerity and with love towards God, have sought for and to a greater or lesser extent, found only the kingdom of the perfect man, and have neglected to seek for and missed the kingdom of the divine angel.

Then the only way to the celestial kingdom is simply this: that men shall believe with all the sincerity of their minds and souls that this great Love of the Father is waiting to be bestowed upon each and all of them, and that when they come to Him in faith and earnest aspirations, this Love will not be withholden from them. In addition to this belief, pray with all the earnestness and longings of their souls that He will open up their souls to the inflowing of this Love, and that then may come to them the Holy Spirit to bring this Love into their souls in such abundance that their souls may be transformed into the very Essence of the Father's Love.

The man who will thus believe and pray will never be disappointed, and the way to the kingdom will be his as certainly as the sun shines day

514

by day upon the just and the unjust alike. No mediator is needed, nor are the prayers or ceremonies of priests or preachers, for God comes to man, Himself, and hears his prayers and responds thereto by sending the Comforter, which is God's messenger for conveying into the souls of men this great Divine Love.

I have thus explained the only way to the celestial kingdom of God and to the Divine Nature in His Love; and there is no other way whereby it is possible to reach this kingdom and the certain knowledge of immortality. So, I implore men to meditate on these great truths, and in meditating believe, and when believing, pray to the Father for the inflowing into their souls of this Divine Love, and in doing so they will experience belief, faith, possession and ownership of that which can never be taken from them, not in all eternity.

I am a progressing spirit, and as I grew in Love and knowledge and wisdom when on earth, I am still growing in these qualities. When the Divine Love and mercy of the Father comes to me it comes with the assurance that never in all eternity will I cease to progress towards the very fountainhead of the attributes of the Father, the only God, the All in All.

I have finished and feel that you have received my messages as I intended, and I am pleased. I will not write more, and with my love and blessings, will say good night.

Your brother and friend,

Jesus

THE END OF THE NEW TESTAMENT OF SPIRITUALISM

INDEX

A

Aaron, 254-255
Abortion, 14
Abortionist, 87
Accretion, 464
Accusers, 444
Adam, 139, 242, 319, 328
Adultery, 444, 502
Agnostic, 50, 73, 165
Agnosticism, 336
Ahab, 269
Ahasuerus, 280
Air, 128, 364, 420, 422
Airships, 222
Aleyabis, 219
Allah, 107, 126
Allies, 105-107, 109, 131, 133
Almighty, 187, 256-257, 367
Alphaeus, 289-290, 459
Altar, 269
Amalekites, 257
Aman, 242, 246, 249-250
America, 98, 346
American, 91
Amon, 242, 247-250
Amos, 502
Amoulomol, 220
Anaxylabis, 231-232
Andrew, 327, 455
Animals, 90, 206, 252, 304, 361, 467
Anoint, 278
Anointed, 299, 439, 441
Anointing, 181, 287, 328
Anthropomorphic, 508
Apostle, 311, 319, 324, 377, 388, 396, 408, 448
Apple, 250
Arabia, 241
Ark, 134

Armageddon, 497-498
Armament, 106
Armies, 106-109, 496
Army, 113
Arrest, 279-280, 448-450, 456
Arrested, 261, 318, 448
Asia, 318, 500
Assyria, 228
Assyrian, 239
Assyrians, 229
Astrologers, 440
Astronomy, 193
Atheist, 73
Atlantian, 220-222
Atlantis, 220, 222
Atonement, 120, 388-389
Atmosphere, 52, 85, 286, 351, 363, 432
Atom, 468
Atoms, 191
Authorities, 442
Automobiles, 222

B

Baal, 269, 502
Bacon, 196, 199, 202, 204
Baptism, 179, 277, 439
Baptized, 277, 282, 457
Barnabas, 318
Barton, 86-87
Baruch, 185
Bathsheba, 502
Battle, 107, 131, 229, 497-498
Battles, 109, 119, 257
Beatitude, 76, 343
Beauharnais, 96
Bethesda, 444
Bethlehem, 436-437, 449, 451
Betray, 386-387
Betrayal, 280, 297, 387, 448-449
Betrayed, 295, 449
Betraying, 295-296
Bewildered, 113, 287, 291, 456
Bible, 68, 119, 138, 158, 170, 190, 223,

Virtues, 288
Virtuous, 217, 501
Vision, 136, 326, 335, 439, 471, 474
Visions, 6, 171, 383-384
Visit, 14, 27, 80, 93, 105-106, 398, 459
Visitation, 358
Visitations, 211
Voices, 78, 95, 272
Void, 75, 234, 464
Voyage, 90

W

Wanderers, 177
Wandering, 83-84, 169
Wanderings, 51, 212, 314
Wars, 421
Wash, 55, 392
Washed, 120, 389
Washington, 48, 112-113, 115
Waterloo, 106
Waters, 135, 421, 432
Waves, 321
Wayshower, 360
Wealth, 99, 166
Wedding, 418
Whitefield, 145-146, 148
Widows, 421
Wild, 121, 123
Wilderness, 276, 283
Wilhelm, 190, 193
Witch, 261
Wither, 445, 454
Withered, 321, 453
Witness, 265, 267, 451-452
Witnessed, 452
Wonderment, 81
Wonders, 79, 133, 237, 264, 321, 332
Worldly, 215, 260
Worlds, 143, 260, 304, 314, 420
Worshiper, 101, 276, 368
Worshippers, 118-119, 234, 253, 299, 382
Wrathful, 329, 391, 503-504

Y

Yahweh, 503, 505
Yoke, 462
Younger, 22, 136, 286, 448, 498
Youth, 217, 278, 285, 448-449

Z

Zealot, 287
Zealously, 299, 451
Zone, 348-349
Zoroaster, 219, 314

GLOSSARY

A

Agnostic - A person who holds the view that any ultimate reality (as God) is unknown and probably unknowable.

Almighty - A reference to God as having absolute power over all.

Alphaeus - An assumed name taken by Jesus's father Joseph to disguise his identity.

Amalekites - A member of an ancient nomadic people living south of Canaan.

Aman - The name of the first human man.

Amon - The name of the first human woman.

Angel - The spirit2 of a human that has been transformed into the divine; superior in beauty, power and intelligence.

Anthropomorphic - In reference to God as described or thought of as having a human form or human attributes.

Apostle - One of an authoritative New Testament group sent out to preach the gospel and made up especially of Christ's twelve original disciples and Paul.

Armageddon - The site or time of a final and conclusive battle between the forces of good and evil.

Atheist - One who denies the existence of God.

Atlantis - A fabled continent in the Atlantic that sank beneath the sea.

Automatic Writing - Writing produced without conscious intention as if of telepathic or mediumistic origin.

B

Baal - Any of numerous Canaanite and Phoenician local deities.

Baptism - A Christian sacrament marked by ritual use of water and admitting the recipient to the Christian community.

Barnabas - A companion of the apostle Paul on his first missionary journey.

Beatitude - Any of the declarations made in the Sermon on the Mount by Jesus.

Born Again - of, relating to, or being a usually Christian person who has made a renewed or confirmed commitment of faith especially after an intense religious experience.

Brahman - A Hindu of the highest caste traditionally assigned to the priesthood.

C

Canaan - An ancient region corresponding vaguely to later Palestine.

Canon - A regulation or dogma decreed by a church council.

Canonical - Conforming to a general rule or acceptable procedure.

Capernaum - A city of ancient Palestine on northwest shore of Sea of Galilee.

Catholic - Of, or relating to, or forming the ancient undivided Christian church.

Celestial - Of, or relating to, or suggesting heaven and divinity.

Celestials - Relating to the inhabitants of the heavenly realm.

Celestial Heavens or Spheres - The realm located immediately above the seven numbered spheres.

Cleophas - Another assumed name taken by Jesus's father to disguise his identity.

Comforter - God's Love that brings one solace.

Confucius - Chinese teacher and philosopher; became the most revered person in Chinese history; his teachings form the basis of Confucianism.

Corinthians - A native or resident of Corinth Greece.

Covenant - A formal, solemn, and binding agreement.

Creator - God who brings something new or original into being.

D

Damascus - Capital of Syria located in the southwestern part of the country, it has been called the "pearl of the East. This ancient city boasts great religious significance.

David - A Hebrew shepherd who became the second king of Israel in succession to Saul according to biblical accounts.

Decalogue - The ethical commandments of God given according to biblical accounts to Moses by voice and by writing on stone tablets on Mount Sinai.

Deity - The rank or essential nature of God. One exalted or revered as supremely good or powerful.

Dematerialize - To cause to become or appear to lose materiality.

Divine - Of, relating to, or proceeding directly from God.

Divine Love - The very substance or essence of God.

Discourse - A formal and orderly and usually extended expression of thought on a subject.

Discarnate - Of having no physical body.

Dogma - a doctrine or body of doctrines concerning faith or morals formally stated and authoritatively proclaimed by a church.

E

Earth Plane - The space in the spirit world that is between the earth and the first sphere.

Ecclesiastes - A book of wisdom literature in canonical Jewish and Christian Scripture

Ecclesiastical - Of or relating to a church especially as an established institution

Ego - The self the real person.

Enlightenment - A state of being freed from ignorance and misinformation.

Ephesians - A letter addressed to early Christians and included as a book in the New Testament.

Episcopalian - An adherent of the episcopal form of church government.

Esau - The elder son of Isaac and Rebecca who sold his birthright to his twin brother Jacob.

Esoteric - Designed for or understood by the specially initiated alone.

Ethereal - Lacking material substance marked by unusual delicacy or refinement.

Eternal - Having infinite duration relating to eternity seemingly endless.

Ethical - Involving or expressing moral approval or disapproval conforming to accepted standards of conduct.

Eucharist - A Christian sacrament in which consecrated bread and wine are consumed as memorials of Christ's death or as symbols for the realization of a spiritual union between Christ and communicant or as the body and blood of Christ.

Evangelizing - To preach the gospel.

F

Faith - A firm belief in something for which there is no proof especially in a system of religious beliefs.

Foreordained - To dispose or appoint in advance.

Fountainhead - The source of something that flows.

Free Will - Freedom of humans to make choices that are not determined by prior causes or by divine intervention.

G

Galilee - The northernmost region of ancient Palestine.

Gentile - A person of a non-Jewish nation or of non-Jewish faith.

Ghost - The soul of a dead person believed to be an inhabitant of the unseen world or to appear to the living in bodily likeness.

Goddess - A woman whose great charm or beauty arouses adoration.

Golgotha - The place outside ancient Jerusalem where Jesus was crucified.

Grace - A divine virtue coming from God given to humans for their regeneration or sanctification.

H

Harbinger - A person sent ahead who foretells what is to come.

Heathen - An unconverted member of a people or nation that does not acknowledge the God of the Bible.

Heaven - A realm of the spirit world of everlasting communion with God.

Hell - The lowest realm of the spirit world, a place where compensation takes place for wrongs done on the earth.

Holy Spirit - The energy from God that has to do exclusively with His relationship with His children.

Human Love - The love that every human being has endowed in their soul.

I

Iconoclastic - One who attacks settled beliefs or institutions.

Immortal - the quality or state of being whereby one is guaranteed to exist as long as God exists.

Incarnate - Invested with bodily and especially human nature and form.

Individualize - Being an individual or existing as an indivisible whole, existing as a distinct entity.

Infinite - Immeasurably or inconceivably great or extensive.

Instantaneous - Occurring, or acting without any perceptible duration of time.

Instinct - A natural or inherent aptitude, impulse, or capacity.

Intellect - The power of thought and reason as distinguished from the power to feel and to will, the capacity for knowledge.

Interpolated - To alter or corrupt (as a text) by inserting new or foreign matter.

J

Jehovah - Judeo-Christian name for God, derived from Yahweh.

Joppa - Ancient city in western Israel.

Josephus - Jewish historian; under patronage of emperors Vespasian, Titus, and Domitian.

K

Karma - In Indian philosophy, the influence of an individual's past actions on future lives, or incarnations.

Kingdom - The spiritual realm created at the time of Jesus's birth.

L

Lazarus - Friend of Jesus and brother to Mary and Martha, who was healed by Jesus.

Lucifer - Used as a name of the devil.

M

Malefactor - one who commits an offense against the law.

Manifest - Readily perceived by the senses and especially by the sight.

Martyr - A person who voluntarily suffers death as the penalty of witnessing to and refusing to renounce a religion.

Materialization - To come into existence especially suddenly.

Medium - An individual held to be a channel of communication between the earthly world and a world of spirits.

Mediumship - The capacity, function, or profession of a spiritualistic medium.

Messenger - One who bears a message.

Messiah - The king and deliverer of the Jews.

Metaphysical - Of or relating to the

transcendent or to a reality beyond what is perceptible to the senses.

Millennium - The thousand year period during which holiness is to prevail and Christ is to reign on earth.

Miraculous - The suggesting of a miracle.

Mortal - Relating to a human of the earth.

Mystical - Having a spiritual meaning or reality that is neither apparent to the senses nor obvious to the intelligence.

Mysticism - The belief that direct knowledge of God, spiritual truth, or ultimate reality can be attained through subjective experience (as intuition or insight).

Myth - A person or thing having only an imaginary or unverifiable existence

Mythical - Existing only in the imagination.

N

Natural Love - The same as human love.

New Birth - The flowing into the soul of the Divine Love of God, so that soul becomes, as it were, a part of God in His divinity.

New Covenant - An agreement between God and the people of Israel, higher than that of righteousness in conduct brought by Moses, but the Love and Grace of God for His children.

Nirvana - A state of utmost bliss.

O

Obsession - An obsessive compulsive disorder that can be caused by spirit influence.

Occult - Matters regarded as involving the action or influence of supernatural or supernormal powers or some secret knowledge of them.

Omnipotent - Having virtually unlimited authority or influence.

Omnipresent - present in all places at all times

Omniscience - Having infinite awareness, understanding, insight complete knowledge.

Oracle - A person (as a priestess of ancient Greece) through whom a deity is believed to speak

Oversoul - The absolute reality and basis of all existences conceived as a spiritual being, God.

P

Patriarch - One of the scriptural fathers of the human race or of the Hebrew people.

Pentecost - A Christian feast on the seventh Sunday after Easter commemorating the descent of the Holy Spirit on the apostles.

Pharisees - A member of a Jewish sect of the intertestamental period noted for strict observance of rites and ceremonies of the written law and for insistence on the validity of their own oral traditions concerning the law.

Phenomenon - An object or aspect known through the senses rather than by thought or intuition

Philosophy - A discipline comprising as its core logic, aesthetics, ethics, metaphysics, and epistemology.

Pious - Marked by or showing reverence for deity and devotion to divine worship.

Prophecy - A prediction of something to come.

Psalms - Book of the Old Testament composed of sacred songs, or of sacred poems meant to be sung.

Psychic - Lying outside the sphere of physical science or knowledge, immaterial, or spiritual in origin.

Psychology - The science of mind and behavior.

R

Rebirth - Spiritual regeneration.

Redeemer - Jesus whose life, death, and resurrection is the basis of the Christian message of salvation.

Reincarnation - The belief in the rebirth of the soul in one or more successive existences.

Resurrection - The rising of Christ from the dead.

an act of revealing or communicating divine truth b : something that is revealed by God to humans
Revelations - An apocalyptic writing addressed to early Christians of Asia Minor and included as a book in the New Testament.

S

Sacrament - A Christian rite (as baptism) that is believed to have been ordained by Christ and that is held to be a means of divine grace or to be a sign or symbol of a spiritual reality.

Sadducees - A member of a Jewish party of the intertestamental period consisting of a traditional ruling class of priests and rejecting doctrines not in the law (as resurrection, retribution in a future life, and the existence of angels).

Saint - One officially recognized especially through canonization as preeminent for holiness.

Sanhedrin - The supreme council and tribunal of the Jews during postexilic times headed by a high priest and having religious, civil, and criminal jurisdiction.

Seance - A spiritualist meeting to receive spirit communications.

Seer - A person credited with extraordinary moral and spiritual insight.

Sepulcher - A place of burial.

Silver Cord - An etheric cord that connects the soul with the central nervous system of the physical body.

Soulmate - A person who is one half of a single soul.

Soul Perceptions - Senses that are beyond the five physical senses that allows a soul to perceive things of the spiritual.

Soul Spheres - Spheres three, five and seven, whose inhabitants are progressing by the means of receiving

God's Divine Love into their souls.

Soul Substance - In reference to the Divine Love.

Spheres - The seven levels of spirit habitation surrounding the earth. They co-exist with what we call the earth's atmosphere and beyond into outer space. They range from darkness nearest the earth to light in the spiritual heavens..

Spirit 1 - The animating or vital energy that gives life to physical organisms.

Spirit 2 - In reference to a human soul that has passed into the spirit world and his physical body has been replaced with a spirit body for his existence in the spiritual world.

Spirit Body - The active energy of the soul which gives a spirit2 its appearance.

Spiritualism - A religion based upon the continuity of life after physical death and the communication between spirits and mortals.

Spiritualist - A person who subscribes to the principles of Spiritualism.

Spirituality - Relating to, consisting of, or affecting that which is not corporeal.

Spiritual Healing - The healing of a person through the means of conveying spiritual energy from the spirit world.

Spiritual Spheres - Spheres two, four, and six, whereby spirits are progressing through either the purification of their human love or the development of their intellect.

Spirit World - An invisible universe that co-exists with the physical universe at a higher vibration.

Subconscious - Existing in the mind but not immediately available to consciousness.

Sublimated - To pass directly from the solid to the vapor state.

Subspheres - Spheres one through six each have seven planes of habitation or subspheres.

Supernatural - Of or relating to an order of existence beyond the visible observable universe.

Superstition - A belief or practice resulting from ignorance, fear of the unknown, trust in magic or chance, or a false conception of causation.

T

Talmud - The authoritative body of Jewish tradition comprising the Mishnah and Gemara.

Theological - The study of religious faith, practice, and experience; especially the study of God and of God's relation to the world.

Theosophy - The teachings of a modern movement originating in the U.S. in 1875 and following chiefly Buddhist and Brahmanic theories especially of pantheistic evolution and reincarnation.

Thessalonians - The inhabitants of ancient Thessalonica, or either of two letters written by St. Paul to the Christians of Thessalonica and included as books in the New

Testament.

Transcendent - Extending or lying beyond the limits of ordinary experience and knowledge.

Transfiguration - a change in form or appearance; observed as a Christian feast in commemoration of the transfiguration of Christ on a mountaintop in the presence of three disciples

Transubstantiation - to change into another substance; the miraculous change by which according to Roman Catholic and Eastern Orthodox dogma the eucharistic elements at their consecration become the body and blood of Christ while keeping only the appearances of bread and wine.

Tripartite - Composed of three corresponding parts or copies.

U

Universalist - The principles and practices of a liberal Christian denomination founded in the 18th century originally to uphold belief in universal salvation and now united with Unitarianism.

Universe - The whole body of things and phenomena observed or postulated.

V

Vacuum - A space absolutely devoid of matter.

Variegated - To diversify in external appearance especially with different colors.

Visions - Something seen in a dream, trance, or ecstasy; especially; a supernatural appearance that conveys a revelation.

Visitation -In reference to the appearance of a supernatural being.

Void - Being without content or occupant.

W

Wayshower - A person who shows other the way to spiritual enlightenment.

Y

Yahweh - The God of the Israelites, his name being revealed to Moses as four Hebrew consonants (YHWH) called the tetragrammaton.

Z

Zealot - A member of a fanatical sect arising in Judea during the first century A.D. who militantly opposed the Roman domination of Palestine.

Zoroaster - The founder of Zoroastrianism; reputed author of the GAthAs, oldest and holiest part of the Avesta.

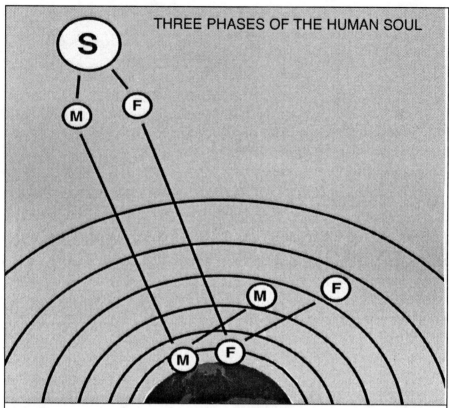

THREE PHASES OF THE HUMAN SOUL

PHASE I

The human soul is made of a high vibrational substance that exists high up in the spirit world. Just prior to incarnation the soul splits into its male and the female components - these are soulmates. God's purpose of soulmates is for the complete and eternal happiness of His children.

PHASE II

When a suitable receptacle (fetus) is made by a man and a woman God sends a soul to inhabit it of the correct gender. This is regardless of the conditions that soul may be subject, due to the position that its parents occupy in the material world.

PHASE III

When the physical body dies there is a breaking of the silver cord, and by the laws of attraction and compensation the soul is draw to a level that is comparable with its condition and vibration. It is at this time the spirit experiences a life recall, its purpose is so that the new spirit will realize the reason for the position that it occupies in the spirit world.

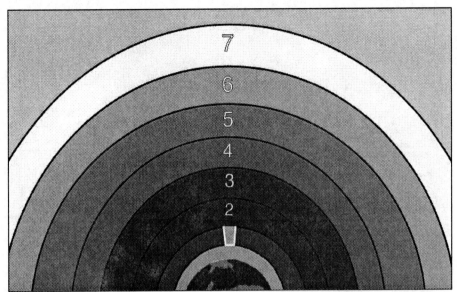

SEVEN SPHERES OF THE SPIRIT WORLD

The spirit world is comprised of seven numbered spheres. They are called spheres because they completely encompass the earth which is a globe. The vibration and the amount of light the spheres contain increases the farther the sphere is from the earth.

The spirit world co-exists with the earth's atmosphere and outer space only at a higher vibration. The first six spheres have seven planes or degrees of habitation in each. There is a place in the spirit world that is comparable to the vibration and condition of every mortal on the earth, as well as, every spirit in the spirit world. The lines of demarcation between the planes are solid and the spirit cannot pass above until its vibration is comparable.

The spirit world is a very busy place, each year some 52 million people go there - that is 142,000 per day. There are people who are convinced that what you believe your destiny to be after death is what you will get. I say different, that God the creator of the human soul has specific laws that govern the soul's position and its privileges in the afterlife.

Notice the gray area closest the earth this is the buffer zone, spirits do not live there they use it for their visitations to the earth plane. The tunnel which connects the buffer zone with the second sphere is to insulate the new spirit from seeing the penalties being paid by the inhabitants of the first sphere. The penalties are equal to the crime, thus the tunnel is God's design to spare the new spirit from seeing this torment on the way to its lovely spirit home.

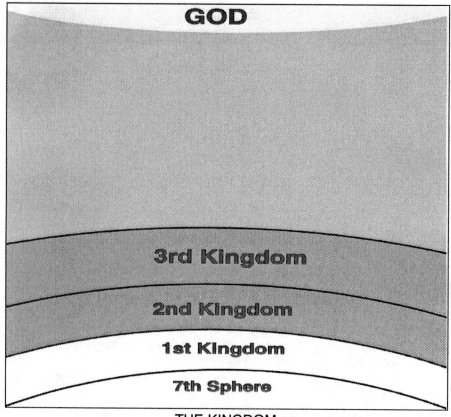

GOD

3rd Kingdom

2nd Kingdom

1st Kingdom

7th Sphere

THE KINGDOM

Directly above the 7th sphere is the kingdom. The kingdom has three numbered spheres and then it just goes on to God. The kingdom is clearly the central theme of Jesus's ministry while on earth, for it is mentioned in the New Testament 163 times. Two examples are: repent ye for the kingdom of heaven is at hand and seek ye first the kingdom of God and all shall be added unto you. The kingdom is a new realm, it is just over 2000 years old and was created by God when Jesus was born. It is not completed but is still under construction. However, it is not being built with bricks and mortar, but with the soul's of God's children transformed into Divine Angels. When the kingdom is completed it will close for a time and then all the suffering of both worlds will cease for all eternity. It will be as if the City of God has been lowered to the earth.

God is at the end of the spirit world, you might say He is its ceiling. This is so, because the spiritual light comes from above and God is the source of the light.

GOD

SPIRIT OF GOD

God is a Soul, not the soul that is the created human, but the Soul that is Deity. From God's Soul there emanates two very distinct rays of light that affects mortals and spirits alike. The spirit of God blankets the entire universe that God governs. In this spirit we live and move and have our being. This spirit is the glue of the universe, and is how God makes matter conform to His will when He creates, and is how He sustains the systems that he has put into place to maintain the harmony of the universe. God's attributes are manifested everywhere by this spirit, and it is this spirit which makes Him all knowing and everywhere present. For in a sense this spirit reports back to God everything that is taking place in the universe.

GOD

DIVINE OR HOLY SPIRIT

The Divine Spirit which is God's other spirit has nothing to do with the governing of the physical universe, it has to do exclusively with God's relationship with His children. This ray of light carries in it God's Divine Qualities of power, wisdom, goodness, justice, mercy, and Love. Once implanted in the human soul that soul becomes divine itself. It may lie dormant for a time, but can be awakened by the exercise of the will. It usually comes on an individual, but it can also come to a group as in the case of the Pentecost of the New Testament. Divine Love can never be removed for it has been earned. No human can give their Divine Love to another, it can be expressed and felt, but only God can bestow Divine Love on the human soul.

THE TWO LOVES

HUMAN LOVE		DIVINE LOVE
ENDOWED	←——→	BESTOWED
IMAGE & LIKENESS	←——→	SUBSTANCE & ESSENCE
PURIFICATION	←——→	TRANSFORMATION
BELIEF OF MIND	←——→	FAITH OF THE SOUL
KNOWLEDGE	←——→	WISDOM
HAPPINESS	←——→	JOYOUS FULFILLMENT
LIMITED PROGRESS	←——→	UNLIMITED PROGRESS
ENLIGHTENMENT	←——→	THE CHRIST PRINCIPLE
ETERNAL LIFE	←——→	IMMORTAL LIFE

In the universe of being there are two very wonderful and distinct loves. The human or natural love is endowed in the soul, it need not be prayed for or acquired. Although, it is not in its original pristine condition and needs to be purified through good thoughts and deeds. Divine Love is not self generated from within, it bestowed by God from without. Divine Love affords the soul the greatest benefits and happiness. It is greater than enlightenment for it is the Christ Principle. The difference between eternal life of the natural love and immortal life of the Divine Love is that all souls are eternal, and will in all likelihood exist forever, but with immortal life the soul is guaranteed to exist as long as God exists.

PSYCHIC INFLUENCES IN THE BIBLE

Compiled by Austin D. Wallace 1951

Apports

Numbers 11:31, 17:8
Psalms 78:24
Ezekiel 2:9

Casting Out Spirits

I Samuel 16:23
Matthew 8:16
Mark 5:8
Acts 5:16, 8:7, 16:18, 19:12

Clairaudience

Ezekiel 13:13

Clairvoyance

Genesis 15:1
Exodus 24:10
II Kings 6:12
Jeremiah 1:11, 1:13
Ezekiel 8:3
Daniel 2:19, 3:25
John 21:6
Acts 9:10 9:12, 16:9

Dreams

Genesis 28:12, 31:11, 31:24, 37:5, 37:9
Samuel 28:15
Job 33:15
Matthew 1:20, 2:13, 27:19

Fire Manifestations

Genesis 19:24
Exodus 3:2, 14:24
Judges 15:14
Daniel 3:22
Acts 2:3, 7:30

Gift of Healing

Matthew 10:8
Luke 9:2, 10:9
I Corinthians 12:9, 12:28

Healings

I Kings 17:22
II Kings 4:35, 5:14
Matthew 8:13, 12:13
Luke 5:17, 9:11, 17:14
John 5:8-9
Acts 3:7-8, 9:18,14:10, 28:8-9

Holy Spirit

Joel 2:28
Acts 2:4, 2:17, 4:31, 9:17

Independent Spirit Voice

Genesis 21:17, 22:11, 22:15
Exodus 19:3, 20:1
Judges 2:1 13:3
I Samuel 3:4, 9:15
I Kings 19:5
Job 4:12
Ezekiel 1:24, 1:25, 1:28 , 13:13
Matthew 17.5
John 12: 28-30
Acts 7:31, 9:7, 11:7-9

Independent Writing

Exodus 24:12, 31:18, 34:1
Deuteronomy 9:10
II Chronicles 21:12
Daniel 5:5

Inspirational Speaking

Mark 13:12

Levitation

I Kings 18:12

Ministering of Angels

Genesis 21:7 32:1, 32:24
Joshua 5:13-14
I Kings 19:5-7
Luke 1:26, 2:9, 2:13, 4:10
Acts 5:19, 8:26 , 12:7

Names of Controls

Genesis 32:29
Judges 13:17
Job 26:4
Mark 5:9

Physical Phenomena

Genesis 30:30
Exodus 4:3
Judges 6:40
I Kings 19:5-7, 19:11-12
II Kings 3:15
Matthew 8:26
Acts 12:7

Prophesy

Exodus 4:17
I Samuel 10:6
Ezekiel 14:13
Luke 1:67-68

Seances

John 20:19
Acts 2:1-4

Spirit Guidance

Exodus 4:15-16
Acts 11:12
Galatians 2:2

Spirit Light

Genesis 15:17
Exodus 34:29
Ezekiel 1:28
Acts 9:3

Spirit Manifestation

Genesis 3:8, 18:1, 19:1
I Samuel 28:13-14
II Kings 3:15
Ezekiel 2:2
Luke 1:11
John 21:4, 21:14

Spirit Materialization

I Kings 19:6
Luke 25:15-16
Acts 26:16

Spirit Power

Daniel 6:22
Matthew 28:2
Acts 5:19

Spiritual Gifts

Daniel 2:26
John 14:26
Acts 2:17
Luke 10:19-20
I Corinthians 12:1,4

Tongues

I Corinthians 14:18

Trance

Genesis 15:12
Numbers 24:4
Daniel 8:18, 10:9
Acts 10:10, 22:17

Trumpet Mediumship

Revelations 1:10 , 4:1

BOOK LIST

The New Testament of Spiritualism is a work that contains a selection of messages from the original published books received by both mediums, Mr. James Padgett and Dr. Daniel Samuels. The New Testament of Spiritualism contains many of the most profound messages, however, it by no means contains all the material that was received. The six original books below contain many more informative and interesting messages. If you would like to continue reading you may order the following books.

The following four volumes constitute the complete original
published works of James E. Padgett.

1. *Volume I* - Published 1940, paperback 383 pgs, contains 102 messages.
    This first volume has an extensive introduction by its publisher, Dr. Leslie R. Stone. He reflects on the circumstances surrounding his friendship with the medium, and as witness during his writing sessions. This volume contains the largest and most powerful of the messages. Some of the subjects covered are: who and what is God, the holy spirit, atonement, the human soul, heaven and hell, and many other deeply religious topics.

2. *Volume II* - Published 1954, paperback 391 pgs, contains 285 messages.
    This could very well be the most spiritual and interesting of the volumes. It contains messages about the creation of the world, the origin of man, the devolution and evolution, reincarnation and much more. This volume contains deep insight into many spiritual subjects not to be found elsewhere.

3. *Volume III* - Published 1969, paperback 404 pgs, contains 408 messages.
    This volume contains messages from the famous and not so famous.

Spirits from many lands tell about their lives on earth, their homes and activities in the spirit world. The subjects of the human soul and its soulmate are well covered in this volume.

4. *Volume IV* - Published 1972, about the same size as Vol III.
This volume contains messages mostly from relatives and friends of Mr. Padgett, Dr. Stone and Mr. Eugene Morgan (a friend of theirs). These messages are of a more personal than spiritual nature.

These four volumes are $14.95US/£9.95UK each plus postage.

The following two booklets constitute the complete original published works of Dr. Daniel G. Samuels.

5. *New Testament Revelations* - Published 1966, oversize booklet 125 pgs, contains 53 messages.
This provocative collection reinterprets many important New Testament subjects, it discusses the Oahspe Bible, reincarnation, and more.

6. *Old Testament Sermons* - Published 1957, two-oversize booklets 100 pgs, contains 76 messages.
These booklets contain a wealth of historical and religious information for those students of the Old Testament.

These booklets are $11.95US/£7.95UK each plus postage.

The following three books were compiled from or based on the original volumes by both mediums.

7. *The Genuine Jesus* - Published in 1999, paperback 109 pgs, contains 50 messages .... $8.95US/£5.95UK plus postage
An autobiography of Jesus's life told in the first person. The story follows the chronology of the New Testament Gospels, however, with dramatic changes in the events. It begins with his birth and formative years, and goes through to his ministry, his death, and his resurrection. This book also contains some of his most important teaching that he brought to earth, but were lost or altered with time.

8. *The Lost Teachings of Spiritualism* - Published 2004, paperback.
.... $7.95US/£4.95UK plus postage
This book is based on the evening slide lecture Alan has presented in the US, the UK, and Canada. The information contained in this book comes from the teachings received by both mediums, as well as from Alan's spiritual experiences and from his guides.

9. *The New Testament of Spiritualism* - Published 2003, paperback
515 pgs, contains 167 messages........ $16.95US/£9.95UK plus postage
A collection of the most important and interesting of the messages taken from the works of both mediums.

ORDERING INSTRUCTIONS

1. Please select the postage from the table below and add it to the cost of the book(s) you desire. Include the name and number of the book to insure accuracy.

   Within the US: $2.00 surface or $4.00 air.

   To Canada: $4.00 surface or $7.00 air (US dollars equivalent)

   To the UK and most countries: £3.50 surface (4-6 weeks) or £6.00 air (2 - 3 days)

   Note: In many cases two or more books can go for the same postage as one book. If the above postage information does not apply to your order please contact me for the correct postage.

2. Please enclose a check, bank draft or money order indorsed to Ross Publications. If you intend to pay in other than dollars or pounds please calculate the equivalent in your currency (Canada, Australia, New Zealand, South Africa and all Euro countries), all other countries please pay either in US dollars or GB pounds.

3. Mail your order and payment to the address below.
   Thank you.
   Alan Ross

ROSS PUBLICATIONS

1438 W. Lantana Rd. #401 561 833-0384
Lantana, FL 33462 USA ROSS PUBLICATIONS alanross@aol.com

www.thegenuinejesus.com